LISTOMANIA

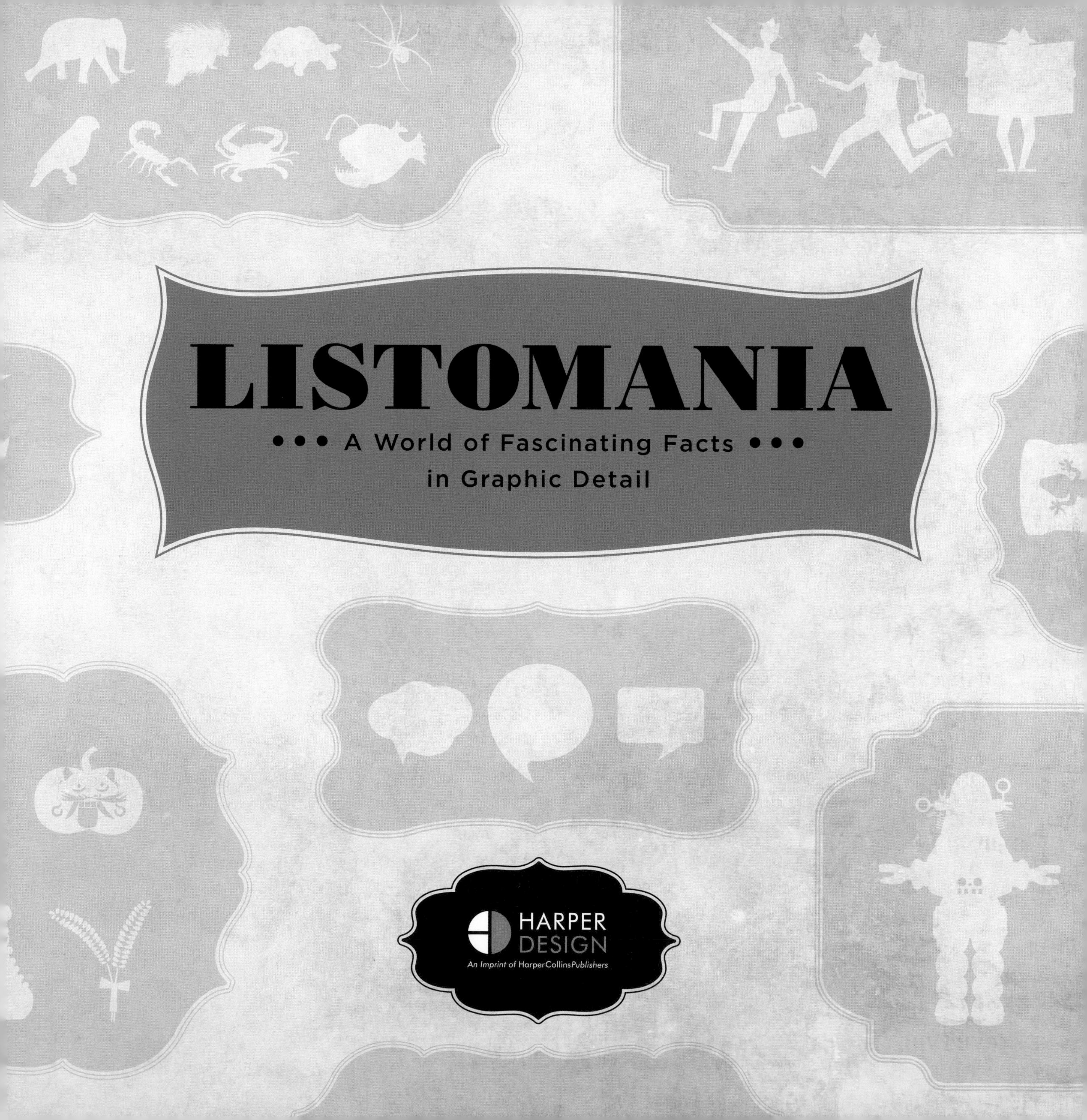

LISTOMANIA

••• A World of Fascinating Facts •••
in Graphic Detail

HARPER DESIGN
An Imprint of HarperCollinsPublishers

CONTENTS

242 THINGS THAT HAVE COME, GONE, AND STAYED

229 QUESTIONABLE ACTIONS AND IDEAS

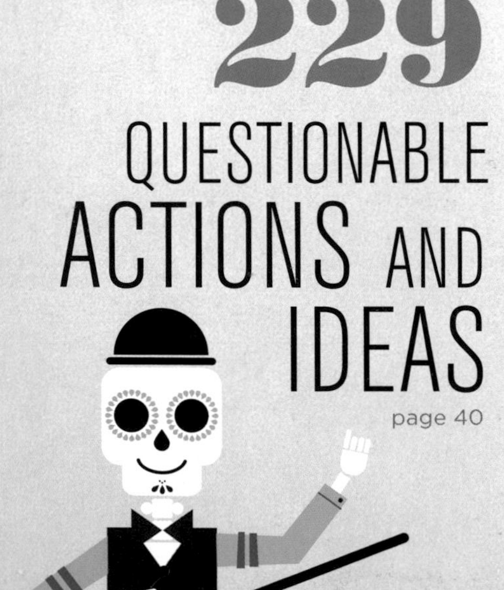

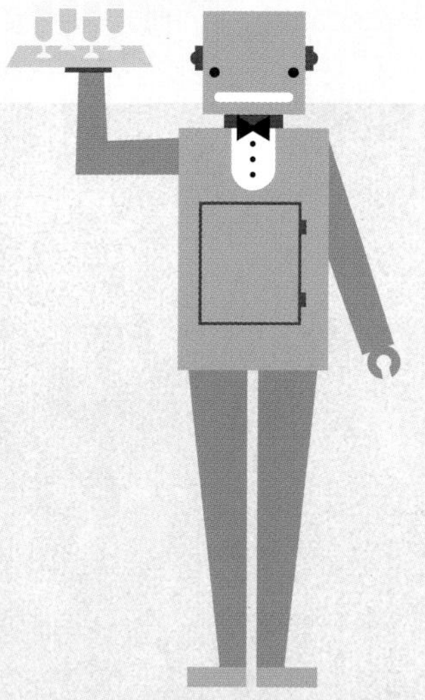

446 GOOD, BAD, POPULAR, AND UNPOPULAR ITEMS

382 GREAT (AND NOT SO GREAT) KINDS OF ENTERTAINMENT

267 THINGS YOU MIGHT EAT OR DRINK (OR NOT)

218 CREATURES BOTH REAL AND IMAGINARY

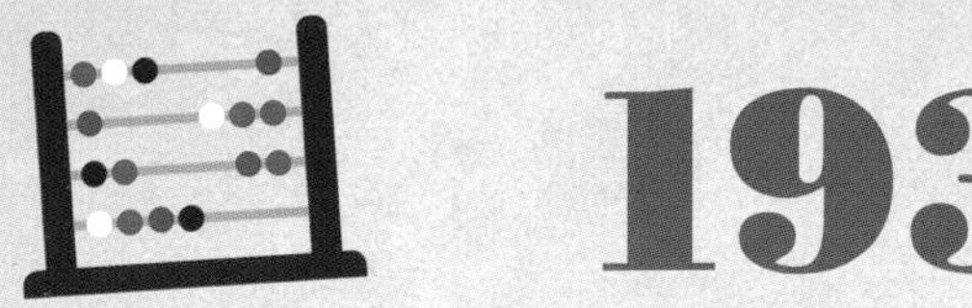

193 HEIGHTS AND DEPTHS OF HUMAN BEHAVIOR

1,333 AMAZING THINGS ABOUT THIS BOOK

5 THINGS WE SHOULD COP TO RIGHT NOW

A NOTE FROM YOUR HUMBLE PUBLISHER

This book is an absolute joy and will grace your coffee table quite nicely, if we do say so ourselves. That said, here are some things you should know before embarking upon the thrill-a-minute adventure that is *Listomania.*

1 THIS BOOK IS ALREADY OUT OF DATE

You can't make a book about the biggest, fastest, and weirdest without knowing that the day after the book comes out, something bigger, faster, or weirder will turn up. Hopefully, none of those late-breaking events will involve new alien attacks (see page 240) or fresh acts of cannibalism (check out page 210).

2 OUR FACT-CHECKERS ARE REALLY AWESOME . . .

But that doesn't mean we didn't get anything wrong. After all, do you know how hard it is to find someone who speaks fluent Volapük (see the sample on page 20)? If you find something wrong, let us know! We'll thank you profusely.

3 SOME THINGS ARE A MATTER OF OPINION

Some of the facts in the book are indisputable. Others . . . not so much (for instance, believe nothing on page 222). If you really disagree with us about, say, the sexiest movie villains ever (listed on page 175), drop us a line and let us know whom you would have chosen. You might become one of our Listomaniacs for the next book.

4 **THERE IS WAY TOO MUCH COOL STUFF IN THE WORLD TO FIT INTO ONE BOOK**

When we had to choose between authoritative and fun, we went for fun every time—even if it made the list a little more random. If you don't find anything that surprises you in the pages that follow, we would be, well, very surprised! Ideally, at least something will make you say, "Oh, I never looked at it like that before." (Check out page 66).

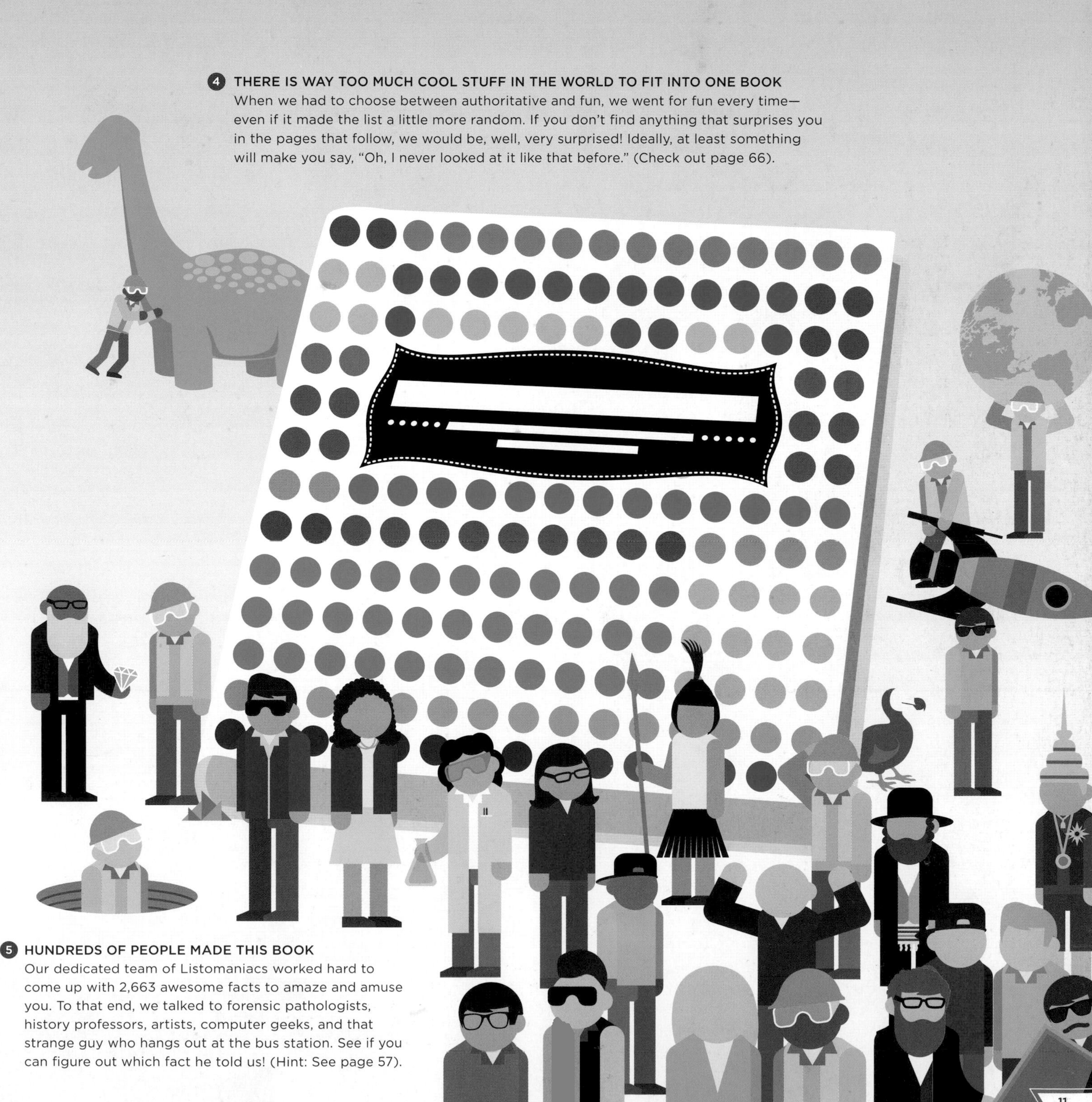

5 **HUNDREDS OF PEOPLE MADE THIS BOOK**

Our dedicated team of Listomaniacs worked hard to come up with 2,663 awesome facts to amaze and amuse you. To that end, we talked to forensic pathologists, history professors, artists, computer geeks, and that strange guy who hangs out at the bus station. See if you can figure out which fact he told us! (Hint: See page 57).

242 THINGS THAT HAVE COME, GONE, AND STAYED

Here today, gone tomorrow . . . this chapter explores things that have faded away (like the Aztec empire), things that have dropped out of the sky (rain of frogs, anyone?), and things that we've managed to lose somehow (like a lonely toothbrush floating out there in space). From mysterious disappearances to brand-new languages to mind-blowing migrations, it's all here—for now.

12 NOTABLE BEGINNINGS

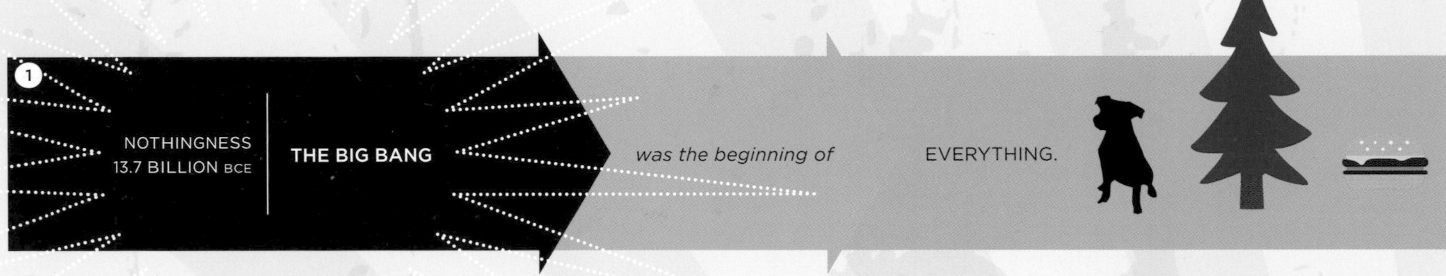

1 NOTHINGNESS 13.7 BILLION BCE | **THE BIG BANG** *was the beginning of* EVERYTHING.

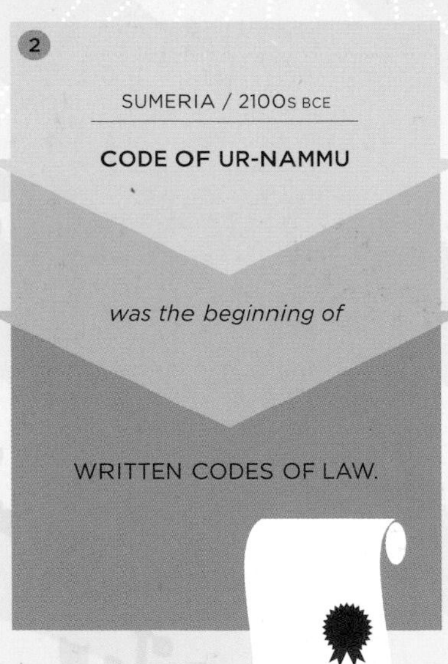

2 SUMERIA / 2100s BCE

CODE OF UR-NAMMU

was the beginning of

WRITTEN CODES OF LAW.

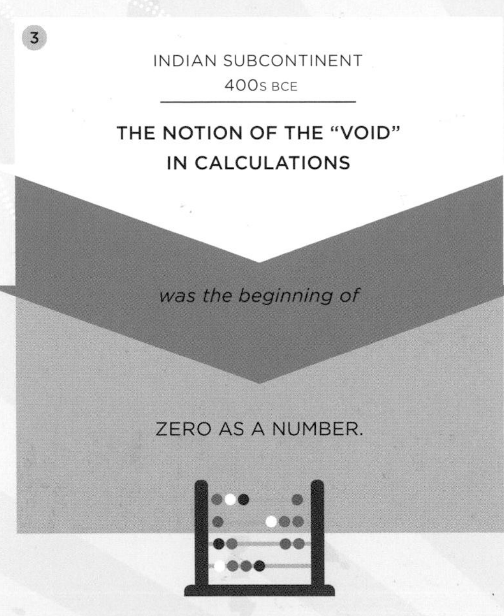

3 INDIAN SUBCONTINENT 400s BCE

THE NOTION OF THE "VOID" IN CALCULATIONS

was the beginning of

ZERO AS A NUMBER.

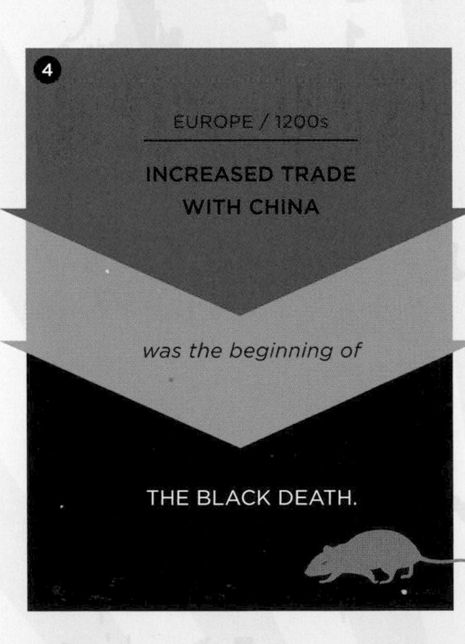

4 EUROPE / 1200s

INCREASED TRADE WITH CHINA

was the beginning of

THE BLACK DEATH.

5 ENGLAND 1796 | **EDWARD JENNER'S INVESTIGATION OF WHY MILKMAIDS DIDN'T GET SMALLPOX** *was the beginning of* VACCINATIONS.

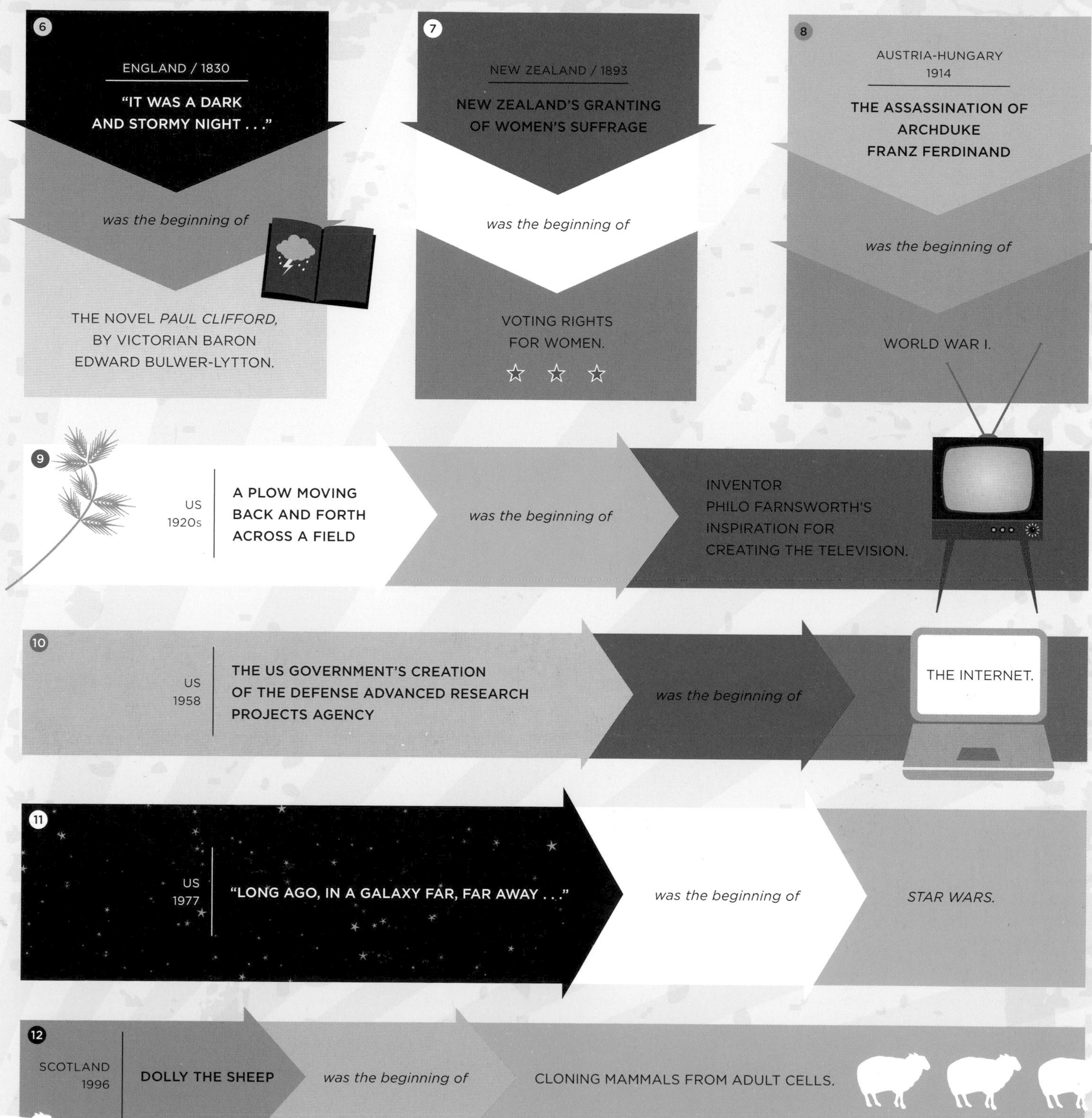
6
ENGLAND / 1830
"IT WAS A DARK AND STORMY NIGHT . . ."
was the beginning of
THE NOVEL *PAUL CLIFFORD,* BY VICTORIAN BARON EDWARD BULWER-LYTTON.
7
NEW ZEALAND / 1893
NEW ZEALAND'S GRANTING OF WOMEN'S SUFFRAGE
was the beginning of
VOTING RIGHTS FOR WOMEN.
8
AUSTRIA-HUNGARY 1914
THE ASSASSINATION OF ARCHDUKE FRANZ FERDINAND
was the beginning of
WORLD WAR I.
9
US 1920s
A PLOW MOVING BACK AND FORTH ACROSS A FIELD
was the beginning of
INVENTOR PHILO FARNSWORTH'S INSPIRATION FOR CREATING THE TELEVISION.
10
US 1958
THE US GOVERNMENT'S CREATION OF THE DEFENSE ADVANCED RESEARCH PROJECTS AGENCY
was the beginning of
THE INTERNET.
11
US 1977
"LONG AGO, IN A GALAXY FAR, FAR AWAY . . ."
was the beginning of
STAR WARS.
12
SCOTLAND 1996
DOLLY THE SHEEP
was the beginning of
CLONING MAMMALS FROM ADULT CELLS.

18 THINGS THAT FELL from the sky

❶ **MEAT**
US / 1876
Falling chunks of meat over Kentucky were identified—by brave souls who tasted them—as mutton or venison. It's theorized that the meat came from vomiting vultures.

❷ **BLUE ICE**
US / 2002
Numerous reports have been made of "blue ice" (frozen bathroom waste) falling from airplanes. In this case, a Pennsylvania home was blanketed with it.

❸ **EGGS**
HAITI / 1786
A large number of small, black eggs fell over Port-au-Prince. They hatched the following day; inside were tadpole-like creatures that never grew into frogs.

❹ **UNIDENTIFIED BLOOD**
COLOMBIA / 2008
Citizens of Choco reported red rain, and a scientist confirmed that the mysterious liquid was blood. Local priests held that this phenomenon might be a warning from God.

❺ **HUGE BALL OF ICE**
BRAZIL / 2005
No one is sure why "megacryometeors" exist, but they've fallen in sizes ranging from 1 pound (0.5 kg) to this behemoth, which weighed 440 pounds (200 kg) and crashed through a factory roof.

❻ **SPIDERS**
ARGENTINA / 2007
A rain of spiders, each about 4 inches (10 cm) across, fell in the Salta province. This horrifying event is notable because it was captured on film.

❼ **FROZEN SQUID**
FALKLAND ISLANDS / 1997
A Korean fisherman in the water off the Falklands spent two days in a coma after a single frozen squid dropped out of the sky, knocking him unconscious.

❽ **JELLY**
SCOTLAND / 2009
Jelly-like blobs have rained down on a number of regions around the globe, including the Scottish moors. No one knows what they are.

❾ **SHELLFISH**
ENGLAND / 1881
A thunderstorm over Worcester in the south of England showered several tons of hermit crabs and periwinkles (a snail-like mollusk).

❿ **TOADS**
FRANCE / 1794
Vast numbers of toads fell on soldiers camped near the village of Lalain. Of all strange rains, frogs and toads are the most common curiosities to fall from the sky.

⓫ **MONEY**
GERMANY / 1976
Bank notes totaling US $1,450 fluttered over Limburg and were picked up by two clergymen. Cash showers have gone down in Russia, the United States, and elsewhere.

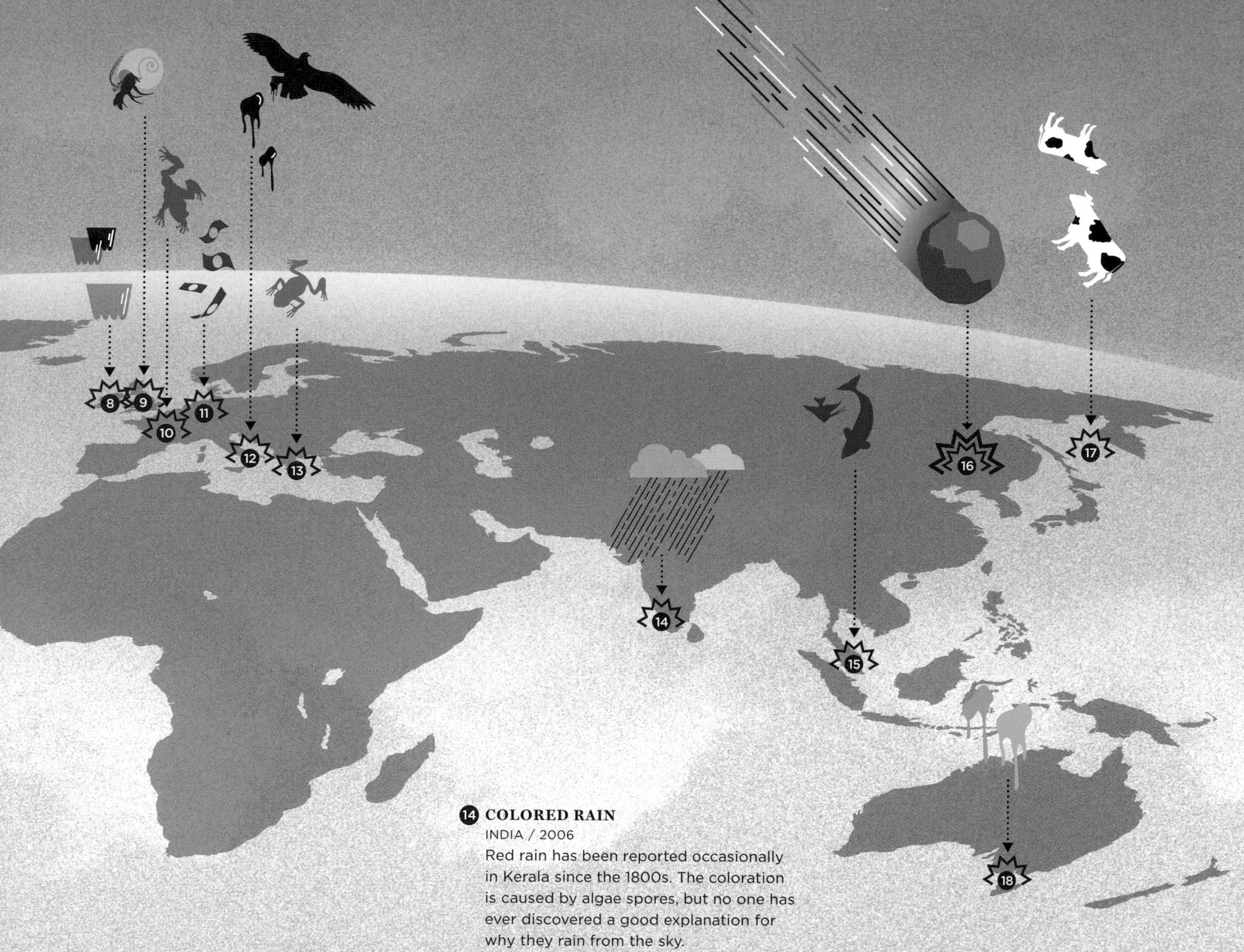

14 COLORED RAIN
INDIA / 2006
Red rain has been reported occasionally in Kerala since the 1800s. The coloration is caused by algae spores, but no one has ever discovered a good explanation for why they rain from the sky.

12 BIRDS' BLOOD
ITALY / 1890
Birds' blood rained down on a town in Calabria. It's theorized that birds were torn apart by high winds, but there were no such winds, and no pieces of birds fell.

13 FROGS
GREECE / 1981
A species of small green frogs native to North Africa came down unexpectedly on the citizens of Nafplion, a city in southern Greece.

15 FISH
SINGAPORE / 1861
Following an earthquake, numerous fish as long as 12 inches (30 cm) poured from the heavens. The connection to the earthquake has never been explained.

16 ENORMOUS METEORITE
CHINA / 1976
"Meteorite 1," now on display at the Jilin Meteorite Museum in Jilin City, weighs 2 tons (1,800 kg). It is one of nearly 170 other meteorites that fell near Jilin.

17 COWS
RUSSIA / 1997
Claims that a Japanese fishing boat was destroyed by falling cows prompted fraud accusations. Some proposed that the cows had been dropped from a cargo plane.

18 SLIME
AUSTRALIA / 1996
Tasmanians in a small town awoke one morning to find it coated in slime. They now celebrate the anniversary of "Slime Day" each year by throwing jelly.

11 LOST CIVILIZATIONS

1 **SUMER**
MIDDLE EAST
5000s–2000s BCE

2 **MINOAN**
SOUTHERN EUROPE
2700s–1500s BCE

3 **HARAPPA**
INDIAN SUBCONTINENT
3300s–1300s BCE

4 **NOK**
AFRICA
1000s BCE–500s CE

5 **MAYA**
CENTRAL AMERICA
2600s BCE–900s CE

6 **ANASAZI**
NORTH AMERICA
1200s BCE–1300s CE

EASY COME, NOT SO EASY GO

When an ancient civilization vanishes, the cause of its demise often remains a mystery. Below are some guesses from modern science as to what may have happened to a few of the most famous extinct cultures.

7 POLYNESIANS OF THE PITCAIRN ISLANDS
SOUTH PACIFIC
1000s–1400s

8 AZTEC
CENTRAL AMERICA
1200s–1500s

9 INCA
SOUTH AMERICA
1200s–1572

10 RAPA NUI
SOUTH PACIFIC
300s–1800s

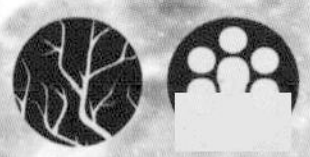

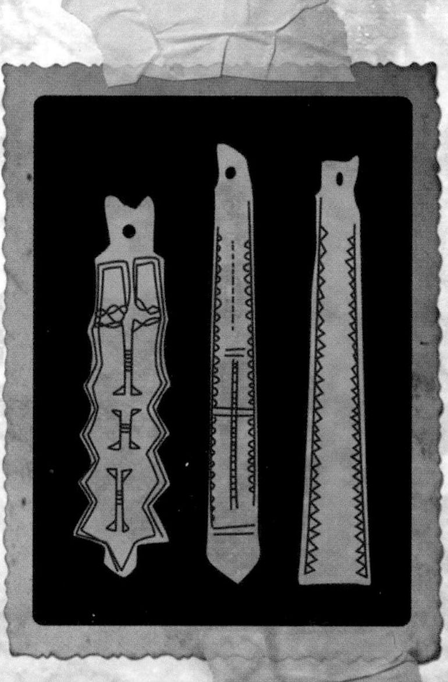

11 BEOTHUK
NORTH AMERICA
1500s–1829

WHAT HAPPENED?

- ENVIRONMENTAL COLLAPSE
- NATURAL DISASTER
- INVASIONS
- DISEASE
- OVERPOPULATION
- UNKNOWN

13 INVENTED LANGUAGES

KAFUGGO! SNIPPA BLOP!

BUT I'M JUST TRYING TO HELP, DAMN IT!

GRAMMELOT

1500s

A gibberish language developed for use in satirical theater, it allowed performers to avoid censorship, and also to get their point across no matter what language the audience spoke.

VOLAPÜK

1880

Created by Johann Martin Schleyer, a Roman Catholic priest in Germany. He dreamed God had told him to create an international language.

O FAT OBAS, KEL BINOL IN SÜLS, PAISALUDOMÖZ NEM OLA.

OUR FATHER, WHO ART IN HEAVEN, HALLOWED BE THY NAME.

UNU BIERON, MI PETAS.

ONE BEER, PLEASE.

ESPERANTO

1887

Easily the most recognized new language, Esperanto was intended to be an international, politically neutral tongue that most people could easily learn.

VENDERGOOD

1906

Created by child prodigy William James Sidis at the age of eight, this arcane, difficult-to-pronounce tongue has been used to send encrypted messages.

QUEN DISEOIS-NAR?

WHAT DO YOU LEARN?

I WILL KILL YOU TOMORROW.

AUI

1962

Psychiatrist John W. Weilgart claims to have learned this language from a diminutive green alien. It's evidently universal throughout the cosmos.

NADSAT

1962

Used by members of the teen subculture in the novel *A Clockwork Orange,* Nadsat is basically English with some borrowed words from Russian.

PEETING THE OLD MOLOKO WITH SYNTHEMESC.

DRINKING MILK SPIKED WITH DRUGS.

1 M 4 7074L N008.

I AM A TOTAL NEWBIE.

L33TSPEAK

1980

Developed as an "insider" language by hackers in the early days of the Internet, this jokey language replaces letters with numbers, among other humorous inventions.

TALOSSAN

1980

Created by R. Ben Madison for his micronation (the Kingdom of Talossa), this language has more than 28,000 words and plenty of pop-culture references.

TU FOST S'ASCARH VIENSA FRAGA: "¿SENTIÉU CEASTLIVÉU?" SA, ¿SENTIETZ-TU, BRAGARTAC'H?

YOU'VE GOT TO ASK YOURSELF ONE QUESTION: "DO I FEEL LUCKY?" WELL, DO YOU, PUNK?

BÍI RIL LÁMÁLA WITH RULETH WA.

THE WOMAN STROKES THE CAT.

LÁADAN

1982

Science-fiction author and feminist linguist Suzette Haden Elgin constructed this tongue to provide an alternative to male-centered language.

KLINGON

1984

The fictional Klingons in the *Star Trek* universe speak this language. Many die-hard fans can converse in Klingon, and even attend Klingon language camps.

TOH, CHOVNATLH DOJ GHAH TLHINGAN'E'.

A KLINGON IS AN IMPRESSIVE SPECIMEN.

NASA PONA!

PARTY ON!

TOKI PONA

2001

This minimalist language focuses on basic concepts and elements. The entire language has only 123 words; its simplicity is rumored to bring speakers happiness.

OOU

2003

Sonja Elen Kisa designed this deliberately ambiguous language. Its writing system is made up of punctuation marks, and the sounds are composed solely of vowels.

I LOVE YOU.

F-AY-VRRTEP FÌ-TSENGE LU KXANÌ!

THESE DEMONS ARE FORBIDDEN HERE!

NA'VI

2009

The constructed language of the Na'vi people in the 2009 film *Avatar* was created by celebrity linguistics consultant Paul Frommer, who was on hand during filming to help with pronunciation.

11 LANGUAGES FAR FROM HOME

YOU'VE COME A LONG WAY, BABY

Languages are living things—and sometimes living things end up far away from where they were born. Here are eleven languages and dialects that migrated great distances with their speakers, and some of the fascinating facts behind their voyages.

WALLOON

4,100 MI / 6,600 KM

Walloon is spoken in a small district in the US state of Wisconsin, owing to fairly large-scale immigration there from Belgium in the 1800s.

VERY FEW SPEAKERS

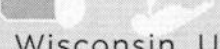

WOLOF

2,600 MI / 4,200 KM

France colonized much of western Africa in the 1800s. In the 1900s, some West Africans immigrated to France, bringing Wolof with them.

39,000 SPEAKERS

KABUVERDIANU

2,500 MI / 4,000 KM

Cape Verde was colonized by the Portuguese; this language is an Afro-Portuguese creole.

394,000 SPEAKERS

HAKKA CHINESE

10,200 MI / 16,500 KM

Starting in 1854, Chinese laborers were brought in to build the Panama Railway.

6,000 SPEAKERS

GERMAN

8,100 MI / 13,000 KM

A large number of Germans emigrated to Chile in the mid-1800s.

150,000 SPEAKERS

WELSH

7,500 MI / 12,100 KM

Due to Argentina's encouragement of European settlement in the 1800s, there are more Welsh speakers in Argentine Patagonia than in Wales.

25,000 SPEAKERS

JAVANESE

12,200 MI / 19,600 KM

Many Indonesians were brought to plantations as indentured servants during colonial times.

60,000 SPEAKERS

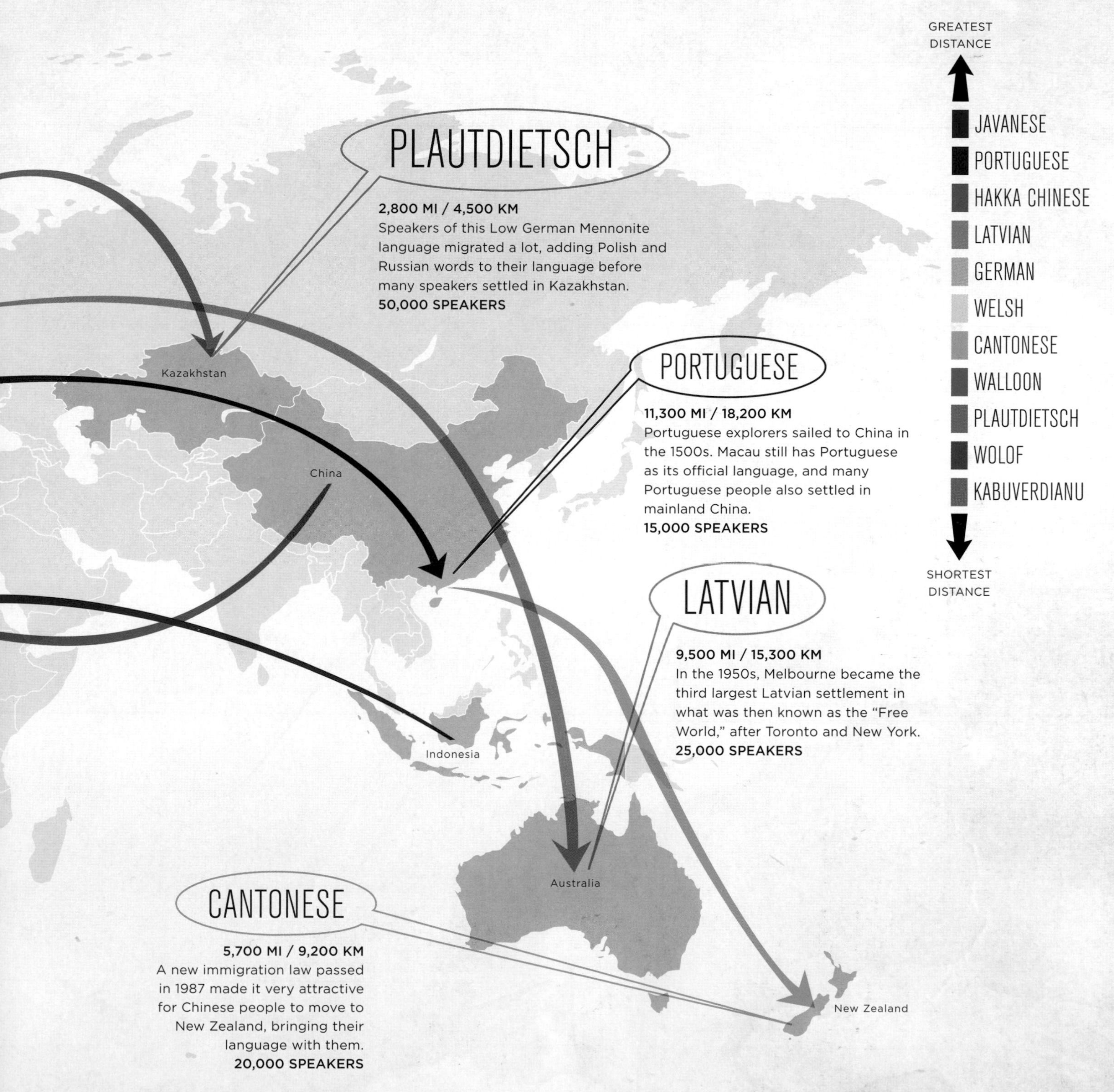
GREATEST DISTANCE
JAVANESE
PORTUGUESE
HAKKA CHINESE
LATVIAN
GERMAN
WELSH
CANTONESE
WALLOON
PLAUTDIETSCH
WOLOF
KABUVERDIANU
SHORTEST DISTANCE
PLAUTDIETSCH
2,800 MI / 4,500 KM
Speakers of this Low German Mennonite language migrated a lot, adding Polish and Russian words to their language before many speakers settled in Kazakhstan.
50,000 SPEAKERS
Kazakhstan
China
PORTUGUESE
11,300 MI / 18,200 KM
Portuguese explorers sailed to China in the 1500s. Macau still has Portuguese as its official language, and many Portuguese people also settled in mainland China.
15,000 SPEAKERS
LATVIAN
9,500 MI / 15,300 KM
In the 1950s, Melbourne became the third largest Latvian settlement in what was then known as the "Free World," after Toronto and New York.
25,000 SPEAKERS
Indonesia
Australia
CANTONESE
5,700 MI / 9,200 KM
A new immigration law passed in 1987 made it very attractive for Chinese people to move to New Zealand, bringing their language with them.
20,000 SPEAKERS
New Zealand

10 COLORS THAT FADED AWAY

1 IVORY BLACK
ANTIQUITY–MODERN TIMES
This deep blue-black was made from the burned and charred waste of ivory. It fell out of use as ivory did.

2 CAPUT MORTUUM
1700s–1800s
A tarry brown pigment made of ground-up Egyptian mummies, "caput mortuum" means "worthless remains."

3 VERMILION
ANTIQUITY–MODERN TIMES
The color of the mercuric sulfide cinnabar, vermilion was beautiful but rare, unstable, and toxic.

4 RED DYE #3
MODERN TIMES
The US government banned this red food and cosmetics dye in 1990 for being carcinogenic.

5 REALGAR
ANTIQUITY–MODERN TIMES
Realgar is a highly toxic arsenic sulfide that was once the only pure orange pigment available.

6 INDIAN YELLOW
1400s–1800s
Supposedly made from the urine of cows only fed mango leaves, this color would have become rare due to its poor effects on cattle.

7 LEAD WHITE
ANTIQUITY–RENAISSANCE
White paint that got its color from lead was a great pigment, but deadly.

8 VERDIGRIS
ANTIQUITY–1800s
A moderately transparent bluish green with low stability, verdigris is a copper acetate, and quite toxic.

9 CHARTRES BLUE
1300s
This blue, used to color stained glass in France's Chartres Cathedral, proved incredibly difficult to make.

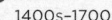

10 SMALT
1400s–1700s
Made from ground-up glass and cobalt, this blue was complicated to manufacture and faded easily.

 UNSTABLE INGREDIENTS

 COMPLICATED INGREDIENTS OR METHOD

 DETAILS OF MANUFACTURE LOST TO TIME

 POISONOUS OR HARMFUL TO HEALTH

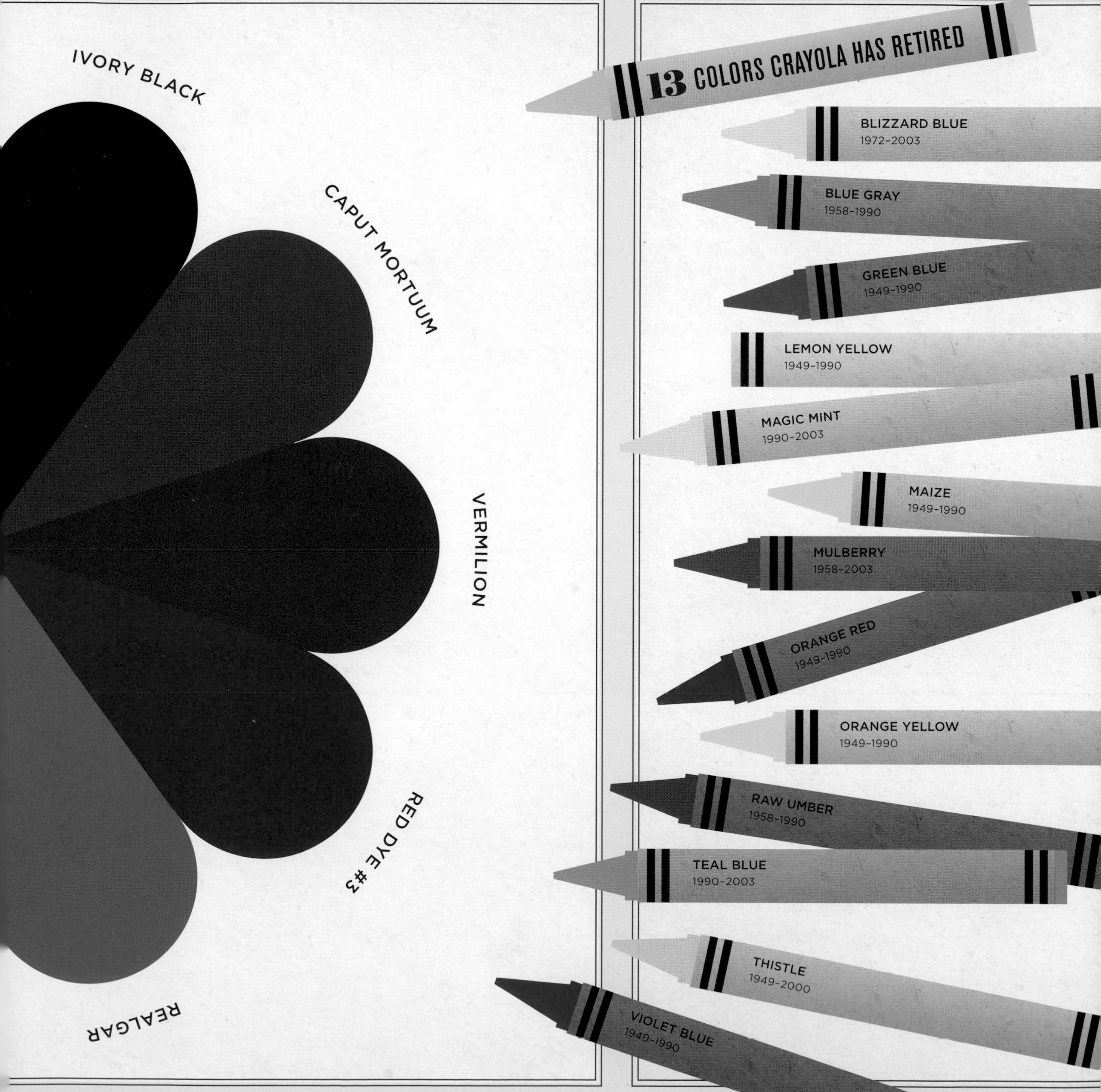
IVORY BLACK
CAPUT MORTUUM
VERMILION
RED DYE #3
REALGAR
13 COLORS CRAYOLA HAS RETIRED
BLIZZARD BLUE
1972–2003
BLUE GRAY
1958–1990
GREEN BLUE
1949–1990
LEMON YELLOW
1949–1990
MAGIC MINT
1990–2003
MAIZE
1949–1990
MULBERRY
1958–2003
ORANGE RED
1949–1990
ORANGE YELLOW
1949–1990
RAW UMBER
1958–1990
TEAL BLUE
1990–2003
THISTLE
1949–2000
VIOLET BLUE
1949–1990

9 THINGS THAT WERE LOST IN SPACE

1 SATELLITE *VANGUARD I*
1964
Sent up in 1958, it's been orbiting without communication since 1964.

2 TOOTHBRUSH
1965
On the 14-day *Gemini 7* flight, Jim Lovell lost his toothbrush. Luckily, crewmate Frank Borman was willing to share his.

3 GLOVE
1965
Lost during the first US space walk, the glove stayed in orbit for a month with a speed of 17,400 miles per hour (28,000 km/h), making it the most dangerous garment in history.

4 FOOT ANCHOR
2001
Used to tether astronauts to the shuttle's robotic arm, this piece of hardware drifted away during a space walk. Later, the shuttle had to change orbit to avoid hitting it.

15 THINGS THAT WE'VE SHOT INTO SPACE

1 CHIMP
1961
Enos was the first chimp sent into orbit by the United States.

2 BULLFROGS
1970
Two bullfrogs were launched on a one-way mission to help us understand space motion sickness.

3 MICE
1972
Apollo 17 carried five pocket mice. They orbited both the Earth and the Moon.

4 GOLDEN PLAQUES
1972–1973
A pair of gold-anodized aluminum plaques were placed on board the *Pioneer* spacecrafts. They show images of humans, equations, and more.

5 GOLDEN RECORDS
1977
The Voyager Golden Records contain sounds and images selected to portray the diversity of life and culture on Earth, including heartbeats, music, and nature sounds.

6 PAINTING
1980
The first painting to orbit the Earth was by Russian artist Andrei Sokolov. It was carried aboard the Soviet Mir space station.

5 SPATULA
2006
Astronauts lost a spatula while testing a way to repair the space shuttle.

6 CAMERA
2007
It floated off as astronaut Suni Williams performed repairs on the shuttle.

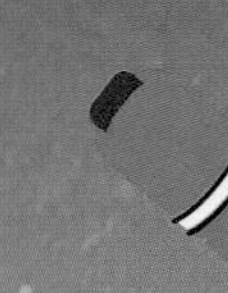

7 AMMONIA TANK
2007
This huge tank was jettisoned from the space station after its climate control was upgraded.

15 GOLF BALLS
1971
Astronaut Alan Shepard hit two golf balls off the surface of the moon.

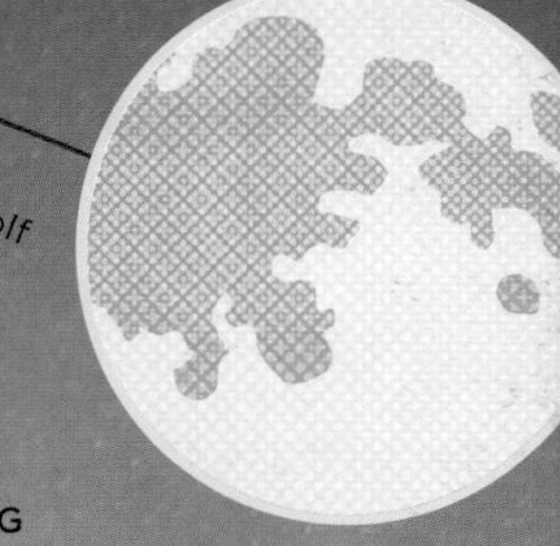

8 TOOL BAG
2008
Contained two grease guns, a putty knife, and cloth mitts.

9 ORB-WEAVER SPIDER
2008
Two spiders were sent by NASA to live in the International Space Station. One went missing.

7 SCULPTURE
1993
The first sculpture designed for a human habitat in orbit was Arthur Woods's *Cosmic Dancer*, which was sent to Mir.

8 TIMOTHY LEARY'S ASHES
1997
The capsule carrying the psychedelic visionary's remains stayed in orbit for six years; it burned up on reentry.

9 SWEET POTATO SEEDS
2005
As part of China's second manned space mission, sweet potato seeds were flown into space to test whether space-grown foods had bonus health benefits.

10 *STAR TREK* ACTOR'S ASHES
2007
Two years after the 2005 death of James Doohan (Scotty in the *Star Trek* series), the actor's ashes were launched into space.

11 LIGHTSABER
2007
In 2007, Luke Skywalker's lightsaber made the trip into space on board the space shuttle *Discovery*.

12 COMPUTER VIRUS
2008
A Windows virus known as Gammima was accidentally carried to the space station on laptops.

13 HELA CELLS
2009
The cells of cancer victim Henrietta Lacks were sent into space to test the effects of atomic radiation.

14 PIECE OF "NEWTON'S TREE"
2010
Wood from the apple tree that inspired Newton's discovery of gravity made the trip into Earth's orbit as part of the Royal Society's celebration of its 350th anniversary.

11 PEOPLE WHO MYSTERIOUSLY VANISHED

LOUIS LE PRINCE
FRANCE / 1890
This film pioneer vanished from a train near Dijon. His body and luggage were never found.

DOROTHY ARNOLD
US / 1910
The perfume heiress was last spotted buying a book of epigrams and a bag of candy. Rumor is she never came back from a stroll in Central Park.

AMBROSE BIERCE
MEXICO / 1913
While reporting on the Mexican revolution, the pioneering journalist and satirist vanished without a trace.

ALEJANDRO BELLO SILVA
CHILE / 1914
His disappearance during a qualifying exam flight over central Chile inspired the saying "more lost than Lieutenant Bello."

ARTHUR CRAVAN
MEXICO / 1918
The French proto-Dadaist writer and art critic disappeared near Salina Cruz, Mexico, and is believed to have drowned.

AMBROSE SMALL
CANADA / 1919
The millionaire was last seen at his theater, the Grand Opera House, in Toronto. It is rumored that he was killed by his wife.

WALLACE FARD MUHAMMAD
US / 1934
The controversial founder of the extremist Nation of Islam left Detroit for Chicago one day and was never heard from again.

AMELIA EARHART
PACIFIC OCEAN / 1937
The pioneering aviatrix vanished over the Central Pacific. It is clear that her plane crashed, but no debris was conclusively identified.

SUBHAS CHANDRA BOSE
TAIWAN / 1945
One of the most prominent leaders of the Indian Independence Movement, he vanished after a supposed plane crash.

MICHAEL ROCKEFELLER
NEW GUINEA / 1961
After he disappeared during an archaeology expedition in New Guinea, many speculated that he was eaten by the local people.

JIMMY HOFFA
US / 1975
An American labor leader with ties to the Mafia, he disappeared after a meeting with two men he suspected of being mobsters.

38 NEW COUNTRIES

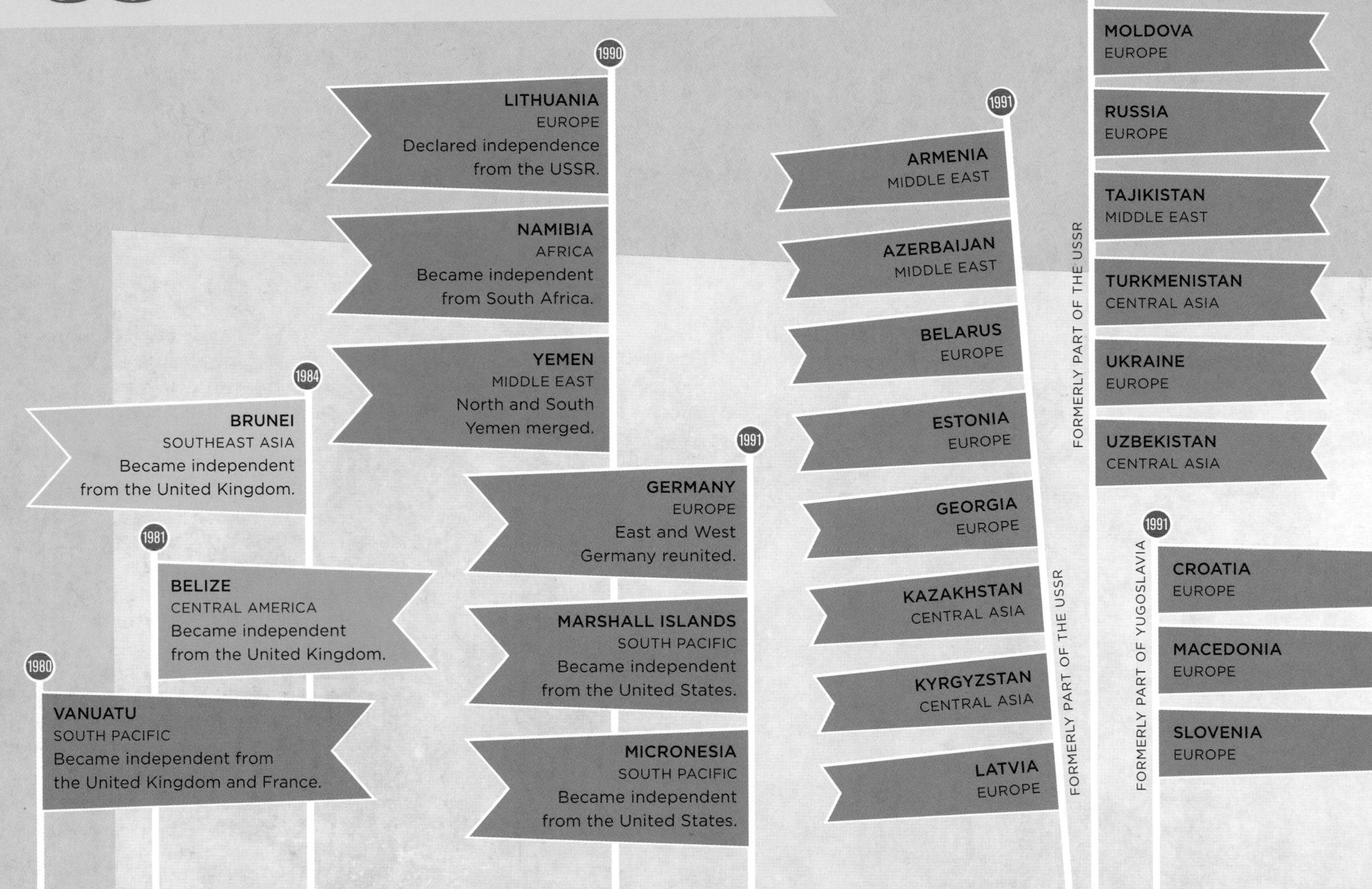

10 FORMER COUNTRIES

1. **BENGAL**
   SOUTHEAST ASIA
   An independent kingdom from 1338 to 1539, this area has seen many rulers; it is now part of Bangladesh and India.

2. **THE HURON CONFEDERACY**
   NORTH AMERICA
   This Native American nation of Canada's Great Lakes region was conquered by the Iroquois Nation in 1649.

3. **THE DUTCH REPUBLIC**
   EUROPE
   A confederation of states that was formed in 1581 and lasted more than 200 years, until the French overtook it in 1795.

4. **KINGDOM OF NAPLES**
   EUROPE
   This southern part of the Italian peninsula was a sovereign nation from 1282 to 1816, when it merged with Sicily, and then Italy.

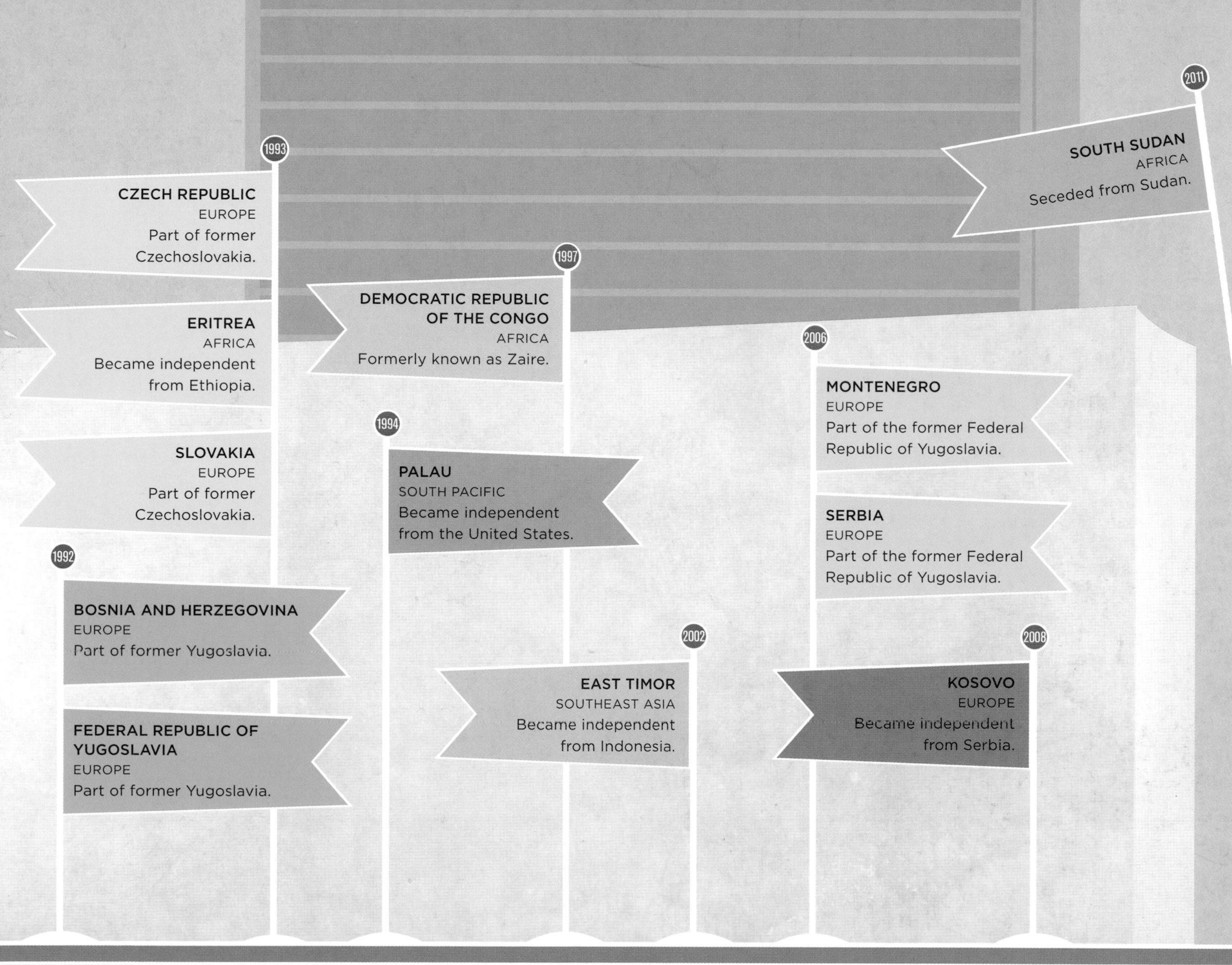

5 **CHAMPA**
SOUTHEAST ASIA
Found in what is now southern and central Vietnam, Champa gradually lost territory to Vietnam, and was no more by 1832.

6 **GRAN COLOMBIA**
SOUTH AMERICA
This coalition spanned what is now Colombia, Panama, Venezuela, and Ecuador; the latter two seceded in 1830.

7 **HAWAII**
SOUTH PACIFIC
Western business leaders overthrew this island kingdom's monarchy in 1893. It became a US territory in 1898.

8 **THE OTTOMAN EMPIRE**
EURASIA
The empire once encompassed parts of Eastern Europe, Asia, and North Africa. It was slowly disbanded by 1923.

9 **PRUSSIA**
EUROPE
A former duchy that once included much of northern Germany and western Poland, it was folded into Germany in 1933.

10 **UNITED ARAB REPUBLIC**
AFRICA
Syria and Egypt merged in 1958 to become a unified country; Syria abandoned the alliance in 1961.

THINGS THAT USED TO BE VALUABLE

FOR WHAT IT'S WORTH
Some items retain their value for centuries; others have a brief moment of great worth and then go back to a more mundane status. Below are some once-valuable items and their perceived equivalents in their heyday.

1 **SALT**
GHANA / 300s
Salt = its weight in gold

2 **TULIPS**
HOLLAND / 1637
1 tulip bulb = 10 times an average annual salary

3 **PEPPERCORNS**
ROME / 400s
1 ton (900 kg) peppercorns = part of ransom for Rome's safety

4 **ENSUBA (POTATO MASHERS)**
BAFIA (CAMEROON) / 1800s
30 potato mashers = 1 wife

5 **TRADE BEADS**
EUROPE / 1500s–1900s
1 handful beads = 1 slave

6 **OSTRICH PLUMES**
LONDON / 1903
1 plume = twice its weight in gold

7 **GOURDS**
HAITI / EARLY 1800s
1 gourd = 20 pigs

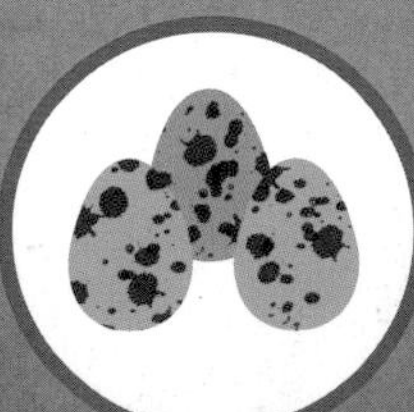

8 **MURRE EGGS**
SAN FRANCISCO / MID-1800s
1 Murre egg = ½ a day's average wages for a working man during the Gold Rush

9 SILK
CHINA / HAN DYNASTY (206 BCE–220 CE)
1 bolt silk = 1 year's taxes

10 MUREX DYE
PHOENICIA / 300s
1 pound (500 g) cloth dyed with murex = a year's wages

11 VIRGINITY
JAPAN / 1603–1959
Mizuage (the incredibly controversial practice of paying for a geisha's virginity) = more than an average year's wages

12 AIR TRAVEL
US / 1939
First round-trip ticket from New York to France = a new car

13 ONLINE CONNECTIVITY
EVERYWHERE / 1991
1 hour online time = several hours' wages at minimum wage

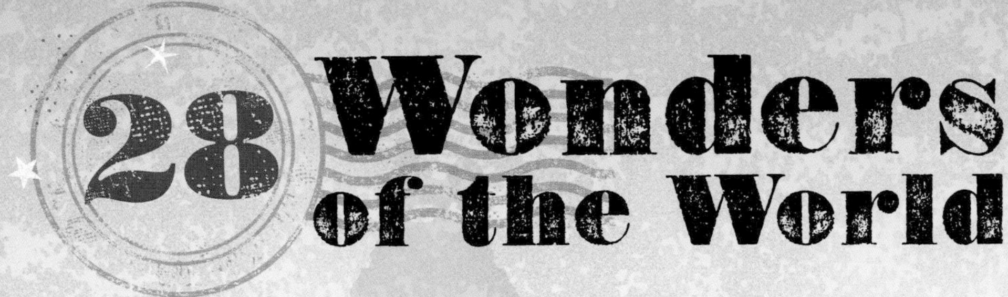

28 Wonders of the World

7

WONDERS OF THE ANCIENT WORLD

1. **GREAT PYRAMID OF GIZA**
   EGYPT
2. **HANGING GARDENS OF BABYLON**
   MODERN-DAY IRAQ
3. **STATUE OF ZEUS AT OLYMPIA**
   GREECE
4. **TEMPLE OF ARTEMIS AT EPHESUS**
   MODERN-DAY TURKEY
5. **MAUSOLEUM AT HALICARNASSUS**
   MODERN-DAY TURKEY
6. **COLOSSUS OF RHODES**
   GREECE
7. **LIGHTHOUSE OF ALEXANDRIA**
   EGYPT

7

WONDERS OF THE MEDIEVAL WORLD

1. **STONEHENGE**
   ENGLAND
2. **COLOSSEUM**
   ROME
3. **CATACOMBS OF KOM EL SHOQAFA**
   EGYPT
4. **GREAT WALL OF CHINA**
   CHINA
5. **PORCELAIN TOWER OF NANJING**
   CHINA
6. **HAGIA SOPHIA**
   TURKEY
7. **LEANING TOWER OF PISA**
   ITALY

WHAT A WONDERFUL WORLD

Some must-see spots are universally agreed upon—like those of the ancient world, which haven't been questioned since the Greeks first selected them. But other groups have chimed in with their own picks for awesome sites: CNN published their favorite natural marvels, while the American Society of Civil Engineers called out modern architecture's most noteworthy feats. There's just one list that's baffling in origin: Whoever picked the most majestic medieval wonders remains as mysterious as the medieval ages themselves.

7 WONDERS OF THE NATURAL WORLD

1. **GRAND CANYON**
   US
2. **GREAT BARRIER REEF**
   AUSTRALIA
3. **HARBOR OF RIO DE JANEIRO**
   BRAZIL
4. **MOUNT EVEREST**
   NEPAL
5. **AURORAS BOREALIS AND AUSTRALIS**
   THE SKY
6. **PARICUTÍN VOLCANO**
   MEXICO
7. **VICTORIA FALLS**
   ZIMBABWE / ZAMBIA BORDER

7 WONDERS OF THE MODERN WORLD

1. **CHUNNEL**
   UK / FRANCE
2. **CN TOWER**
   CANADA
3. **EMPIRE STATE BUILDING**
   US
4. **GOLDEN GATE BRIDGE**
   US
5. **ITAIPÚ DAM**
   BRAZIL / PARAGUAY BORDER
6. **ZUIDERZEE WORKS**
   NETHERLANDS
7. **PANAMA CANAL**
   PANAMA

8 ANIMALS THAT DARWIN ATE

CHECK, PLEASE

In his comings and goings around the globe, naturalist Charles Darwin developed an old-fashioned appreciation for animals: by eating them. He introduced any number of animals to museums, laboratories, and even the dinner table.

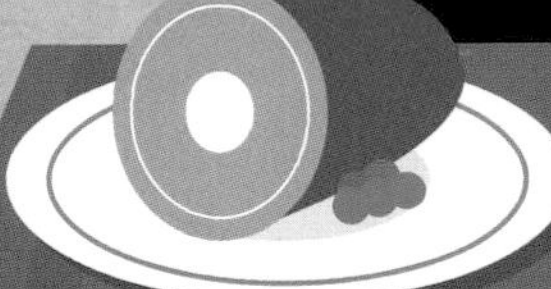

ARMADILLO

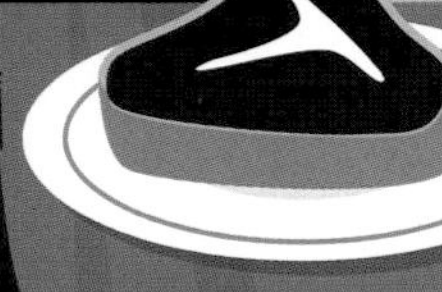

Darwin pronounced that this big cat tasted exactly like veal.

PUMA

When treated to this large rodent in South America, Darwin wrote that it was the best meat he ever tasted.

AGOUTI

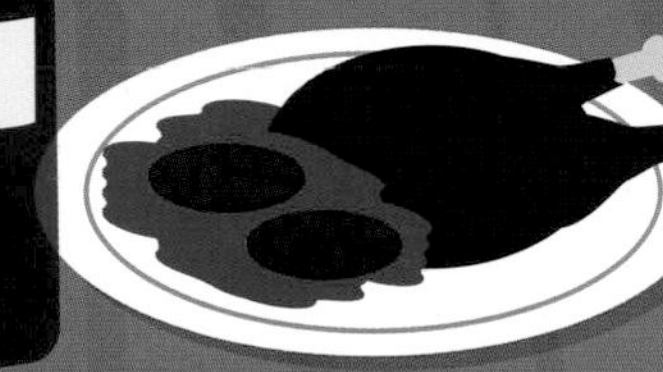

Every adventurous appetite finds its limits. Brown owl, evidently, was "indescribable."

BROWN OWL

Darwin classified this new species while dining on it one Christmas on the HMS *Beagle*.

DARWIN'S RHEA

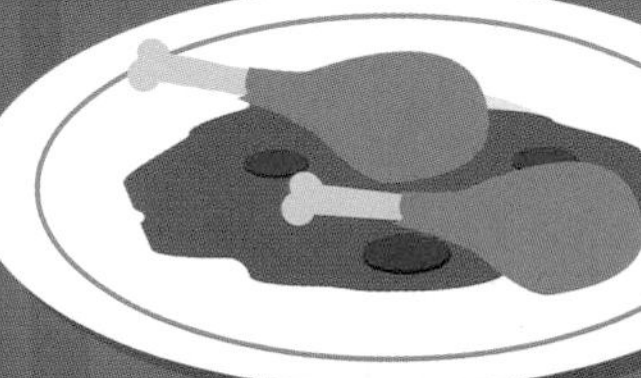

Darwin tried this heron-like bird while he was a member of the Gourmet Club at Cambridge.

BITTERN

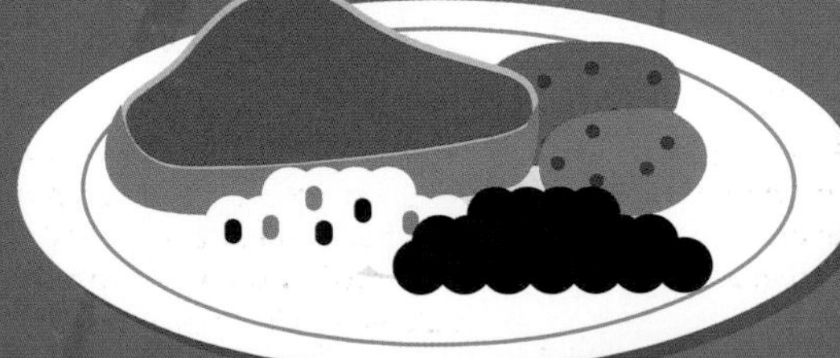

GALÁPAGOS LAND IGUANA

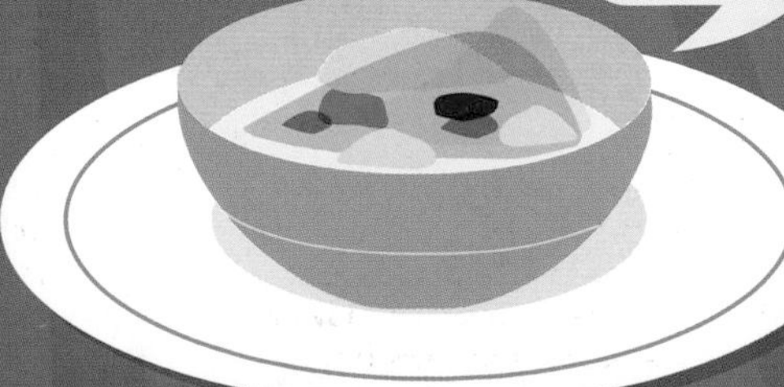

So delicious that he brought 48 as provisions on his return trip.

GALÁPAGOS TORTOISE

12 ANIMAL INTERLOPERS

1 WILD BOAR
FROM: EURASIA
TO: THE AMERICAS
Imported as a food animal and for sport hunting; they damage native plants and crops.

2 CHINESE MITTEN CRAB
FROM: EASTERN ASIA
TO: EUROPE AND NORTH AMERICA
Introduced as a delicacy, these pesky crustaceans compete with local species, and their burrowing damages embankments and clogs drainage systems.

3 CANE TOAD
FROM: HAWAII
TO: AUSTRALIA
Imported to control insect pests, they bred massively, have no local predators, and are poisonous to local wildlife who try to eat them.

4 NILE PERCH
FROM: TROPICAL AFRICA
TO: EAST AFRICA
Introduced as a food fish from one region of Africa to another, they wiped out local native fish. However, they have become an important food source, as planned.

5 SMALL ASIAN MONGOOSE
FROM: SOUTHEAST ASIA
TO: VARIOUS PLACES WORLDWIDE
Brought to kill rats and poisonous snakes, they also kill birds, eat their eggs, and breed prolifically.

6 POLYNESIAN RAT
FROM: SOUTHEAST ASIA
TO: THROUGHOUT THE PACIFIC
Stowaways on ships, the rodents are responsible for many of the extinctions in the Pacific's native bird and insect species.

7 AFRICANIZED HONEYBEES
FROM: AFRICA
TO: THE AMERICAS
Imported and bred with European honeybees to increase honey production, they are more aggressive and produce less honey.

8 KHAPRA BEETLE
FROM: SOUTHERN ASIA
TO: WARM REGIONS WORLDWIDE
Probably accidentally shipped with grain, these little insects are one of the world's most destructive pests of grain products and seeds.

9 BURMESE PYTHON
FROM: SOUTHEAST ASIA
TO: US
As escaped or released pets, these carnivorous snakes can grow up to 16 feet (5 m) long.

10 MYNAH BIRD
FROM: ASIA
TO: WORLDWIDE
Imported as pets, they are omnivorous, can threaten local ecosystems, and are particularly problematic in Australia.

11 CRAB-EATING MACAQUE
FROM: SOUTHEAST ASIA
TO: EASTERN PACIFIC
Brought as pets or experimental animals, they are now a threat to native wildlife on islands where resources have become scarce.

12 CHILLI THRIP
FROM: SOUTHEAST ASIA
TO: WARM REGIONS WORLDWIDE
Tiny and dainty looking, the dreaded thrip attacks more than 100 crops, resulting in widespread defoliation and crop loss.

10 EXTREME ANIMAL MIGRATIONS

1 **BAR-TAILED GODWIT**
This bird flies 6,800 miles (11,000 km) without stopping to feed or sleep. It consumes half its body weight before the trip from New Zealand to Alaska.

LONGEST NONSTOP MIGRATION

2 **MONARCH BUTTERFLY**
These butterflies migrate 4,300 miles (6,900 km) during the course of several generations.

MULTIGENERATIONAL MIGRATION

3 **KRILL**
This tiny but crucial ecosystem member makes daily migrations between the ocean's surface and 1,500 feet (450 m) below, swimming 4,500 times its body length. The phenomenon was first observed near Bermuda, but happens in all oceans.

DEEPEST MIGRATION

LARGEST MIGRANT

4 **BLUE WHALE**
Its migration pattern remains something of a mystery, but this giant often travels more than 5,000 miles (8,000 km).

LONGEST LIFETIME MIGRATION

5 **MANX SHEARWATER**
This bird migrates 9,000 miles (14,500 km) each winter. It can live to be 55 years old and travel up to 500,000 miles (800,000 km).

MOST MISUNDERSTOOD MIGRATION

6 LEMMING
Lemmings do not commit mass suicide over cliffs, as many people believe. However, they have such high reproduction rates that the occasional population boom causes mass migrations in search of food. The inevitable deaths along the way may explain this myth's origins.

HIGHEST MIGRATION

7 BAR-HEADED GOOSE
This goose flies as high as 6 miles (9.5 km) and can travel 1,000 miles (1,600 km) in a single day by riding a jet stream over the Himalayas, completing its migration.

LONGEST MIGRATION

8 ARCTIC TERN
This bird travels 34,000 miles (54,700 km) from pole to pole, with a few stops along the way.

DEADLIEST MIGRATION

9 WILDEBEEST
More than 250,000 wildebeests die during each migration; many drown or are eaten by crocodiles as they search for fresh sources of food and water.

LONGEST INSECT MIGRATION

10 GLOBE-SKIMMER DRAGONFLY
Every year, millions of dragonflies migrate up to 11,000 miles (17,700 km) around the Indian Ocean in order to follow the monsoon.

1
2
3

QUESTIONABLE ACTIONS AND IDEAS

Whether it's surfing down volcanoes, bathing in crocodile dung, or trying to figure out who really controls the world, people have come up with some really wacky ideas over the years. In this chapter, you'll read about some of these truly ill-advised concepts—from history (who was Ponzi and why did people give him so much money?), medicine (what's up with those leeches anyway?), and beyond (who really thought the monokini was a good idea?).

1 FREE-RIDING MOTOCROSS
Motocross daredevils perform their crazy flips and jumps on public land with no medics and few, if any, spectators.

2 ELEVATOR SURFING
Surfers ride on top of elevators in skyscrapers, sometimes jumping from elevator to elevator, risking life and limb.

3 BASE JUMPING
The name stands for Buildings, Antennae, Spans (bridges), and Earth (cliffs). It involves parachuting from low heights.

4 HELI-SKIING
Skiers take a helicopter to trails too extreme to reach via lift, then make their way back through an unpredictable terrain.

5 SPEED SKIING
Skiers take off at breakneck speed in a straight line down a mountain slope. It's one of the fastest nonmotorized sports.

6 VOLCANO BOARDING
Participants race down an active volcano on a snowboard-like plank, reaching up to 50 miles per hour (80 km/h).

7 WINGSUIT FLYING
Flyers glide in a special winged suit that creates extra lift. Sometimes they fly close to mountain faces.

8 BULL RIDING
Riders attempt to stay on the backs of angry, untrained bulls for a set amount of time in a rodeo setting.

9 STREET LUGE
Lying face up and feet forward on modified skateboards, riders race down paved hills and city streets at high speeds.

10 CAVE DIVING
Scuba divers make their way through narrow, winding underwater caves without a clear emergency escape route.

11 COMPETITIVE APNEA
Swimmers compete to stay underwater the longest on a single breath without the assistance of scuba equipment.

4
5
6
7
8
9
10
11

18 DUBIOUS BEAUTY TREATMENTS

MEN

1 **HAIR TRANSPLANTS**
Transplants are used to thwart baldness the world over these days.

2 **CROCODILE-DUNG BATHS**
The ancient Greeks found these baths relaxing and good for the skin.

3 **NIPPLE REMOVAL**
A modern-day "extreme body modification" in which the nipples are surgically removed.

4 **CURVE ENHANCEMENTS**
The Dinka tribe of the Sudan wear bright, beaded corsets that fit tightly, emphasizing their chests and buttocks.

UNISEX

5 **LEAD EYELINER**
Ancient Egyptians of both sexes wore eye makeup made from lead powder and copper ore.

6 **LIP PLATES**
People around the world and throughout history have used large lip piercings to signify their class or status—or enhance their beauty.

7 **BOTOX**
Modern seekers of the fountain of youth inject this toxin, which temporarily paralyzes muscles to smooth wrinkles.

8 **BEER BATHS**
Around the world, beer baths are believed to relax muscles and rejuvenate pores.

9 **GOLDFISH PEDICURE**
This treatment, developed in Japan and now available worldwide, consists of having your calluses nibbled off by hungry little fish.

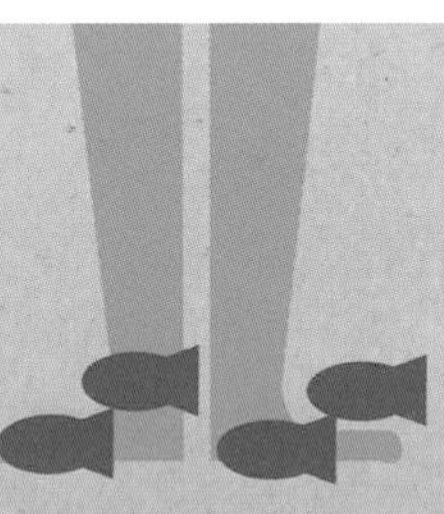

WOMEN

10 NIGHTINGALE-DUNG FACIALS
From ancient times until today, salons in Japan have used nightingale-dung facials to bleach and brighten skin.

18 LARD FOR STYLING
In Elizabethan England, lard was used to set wigs; it often resulted in rats infesting the hairpiece.

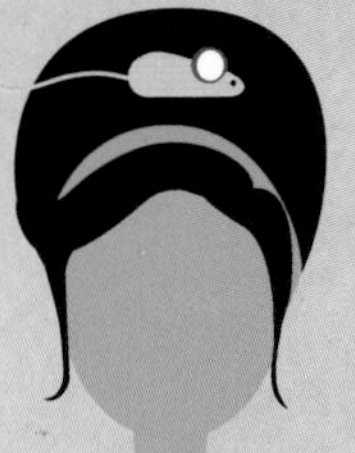

11 STRING BREAST IMPLANTS
In the 1990s, fiber "strings" were implanted into women's breasts; the resulting inflammation caused breasts to swell up to 25 pounds (11.5 kg) each.

17 LEECHES
Renaissance beauties placed leeches on their ears to drain blood from their faces for a fashionably pale complexion.

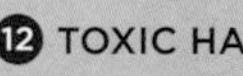

12 TOXIC HAIR DYE
Dyes of lead, lye, and sulfur were used to dye hair red or blond in Elizabethan England.

16 PUBIC-HAIR IMPLANTS
Abundant pubic hair is associated with fertility in South Korea, where implants are available.

13 SNAIL SLIME FACIALS
In some places in South America, snail slime is used to make skin soft.

15 BULL-SEMEN HAIR TREATMENT
A trendsetting London salon has pioneered this innovative hair rinse.

14 LEAD-BASED FOUNDATION
In the 1500s, Europeans tried lead-based products to achieve pale skin, but it unhappily led to gout, facial paralysis, scarring, and anemia.

4 NATIONAL BORDERS WHERE TRAFFIC SWITCHES SIDES

THE RULE OF THE ROAD

In most places, motorists drive on the right side of the road. Still, there are a fair number of nations where cars drive on the left. What happens when those roads meet at the nations' shared border? Hopefully, not head-on collisions. Here are four places that handle this issue, and their preferred traffic tactics.

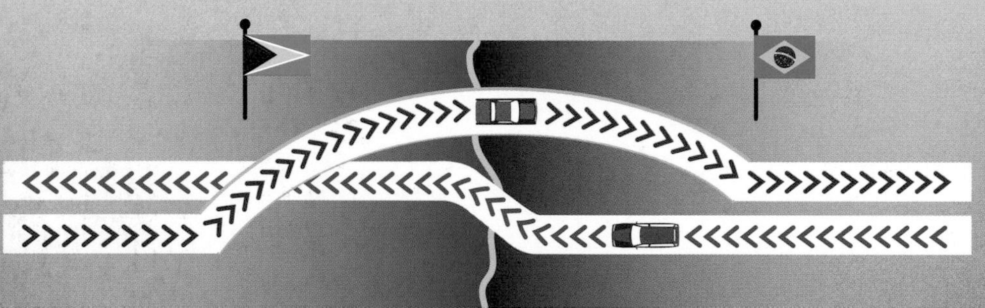

1

GUYANA AND BRAZIL

Crossover bridges span the Takutu River, shunting traffic to the proper lane as drivers cross between left side-loving Guyana and right side-revering Brazil.

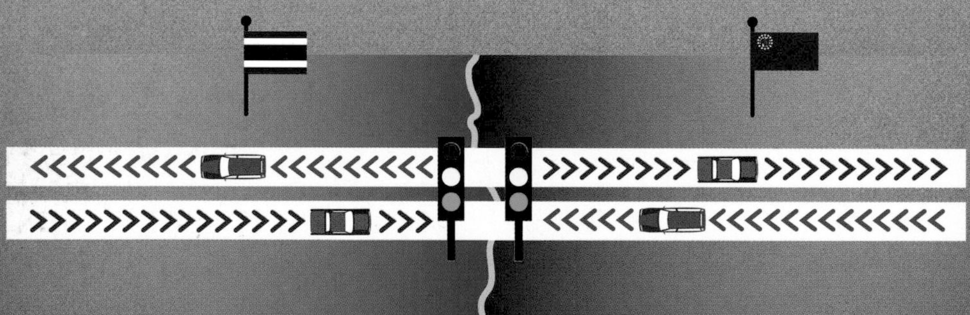

2

THAILAND AND LAOS

Lights let drivers know when to switch sides along the rather lengthy border between Thailand (where motorists drive on the left) and Laos (where drivers favor the right).

@#%!

3

HONG KONG AND MAINLAND CHINA
Lane-changing roundabouts help out along the borders between right side-driving Hong Kong and left side-driving mainland China.

4

KENYA AND ETHIOPIA
Signposts in the border town of Moyale guide low-volume traffic through the crossover between Kenya (a left side-driving country) and Ethiopia (a right side-driving country).

7 MILITARY BLUNDERS

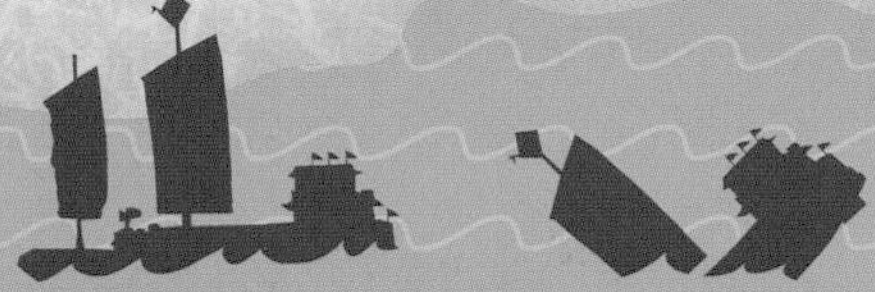

2 SICILIAN EXPEDITION
ATHENS VS. SPARTA / 415 BCE
The great Athenian general Alcibiades had planned a major assault against Spartan Sicily. Then he was accused of vandalism back home and recalled from command to stand trial. The assault went downhill from there for the Athenians.

1 BATTLE OF THE RED CLIFFS
CAO CAO VS. LIU BEI AND SUN QUAN / 208
Northern warlord Cao Cao's forces won many decisive victories over Liu Bei and Sun Quan, but then he attempted an attack via the Yangtze River. His troops became seasick, and he moored his boats to one another to reduce turbulence. His adversary was able to set the string of boats alight, destroying his entire fleet.

3 BATTLE OF DYRRHACHIUM
POMPEY VS. JULIUS CAESAR / 48 BCE
In this attempt at starting a civil war against Caesar (his father-in-law), Pompey had the Roman senate's backing, and his troops outnumbered Caesar's. However, when victory seemed imminent, Pompey feared a trap because it seemed too easy, and withdrew. Caesar took the advantage.

4 BATTLE OF STIRLING BRIDGE
ENGLAND VS. SCOTLAND / 1297
The English had bested the Scottish aristocracy and believed that they now faced a mere rabble. But their commander overslept, and instead of going a bit farther to ford a river 60 horses abreast, they chose to face the Scots on a narrow bridge that only allowed two horses at a time to cross. The Scots' infantry were able to pick the English off as they approached.

5 BATTLE OF LITTLE BIGHORN
GENERAL CUSTER VS. SIOUX INDIANS / 1876
Custer had several new Gatling guns when he set out to uproot a "small Indian village." Unfortunately, he left the guns behind, as he felt they would hamper mobility. Custer's 250 men were grossly outnumbered and overtaken by the Sioux. Had he taken the guns with him, the Sioux wouldn't have had a chance. Instead, the only survivor of this battle was a horse.

6 PEARL HARBOR
JAPAN VS. US / 1941
While the attack on Pearl Harbor was a decisive victory for Japan at the time, it did not achieve the intended goal of discouraging the United States from joining the war. Instead, the attack convinced isolationists that the time had come to join the battle, leading eventually to the destruction of Hiroshima and Nagasaki.

7 OPERATION TYPHOON
GERMANY VS. RUSSIA / 1941
The German drive toward Moscow in 1941 failed in part due to a lack of proper winter attire and vehicle antifreeze.

 WORST WEAPONS

1 **TYPE 94 SHIKI KENJU PISTOL**
JAPAN / WORLD WAR II
Highly unstable, this pistol accidentally fired when holstered or loaded too vigorously. Soldiers were forced to carry it into battle unloaded for safety, and then had to load it as needed during the fight.

2 **ME163 KOMET**
GERMANY / WORLD WAR II
The first and only operational rocket fighter had no landing gear, and its unstable fuel caused many fires and explosions. While 370 were built, they shot down a total of just ten Allied craft.

3 **MACADAM SHIELD SHOVEL**
CANADA / WORLD WAR I
This miniature shovel had a hole in it that fit a rifle's barrel. The hole was too low to allow for a good shot, and the shovel itself was not bulletproof—a real problem for a shield.

4 **ANTI-TANK DOGS**
RUSSIA / WORLD WAR II
The Russian army attempted to train dogs to run under tanks with bombs secured to their backs, which they would drop off at enemy targets and detonate. Unfortunately, the dogs showed a preference for Russian tanks, and the plan was quickly abandoned.

5 **M28 DAVY CROCKETT**
US / COLD WAR
One of the smallest nuclear weapons ever built, this was essentially a bazooka that shot nukes. It was determined (after production but before deployment) that the mini-warhead would produce lethal radiation within a half mile of where it landed, and the targeting was not very accurate.

6 **STICKY BOMB**
UK / WORLD WAR II
This hand grenade was designed to be sticky, so that soldiers could easily adhere it to enemy tanks. Unfortunately, it did not stick to tanks if they were dusty or dirty, and it did tend to stick to the soldier who was placing it.

7 **ACOUSTIC KITTY**
US / COLD WAR
The CIA tried to turn a cat into a spy by surgically implanting batteries and a listening device in its body, using the tail as an antenna. On the radio cat's first test run, it was run over by a taxi.

6 SUPERSTITIONS ABOUT BROOMS

1. Don't sweep your home at night; it means you are sweeping away wealth. (West Africa)
2. A single woman will not marry if someone sweeping the floor brushes her shoes. (Mexico)
3. A man hit with a broom will become impotent unless he retaliates sevenfold. (Nigeria)
4. Don't move an old broom into a new house—it swept up all the bad luck in the old house. (United States)
5. Hit a girl with a broom on the day of her first period so that she won't have trouble giving birth. (Russia)
6. A broom should never touch the head; this is very bad luck. (China)

6 SUPERSTITIONS ABOUT FINERY

1. When a necklace breaks, a member of the family who is sick will die. (China)
2. When you give a purse as a gift, put a little money inside. Giving it empty causes bad financial luck. (Russia)
3. If you put a piece of snakeskin into your wallet, you are going to become rich or find money. (Japan)
4. If you get your shirt wet while doing dishes, it means you'll marry a drunk. (Ireland)
5. A pregnant lady should never wear a *lei*, or the umbilical cord might choke her baby. (Hawaii)
6. Don't place your handbag on the floor or else the money inside will disappear. (Poland)

6 SUPERSTITIONS ABOUT NATURE

1. If it rains on a couple's wedding, it means that they will be wealthy in life. (Russia)
2. If a pregnant woman walks outside during a lunar eclipse, her baby may be born part wolf. (Mexico)
3. Finding an owl in the house is a sign of impending death in the family. (Italy)
4. It is unlucky to look upon a lone magpie; if you do, salute it or you will have bad luck. (England)
5. If black ants frequent a house, it means that its owner will be rich. (Philippines)
6. It is bad luck to cross a stream carrying a cat. (France)

1. If a lamp goes out in the same room in which a dead person is kept before burial, it means another member of the family will soon face death. (Indonesia)
2. A single woman should never sit with the corner of a table pointing at her, as this means she will never wed. (Hungary)
3. A boy, preferably born under the Chinese sign of the dragon, must roll across a newlywed couple's bed to ensure that they'll have a baby boy. (China)
4. If you sleep with your head to the north, you will have bad luck. Only dead people lie with their heads to the north. (Japan)
5. It is bad luck to sleep with one's head facing west, as only the dead lie like that. (Africa)
6. Don't sleep in a room with your feet facing the door because this is the way you will be carried out when you die. (Italy)
7. Leaving the windows of the bedroom open on November 1 brings you very bad luck. The spirits of the dead run free on that day, and will hide in your bed. (Spain)
8. To protect their unborn baby from evil spirits, pregnant women should place a knife under their bed. (China)
9. If you play an organ with a pedal while pregnant, you will have a baby girl. (Philippines)

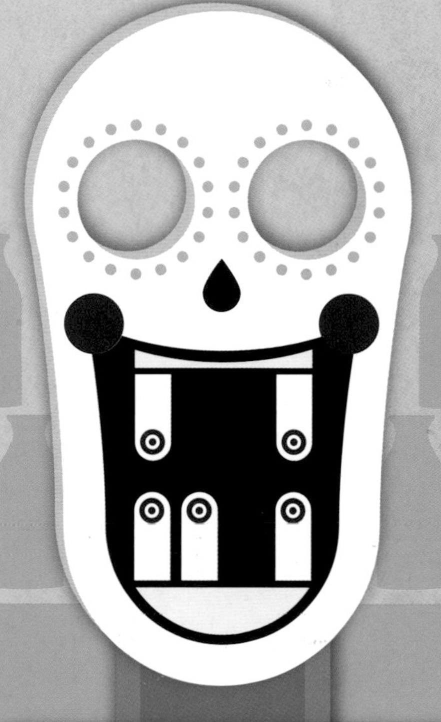

1. If you clip your nails after the sun goes down, you will not have the chance to see your parents before they die. (Japan)
2. If your right hand itches, that means you'll receive unexpected money. But if your left hand itches, that means you'll lose money unexpectedly. (Turkey)
3. If you dream that one of your teeth is being pulled out, this means that a family member will die. (Philippines)
4. If you dream of your teeth falling out, you will lose money. (Europe)
5. An unmarried woman should avoid washing her hair on a Saturday or she will marry a difficult-to-please man. (Indonesia)

6 SUPERSTITIONS ABOUT **FOOD**

1. If you eat all of the corners of your bread, you will have a good relationship with your mother-in-law. (Romania)
2. Don't eat damaged or asymmetrical food when pregnant or your baby will be ugly. (Korea)
3. Immediately after someone dies, the crops in the storehouse should be shoveled and the wine in the cellar shaken; otherwise the grain will not grow and the wine will go sour. (Germany)
4. If a pregnant woman craves fish and doesn't eat it, her baby will be born with the head of a fish. (Canada)
5. After eating a soft-boiled egg, push the spoon through the empty shell's bottom to let out the devil. (England)
6. Throwing rice at a newly married couple encourages any jealous spirits that might be hovering nearby to eat, rather than bother the bride and groom. (China)

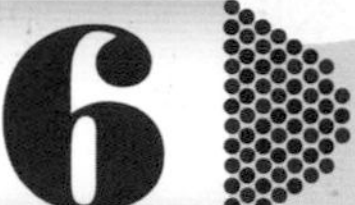

ADDICTIVE SUBSTANCES RANKED

KICKING THE HABIT

It's difficult to definitively name the world's most addictive substance, but Dr. Jack E. Henningfield of the National Institute on Drug Abuse and Dr. Neal L. Benowitz of the University of California at San Francisco have created this fascinating system, which weighs five factors: withdrawal symptoms, tendency to keep using the drug once one is already high, tendency to develop a tolerance, difficulty "staying quit," and how intoxicated the drug makes the user each time.

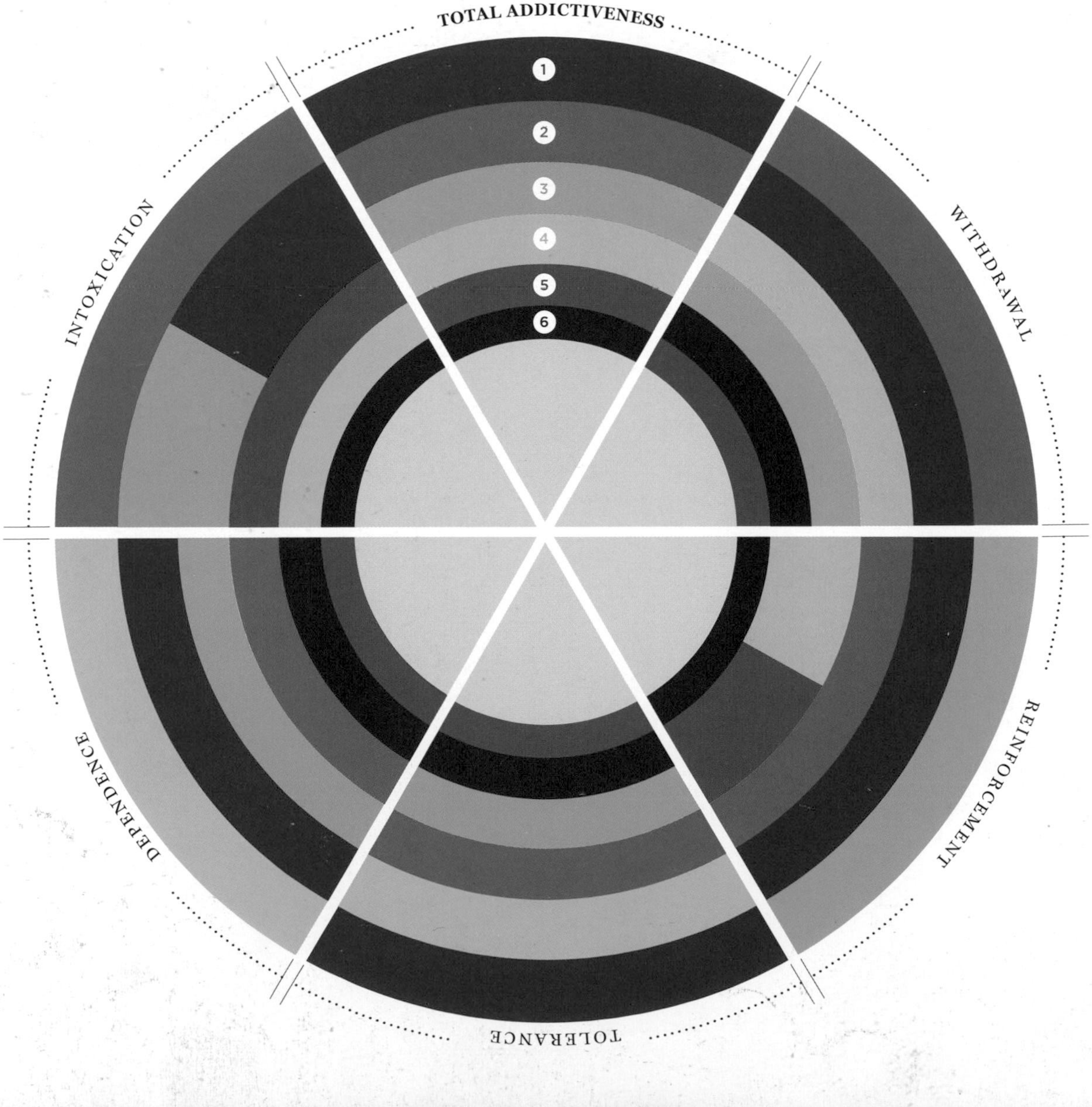

TOTAL ADDICTIVENESS
The overall assessment of how habit-forming a drug is

WITHDRAWAL
The severity of symptoms when trying to quit

REINFORCEMENT
The tendency for a person to keep doing a drug after the first time

TOLERANCE
The need to keep increasing dose to get the same effect

DEPENDENCE
The difficulty in quitting or "staying quit"

INTOXICATION
How intoxicated the user gets per use

TOTAL ADDICTIVENESS
1
2
3
4
5
6
WITHDRAWAL
REINFORCEMENT
TOLERANCE
DEPENDENCE
INTOXICATION

12 PRODUCTS THAT RADIATION "IMPROVED"

GETTING THAT HEALTHY GLOW

Soon after the discovery of radium, it became fashionable to add it to almost everything—before scientists learned that radiation can cause cancer and other health problems.

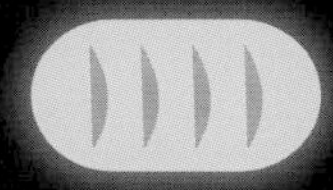

1. **RADIUM BREAD**
CZECHOSLOVAKIA / 1920
These loaves were made with water containing only trace amounts of radiation, and weren't considered notably dangerous.

2. **RADIUM EMANATION BATH SALTS**
US / 1925
These bath salts were advertised as a treatment for nervousness, insomnia, exhaustion, arthritis, and rheumatism.

3. **THO-RADIA SKIN CREAM**
FRANCE / 1930s
This toiletry article contained thorium and radium, which were supposed to erase facial wrinkles.

4. **RADIUM CHOCOLATE**
GERMANY / 1930s
The makers of these chocolate bars—which were "enhanced" with radioactive materials—boasted of the treats' "rejuvenation power."

5. **DORAMAD TOOTHPASTE**
GERMANY / 1930s
This dental-hygiene product was offered to the public with the slogan "Keep Your Health with Radium Radiation."

6. **PURE RADIUM WATER**
US / 1930s
Radium-"infused" water was touted as a remedy for senility, rheumatism, eczema, flatulence, and stomach troubles.

7. **RADIENDOCRINATOR**
US / 1930
These metal wafers were intended to be worn tucked under the scrotum for "invigoration."

8. **VITA RADIUM SUPPOSITORIES**
US / 1930
Radium-treated suppositories were administered to men to stimulate "the weakened organs that needed vitalizing aid."

9. **CARADIUM HAIR TREATMENT**
UK / 1934
Ads claimed it "restores, right from the roots, the natural color, health, and beauty to your hair."

10. **NUTEX RADIUM**
US / 1940s
To improve their effectiveness, condoms were impregnated with radium.

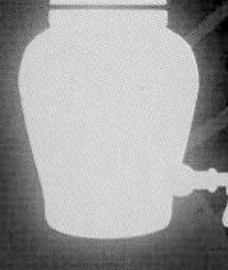

11. **RADIUM SPA**
US / 1950s
Water jugs were made with a radioactive base so that radiation seeped into a family's supply of drinking water overnight.

12. **GILBERT ATOMIC ENERGY LAB**
US / 1950s
Designed for the "junior scientist," this toy set featured a Geiger counter, radioactive ores, and a spinthariscope that showed radioactive decay.

18 THINGS THAT WE SHOULD HAVE BY NOW

3 WORLD PEACE

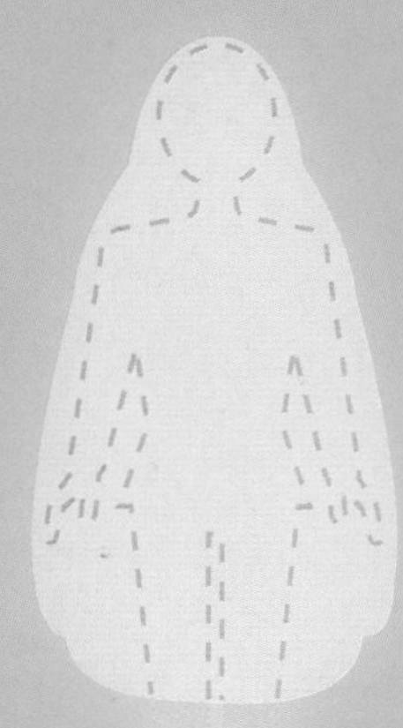

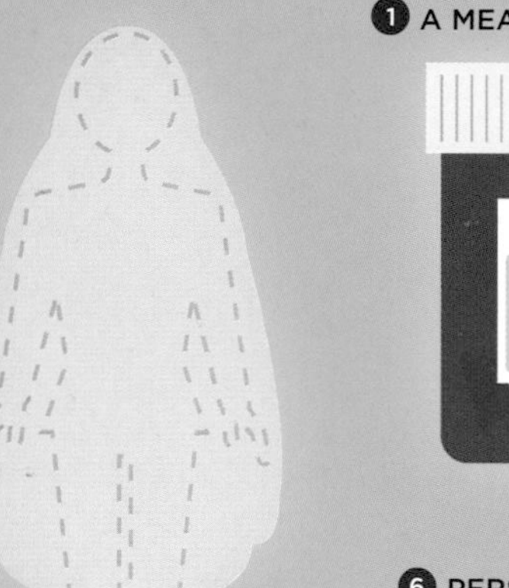

5 INVISIBILITY CLOAK

1 A MEAL IN A PILL

2 A CURE FOR CANCER, HIV/AIDS, HEART DISEASE, INFLUENZA, DIABETES, AND THE COMMON COLD

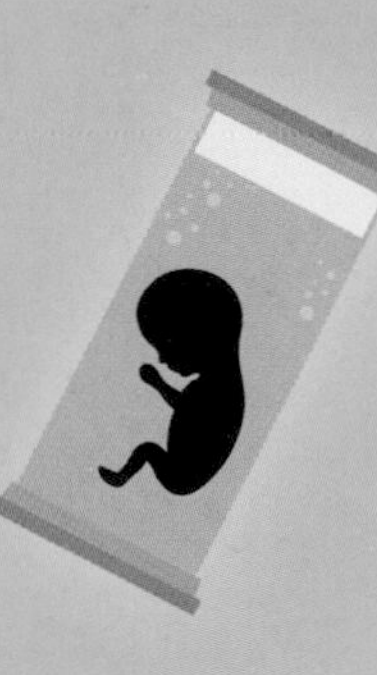

4 WOMB-FREE GESTATION

6 PERSONAL CLONES

7 ARTIFICIAL INTELLIGENCE

8 JET PACKS

11 ROBOT SERVANTS

12 IMMORTALITY

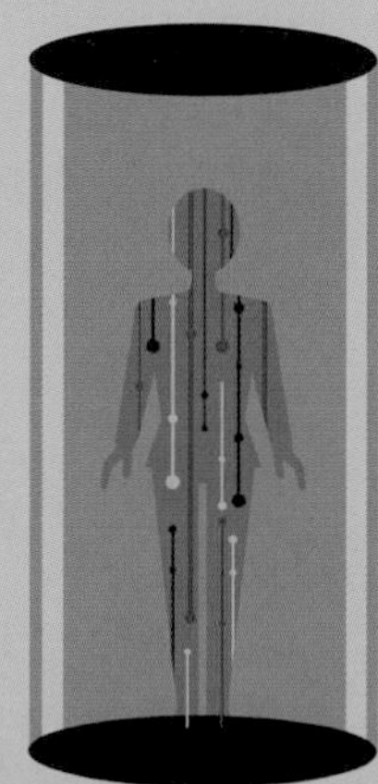

9 TELEPORTATION

10 COLD SLEEP (HIBERNATION DURING INTER-STELLAR TRAVEL)

13 COLONIES ON MARS

14 FLYING CARS

15 TIME TRAVEL

16 FASTER-THAN-LIGHT TRAVEL

17 THE HOLODECK

18 LASER GUNS

9 THINGS WE THOUGHT WERE GOING TO BE EASY

1. **ALCHEMY**
   ALCHEMISTS / THE MIDDLE AGES AND RENAISSANCE
   The belief that elements can be changed into more precious substances (say, lead to gold) has persisted for centuries.

2. **INVADING AFGHANISTAN**
   VARIOUS EMPIRES / THROUGHOUT HISTORY
   Genghis Khan, the British Empire, the USSR, and the United States all thought this military expedition would be a cinch.

3. **STEAM POWER**
   INVENTORS / THE MIDDLE AGES AND RENAISSANCE
   For more than 300 years inventors struggled to perfect steam power, but no viable version was created until 1712.

4. **HOLDING THE MAGINOT LINE**
   FRANCE / 1914–1918
   This massive, fortified wall was built to bar Germans from invading France in World War II. They just went around it.

5. **THE EQUAL RIGHTS AMENDMENT**
   CIVIL RIGHTS ACTIVISTS / 1970s
   US states refused to ratify a seemingly "no brainer" bill to mandate equal pay and other rights for women.

6. **THE PAPERLESS OFFICE**
   BUSINESSES WORLDWIDE / 1990–PRESENT
   Computers were supposed to eliminate paper waste. Apparently, no one really thought about printouts.

7. **CONTROLLING CANE BEETLES**
   AUSTRALIA / 1937
   Toads were imported to prey on sugar cane–eating beetles. The toads are now pests and the beetles still wreak havoc.

8. **GETTING EVERYONE TO USE THE METRIC SYSTEM**
   GLOBAL / 1970s
   The United States, Myanmar, and Liberia are the only nations not currently using the metric system.

9. **COLD FUSION**
   SCIENTISTS / 1980s
   If nuclear fusion could be achieved at low temperatures, it could revolutionize the energy industry. No luck so far.

9 Groups Falsely Believed to Rule the World

1

THE VATICAN

The Vatican has long been surrounded by conspiracy theories—most suggesting that members of the Catholic Church's inner circle are the world's puppeteers.

2

THE UNITED NATIONS

Ever since the United Nations was founded in 1945, there have been theories that the organization is actually a sinister plot to unite the world under one fascist leader.

3

THE JESUITS

Jesuits have been accused of undue influence over the Catholic Church and on governments, and of starting wars throughout the world to gain power.

4

THE ROTHSCHILD FAMILY

This banking family with German-Jewish roots has controlled vast finances since the 1700s and has been elevated to nobility in Austria and the United Kingdom. It may or may not, in fact, rule the world.

5

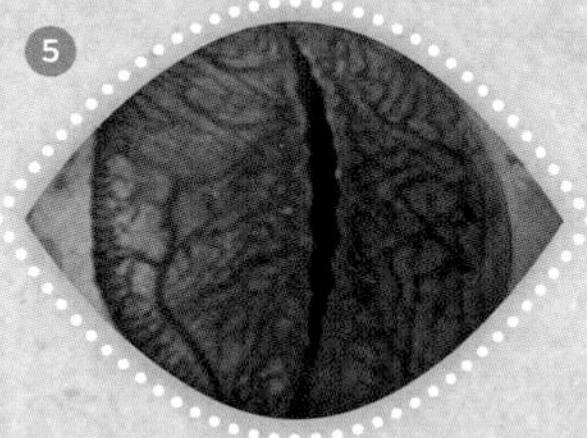

REPTILIAN ALIENS

Believers say that shape-shifting reptilian aliens may have replaced several heads of state, including Dick Cheney. Princess Di evidently knew of their existence, which was why she was eliminated.

6

THE FREEMASONS

This group allegedly seeks to destroy the world so it can be rebuilt more perfectly; since its inception in the late 1500s, it has supposedly long infiltrated nearly all aspects of government at every level.

7

THE ILLUMINATI

A Bavarian freethinking movement dating back to the 1700s, it is believed to control world governments and media, and has members at the highest levels of state.

8

THE JEWISH ELITE

For centuries, Jewish people have been the target of conspiracy theories. Recently, such theories have included manipulating the world financial system and the media.

9

THE BILDERBERG GROUP

This cabal of the wealthy and powerful has been secretly meeting since 1954 at the Netherlands' Hotel de Bilderberg to do business, or perhaps to control the world.

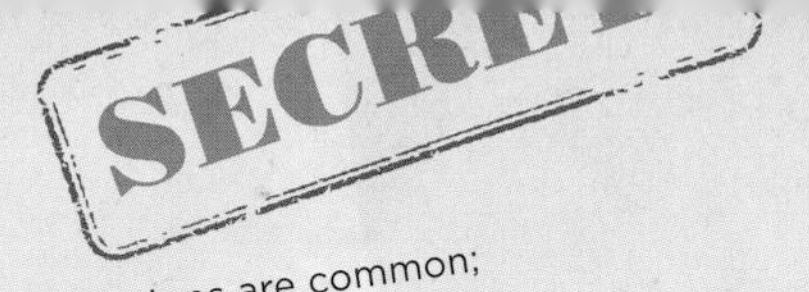

FAMOUS CONSPIRACY THEORIES

1. The Moon landings were faked at a soundstage in the Nevada desert.

2. John F. Kennedy was killed by a shadowy conspiracy involving the CIA, the FBI, the Mafia, his own vice president Lyndon B. Johnson, Cuban operatives, and the Russians—all working together.

4. In 1947, an alien spacecraft crash-landed in Roswell, Nevada, at Area 51. The government evidently still has the alien corpses and is performing unspeakable experiments on them.

5. Space agencies are covering up evidence of life on Mars.

6. "The Man" wants marijuana to be illegal—the real reason pot is against the law is because the hemp plant is so useful that it threatens the paper, rope, pharmaceutical, and cloth industries.

8. The September 11 attacks in 2001 were an inside job—the US government staged it all so as to justify going to war.

9. Airplane contrails are actually the government secretly spraying various chemicals on populations and crops for mysterious purposes.

10. Denver International Airport is the center of a New World Order, and there's a massive city under it.

11. Jesus Christ was married and had at least one child.

12. A secret form of energy, called "Vril," is used and controlled by a subterranean society of matriarchal, socialist, utopian superior beings. In World War II, Germany used this technology to create flying saucers.

13. An automobile that runs on water was invented, but auto manufacturers suppressed it.

14. The 2004 Indonesian tsunami was actually caused by a "tsunami bomb," a nuclear device set off underwater for nefarious purposes.

16. The 2010 Haitian earthquake was caused by nuclear weapons testing.

17. Digital TV signals enable mind control by the government.

18. AIDS was actually developed by the US government as a form of biological warfare.

19. Barack Obama is a sleeper agent in a Muslim plot to rule the United States.

20. UFO abductions are common; witnesses are hushed up by government "men in black."

21. A sacred menorah stolen in 70 CE is still kept in the Vatican.

22. US President Franklin D. Roosevelt knew about Japan's plan to attack Pearl Harbor in 1941, but kept quiet because he knew the attack would make Americans supportive of World War II.

23. Water fluoridation causes mental illness and susceptibility to government brainwashing.

24. The USSR sent many cosmonauts into space before Yuri Gagarin, who is credited with being the first human in space. All died and the accidents were covered up.

25. Phar Lap, the champion New Zealand and Australian racehorse, was poisoned in 1932 by US thugs.

26. The plays attributed to William Shakespeare were actually written by Edward de Vere, Christopher Marlowe, Sir Francis Bacon, or a group of any or all of the above.

4 CRAZY THINGS GOVERNMENTS ACTUALLY DID

1. **THE SUN GUN**
GERMANY / 1940s
Wartime physicists designed (but never made) a giant mirror, intending to send it into orbit and use it to burn cities to the ground, boil reservoirs, and wreak general havoc.

2. **SOCIALIST *GODZILLA***
NORTH KOREA / 1978
Kim Jong-Il kidnapped a South Korean filmmaker and forced him to realize the dictator's visions, including *Pulgasari*, a "socialist *Godzilla*," in 1985. The director and his wife finally escaped in 1986.

3. **OPERATION FREEDOM**
US / 1966
The CIA attempted to kill Fidel Castro with a poisoned cigar slipped into his briefcase at a United Nations meeting. When this failed, exploding and LSD-drugged cigars were also considered.

4. **IMELDA MARCOS VS. THE BEATLES**
THE PHILIPPINES / 1966
After the group inadvertently missed a lunch with First Lady Imelda Marcos, the government withdrew security support and the band was hounded and attacked in public.

6 SCIENTISTS WHO EXPERIMENTED ON THEMSELVES

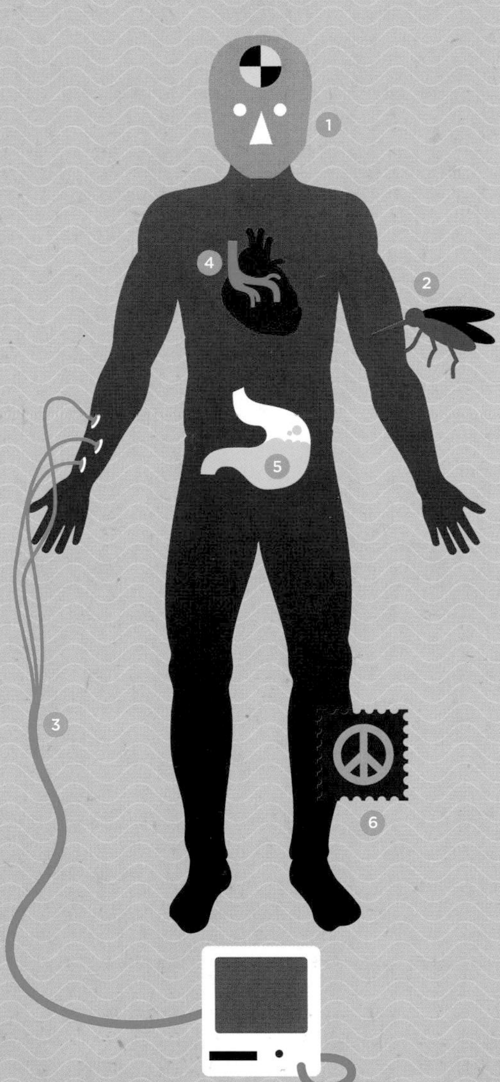

1 **DR. JOHN STAPP**
US / 1940s
For years, scientists believed that humans could withstand no more than 18 times the force of gravity. Then Dr. John Stapp subjected his body to up to 46 times the force of gravity in his "rocket sled" experiments, which proved crucial to improving vehicular and aerodynamic safety.

2 **DR. JESSE WILLIAM LAZEAR**
US / 1900
While studying the transmission of yellow fever in Cuba, Dr. Jesse William Lazear experimented on himself, knowingly letting fever-infected mosquitoes bite him and then not telling his colleagues. He died at the age of 34; his research later was recognized as invaluable in treating yellow fever.

3 **DR. KEVIN WARWICK**
UK / 2002
Cybernetics professor Dr. Kevin Warwick had an array of 100 electrodes implanted directly into the nerves of his arm. Over a three-month period, he conducted a number of experiments linking his nervous system with the Internet, most notably to control a robot arm located thousands of miles away.

4 **DR. WERNER FORSSMANN**
GERMANY / 1929
Colleagues worried that Dr. Werner Forssmann's idea for a heart catheter could be deadly. To prove them wrong, he anesthetized his own lower arm and inserted a cannula, threading it to his heart. He then walked to the hospital's X-ray department to get an image.

5 **DR. BARRY MARSHALL**
AUSTRALIA / 1984
After failed attempts to infect piglets in 1984, Dr. Barry Marshall drank a petri dish of *Helicobacter pylori* collected from a patient. He then developed gastritis, achlorhydria, stomach discomfort, nausea, vomiting, and halitosis, confirming his hypothesis that bacteria causes ulcers. He won the Nobel Prize.

6 **DR. ALBERT HOFMANN**
SWITZERLAND / 1943
Dr. Albert Hofmann created LSD in a lab in 1938, but the drug wasn't used until 1943, when he accidentally absorbed some of it through his skin. He then tried a large enough dose to result in the first LSD trip, and had a very interesting bike ride home. He called LSD "medicine for the soul."

7 UNETHICAL THINGS DONE IN THE NAME OF SCIENCE

1 APE-MAN

GUINEA / 1927

Russian scientist Ilya Ivanovich Ivanov first attempted to artificially inseminate female apes with human sperm. Next he hoped to inseminate human female volunteers with ape sperm, but authorities intervened.

2 TUSKEGEE SYPHILIS EXPERIMENT

US / 1932–1972

A state-run public health service recruited 399 poor African-Americans with syphilis, hoping to find a cure. After a treatment was discovered, the men were not given it so that scientists could study their decline.

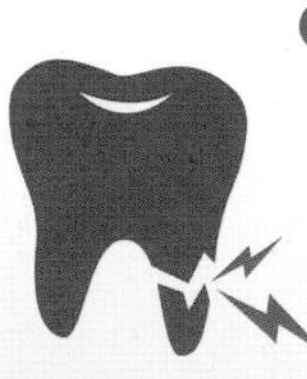

3 VIPEHOLM EXPERIMENT

SWEDEN / 1947–1949

Patients at a mental hospital were fed sweets as part of a study on dental cavities, which ultimately ruined their teeth. Devised by the dentistry field and candy companies, the study was ruled unethical.

4 TWO-HEADED DOG

USSR / 1950s

Vladimir Petrovich Demikhov did a number of experiments involving dog head transplants, creating up to 20 two-headed dogs that survived briefly after the procedure, with both heads fully functional.

5 SEX AND DRUGS

US / 1950s

In Operation Midnight Climax, prostitutes were paid by the CIA to entice clients back to a disguised headquarters. Once inside, the johns were given LSD and observed in an ill-advised study on surveillance, sex, and mind-altering substances.

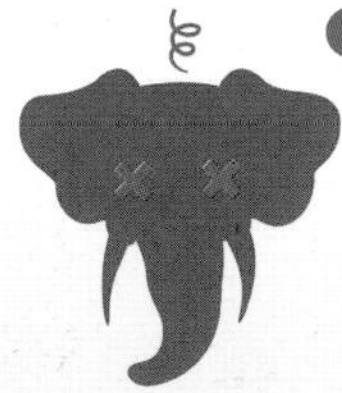

6 ELEPHANT ON LSD

US / 1962

Tusko, a zoo elephant, was dosed by researchers with 0.01 ounces (285 mg) of LSD (about 3,000 times a human dose, and the highest dose ever given to any creature). He appeared very agitated for a few minutes, then fell over dead.

7 ELECTRIFIED CORPSES

ITALY / 1803

Galvanist Giovanni Aldini (nephew of the anatomy professor Galvani) toured Europe displaying what happens when corpses are shocked with electricity. His most famous demonstration occurred when he placed rods connected to a battery on the face of a murderer's corpse, causing it to create expressions. His grand finale was to stick an electrode up the corpse's rectum, whereupon the corpse broke into a ghastly dance.

13 BIGGEST FLOPS

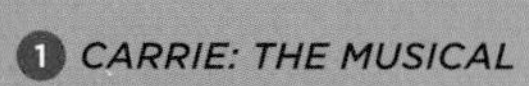

1 *CARRIE: THE MUSICAL*
THEATER / 1988
The lavish production closed 72 hours after it opened on Broadway, losing at least US $7 million. "They're all gonna laugh at you," indeed.

2 THE *SPRUCE GOOSE*
AVIATION / 1947
Legendary aviation eccentric Howard Hughes created this—the largest flying boat ever made—for World War II, though it wasn't completed until after the war ended. Made of wood due to a wartime materials restriction, it flew one test flight, and never flew again—the war ended and there was no perceived use for it.

3 *CUTTHROAT ISLAND*
CINEMA / 1995
This big-budget pirate film lost almost US $150 million, bankrupted a production company, and hurt a lot of careers.

4 PETS.COM
INTERNET / 2000
Opened in 1999 and closed in 2000, this short-lived site has come to exemplify the dot-com bust. With no business plan, the company spent US $11.8 million on advertising in its first year, but only earned US $619,000. It lost money on almost every sale, especially once it started offering free shipping on heavy items, such as cat litter and pet food.

5 EDSEL
AUTOMOBILE / 1958
This Ford model lost millions for the US car company. It was not a dreadful car, just too expensive for a recession, not very sexy, and saddled with a terrible name. It never caught on, and the company lost the US $4 million it had spent developing its big new thing.

6 AQUA DOTS
TOYS / 2007
These seemingly innocent plastic beads were supposed to set into a neat design when sprayed with water. Instead, they exuded a chemical not unlike GHB, the club and date-rape drug.

7 THE *TITANIC*

SHIP / 1912

One of the most famous disasters of all time, the luxury liner—touted as "unsinkable"—hit an iceberg and sank on its maiden voyage, killing 1,517 people.

8 CATHÉDRALE SAINT-PIERRE DE BEAUVAIS

ARCHITECTURE / 1272

Designed in the thirteenth century to be the tallest cathedral in the world, Saint-Pierre was plagued by decisions that placed grandiose elements over functionality—in fact, part of the structure collapsed only 12 years into its construction. While it has been used for centuries, it was never completed.

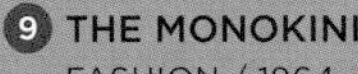

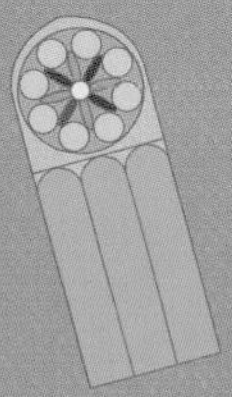

9 THE MONOKINI

FASHION / 1964

After the success of the bikini, could a smaller bathing suit be far behind? Designed by Rudi Gernreich, the monokini had only two small straps over the shoulders, baring the breasts. Other less scandalous versions have made it into the marketplace, with slightly more success.

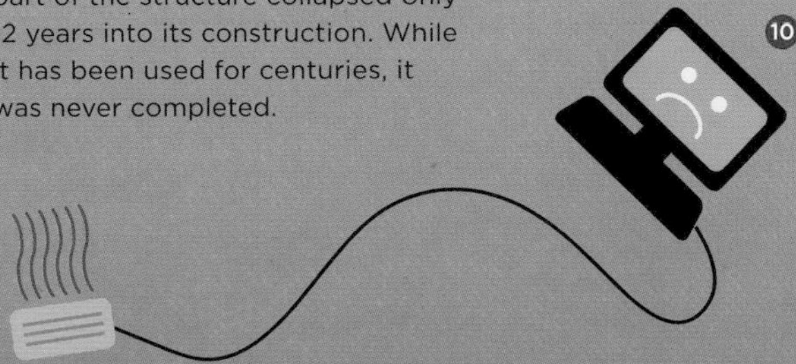

10 Y2K

CULTURE / 2000

The world was supposed to end when all the computer clocks reset. It did not.

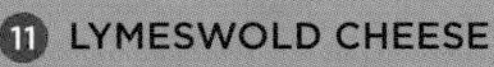

11 LYMESWOLD CHEESE

CUISINE / 1982

Developed as a "new cheese" to use British milk surpluses, this Brie-like cheese generated initial buzz, which perhaps led the manufacturers to release stocks before they were ready for consumption. The cheese's reputation suffered, and it was allowed to die a quiet death.

12 iSMELL

ELECTRONICS / 2001

This shark fin-shaped computer-peripheral device was designed to emit a smell (128 were available) to go with sites visited or e-mails opened. The idea behind it was that the all-important olfactory experience was missing from Internet use. A perfume manufacturer, for example, could embed a scent into a piece of advertising or its Web site. The product never made it past prototype.

13 LYNDON LAROUCHE

POLITICS / 1976–2004

This controversial and stalwart right-winger ran in every US presidential race from 1976 to 2004. (In 1992, he even ran from a prison cell, where he was serving time for fraud and tax violation.) His views on race, religion, and sexual orientation are not progressive, but his "LaRouche movement" has amassed a sizable cult following.

HOW DOES A PONZI SCHEME WORK, ANYWAY?

A Ponzi scheme is a fraudulent investment operation that pays returns to separate investors from their own money or money paid by subsequent investors, rather than from any actual profit earned. In this simplified example, the schemer starts by taking US $100 from investors, promising to double it within a month. But instead of investing their money, he pays them with funds from larger, successive rounds of investors.

THE SCHEMER

FIRST ROUND
2 INVESTORS

In the first month, the schemer takes US $100 each from the first two investors.

SECOND ROUND
4 INVESTORS

Because the schemer pockets US $200, he needs to find US $400—four investors—in the next month to pay returns to the first two investors.

THIRD ROUND
8 INVESTORS

In the third month, he owes US $800, so he has to find eight new investors. He'll have to get more than US $100 from each of them if he wants to keep skimming money for himself.

FOURTH ROUND
16 INVESTORS

In the next month, he'll need 16 investors. And so on.

1900 1905 1910 1915 1925 1935 1940 1945 1950 1955 1960 1965

1899
William F. Miller / US
Modern-day US $25 million

1920
Charles Ponzi / US
Modern-day US $130 million

1930
Ivar Kreuger / Sweden
Modern-day US $1.5 billion

1970
Dona Branca / Portugal
Modern-day US $600 million

BERNIE MADOFF'S PONZI SCHEME

How big *was* the pile of money that Bernie Madoff made off with? Well, it was so big that we couldn't even show it on the main chart. Here's how it all stacks up.

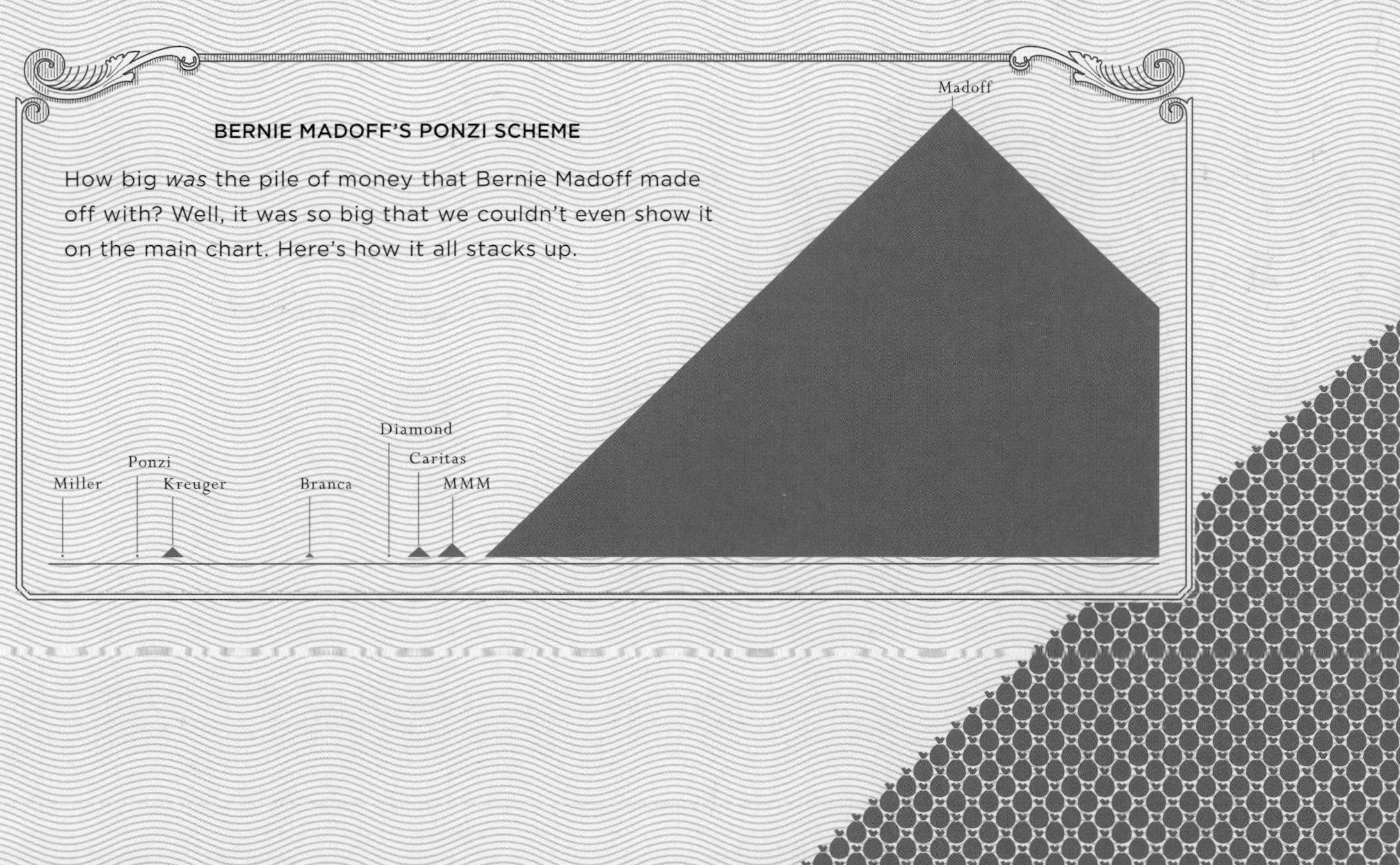

1975 1980 1995 2000 2005 2010

1986
Diamond Mortgage / US
Modern-day US $100 million

1992
Caritas Company / Romania
Modern-day US $1.5 billion

1994
MMM Co. / Russia
Modern-day US $2 billion

2008
Bernard Madoff / US
Modern-day US $65 billion

BIZARRE MEDICAL CURES THAT WORK

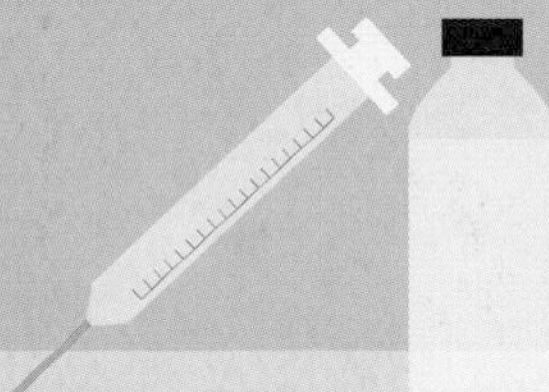

1 INSULIN COMA THERAPY
In the United States during the mid-1900s, doctors treated mental-illness patients by inducing a daily insulin coma.

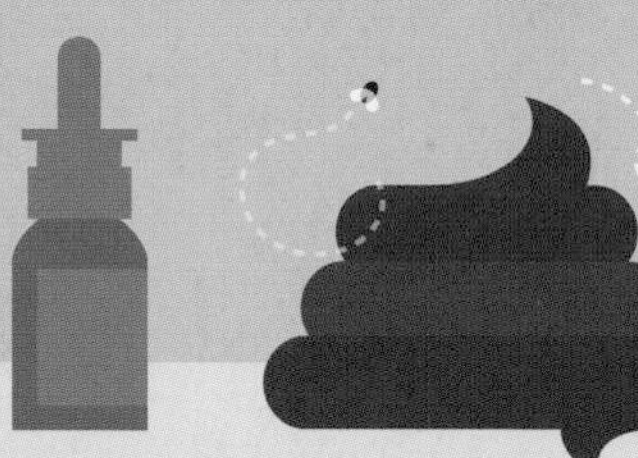

2 FECAL BACTERIOTHERAPY
In a last-ditch treatment for people with severe intestinal problems, fecal matter from a healthy donor is placed in the ailing patient's colon.

3 HIRUDOTHERAPY
Leeches are now used to keep blood from coagulating during surgeries on tiny vascular tissue. In reconstructive surgery, they help renew blood flow to reattached body parts.

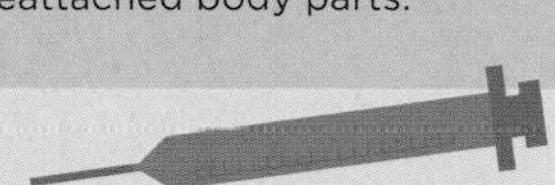

4 TOOTH-EYE IMPLANT
This experimental procedure involves implanting a fractional piece of a tooth into a nonfunctioning eye (as part of a new, artificial cornea) to restore sight.

5 VODKA DEODORIZER
Stinky feet can be freshened up with a wipe from a vodka-soaked cloth—its alcohol kills odor-causing fungus.

6 DUCT TAPE
Some swear by duct tape for more than household fixes; for example, covering a wart with the sticky stuff may be more effective than freezing it off.

7 MAGGOT DEBRIDEMENT THERAPY
Maggots are introduced into a wound to eat dead or rotting flesh. Bonus: Their excrement also kills harmful bacteria.

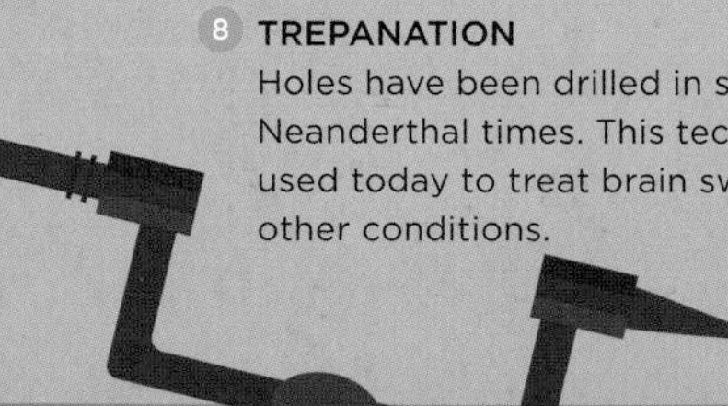

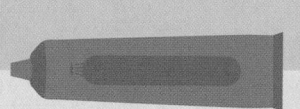

8 TREPANATION
Holes have been drilled in skulls since Neanderthal times. This technique is used today to treat brain swelling and other conditions.

9 HELMINTHIC THERAPY
Deliberate infestation with a parasitic worm seems to have positive effects on many conditions, like ulcers, multiple sclerosis, asthma, eczema, dermatitis, and hay fever.

8 BIZARRE MEDICAL CURES THAT DON'T

1 PSYCHIC SURGERY
"Surgeons" supposedly reach magically into a person's body and remove "tumors" and "bad spirits" (actually fake blood and chicken parts), all without leaving a wound.

2 PUPPY BLOOD
A book published in the 1700s claimed that one could cure acne by applying a potion made from the blood of two puppies mixed with white wine.

3 URINE THERAPY
Urine was once considered a general health tonic, consumed directly to cure strep throat and applied as a poultice for athlete's foot and broken bones.

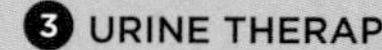

4 FROG SMOOTHIE
A blended concoction of frog skin, broth, honey, and aloe is said to cure impotence. Popular in Peru.

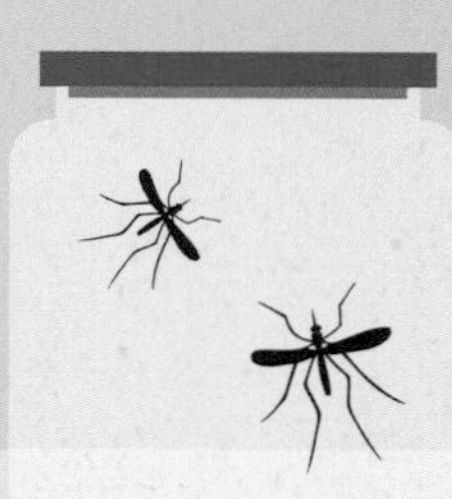

5 MALARIOTHERAPY
Much to the medical community's chagrin, Henry Heimlich (inventor of the abdominal thrust) claimed that malaria parasite injections are effective against cancer, Lyme disease, and HIV.

6 LOTUS BIRTH
Some cultures leave a baby's umbilical cord and placenta attached for several days until it rots off. Others believe this increases risk of infection.

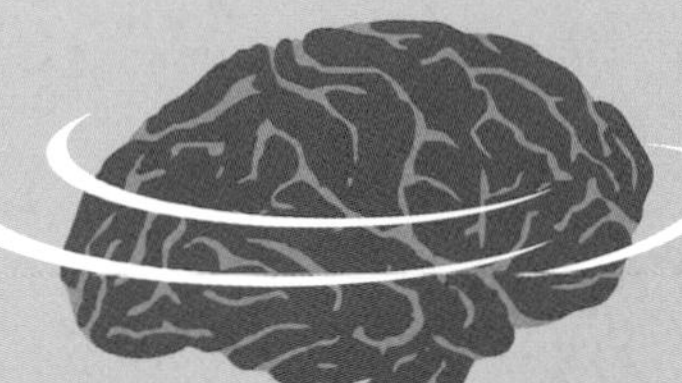

7 ROTATIONAL THERAPY
American physician Benjamin Rush believed that spinning patients in specially constructed chairs would reduce brain congestion and, in turn, cure mental illness.

8 MALARIA SPIDER CURE
In Europe during the 1700s, it was believed that consuming compressed spider webs could treat malaria. Some versions of the cure even involved swallowing the spider alive.

12 THINGS THAT RUINED IT FOR EVERYONE

1 THE INQUISITION
RUINED
HEALTH IN THE MIDDLE AGES
EUROPE / 1300s

As part of the Inquisition, cats were killed in vast numbers due to their association with witchcraft. The cats were key to controlling rats, which, then unchecked, bred and spread plague everywhere.

2 CATHOLIC MISSIONARIES
RUINED
THE MAYAN CODICES
LATIN AMERICA / 1500s

Vast numbers of books depicting Mayan life and religion existed for 600 years before the conquistadors arrived. These books were destroyed as part of the conquest's goal to eliminate native culture.

3 CHERNOBYL
RUINED
NUCLEAR POWER
USSR / 1986

Many believe that nuclear power could be a clean and relatively safe option, but the Chernobyl disaster put a halt to a lot of research. Ironically, this may have made existing, aging plants even less safe.

4 INCOMPETENT TERRORISTS
RUINED
CONVENIENT AIR TRAVEL
WORLDWIDE / 2000s

The shoe bomber, the people who tried to mix bombs from fluids, and the underpants bomber all failed at terrorism, but did manage to make air travel increasingly annoying for everyone else.

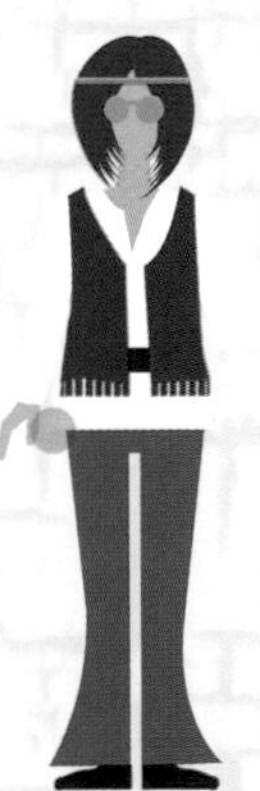

5 THE MANSON FAMILY
RUINED
BEING A HIPPIE
US / 1969

Hippies might have been laughed at for their peace-loving attitudes and colorful attire, but it took mentally deranged killer Charles Manson to make people start fearing them.

6 VLADIMIR LENIN
RUINED
COMMUNISM
USSR / 1917–1924

The basic tenets of Communism were so warped by its most enthusiastic early adopter that the "socialist paradise" laid out in *Das Kapital* will probably never be established as described.

7 THE *HINDENBURG*

RUINED

LIGHTER-THAN-AIR TRAVEL

US / 1937

Dirigibles were a promising form of transport, and helium-filled ones were safe. Still, the dramatic explosion of the hydrogen-filled *Hindenburg* ruined their popularity.

8 THE CULTURAL REVOLUTION

RUINED

CENTURIES OF CULTURE AND PROGRESS

CHINA / 1966–1976

The Red Guard destroyed countless ancient buildings, artifacts, antiques, books, and paintings. Doctors, teachers, and other "counterrevolutionaries" were killed, imprisoned, or forced to flee.

9 AIDS

RUINED

CASUAL SEX

WORLDWIDE / 1980s

The sexual revolution bloomed for only a couple of decades before AIDS put the fear back into hooking up.

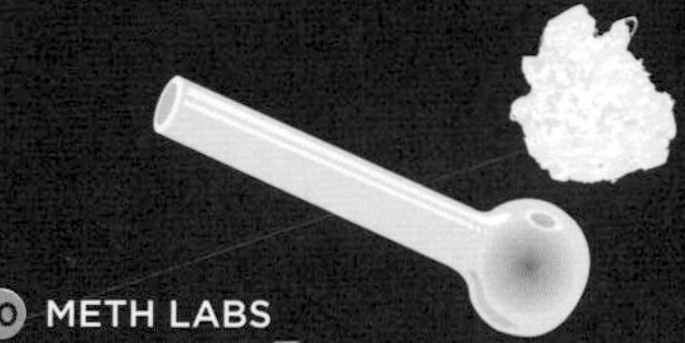

10 METH LABS

RUINED

ALLERGY RELIEF

US / 1990s

Pseudoephedrine, the key ingredient in some of the most effective allergy and cold treatments, can be used to make meth. Some states have banned the sale of medicines containing this drug.

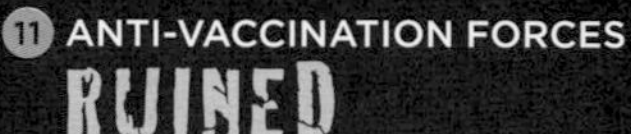

11 ANTI-VACCINATION FORCES

RUINED

NOT HAVING WHOOPING COUGH

US / 1988

A number of diseases were close to being well under control when fears about vaccination scared some parents into allowing their children to forgo shots, resulting in a resurgence of nearly eradicated illnesses.

12 JULIUS CAESAR

RUINED

THE LIBRARY AT ALEXANDRIA

EGYPT / 48 BCE

The largest and most important library in the ancient world was a priceless resource until Julius Caesar burned it down by accident.

水
!!!

446 GOOD, BAD, POPULAR, AND UNPOPULAR ITEMS

What's the best country to live in if you're unemployed? The worst thing a beauty queen ever did? How about the most widely read novel ever? From the worst natural disasters to the most butchered karaoke songs in Korea, this chapter makes dozens of shameless value judgments . . . some indisputable (like the most dangerous hiking trail in the world), others less so (a sampling of the world's most popular names).

14 BEAUTY QUEEN SCANDALS

ARGENTINA

AUSTRIA

SPAIN

WALES

GERMANY

AMERICA

PHILIPPINES

1 1960

Miss Argentina's fondness for liquor nearly got her disqualified from the Miss World pageant.

2 1969

Miss Austria was nearly dethroned because she posed for nude photos.

3 1974

Spain's first Miss Universe renounced her title after tossing her crown out of a window.

4 1974

Miss Wales resigned as Miss Universe after judges discovered that she was an unwed mother.

5 1980

Miss Germany resigned as Miss World after nude photos were found; her "reign" was only 18 hours long.

6 1984

Unauthorized photos surfaced in a magazine; she's enjoyed a successful music and acting career.

7 1994

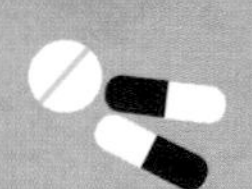

Miss Philippines International was caught "importing" amphetamines into Guam.

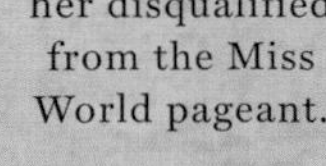

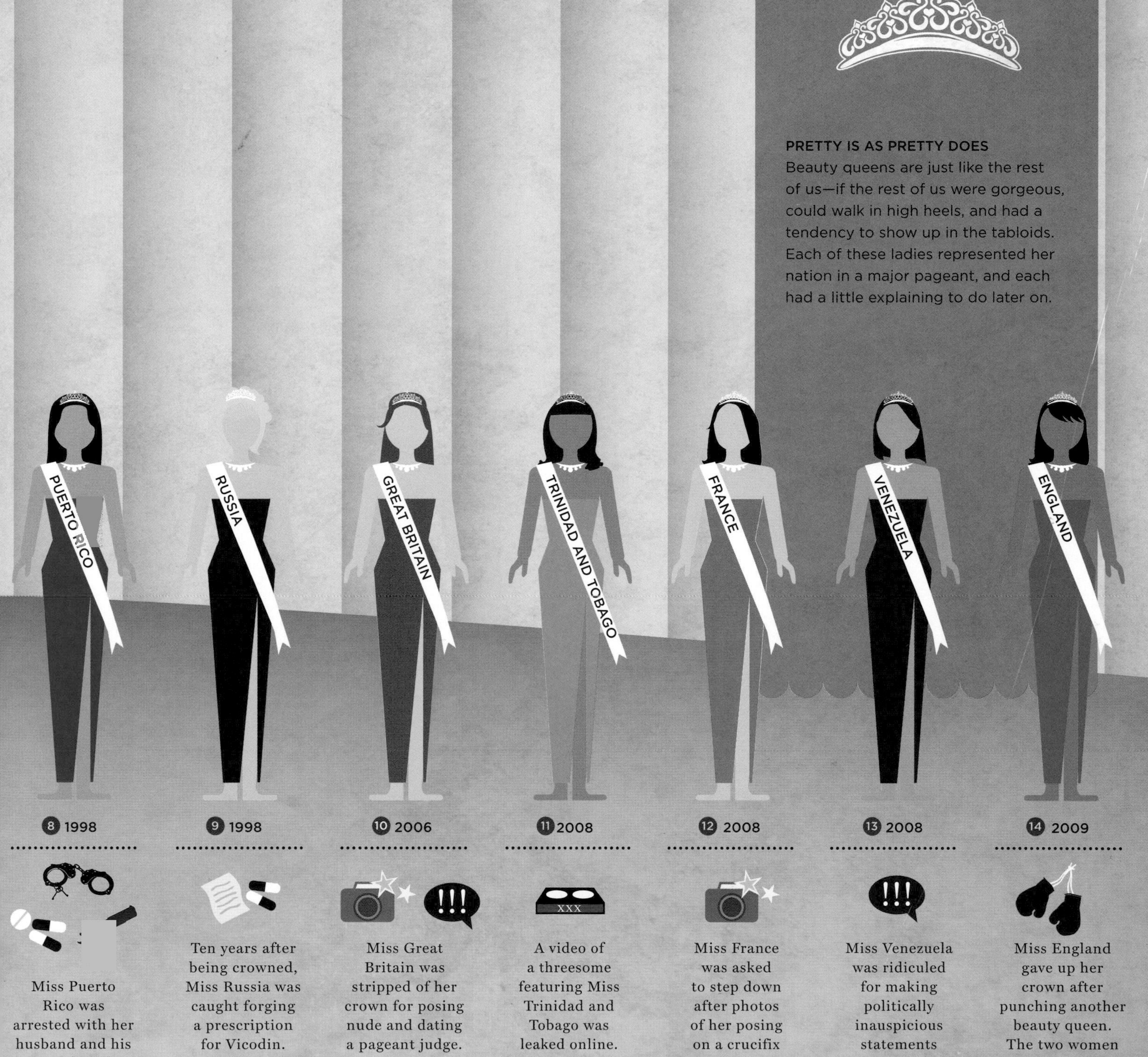

PRETTY IS AS PRETTY DOES

Beauty queens are just like the rest of us—if the rest of us were gorgeous, could walk in high heels, and had a tendency to show up in the tabloids. Each of these ladies represented her nation in a major pageant, and each had a little explaining to do later on.

8 1998

Miss Puerto Rico was arrested with her husband and his cartel friends, who were all carrying drugs and firearms.

9 1998

Ten years after being crowned, Miss Russia was caught forging a prescription for Vicodin.

10 2006

Miss Great Britain was stripped of her crown for posing nude and dating a pageant judge.

11 2008

A video of a threesome featuring Miss Trinidad and Tobago was leaked online.

12 2008

Miss France was asked to step down after photos of her posing on a crucifix in a bikini were leaked.

13 2008

Miss Venezuela was ridiculed for making politically inauspicious statements while touring Guantánamo.

14 2009

Miss England gave up her crown after punching another beauty queen. The two women were evidently fighting over a bodybuilder.

YEARS' MOST POPULAR WEB SITES

1997

1. GEOCITIES
   WEB HOSTING SERVICE
2. YAHOO
   WEB PORTAL
3. STARWAVE
   WEB SITE DEVELOPER
4. EXCITE
   WEB PORTAL
5. CNN
   NEWS
6. ALTA VISTA
   SEARCH ENGINE
7. AMERICA ONLINE
   WEB PORTAL
8. CNET
   TECHNOLOGY NEWS
9. NEW YORK TIMES
   NEWS
10. ZIFF DAVIS MEDIA
    TECHNOLOGY NEWS

1999

1. AMERICA ONLINE
   WEB PORTAL
2. MICROSOFT
   WEB PORTAL
3. YAHOO
   WEB PORTAL
4. LYCOS
   SEARCH ENGINE
5. GO NETWORK
   WEB PORTAL
6. GEOCITIES
   WEB HOSTING SERVICE
7. EXCITE
   WEB PORTAL
8. TIME WARNER ONLINE
   MEDIA COMPANY
9. BLUE MOUNTAIN ARTS
   ONLINE GREETING CARDS
10. ALTA VISTA
    SEARCH ENGINE

2001

1. MSN
   WEB PORTAL
2. YAHOO
   WEB PORTAL
3. EBAY
   E-COMMERCE
4. NEOPETS
   ENTERTAINMENT
5. GOTO
   SEARCH ENGINE
6. AMERICA ONLINE
   WEB PORTAL
7. GO NETWORK
   WEB PORTAL
8. PASSPORT
   WEB PORTAL
9. EXCITE
   WEB PORTAL
10. GEOCITIES
    WEB HOSTING SERVICE

1. **GOOGLE**
   SEARCH ENGINE
2. **YAHOO**
   WEB PORTAL
3. **EBAY**
   E-COMMERCE
4. **INTERNET EXPLORER**
   WEB BROWSER
5. **USA TODAY**
   NEWS
6. **NETSCAPE**
   WEB BROWSER
7. **GO NETWORK**
   WEB PORTAL
8. **PASSPORT**
   WEB PORTAL
9. **EXCITE**
   WEB PORTAL
10. **GEOCITIES**
    WEB HOSTING SERVICE

2005

1. **YAHOO**
   WEB PORTAL
2. **GOOGLE**
   SEARCH ENGINE
3. **MYSPACE**
   SOCIAL NETWORKING
4. **MSN**
   WEB PORTAL
5. **EBAY**
   E-COMMERCE
6. **AMAZON**
   E-COMMERCE
7. **CRAIGSLIST**
   E-COMMERCE
8. **CNN**
   NEWS
9. **GO NETWORK**
   WEB PORTAL
10. **LIVE**
    WEB PORTAL

2007

1. **YAHOO**
   WEB PORTAL
2. **GOOGLE**
   SEARCH ENGINE
3. **MYSPACE**
   SOCIAL NETWORKING
4. **MSN**
   WEB PORTAL
5. **YOUTUBE**
   VIDEO HOSTING
6. **EBAY**
   E-COMMERCE
7. **FACEBOOK**
   SOCIAL NETWORKING
8. **WINDOWS LIVE**
   WEB PORTAL
9. **CRAIGSLIST**
   E-COMMERCE
10. **WIKIPEDIA**
    ENCYCLOPEDIA

2009

1. **GOOGLE**
   SEARCH ENGINE
2. **YAHOO**
   WEB PORTAL
3. **YOUTUBE**
   VIDEO HOSTING
4. **LIVE**
   WEB PORTAL
5. **FACEBOOK**
   SOCIAL NETWORKING
6. **MSN**
   WEB PORTAL
7. **WIKIPEDIA**
   ENCYCLOPEDIA
8. **BLOGGER**
   WEB HOSTING SERVICE
9. **MYSPACE**
   SOCIAL NETWORKING
10. **YAHOO.CO.JP**
    WEB PORTAL

10 DANGEROUS TOURIST SPOTS

1 NORTHERN AUSTRALIA

MOST DANGEROUS DIP

The rivers of northern Australia contain tiny, deadly box jellyfish that are responsible for more deaths in Australia than sharks, snakes, and saltwater crocodiles combined. These little killers converge around the same river mouths and shallow coastal waters that appeal to swimmers and wading tourists.

3 MOUNT HUASHAN, CHINA

MOST DANGEROUS HIKE

Exposed, narrow, and treacherous pathways zigzag up most of the 7,085 feet (2.2 km) of sheer rock face on Mount Huashan in central China. One section is no more than a series of chains and planks bolted into the cliffside. It's not surprising that as many as 100 people die each year on the trail.

2 NEW SMYRNA BEACH, FLORIDA

MOST SHARK ATTACKS

New Smyrna Beach has been rated North America's top beach for shark attacks, beating out North Shore, Oahu, in Hawaii (the second-place contender), based on the number of people bitten. In 2008, the beach set a new record with 24 shark bites recorded.

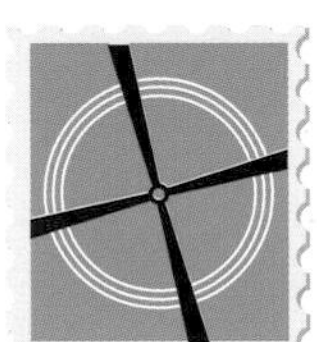

4 KAUA'I, HAWAII

MOST DANGEROUS SIGHTSEEING FLIGHT

In the span of just a few days in 2007, two helicopter crashes on the island took the lives of five passengers. And in the three years before, an additional nine people died. Since 1981, some 55 people have died in helicopter sightseeing tours in Hawaii.

5 MONT BLANC, FRENCH ALPS

MOST DANGEROUS MOUNTAINEERING

The highest summit in the Alps at 15,782 feet (4.8 km), Mont Blanc has a history of ice avalanches, falling rocks, and scary weather. Climbers face destabilizing winds of more than 60 miles per hour (97 km/h), as well as temperature drops of at least 11°F (6°C) every 3,280 feet (1 km). Mont Blanc claimed 58 lives in 2008, with ten more missing and presumed dead.

8 HOWICK FALLS, SOUTH AFRICA

MOST DANGEROUS WATERFALL

This gorgeous waterfall drops approximately 310 feet (95 m) into the Umgeni River. It is known in the native language as "the Tall One," and has claimed at least 40 lives. Some of these were doubtlessly suicides, but accidents and murders have also gone down, contributing to the falls' renown.

6 NORTH YUNGAS ROAD, BOLIVIA

MOST DANGEROUS SCENIC DRIVE

El Camino de la Muerte, or "the Road of Death," once claimed as many as 300 lives each year due to crashes or cars going over the edge—the drop is almost 2,000 feet (609 m). A new, safer alternate route has cut down on the original road's traffic—and its death toll. The perilous stretch is still open to thrill-seekers.

9 MAYON VOLCANO, PHILIPPINES

MOST DANGEROUS PHOTO OP

Mayon has erupted more than 49 times in recorded history and has claimed many lives—77 people died during the 1993 eruption. Still, tourists continually breach security to get great pictures of lava from far too close for safety. Scientists say that the next eruption will likely be a major one.

7 MOUNT COOK, NEW ZEALAND

MOST DANGEROUS NATIONAL PARK

At 12,316 feet (3,754 m) in height, Mount Cook offers up the usual perils (avalanches and crevasses) associated with ice climbing, but it also has severe weather that makes rescue difficult. In total, 245 people have died on Mount Cook since records have been kept.

10 VANUATU

MOST DANGEROUS ISLAND

This lovely island is prone to earthquakes. In 2009, it was hit by three, each of which topped 7.0 on the Richter scale, as well as tsunamis and cyclones. As if that weren't enough, the island also has a number of active volcanoes.

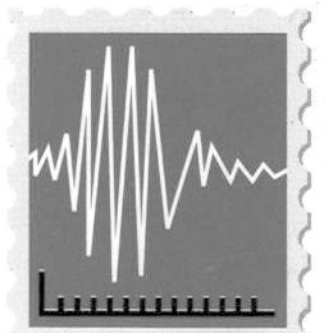

MOST LUCRATIVE HEISTS

CAUGHT

STILL AT LARGE

1 **CENTRAL BANK OF IRAQ**
IRAQ / 2003
SADDAM HUSSEIN

MODERN-DAY US $1,200,000,000

The day before the United States began bombing Baghdad, the soon-to-be-deposed dictator raided the nation's banks and made away with a fortune. About US $650 million was later found hidden in the walls of his palace; the rest was never found.

2 **ISABELLA STEWART GARDNER MUSEUM HEIST**
US / 1990
TWO MEN DRESSED AS POLICE OFFICERS

MODERN-DAY US $500,000,000

Two men knocked on the Boston museum's door at 1:24 AM, the guards opened it, and the thieves tied them up and stole three Rembrandts, a Vermeer, a Chinese bronze beaker, and other precious objects. The museum did not have insurance at the time, and the art has yet to be returned.

3 KNIGHTSBRIDGE SAFE DEPOSIT CENTER
UK / 1987
VALERIO VICCEI AND AN ACCOMPLICE

MODERN-DAY US $175,000,000

Viccei, an Italian lawyer's son who had already committed 50 heists, entered the depository and asked about renting a box. He then drew a gun and cleaned the place out. Forensic evidence led to his eventual arrest.

4 BRITISH BANK OF THE MIDDLE EAST
LEBANON / 1976
A PLO-AFFILIATED GROUP

MODERN-DAY US $150,000,000

Operatives from the Palestine Liberation Organization blasted through the bank's exterior wall, then brought in a team of Corsican locksmiths to break into the vaults. During a two-day period, the robbers loaded trucks full of currency, gold, jewels, and stocks and bonds.

5 KENT SECURITAS CASH MANAGEMENT LTD
UK / 2006
AT LEAST SIX MEN

MODERN-DAY US $100,000,000

Men dressed as police officers abducted the manager of an armored-car company and his family. Under threats to himself and his loved ones, the manager gave the robbers access to cash stored inside the company building. Many gang members were eventually arrested.

6 THE GREAT TRAIN ROBBERY
UK / 1963
RONNIE BIGGS AND CREW

MODERN-DAY US $65,000,000

The gang stormed the train using no guns, preferring to conk the train driver on the head with an iron bar. Thirteen of them were caught, tried, sentenced, and imprisoned. Ringleader Biggs lived as a fugitive for 36 years, finally returning to the United Kingdom voluntarily.

7 NORTHERN BANK
IRELAND / 2004
A LARGE UNIDENTIFIED GANG

MODERN-DAY US $56,500,000

Armed men masquerading as policemen held the families of two bank officials at gunpoint in their homes, then directed the officials to go to work the next day to let the robbers in after hours. The IRA was suspected, but no proof was found.

8 SECURITY PACIFIC NATIONAL BANK
US / 1978
STANLEY RIFKIN

MODERN-DAY US $34,100,000

Stanley Rifkin used wire transfers and a phone to raid the bank and transfer the loot to a Swiss bank account. The bank didn't know it had been hit until the FBI issued a report days later. Rifkin was arrested in the United States after trying to sell diamonds purchased with the stolen cash.

9 DUNBAR ARMORED FACILITY
US / 1997
ALLEN PACE AND FIVE OF HIS CHILDHOOD FRIENDS

MODERN-DAY US $25,700,000

Allen Pace worked for this armored-car company as a regional safety inspector. He and his friends ambushed guards one by one and loaded a waiting rental truck with millions of dollars in 30 minutes. They were caught after a gang member tried to spend cash that was still in the original bank wrappers.

HELLO 16 NAMES IN 8 LANGUAGES

ENGLISH	JOHN	WILLIAM	JAMES	GEORGE	JOSEPH	EDWARD	STEPHEN	ALEXANDER
FRENCH	JEAN	GUILLAUME	JACQUES	GEORGES	JOSEPH	ÉDOUARD	ÉTIENNE	ALEXANDRE
GERMAN	JOHANNES	WILHELM	JAKOB	JÜRGEN	JOSEF	EDUARD	STEFAN	ALEXANDER
ITALIAN	GIOVANNI	GUGLIELMO	GIACOMO	GIORGIO	GIUSEPPE	EDOARDO	STEFANO	ALESSANDRO
SPANISH	JUAN	GUILLERMO	JAIME	JORGE	JOSÉ	EDUARDO	ESTEBAN	ALEJANDRO
SWEDISH	JOHAN	VILHELM	JAKOB	JÖRGEN	JOSEF	EDVARD	STEFAN	ALEXANDER
RUSSIAN	IVAN	VIL'GEL'M	IAKOV	YURI	IOSIF	EDUARD	STEPAN	ALEKSANDR
WELSH	IOAN	GWILYM	IAGO	SIOR	JOSEFF	IORWETH	STEFFAN	ALECSANDER

WHAT'S IN A NAME?

In many cases, names vary widely not just from country to country, but within a nation as well. For example, handles like John and Mary have dozens if not hundreds of variations. Below, you'll find a sampling of names that have really, well, made a name for themselves, turning up across Western languages in slightly different forms. (Note that this isn't a list of the most popular names in the world. If it were, you'd be sure to see "Mohammed" right at the top.)

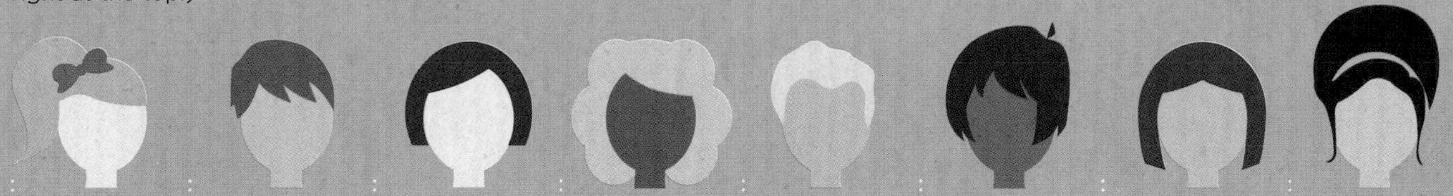

ENGLISH	MARY	LUCY	HELEN	JOANNA	MARGARET	KATHERINE	MATILDA	JANE
FRENCH	MARIE	LUCIE	HÉLÈNE	JEANNE	MARGUERITE	CATHERINE	MATHILDE	JEANNE
GERMAN	MARIE	LUZI	HELENE	JOHANNA	MARGARETE	KATARINA	MATHILDE	JOHANNA
ITALIAN	MARIA	LUCIANA	ELENA	GIOVANNA	MARGHERITA	CATARINA	MATELDA	GIANNA
SPANISH	MARÍA	LUCÍA	ELENA	JUANA	MARGARITA	CATALINA	MATI	JUANA
SWEDISH	MARIA	LUCIA	HELENE	JOHANNA	MARGIT	KATARINA	MATHILDA	JANNA
RUSSIAN	MARIYA	LUZIYA	YELENA	IVANA	MARGARITA	YEKATERINA	MATILDA	IOANNA
WELSH	MARI	LLEUCU	ELLIN	SIÂN	MARGED	CADI	MALLT	SIÂNI

9 CLEVER CRIMES

CRIMINAL MASTERMINDS

The most interesting crimes aren't always the ones that yield the highest returns. Sometimes, it's the sheer brazenness of the scheme or the unusual details that elevate a crime from merely lucrative to truly original.

❶ THE GREAT GOLD ROBBERY
ENGLAND / 1855

A total of 200 pounds (91 kg) of gold was stolen as it was being shipped to the Crimean War front lines. The thieves stole and copied the keys to the safes, boarded the train, replaced the gold with lead shot, and got away clean. The gang fell apart on rivalries; one was sent to Australia as a convict, but the mastermind received only two years for larceny. The gold was never fully recovered.

❷ SISI STAR HEIST
AUSTRIA / 1998

Canadian criminal Gerald Blanchard videotaped the layout of an Austrian castle while on a family holiday. He then parachuted from a small plane to the roof at night, broke in, and switched the jewels with cheap copies. The switch was not discovered for some days. He was eventually caught for other crimes, and admitted that the jewels were hidden in his grandmother's basement in Winnipeg.

❸ MONA LISA CAPER
FRANCE / 1911

Eduardo de Valfierno allegedly had six copies of the *Mona Lisa* made; he then paid Louvre employee Vincenzo Peruggia to steal the original, which he did by simply hiding it under his coat and walking out. After the heist, the copies were delivered to buyers, each of whom believed the painting had been stolen for them. In 1913 Peruggia was caught trying to sell the original.

❹ CATCH ME IF YOU CAN
WORLDWIDE / 1965–1969

Frank William Abagnale Jr. was a con man, impostor, and escape artist who became notorious for successfully passing the modern-day equivalent of US $2.5 million in forged checks, starting when he was only 17 years old. In the process, he successfully impersonated an airline pilot, a doctor, a prison inspector, and a lawyer. He is now a private security consultant.

❺ BANCO CENTRAL BURGLARY
BRAZIL / 2005

A gang of burglars rented an empty property and put up signs claiming that the rental housed a landscaping company (to explain the van-loads of soil they were soon removing daily). They spent three months tunneling 256 feet (78 m)—two city blocks—to a position beneath the bank. They surfaced in the bank on a weekend and made off with almost US $99 million. Most of the money has never been recovered.

❻ THE INNER TUBE ROBBER
US / 2008

A criminal advertised on the online community resource Craigslist, offering to pay strangers to show up outside a given bank dressed in yellow vests, safety goggles, a respirator mask, and blue shirts. About a dozen did and while they milled about, the robber (dressed in the same getup) overpowered an armored car guard and grabbed bags of money. He fled in an inner tube down a nearby creek, but was eventually caught.

❼ D. B. COOPER
US / 1971

"D. B. Cooper" (the name given to him by the press, based on his alias—his real name was never discovered) hijacked a Boeing 727 aircraft, received US $200,000 in ransom, and parachuted from the plane. Despite hundreds of leads through the years, no conclusive evidence has ever surfaced regarding Cooper's true identity or whereabouts, and the bulk of the money has never been recovered.

❽ OPERATION GET RICH OR DIE TRYIN'
US / 2005–2008

For nearly four years, 28-year-old Albert Gonzalez worked as an informant on hackers for the US Secret Service. He was also part of a drug-using gang that committed the biggest data thefts in history, stealing credit and debit card numbers for sale on the black market. The gang targeted major corporations, including a credit card processor, and sold information from nearly 130 million cards.

❾ ANTWERP DIAMOND CENTER ROBBERY
BELGIUM / 2003

Thieves rented office space in the diamond merchants' building and spent three years actually running a diamond business. They then somehow robbed the building's vault, which was protected by infrared heat detectors, a seismic sensor, and a lock with 100 million possible combinations. Mastermind Leonardo Notarbartolo was caught, but the US $100 million worth of gems has never been found.

BEST COUNTRIES TO BE . . .

A MATTER OF OPINION

Some places are better than others—especially if you're, say, a mom or looking to evade your taxes. Here's a breakdown of where you'd thrive if you happen to fall into any of these categories. Bear in mind that some of these are scientific, while others are just great conversation starters.

AN ENTREPRENEUR

These countries keep bureaucratic red tape to a minimum, making it easy to start a company.

1. Singapore
2. New Zealand
3. US
4. Denmark
5. UK
6. Ireland
7. Canada
8. Australia
9. Norway
10. Iceland

AN ARTIST

Grants for the arts and a robust artistic community create shelter for painters, musicians, and writers.

1. Sweden
2. UK
3. Denmark
4. Ireland
5. Australia
6. New Zealand
7. Canada
8. Singapore
9. Switzerland
10. US

A MOTHER

Bring up baby in one of these places and benefit from primo maternity packages and superior health care.

1. Sweden
2. Denmark
3. Finland
4. Austria
5. Germany
6. Norway
7. Australia
8. Netherlands
9. Canada
10. UK

UNEMPLOYED

When you're down and out, these countries help by paying high percentages of workers' previous salaries.

1. Norway
2. Spain
3. France
4. Germany
5. Canada
6. Turkey
7. Japan
8. South Korea
9. UK
10. US

AN AQUATIC CREATURE

These nations protect their surrounding waters, making living in said waters highly pleasant.

1. Colombia
2. Australia
3. US
4. Guinea-Bissau
5. Greenland
6. Romania
7. Mauritania
8. Germany
9. Suriname
10. Jordan

A JOURNALIST

Some places aren't so into freedom of the press. But in these nations, you can report and not do time.

1. Iceland
2. Finland
3. Norway
4. Denmark
5. Sweden
6. Belgium
7. Luxembourg
8. Andorra
9. Netherlands
10. Switzerland

SICK

These places' universal health care, quality treatment, and healthy lifestyles make being sick less sickening.

1. France
2. Italy
3. San Marino
4. Andorra
5. Malta
6. Singapore
7. Spain
8. Oman
9. Austria
10. Japan

A MOVIE FAN

These nations make the most movies; living in one ups your chances of appearing as an extra.

1. India
2. US
3. Japan
4. France
5. Germany
6. Spain
7. Italy
8. South Korea
9. UK
10. Canada

A TAX EVADER

These nations have cultivated lax tax laws in a bid to host the assets of the loaded-but-less-than-ethical.

1. Luxembourg
2. Cook Islands
3. Channel Islands
4. Bermuda
5. Dubai
6. Liechtenstein
7. British Virgin Islands
8. Andorra
9. Vanuatu
10. Switzerland

A SOCCER FAN

Soccer is a serious pastime in these countries, which all have either won or played in the World Cup finals.

1. Brazil
2. Spain
3. Portugal
4. Netherlands
5. Italy
6. Germany
7. Argentina
8. England
9. France
10. Croatia

A VEGETARIAN

If meat isn't on your itinerary, travel in one of these countries, where the national cuisine is veggie heavy.

1. India
2. UK
3. Thailand
4. Turkey
5. Israel
6. Vietnam
7. Malaysia
8. Taiwan
9. Canada
10. Singapore

AN ORGANIC FARMER

These countries have the highest percentage of organically farmed land in the world.

1. Liechtenstein
2. Austria
3. Switzerland
4. Italy
5. Estonia
6. Latvia
7. Sweden
8. Samoa
9. Czech Republic
10. Timor-Leste

A GEEK

Abundant technology jobs and a healthy role-playing-game community make these places great for nerds.

1. US
2. UK
3. Sweden
4. Denmark
5. Switzerland
6. Australia
7. Netherlands
8. Belgium
9. Finland
10. Canada

AN IMMIGRANT

These nations have immigration-friendly laws on the books and regularly grant asylum.

1. Austria
2. Sweden
3. Spain
4. Norway
5. Switzerland
6. New Zealand
7. Ireland
8. Germany
9. Canada
10. US

10 TOP KARAOKE SONGS AROUND THE WORLD

THE SONG DOES NOT REMAIN THE SAME

It's surprisingly tricky to determine a nation's most popular karaoke songs—not only do tastes change, but they vary widely from bar to bar. In Japan (the birthplace of karaoke), aspiring singers can choose from top-10 lists sorted by folk songs, anime themes, J-pop, and more. The lists here give a snapshot of some of the top tunes around the globe.

US

1. "DON'T STOP BELIEVING" / Journey
2. "LIVING ON A PRAYER" / Bon Jovi
3. "SUMMER NIGHTS (DUET)" / John Travolta & Olivia Newton-John
4. "LIKE A VIRGIN" / Madonna
5. "BLACK VELVET" / Alannah Myles
6. "FRIENDS IN LOW PLACES" / Garth Brooks
7. "SANTERIA" / Sublime
8. "BILLIE JEAN" / Michael Jackson
9. "LOVE SHACK" / The B-52s
10. "I LOVE ROCK 'N' ROLL" / Joan Jett & the Blackhearts

ENGLAND

1. "WATERLOO" / ABBA
2. "BOHEMIAN RHAPSODY" / Queen
3. "MY WAY" / Frank Sinatra
4. "I WILL SURVIVE" / Gloria Gaynor
5. "DANCING QUEEN" / ABBA
6. "ANGELS" / Robbie Williams
7. "LIKE A VIRGIN" / Madonna
8. "IT'S RAINING MEN" / Weather Girls
9. "SUMMER NIGHTS (DUET)" / John Travolta & Olivia Newton-John
10. "I SHOULD BE SO LUCKY" / Kylie Minogue

JAPAN

1. "LINDA, LINDA" / The Blue Hearts
2. "SUGOI OTOKO NO UTA" (beer-drinking song)
3. "YOSAKU" / Kitajima Saburo
4. "UE WO MUITE ARUKOU" / Sakamoto Kyu
5. "AFURETE YUKU NO WA KONO KIMOCHI" / Amaetai
6. "GEKKOUKA" / Janne Da Arc
7. "ENDLESS RAIN" / X Japan
8. "MY WAY" / Frank Sinatra
9. "AMAGI-GOE" / Ishikawa Sayuri
10. "ZANKOKU NA TENSHI" / Yoko Takahashi

CHINA

1. "KISS GOODBYE" / Leehom Wang
2. "MY INTUITION" / Rainie Yang
3. "SKY" / Jolin Tsai
4. "WITHOUT YOU" / Karen Mok Man-wai
5. "BIG CITY, SMALL LOVE" / Leehom Wang
6. "DAN REN FANG SHUANG REN CHUANG" / Karen Mok Man-wai
7. "JIE BU DIAO" / Harlem Yu
8. "IDEAL LOVER" / Rainie Yang
9. "LING" / Alan Kuo
10. "THE FIRST MORNING" / Leehom Wang

8 VERY COOL JOBS

LUXURY-BED TESTER

UK / PRESENT

A luxury-bed manufacturer paid bloggers to sleep in their beds and blog about their sleeping experience.

WINE TASTER

WORLDWIDE / ANTIQUITY-PRESENT

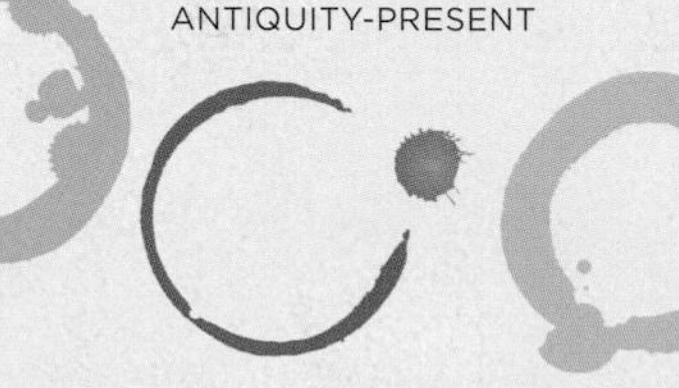

It is traditional for vineyards to employ those rare people with excellent palates to ensure that each vintage is up to par.

PACIFIC ISLAND CARETAKER

AUSTRALIA / 2009

Brit Ben Southall, 34, beat out nearly 35,000 applicants from around the world to spend six months blogging about life on tropical Hamilton Island.

ICE CREAM TASTER

US / PRESENT

An ice-cream taster samples and approves or rejects every flavor produced by trying three cartons from each run on a daily basis.

WATERSLIDE TESTER

WORLDWIDE / PRESENT

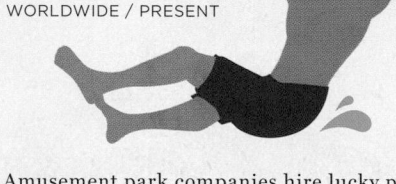

Amusement park companies hire lucky people to travel the world testing out their roller coasters, waterslides, and other rides.

ORGY PLANNER

ROME / ANTIQUITY

The orgy planner arranged wine, women, and song for high society. The job had a number of fairly obvious perks.

MEDICAL MARIJUANA TESTER

ENGLAND / PRESENT

Reviewers critique the quality of pot dispensaries and their products. New reefer-review Web sites are emerging in California and Colorado.

PROFESSIONAL GAMER

WORLDWIDE / PRESENT

Gaming companies hire people to test out the games, evaluate new features, and give quality-assurance feedback.

8 AWFUL JOBS IN HISTORY

SPERM COLLECTOR

WORLDWIDE / PRESENT

This job must be done by hand. It involves inserting an arm into the bull's rectum, stimulating the prostate.

VIOLIN-STRING MAKER

EUROPE / 1500s-1700s

To make the strings, someone had to stretch and dry cat intestines, and then, of course, tune them properly.

POOPER SCOOPER

EUROPE / ANTIQUITY-1800s

Dog refuse was used in tanning leather, and collectors, usually children, were paid modest sums for every bucket delivered to a tannery.

NITPICKER

WORLDWIDE / PRESENT

Entire businesses have sprung up to help finicky parents de-louse their children.

CASTRATO

EUROPE / 1500s-1700s

Boys were castrated around the age of nine to retain the higher-pitched voice that allowed so much beautiful music to be created.

TANNER

EUROPE / ANTIQUITY-1800s

Hides were placed in vats of lime before the rotting flesh and hair could be scraped off. Then they were laid in vats of dog poop "gravy" to soften the leather and remove the lime. Afterward, of course, they needed to be cleaned yet again.

PLAGUE BURIER

EUROPE / 1300s

Those who traveled the streets crying "bring out your dead" not only had to bury tens of thousands of corpses, they also had a 99.9 percent chance of catching the plague.

HYPERBARIC WELDER

WORLDWIDE / PRESENT

Those daring souls who do underwater welding on oil rigs and other such places endure tight, high-pressure spaces underwater, as well as the risks of explosion, electric shock, sharks, and nitrogen poisoning.

20 LARGEST WORLD RELIGIONS

CULTURAL TRADITION

- ABRAHAMIC
- INDIAN
- EAST ASIAN
- NEW RELIGIOUS MOVEMENT

CONFUCIANISM
6.1 MILLION ADHERENTS
ORIGIN: CHINA / 500s BCE

CHEONDOISM
3 MILLION ADHERENTS
ORIGIN: KOREA / 1900s

BAHÁ'Í FAITH
7.6 MILLION ADHERENTS
ORIGIN: IRAN / 1800s

WICCA
1 MILLION ADHERENTS
ORIGIN: UK / 1900s

UNITARIAN UNIVERSALISM
630,000 ADHERENTS
ORIGIN: US / 1800s

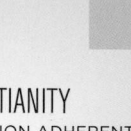

SIKHISM
24 MILLION ADHERENTS
ORIGIN: PUNJAB REGION OF INDIA AND PAKISTAN / 1400s

SHINTO
27 MILLION ADHERENTS
ORIGIN: JAPAN / 2000 BCE–400 BCE

CHRISTIANITY
2.1 BILLION ADHERENTS
ORIGIN: EASTERN MEDITERRANEAN (PRESENT-DAY ISRAEL AND PALESTINE) / MID 1ST CENTURY

RASTAFARIANISM
700,000 ADHERENTS
ORIGIN: JAMAICA / 1930s

SEKAI KYUSEI KYO
1 MILLION ADHERENTS
ORIGIN: JAPAN / 1926

CAO DAI
1 MILLION ADHERENTS
ORIGIN: VIETNAM / 1926

TENRIKYŌ
2 MILLION ADHERENTS
ORIGIN: JAPAN / 1800s

BUDDHISM
400 MILLION ADHERENTS
ORIGIN: NORTHERN INDIA / 500s BCE

HINDUISM
828 MILLION ADHERENTS
ORIGIN: INDIA / 1700–1100 BCE

JUDAISM
18 MILLION ADHERENTS
ORIGIN: EASTERN MEDITERRANEAN (PRESENT-DAY ISRAEL AND PALESTINE) / 1100 BCE

SEICHO-NO-IE
800,000 ADHERENTS
ORIGIN: JAPAN / 1930

AYYAVAZHI
700,000 ADHERENTS
ORIGIN: INDIA / 1800s

JAINISM
6 MILLION ADHERENTS
ORIGIN: INDIA / 800s–500s BCE

TAOISM
50 MILLION ADHERENTS
ORIGIN: CHINA / 500s BCE

ISLAM
1.6 BILLION ADHERENTS
ORIGIN: THE ARABIAN PENINSULA / 600s

8 MICRORELIGIONS

1 **SHAKERS**
ACTIVE WORSHIPPERS: 3
FOUNDED: 1747
Founded in England in 1747, this group believed in sexual abstinence. There is only one active community left; in 2011, there were three members.

2 **BRANCH DAVIDIANS**
ACTIVE WORSHIPPERS: 50–70
FOUNDED: 1958
This group is known for the Waco Siege of 1993, which resulted in the deaths of leader David Koresh, 82 other Branch Davidians, and four federal agents.

3 **AUMISM**
ACTIVE WORSHIPPERS: 400
FOUNDED: 1969
A synthesis of a number of religions (including Buddhism), Aumism is centered in the "holy city" of Mandarom, near Castellane in the French Alps.

4 **SAMARITANISM**
ACTIVE WORSHIPPERS: 712
FOUNDED: 721
Samaritanism is much like Judaism, but adherents claim that their religion is closest to that of the Israelites prior to the birth of Christ.

5 **FEDERATION OF DAMANHUR**
ACTIVE WORSHIPPERS: 1,000
FOUNDED: 1975
A mix of New Age and neopagan beliefs, this movement gained fame in 1992 due to its secret excavation of an extensive underground temple.

6 **CHURCH OF GOD WITH SIGNS FOLLOWING**
ACTIVE WORSHIPPERS: 1,000–5,000
FOUNDED: 1910
This American Protestant sect practices snake handling and drinks poison in worship services; at least 60 documented deaths have occurred.

7 **THE FAMILY INTERNATIONAL**
ACTIVE WORSHIPPERS: 11,200
FOUNDED: 1968
An offshoot of the Jesus movement of the late 1960s, with a hippie-friendly message of free love and spiritual "revolution" against "the System."

8 **SCIENTOLOGY**
ACTIVE WORSHIPPERS: 25,000
FOUNDED: 1952
Founded by former sci-fi writer L. Ron Hubbard, this highly secretive religion has aspects of alienology, self-improvement, and reincarnation.

11 HORRIFIC HUMAN-MADE DISASTERS

1 ST. FRANCIS DAM FAILURE
US / 1928
500 DEAD
This Los Angeles dam was built by a self-taught civil engineer named William Mulholland. Twelve hours after he finished an inspection and declared it safe, the dam failed, unleashing 12 billion gallons (45.4 billion L) of water.

2 MINAMATA DISEASE
JAPAN / 1932
10,000–17,000 AFFECTED
Chisso Corporation released a toxic mercury compound called methyl mercury into the waters of Minamata Bay for more than 30 years; the poisoning caused illness, insanity, and death.

3 LONDON'S KILLER FOG
ENGLAND / 1952
12,000 DEAD
The winter was cold, and Londoners burning coal in their furnaces created a deadly miasma of sulfur dioxide, nitrogen oxides, and soot that blanketed London under almost total darkness for four days.

4 CASTLE BRAVO
MARSHALL ISLANDS / 1954
ENVIRONMENTAL DEVASTATION
A US nuclear test was bigger than expected, and the fallout contaminated inhabited islands, causing sickness and lingering effects, such as a high rate of birth defects.

5 BHOPAL GAS LEAK
INDIA / 1984
18,500 DEAD
A Union Carbide tank holding more than 40 tons (36,300 kg) of toxic chemicals released a gas that coated the ground in a deadly fog; many died instantly, others suffered for years after.

6 CHERNOBYL
USSR / 1986
ENVIRONMENTAL DEVASTATION
Fifty or so people died immediately as a result of the nuclear disaster; some 4,000 died of cancer; an area of the Ukraine was rendered uninhabitable; and more than 300,000 sea animals and birds died.

7 EXXON VALDEZ OIL SPILL
US / 1989
ENVIRONMENTAL DEVASTATION
A shipwreck spilled at least 11 million gallons (41.6 million L) of crude oil into Alaska's waters, contaminating 1,300 miles (2,100 km) of coastline and killing more than 150,000 animals.

8 AL-MISHRAQ FIRE
IRAQ / 2003
TOLL UNKNOWN
A sulfur-plant fire (thought to have been arson) burned for a month, releasing 1 billion tons (910 billion kg) of sulfur oxide, which sickened thousands and devastated the surrounding environment.

9 JILIN EXPLOSIONS
CHINA / 2005
ENVIRONMENTAL DEVASTATION
When a series of huge explosions rocked the Jilin City chemical plant, few died in the explosion, but the resulting water pollution affected tens of thousands of people downriver.

10 DEEPWATER HORIZON SPILL
GULF OF MEXICO / 2010
ENVIRONMENTAL DEVASTATION
When a BP drilling platform exploded, oil flowed into the Gulf for three months, affecting up to 87,000 square miles (225,000 sq km). The long-term environmental effects of this catastrophic spill won't be known for decades.

11 GREAT PACIFIC GARBAGE PATCH
PACIFIC OCEAN / ONGOING
ENVIRONMENTAL DEVASTATION
Some estimate that this huge floating "island" of plastic waste, sludge, and chemicals is larger than the continental United States. Its long-term effect remains to be seen.

14 DEADLIEST NATURAL DISASTERS

THE WORST OF TIMES
Any one of these disaster types could really ruin your day, even in its wimpiest incarnation. These devastating examples, however, show the forces of nature at their most destructive.

1. **EPIDEMIC**
BUBONIC PLAGUE
WORLDWIDE / 1400s–1700s
300 MILLION DEAD

2. **FAMINE**
THE GREAT CHINESE FAMINE
CHINA / 1958–1961
43 MILLION DEAD

3. **FLOOD**
CENTRAL CHINA FLOODS
CHINA / 1931
2.5 MILLION DEAD

4. **EARTHQUAKE**
SHAANXI EARTHQUAKE
CHINA / 1556
830,000 DEAD

5. **CYCLONE**
BHOLA CYCLONE
BANGLADESH / 1970
500,000 DEAD

6. **TSUNAMI**
INDIAN OCEAN TSUNAMI
INDONESIA / 2004
230,000 DEAD

7. **VOLCANIC ERUPTION**
MOUNT TAMBORA
INDONESIA / 1815
92,000 DEAD

8. **HEATWAVE**
EUROPEAN HEATWAVE
EUROPE / 2003
40,000 DEAD

9. **AVALANCHE**
HUARASCARÁN AVALANCHE
PERU / 1970
20,000 DEAD

10. **MUDSLIDE**
VARGAS MUDSLIDE
VENEZUELA / 1999
15,000 DEAD

11. **BLIZZARD**
IRAN BLIZZARD
IRAN / 1972
4,000 DEAD

12. **WILDFIRE**
PESHTIGO WILDFIRE
US / 1871
2,500 DEAD

13. **LIMNIC ERUPTION**
LAKE NYOS LIMNIC ERUPTION
CAMEROON / 1986
1,700 DEAD

14. **TORNADO**
DAULATPUR-SATURIA TORNADO
BANGLADESH / 1989
1,300 DEAD

23 BEST-SELLING BOOKS IN THE WORLD

1. THE BIBLE / 5 BILLION COPIES
2. *QUOTATIONS FROM CHAIRMAN MAO* / 900 MILLION
3. THE QUR'AN / 800 MILLION
4. *XINHUA DICTIONARY* / 400 MILLION
5. *CHAIRMAN MAO'S POEMS* / 400 MILLION
6. *SELECTED ARTICLES OF MAO ZEDONG* / 253 MILLION
7. *A TALE OF TWO CITIES* / 200 MILLION
8. *SCOUTING FOR BOYS* (THE BOY SCOUT'S MANUAL) / 150 MILLION
9. *THE LORD OF THE RINGS* (TRILOGY) / 150 MILLION
10. THE BOOK OF MORMON / 150 MILLION
11. *THE TRUTH THAT LEADS TO ETERNAL LIFE* / 107 MILLION
12. *ON THE THREE REPRESENTATIONS* / 100 MILLION
13. *AND THEN THERE WERE NONE* / 100 MILLION
14. *THE HOBBIT* / 100 MILLION
15. *DREAM OF THE RED CHAMBER* / 100 MILLION
16. *THE LION, THE WITCH AND THE WARDROBE* / 85 MILLION
17. *SHE* / 83 MILLION
18. *THE LITTLE PRINCE* / 80 MILLION
19. *THE DA VINCI CODE* / 80 MILLION
20. *THE CATCHER IN THE RYE* / 65 MILLION
21. *THE ALCHEMIST* / 65 MILLION
22. *STEPS TO CHRIST* / 60 MILLION
23. *MERRIAM-WEBSTER'S DICTIONARY* / 55 MILLION

26 MOST STOCKED LIBRARY BOOKS

1. THE BIBLE / 796,882 LIBRARIES
2. *THE US CENSUS* / 460,628 LIBRARIES
3. *MOTHER GOOSE* / 67,663 LIBRARIES
4. *THE DIVINE COMEDY* / 62,414 LIBRARIES
5. *THE ODYSSEY* / 45,551 LIBRARIES
6. *THE ILIAD* / 44,093 LIBRARIES
7. *HUCKLEBERRY FINN* / 42,724 LIBRARIES
8. *THE LORD OF THE RINGS* (TRILOGY) / 40,907 LIBRARIES
9. *HAMLET* / 39,521 LIBRARIES
10. *ALICE'S ADVENTURES IN WONDERLAND* / 39,277 LIBRARIES
11. *DON QUIXOTE* / 38,485 LIBRARIES
12. *BEOWULF* / 37,914 LIBRARIES
13. THE QUR'AN / 37,080 LIBRARIES
14. *THE NIGHT BEFORE CHRISTMAS* / 33,343 LIBRARIES
15. *GARFIELD* / 33,234 LIBRARIES
16. *TOM SAWYER* / 32,233 LIBRARIES
17. *AESOP'S FABLES* / 32,232 LIBRARIES
18. *ARABIAN NIGHTS* / 31,728 LIBRARIES
19. *MACBETH* / 30,388 LIBRARIES
20. *GULLIVER'S TRAVELS* / 29,066 LIBRARIES
21. *ROBINSON CRUSOE* / 28,669 LIBRARIES
22. *ROMEO & JULIET* / 28,646 LIBRARIES
23. THE BHAGAVAD GITA / 28,588 LIBRARIES
24. *A CHRISTMAS CAROL* / 27,928 LIBRARIES
25. *THE CANTERBURY TALES* / 27,863 LIBRARIES
26. *TREASURE ISLAND* / 27,643 LIBRARIES

20 MOST TRANSLATED BOOKS

1. THE BIBLE / 438 LANGUAGES
2. *PINOCCHIO* / 260 LANGUAGES
3. *PILGRIM'S PROGRESS* / 200 LANGUAGES
4. *THE LITTLE PRINCE* / 180 LANGUAGES
5. *STEPS TO CHRIST* / 140 LANGUAGES
6. THE BOOK OF MORMON / 107 LANGUAGES
7. THE QUR'AN / 102 LANGUAGES
8. *THE ADVENTURES OF TINTIN* / 96 LANGUAGES
9. *THE IMITATION OF CHRIST* / 95 LANGUAGES
10. *THE ALCHEMIST* / 67 LANGUAGES
11. *HARRY POTTER AND THE PHILOSOPHER'S STONE* / 67 LANGUAGES
12. *PIPPI LONGSTOCKING* / 64 LANGUAGES
13. *THE ADVENTURES OF SHERLOCK HOLMES* / 60 LANGUAGES
14. *THE DIARY OF A YOUNG GIRL* / 60 LANGUAGES
15. *THE GOOD SOLDIER ŠVEJK* / 54 LANGUAGES
16. *QUO VADIS* / 50 LANGUAGES
17. *THINGS FALL APART* / 50 LANGUAGES
18. *HEIDI* / 48 LANGUAGES
19. *DON QUIXOTE* / 48 LANGUAGES
20. *THE STRANGER* / 45 LANGUAGES

340 IMPORTANT AND TRIVIAL MEASURES

This chapter goes to great lengths—like that of the world's longest tunnel—and then it plumbs the depths—deepest hole, anyone?—of society's endeavors. From the shortest world leader to the longest song ever, it's all here for you to weigh (like the ton of pepper once paid in ransom), time (how long does it take to hand-build a grand piano), or maybe just endure (longest speech ever? 124 hours!).

23 RANDOM AVERAGES

CARS
The typical number owned by a citizen of the European Union

2

WEEKS
The time most people spend kissing during a lifetime

PEOPLE
The average size of the Chinese household

YEARS
The span by which right-handed people are rumored to outlive lefties

HOURS PER DAY
The time an American spends absorbing information from various media channels

CARS
The average number an American owns in a lifetime

HOURS PER DAY
The time a cat spends sleeping

YEARS
The usual age of death for a human in the Neolithic era

MOONS
The average number for a planet in our solar system

28

YEARS
The human lifespan in classical Rome

100

DECIBELS
The level of a typical pig squeal

130 “FRIENDS”
The number the average Facebook user has

150 POINTS
The average person's bowling score

300 LAUGHS
The number of times a typical 6-year-old laughs each day

345 SQUIRTS
The number of squirts from a cow's udder needed to yield a gallon of milk

437 QUESTIONS
The number asked in a day by a typical 4-year-old child

550 HAIRS
The number of hairs in the human eyebrow

1,500 EGGS
The median number of eggs laid by a queen bee in a day

2,000 CALORIES
The amount an average global citizen consumes in calories from cola drinks each year

5,210 STEPS
The number taken by the average American woman in a day

7,192 STEPS
The number taken by the average American man in a day

6,000,000 DUST MITES
The number living in the average bed

100,000,000,000,000 CELLS
The number in the human body

11 DAILY RATIONS FROM CULTURES ACROSS THE AGES

WHAT'S FOR DINNER?
Food, drink, and various household commodities have been rationed throughout history, usually in times of war or shortages. The figures below reflect daily allotments, although rations are actually handed out on a weekly or monthly basis. In many cases, people didn't receive this much; the rations reflect the government's goals.

1 FOR A ROMAN SOLDIER / 27 BCE–250 CE

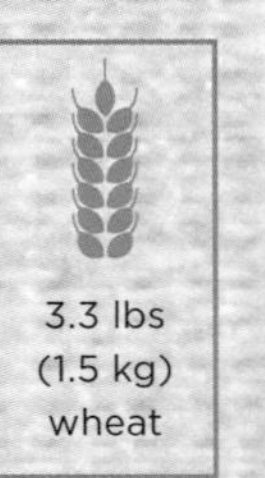

3.3 lbs (1.5 kg) wheat

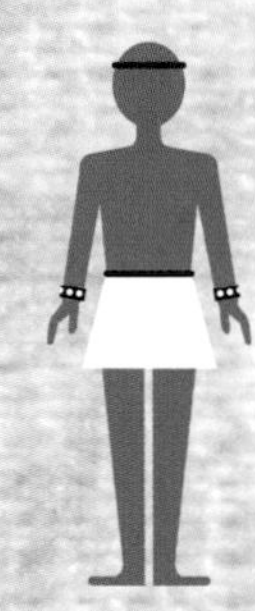

2 FOR AN ITALIAN GALLEY SLAVE / 1100S

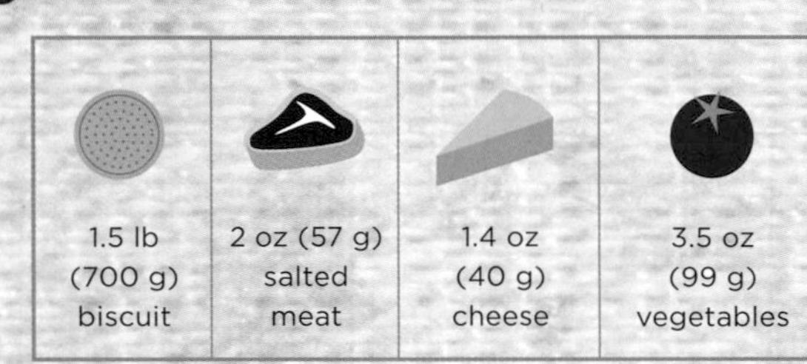

1.5 lb (700 g) biscuit	2 oz (57 g) salted meat	1.4 oz (40 g) cheese	3.5 oz (99 g) vegetables

3 FOR A BRITISH SAILOR / 1800S

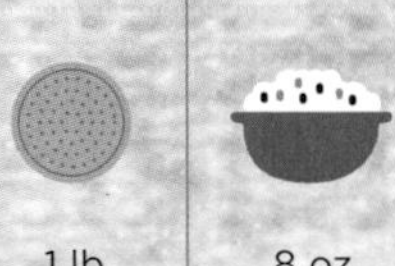

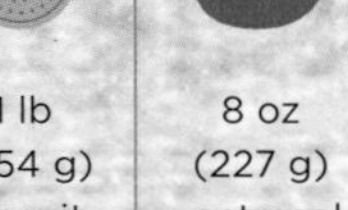

1 lb (454 g) biscuit	8 oz (227 g) oatmeal	1 lb (454 g) pork or beef	1 oz (28 g) butter	1 gallon (3.8 L) beer or 1 pint (473 ml) rum

4 FOR A UNION SOLDIER / CIVIL WAR

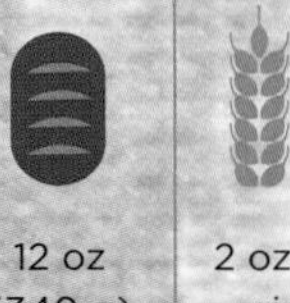

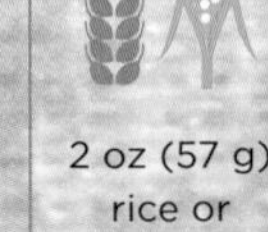

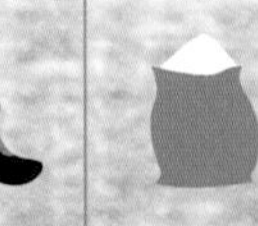

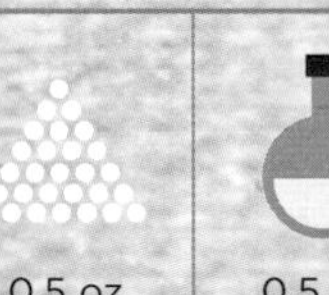

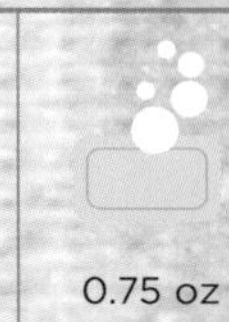

12 oz (340 g) bread	2 oz (57 g) rice or hominy	1.25 lb (500 g) salted meat	3 oz (85 g) beans	2 oz (57 g) sugar	0.5 oz (14 g) salt	0.5 oz (15 ml) vinegar	2 oz (57 g) coffee beans	1 candle	0.75 oz (21 g) soap

5 FOR A BRITISH SOLDIER / WORLD WAR I

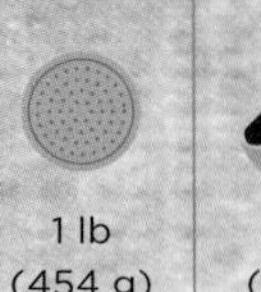

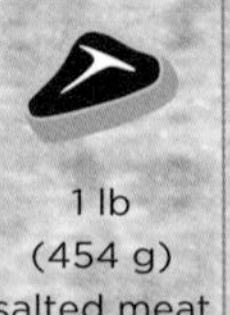

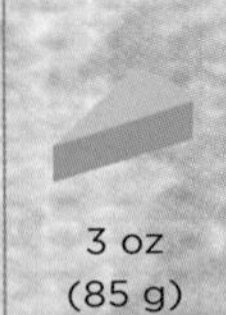

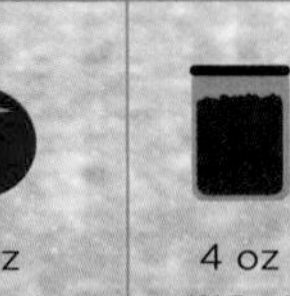

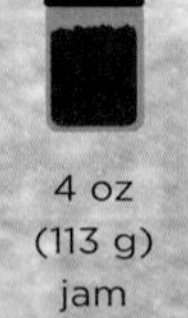

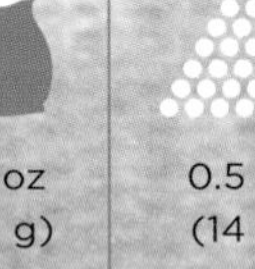

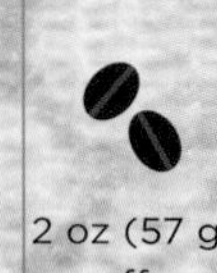

1 lb (454 g) biscuit	1 lb (454 g) salted meat	3 oz (85 g) cheese	8 oz (227 g) vegetables	4 oz (113 g) jam	1.5 oz (43 g) sugar	0.5 oz (14 g) salt	2 oz (57 g) tea	2 oz (57 g) coffee beans

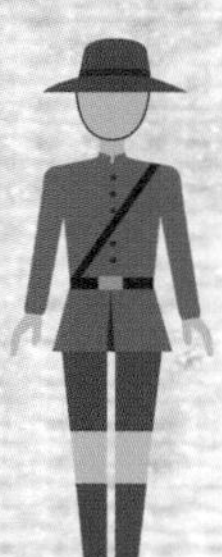

6 FOR AN AUSTRALIAN SOLDIER / WORLD WAR II

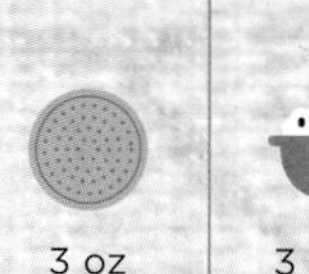 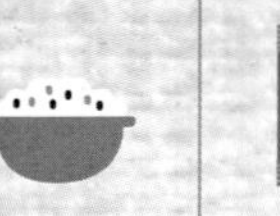   

3 oz (85 g) biscuits	3 packs wheat cereal	1 tin tuna	1 tin corned beef	1 roll mints	1 pack matches

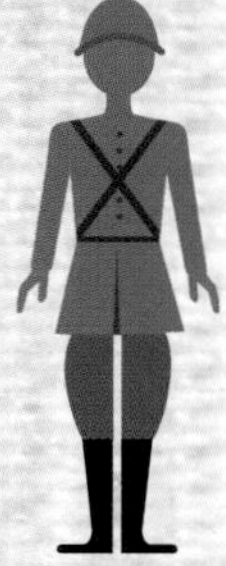

7 FOR A JAPANESE SOLDIER / WORLD WAR II

   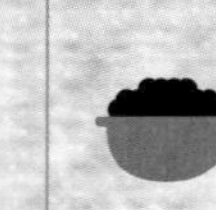  

28 oz (800 g) rice	7.4 oz (210 g) fresh meat or fish	21 oz (600 g) vegetables	2 oz (57 g) pickled radish	1.7 oz (50 ml) shoyu	2.6 oz (74 g) bean paste	0.5 oz (14 g) salt	1 oz (28 g) sugar	0.2 oz (5.7 g) green tea leaves

8 FOR A BRITISH CIVILIAN / WORLD WAR II

0.6 oz (17 g) ham	0.6 oz (17 g) bacon	0.4 oz (11 g) lard	3 oz (85 g) meat	2.3 oz (65 g) sugar	0.5 oz (14 g) sweets	0.25 oz (7 g) jam	0.3 oz (8.5 g) butter	0.3 oz (8.5 g) cheese	0.3 oz (8.5 g) tea leaves

9 FOR A RUSSIAN SOLDIER / COLD WAR

 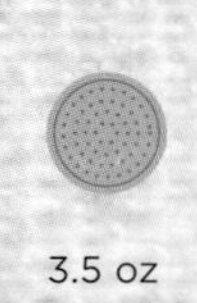 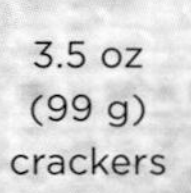    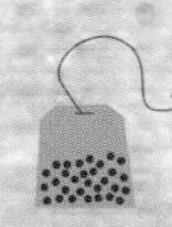

3.5 oz (99 g) crackers	1 can preserved meat	1 can cheese	1 cube sugar	1 tea bag

10 FOR A NORTH KOREAN CIVILIAN / 1970s

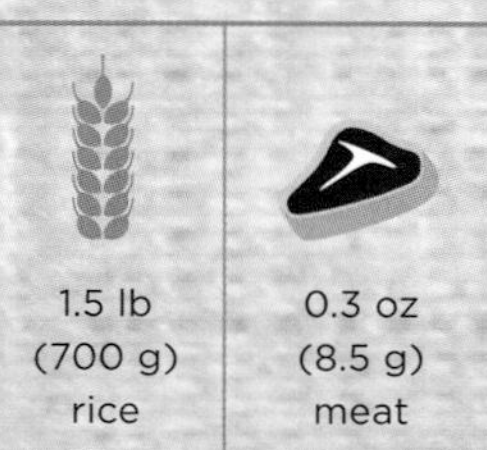

1.5 lb (700 g) rice	0.3 oz (8.5 g) meat

11 FOR A CUBAN CIVILIAN / 2000

    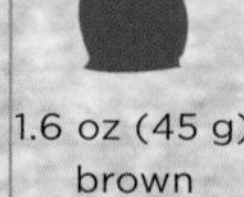 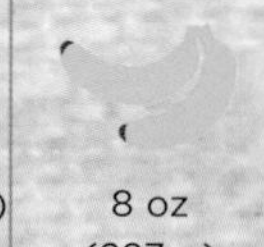 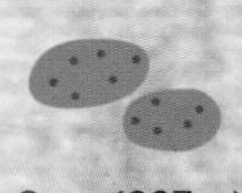 

3.5 oz (99 g) rice	1.6 oz (45 g) sugar	1.6 oz (45 g) brown sugar	8 oz (227 g) bananas	8 oz (227 g) potatoes	1 dozen eggs per month	33 fl oz (1 L) milk for children under 7

MOST WIDELY SPOKEN LANGUAGES

HAVE WORDS, WILL TRAVEL

Some languages really get around, through immigration, emigration, conquest, and general diffusion. These are the globe's most popular languages based on the number of countries that have declared them their "official tongues." Each language is spoken in many more places than are shown here, but these are the places where it's on the books. Exceptions are the United Kingdom, Australia, and the United States, which have no official language but still speak mostly English.

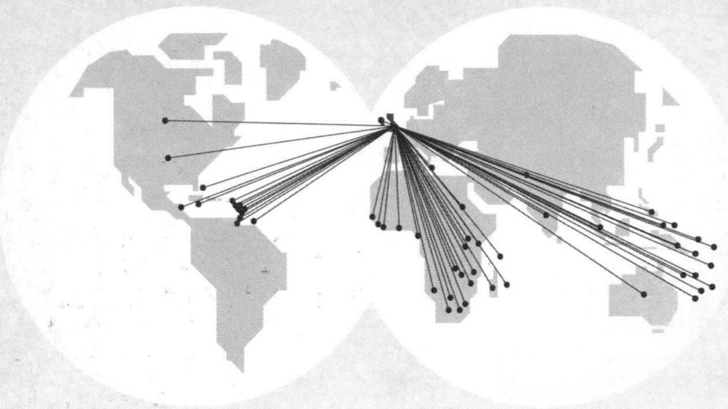

1 ENGLISH

Antigua and Barbuda • Australia • The Bahamas • Barbados • Belize Botswana • Cameroon • Canada • Dominica • Fiji • The Gambia • Ghana Grenada • Guyana • India • Ireland • Jamaica • Kenya • Kiribati • Lesotho Liberia • Madagascar • Malawi • Malta • Marshall Islands • Mauritius Micronesia • Namibia • Nauru • New Zealand • Nigeria • Pakistan • Palau Papua New Guinea • Philippines • Rwanda • Saint Kitts and Nevis Saint Lucia • Saint Vincent and the Grenadines • Samoa • Seychelles Sierra Leone • Singapore • Solomon Islands • South Africa • Sudan Swaziland • Tanzania • Tonga • Trinidad and Tobago • Tuvalu • Uganda United Kingdom • United States • Vanuatu • Zambia • Zimbabwe

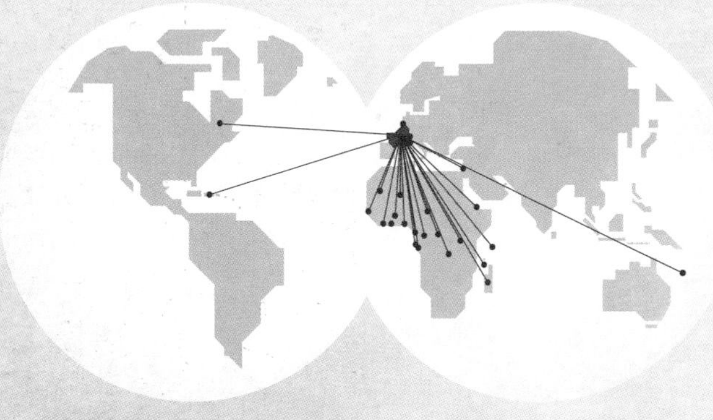

2 FRENCH

Belgium • Benin • Burkina Faso • Burundi • Cameroon • Canada Central African Republic • Chad • Comoros • Côte d'Ivoire • Democratic Republic of the Congo • Djibouti • Equatorial Guinea • France • Gabon Guinea • Haiti • Lebanon • Luxembourg • Madagascar • Mali • Monaco Niger • Rwanda • Senegal • Seychelles • Switzerland • Togo • Vanuatu

3 ARABIC

Algeria • Bahrain • Chad • Comoros • Djibouti • Egypt • Eritrea • Iraq Israel • Jordan • Kuwait • Lebanon • Libya • Mauritania • Morocco • Oman Palestine • Qatar • Saudi Arabia • Somalia • Sudan • Syria • Tunisia United Arab Emirates • Yemen

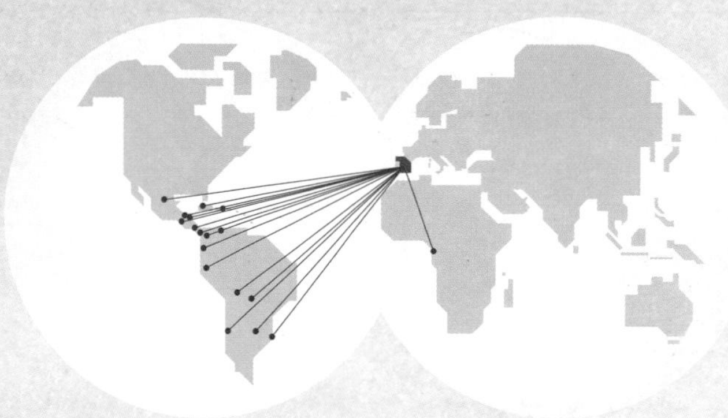

4 SPANISH

Argentina • Bolivia • Chile • Colombia • Costa Rica • Cuba
Dominican Republic • Ecuador • El Salvador • Equatorial Guinea
Guatemala • Honduras • Mexico • Nicaragua • Panama • Paraguay
Peru • Spain • Uruguay • Venezuela

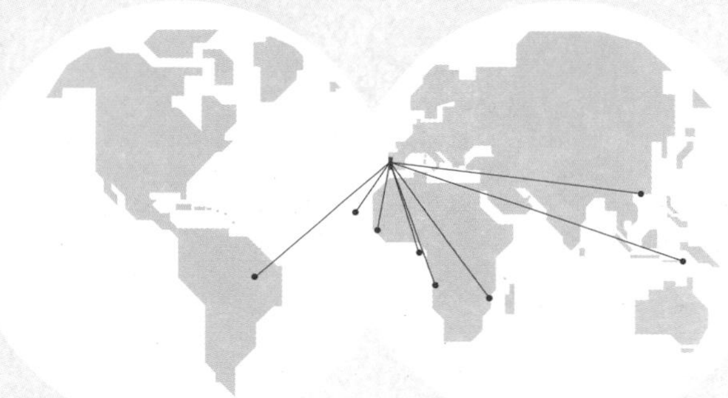

5 PORTUGUESE

Angola • Brazil • Cape Verde
East Timor • Guinea-Bissau
Macau • Mozambique • Portugal
Sao Tome and Principe

6 GERMAN

Austria • Germany • Liechtenstein
Luxembourg • Switzerland

7 RUSSIAN

Belarus • Kazakhstan • Kyrgyzstan
Russia • Ukraine

18 LANGUAGES WITH THE MOST SPEAKERS

	LANGUAGE	NO. OF SPEAKERS, IN MILLIONS
1	MANDARIN	845
2	SPANISH	329
3	ENGLISH	328
4	ARABIC	221
5	HINDI	182
6	BENGALI	181
7	PORTUGUESE	178
8	RUSSIAN	144
9	JAPANESE	122
10	JAVANESE	85
11	WU	77
12	TELUGU	70
13	VIETNAMESE	69
14	FRENCH	68
15	MARATHI	68
16	KOREAN	66
17	TAMIL	65
18	PUNJABI	62

8 Real Million-to-One Odds

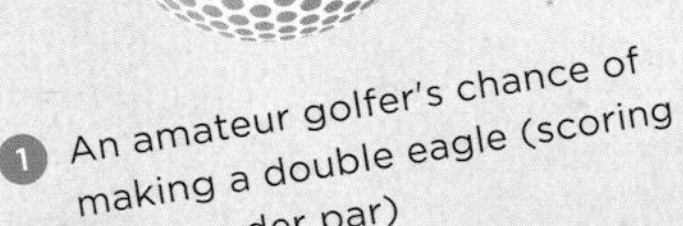

1 An amateur golfer's chance of making a double eagle (scoring three under par)

555
555

2 The odds you'll randomly name the same three-digit number twice in a row

1,000,0

4 The likelihood that a person will die from taking a single ecstasy pill

5 The odds of getting two double-yolk eggs in a half-dozen-egg box

6 The probability that an interracial couple will deliver fraternal twins that appear to be of different races

3 The probability of a major earthquake hitting California's Hayward fault in the next 50 minutes

7 The possibility of growing a half-red, half-green apple

8 The odds of tossing a coin 20 times in a row and getting all heads

14 Unexpected Odds

100 : 1
That the Large Hadron Collider will confirm the existence of God (as given by an online bookmaker)

117 : 1
That you'll fly on a plane with a drunk pilot

200 : 1
That you'll have your identity stolen

250 : 1
That you'll have a child with a genius IQ

6,250 : 1
That you'll be struck by lightning

7,000 : 1
That someone someday will believe you to be possessed by Satan

7,000 : 1
That a given American over the age of 12 will use crack this month

13,000 : 1
That you'll get a hole-in-one in golf, ever

10,000 : 1
That you'll find a four-leaf clover the first time you look

10,000 : 1
That you'll be injured by a toilet this year

700,000 : 1
That you'll be killed by a meteor strike

2 MILLION : 1
That you'll fall overboard on a cruise ship

13 MILLION : 1
That you'll become an astronaut

20 MILLION : 1
That you'll become a saint

5 Largest Empires

WHAT IS AN EMPIRE?

An empire is a collection of territories and people under one sovereign megapower. The world has seen hundreds of empires come and go, but a few stand out as being exemplary in their physical size and number of constituents. The data below are for each empire in the year of its height.

1 **BRITISH EMPIRE**
13 MILLION SQUARE MILES / 33.7 MILLION SQ KM
1922 / 458 MILLION SUBJECTS

The British Empire began colonizing overseas in the late 1500s, and its collection is still the largest empire on historical record. Canada's size gave the empire its huge landmass, while control over India added significantly to its massive population.

2 **MONGOL EMPIRE**
12.7 MILLION SQUARE MILES / 33 MILLION SQ KM
1290 / 100 MILLION SUBJECTS

Genghis Khan became ruler of Mongolia in 1206, unifying tribes and overpowering lands that, by the early 1300s, stretched from the Korean peninsula through Eastern Europe. His empire thrived briefly after his death, but family feuds led to its demise.

3 **RUSSIAN EMPIRE**
14.7 MILLION SQUARE MILES / 38.1 MILLION SQ KM
1866 / 176 MILLION SUBJECTS

From 1721 until the Bolshevik revolution in 1917, Russia ruled an empire that spanned Europe, Asia, and North America. At the beginning of the 1800s, Russia was the world's largest nation.

4 **SPANISH EMPIRE**
12.4 MILLION SQUARE MILES / 32.1 MILLION SQ KM
1781 / 68 MILLION SUBJECTS

At its height, the Spanish Empire controlled most of the Americas, plus a few outposts in Africa. The empire's decline in landmass began after the Louisiana territory was ceded back to the French in 1800.

5 **CHINESE EMPIRE**
9.1 MILLION SQUARE MILES / 23.6 MILLION SQ KM
1790 / 383 MILLION SUBJECTS

The Chinese Empire lasted more than 2,000 years, and reached its height during the Qing Dynasty—which was China's last imperial dynasty—from 1644 until 1912.

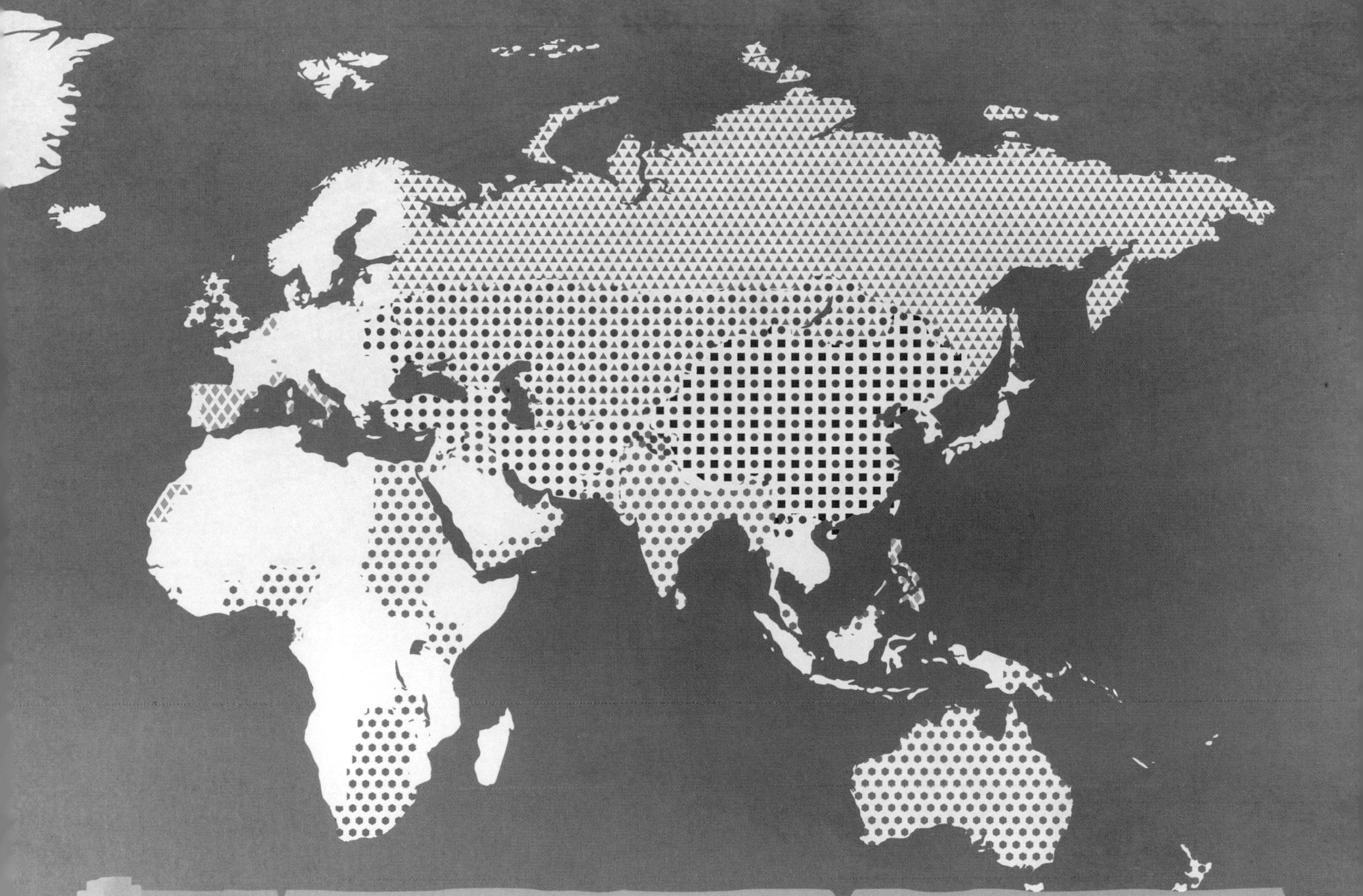

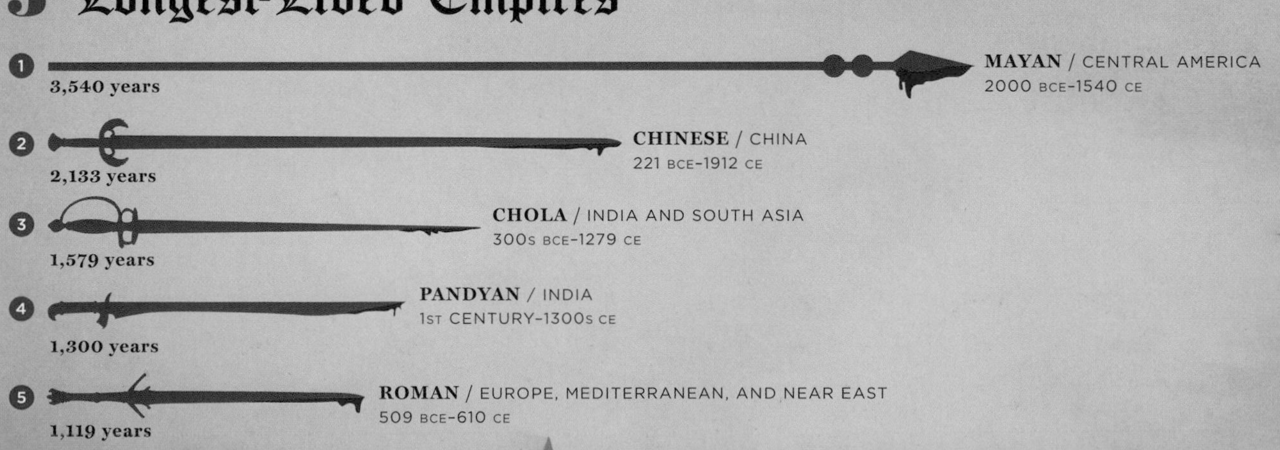
5 Longest-Lived Empires
1
3,540 years
MAYAN / CENTRAL AMERICA
2000 BCE–1540 CE
2
2,133 years
CHINESE / CHINA
221 BCE–1912 CE
3
1,579 years
CHOLA / INDIA AND SOUTH ASIA
300s BCE–1279 CE
4
1,300 years
PANDYAN / INDIA
1st CENTURY–1300s CE
5
1,119 years
ROMAN / EUROPE, MEDITERRANEAN, AND NEAR EAST
509 BCE–610 CE

8 VERY SHORT WORKS OF ART

"The Ladies' Bras"

1 TOP 40 SONG

At 36 seconds, this song by Jonny Trunk is the shortest ever to enter the UK charts, where it reached number 27 in September 2007. The song consists almost entirely of the repeated chorus: "The ladies' bras, the ladies' bras, the ladies' knickers, and the ladies' bras."

"LINES ON THE ANTIQUITY OF MICROBES"

Adam
had 'em.

2 POEM

Often cited as the shortest poem ever penned, this terse verse is alternately known as "Fleas" and has been variously attributed to Shel Silverstein, Ogden Nash, Strickland Gillilan, and "unknown."

breath

3 PLAY

In its entirety, Samuel Beckett's supershort play consists of a quick crying sound, followed by an amplified recording of somebody breathing (which is accompanied by a pulsing of light), and then a second cry. No people are seen on set, but Beckett's stage directions call for there to be rubbish "all scattered and lying" across the stage.

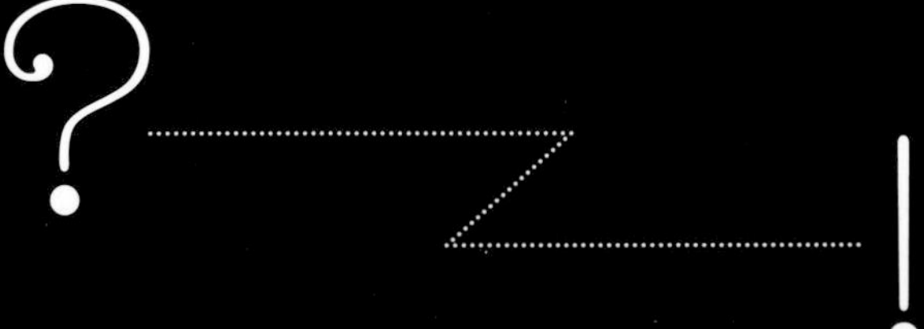

4 CORRESPONDENCE

Victor Hugo had just finished *Les Misérables* and was anxious to know of its success. He telegraphed a single question mark to his publisher, to which the publisher replied with a single exclamation mark. Ironically, *Les Misérables* is incredibly long, coming in at over 1,000 pages for the unabridged French editions.

5 BIBLICAL VERSE

The shortest verse in the King James version of the Bible occurs when Jesus visits the tomb of Lazarus, moments before resurrecting him. It's the shortest in most other popular versions, though it's not the shortest in all languages.

JOHN 11:35

"EL DINOSAURIO"
CUANDO DESPERTÓ,
EL DINOSAURIO
TODAVÍA ESTABA ALLÍ.

"THE DINOSAUR"
When he awoke,
the dinosaur
was still there.

6 SHORT STORY

Noted Guatemalan writer Augusto Monterroso was a master of the short-story form. His very, very short story, "El Dinosaurio," was published in 1959 in his collection, *Obras Completas (y Otros Cuentos)*.

Human Jerky

8 ALBUM

This 1998 album by the goregrind band Cattle Decapitation comes in at 16 minutes, 9 seconds with 18 tracks, including "Decapitation of Cattle," which clocks in at 5 seconds, "Stench from the Dumpster" at 43 seconds, and "Unclogged and Ready for Spewage" at 35 seconds.

The Sands of Time

7 OPERA

This 1993 collaboration between Welsh composer Peter Reynolds and librettist Simon Rees was 3 minutes, 34 seconds in length. It was intended to "match the boiling of an egg" in duration and "to create a piece which bore the same relationship to opera as a miniature does to a full-length portrait."

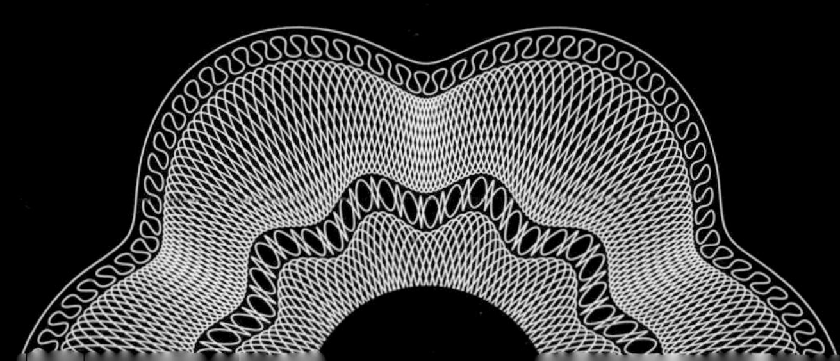

13 SIZABLE SPEECHES

6 HOURS
LORD HENRY BROUGHAM
UK / 1828
Address to the House of Commons

7 HOURS, 10 MINUTES
FIDEL CASTRO
CUBA / 1986
Address to the Communist Party Congress

7 HOURS, 48 MINUTES
V. K. KRISHNA MENON
US / 1957
Defense of India's position on Kashmir

8 HOURS
HUGO CHAVEZ
VENEZUELA / 2007
Annual state of the nation address

15 HOURS
SENATOR WILLIAM V. ALLEN
US / 1893
Filibuster against the Sherman Silver Law

15 HOURS, 31 MINUTES
SENATOR HUEY LONG
US / 1935
Filibuster against aspects of the National Recovery Act

16 SWEEPING SONGS

16:53
"ONLY SKIN"
JOANNA NEWSOM
2006

17:05
"IN-A-GADDA-DA-VIDA"
IRON BUTTERFLY
1968

17:27
"SISTER RAY"
THE VELVET UNDERGROUND
1968

18:19
"THE DECLINE"
NOFX
1999

18:37
"ALICE'S RESTAURANT MASSACREE"
ARLO GUTHRIE
1967

18:42
"BY THE TIME I GET TO PHOENIX"
ISAAC HAYES
1969

9 PROLONGED POEMS

Lines, stanzas, verses, words . . . everyone seems to measure the length of poems differently, so comparisons are tricky. Still, it's clear that these are some long ones.

10,550 LINES
PARADISE LOST
JOHN MILTON
ENGLAND / 1667
The story of Adam and Eve and their expulsion from Paradise

14,233 LINES
THE DIVINE COMEDY
DANTE ALIGHIERI
ITALY / 1321
A journey through Hell, Purgatory, and Paradise

38,736 LINES
ORLANDO FURIOSO
LUDOVICO ARIOSTO
ITALY / 1532
A chronicle of battles between Christendom and the Islamic world

50,000 LINES
THE RAMAYANA
VALMIKI
INDIA / 1000
Shares the teachings of Hindu sages through allegory

22 HOURS, 26 MINUTES
SENATOR WAYNE MORSE
US / 1953
Filibuster against the Tidelands Oil Bill

24 HOURS, 18 MINUTES
SENATOR STROM THURMOND
US / 1957
Filibuster against the passage of America's Civil Rights Act

32 HOURS, 25 MINUTES
REVEREND DONALD THOMAS
US / 1988
Lecture about nutrition for vegetarian athletes

36 HOURS, 31 MINUTES
MUSTAFA KEMAL ATATÜRK
TURKEY / 1927
Congressional address on the independence of Turkey

48 HOURS, 18 MINUTES
PREACHER CLINTON LOCY
US / 1955
Sermon that covered every book in the Bible

93 HOURS
REVEREND DONALD THOMAS
US / 1978
Dissertation on the philosophy of divine nutrition

124 HOURS
LLUIS COLET
FRANCE / 2008
Oration covering Salvador Dalí and Catalan culture, among other topics

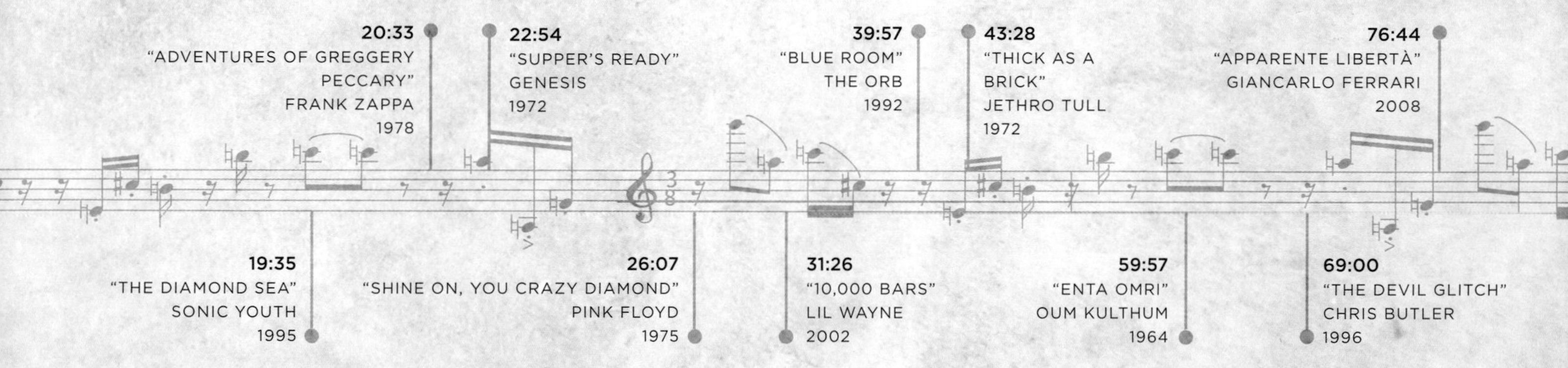

60,000 VERSES
SHAHNAMEH
FERDOWSI
PERSIA / 1000
The history of Persia from the creation of the world up to the Islamic conquest of the region

200,000 LINES
THE EPIC OF JANGAR
AUTHOR UNKNOWN
MONGOLIA / 400
Recounts King Jangar's battle with the evil Mongolian warlord Mangus

100,000 VERSES
MAHABHARATA
VYASA
INDIA / 400 BCE
A heroic tale told in 18 books, said to have been written down by the god Ganesha himself

500,000 LINES
EPIC OF THE MANAS
AUTHOR UNKNOWN
KYRGYZSTAN / 1700
The tale of the hero Manas and his epic battles for the Kyrgyz people

1 MILLION VERSES
THE EPIC OF KING GESAR
AUTHOR UNKNOWN
TIBET / 1000
An ongoing tale of epic battle that is still being modified today

REALLY OLD UNIVERSITIES FROM AROUND THE WORLD

TRULY OLD SCHOOL

Here's a selection of each continent's oldest universities—not to be confused with the world's oldest schools. Some institutions (like Morocco's University of Al-Karaouine, founded in 859) didn't start granting degrees until later.

1088
UNIVERSITY OF BOLOGNA
ITALY

1096
UNIVERSITY OF OXFORD
ENGLAND

1134
UNIVERSITY OF SALAMANCA
SPAIN

1209
UNIVERSITY OF CAMBRIDGE
ENGLAND

1222
UNIVERSITY OF PADUA
ITALY

1538
SANTO TOMÁS DE AQUINO UNIVERSITY
DOMINICAN REPUBLIC

1636
HARVARD UNIVERSITY
US

1693
COLLEGE OF WILLIAM AND MARY
US

1696
ST JOHN'S COLLEGE
US

1701
YALE UNIVERSITY
US

1595
UNIVERSITY OF SAN CARLOS
PHILIPPINES

1645
UNIVERSITY OF SANTO TOMAS
PHILIPPINES

1849
UNIVERSITY OF INDONESIA
INDONESIA

1857
UNIVERSITY OF CALCUTTA
INDIA

1866
AMERICAN UNIVERSITY OF BEIRUT
LEBANON

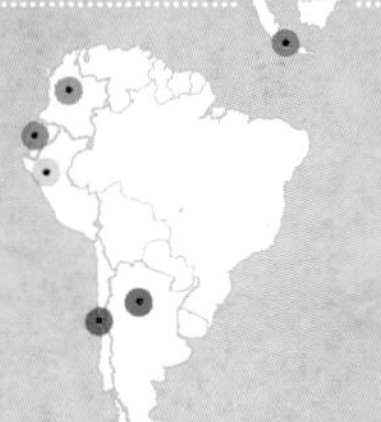

1551
NATIONAL UNIVERSITY OF SAN MARCOS
PERU

1613
NATIONAL UNIVERSITY OF CÓRDOBA
ARGENTINA

1645
SAINT THOMAS AQUINAS UNIVERSITY
COLOMBIA

1826
CENTRAL UNIVERSITY OF ECUADOR
ECUADOR

1842
UNIVERSIDAD DE CHILE
CHILE

1850
UNIVERSITY OF SYDNEY
AUSTRALIA

1853
UNIVERSITY OF MELBOURNE
AUSTRALIA

1874
UNIVERSITY OF ADELAIDE
AUSTRALIA

1887
ROYAL MELBOURNE INSTITUTE OF TECHNOLOGY
AUSTRALIA

1890
UNIVERSITY OF TASMANIA
AUSTRALIA

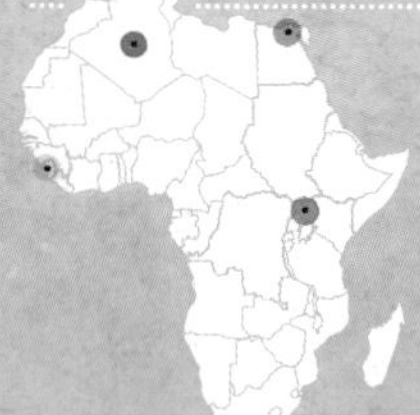

1827
FOURAH BAY COLLEGE
SIERRA LEONE

1829
UNIVERSITY OF CAPE TOWN
SOUTH AFRICA

1908
CAIRO UNIVERSITY
EGYPT

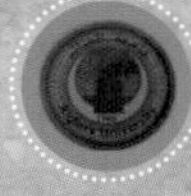

1909
UNIVERSITY OF ALGIERS
ALGERIA

1922
MAKERERE UNIVERSITY
UGANDA

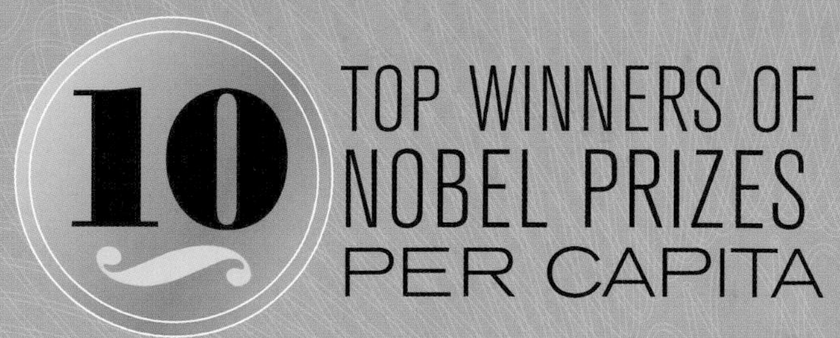

TOP WINNERS OF NOBEL PRIZES PER CAPITA

PRIZE-WINNING NATIONS

It's easy to identify which nations have won the most Nobel Prizes—the United States, the United Kingdom, Germany, France, and Sweden lead the pack. It's more interesting to compare nations' number of Nobel Prizes per capita. By this measure, the tiny Faroe Islands—with only one prize—comes out on top, and the United Kingdom is tenth on the list.

1. **FAROE ISLANDS**
   One Nobel Prize for every 49,000 people
   1 NOBEL PRIZE IN ALL

2. **SAINT LUCIA**
   One Nobel Prize for every 86,850 people
   2 NOBEL PRIZES IN ALL

3. **SWITZERLAND**
   One Nobel Prize for every 302,560 people
   25 NOBEL PRIZES IN ALL

4. **ICELAND**
   One Nobel Prize for every 318,450 people
   1 NOBEL PRIZE IN ALL

5. **SWEDEN**
   One Nobel Prize for every 334,000 people
   28 NOBEL PRIZES IN ALL

6. **NORWAY**
   One Nobel Prize for every 411,925 people
   12 NOBEL PRIZES IN ALL

7. **DENMARK**
   One Nobel Prize for every 427,500 people
   13 NOBEL PRIZES IN ALL

8. **AUSTRIA**
   One Nobel Prize for every 439,825 people
   19 NOBEL PRIZES IN ALL

9. **EAST TIMOR**
   One Nobel Prize for every 533,300 people
   2 NOBEL PRIZES IN ALL

10. **UNITED KINGDOM**
    One Nobel Prize for every 534,550 people
    116 NOBEL PRIZES IN ALL

19 THINGS WE HAVE MADE BIGGER OR SMALLER FOR BEAUTY

1 FOREHEAD
EUROPE / 1300s–1500s
Shaving or plucking hair along the crown gave the illusion of a larger forehead.

2 EYES
EAST ASIA / PRESENT
Plastic surgery is used to "open" the eyelid and make the eyes look larger.

3 PUPILS
ITALY / 1500s
Drops of belladonna (a nasty poison) temporarily made pupils look bigger.

4 NOSE
WORLDWIDE / 500 BCE–PRESENT
Men and women have long operated on their noses to reduce them in size.

5 EARLOBES
WORLDWIDE / ANTIQUITY–MODERN TIMES
Piercing and stretching enlarges and lengthens the earlobes.

6 LIPS
WORLDWIDE / 1960–PRESENT
Injections make lips appear fuller and softer—for a limited time.

7 TEETH
WORLDWIDE / ATIQUITY–MODERN TIMES
Some people undergo "teeth sharpening" to make their teeth smaller or pointed.

8 LIPS
EASTERN AFRICA AND SOUTH AMERICA
ANTIQUITY–MODERN TIMES
Plates are inserted into the lips, stretching them out and enlarging them.

9 NECK
MYANMAR AND SOUTH AFRICA
ANTIQUITY–MODERN TIMES
Women gradually add metal rings to stretch their necks for a longer look.

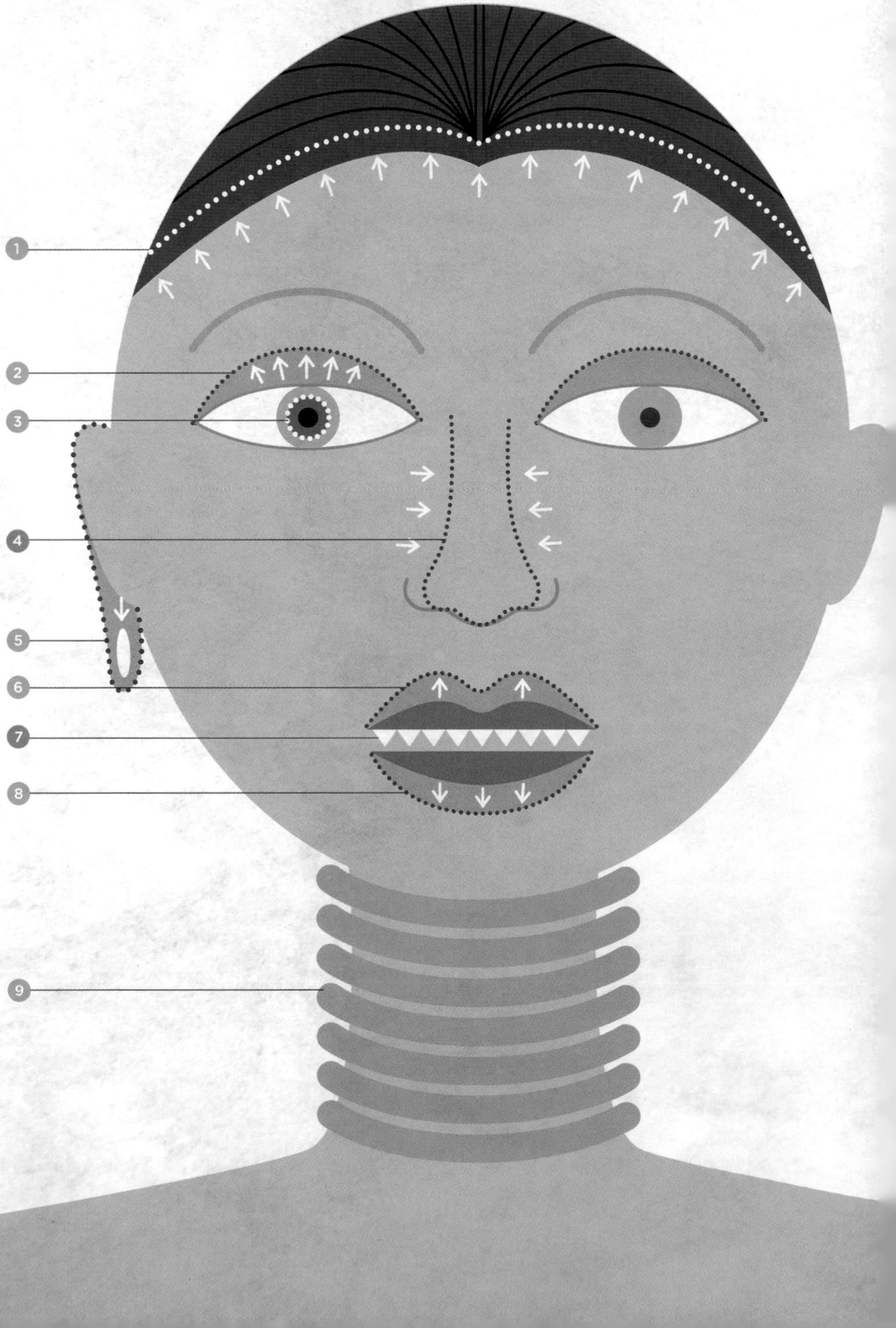

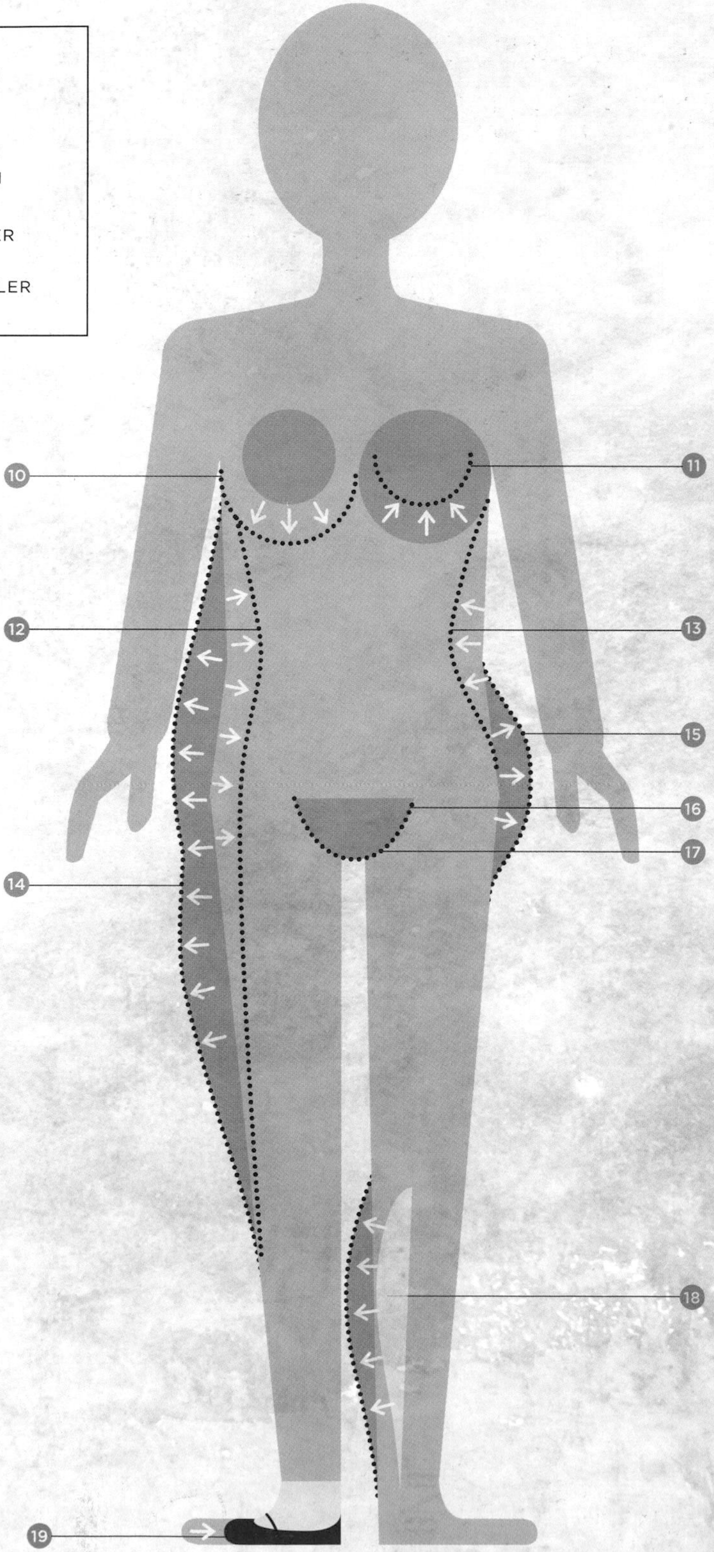

10 BREASTS
WORLDWIDE / 1895–PRESENT
Women get implants or injections to go up a cup size (or three).

11 BREASTS
WORLDWIDE / 1800s–PRESENT
Usually for health reasons, some people have their breasts surgically reduced.

12 ENTIRE BODY, AS DESIRED
WORLDWIDE / 1920s–PRESENT
During liposuction, fat is mechanically suctioned from any portion of the body.

13 WAIST
US AND EUROPE / 1500s–PRESENT
Women lace themselves into corsets for a dramatic silhouette.

14 ENTIRE BODY, AS DESIRED
PACIFIC ISLANDS AND AFRICA
1800s–PRESENT
Women are encouraged or forced to overeat, as fat is a symbol of fertility.

15 BUTTOCKS
WORLDWIDE / 1969–PRESENT
Some have implants inserted into their rears for a rounder appearance.

16 TESTICLES
US AND EUROPE / 1941–PRESENT
There's an implant for everything. These are usually inserted for medical reasons.

17 PENIS
WORLDWIDE / ANTIQUITY–MODERN TIMES
Surgical implants add inches to those gentlemen who would like a few more.

18 CALVES
WORLDWIDE / 1972–PRESENT
Implants are surgically inserted for shapely lower legs.

19 FEET
CHINA / 900s–1900s
In this ritual, the feet of girls are bound so that they remain small.

45 RANDOM DURATIONS

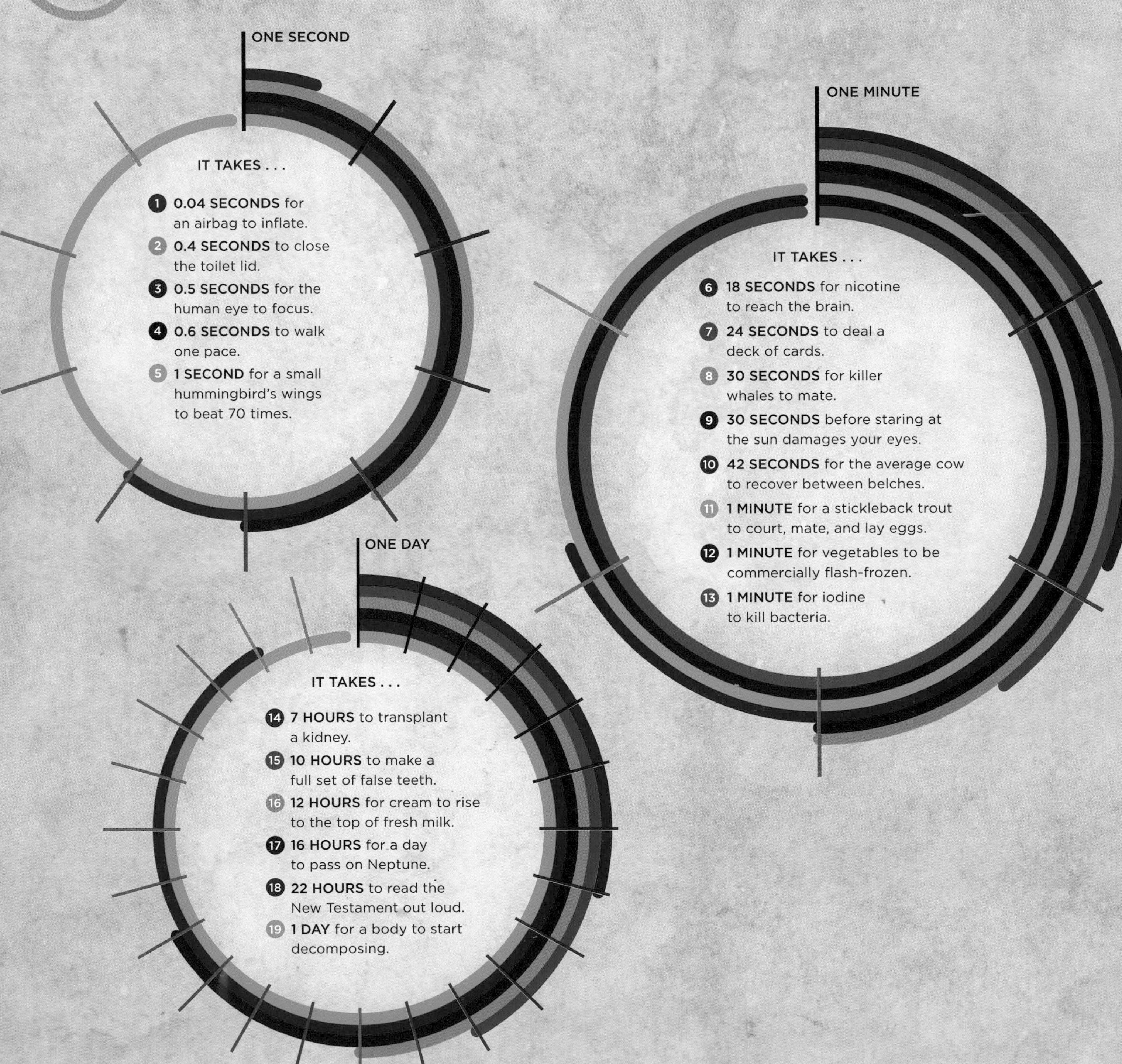

ONE SECOND
IT TAKES . . .
1 **0.04 SECONDS** for an airbag to inflate.
2 **0.4 SECONDS** to close the toilet lid.
3 **0.5 SECONDS** for the human eye to focus.
4 **0.6 SECONDS** to walk one pace.
5 **1 SECOND** for a small hummingbird's wings to beat 70 times.
ONE MINUTE
IT TAKES . . .
6 **18 SECONDS** for nicotine to reach the brain.
7 **24 SECONDS** to deal a deck of cards.
8 **30 SECONDS** for killer whales to mate.
9 **30 SECONDS** before staring at the sun damages your eyes.
10 **42 SECONDS** for the average cow to recover between belches.
11 **1 MINUTE** for a stickleback trout to court, mate, and lay eggs.
12 **1 MINUTE** for vegetables to be commercially flash-frozen.
13 **1 MINUTE** for iodine to kill bacteria.
ONE DAY
IT TAKES . . .
14 **7 HOURS** to transplant a kidney.
15 **10 HOURS** to make a full set of false teeth.
16 **12 HOURS** for cream to rise to the top of fresh milk.
17 **16 HOURS** for a day to pass on Neptune.
18 **22 HOURS** to read the New Testament out loud.
19 **1 DAY** for a body to start decomposing.

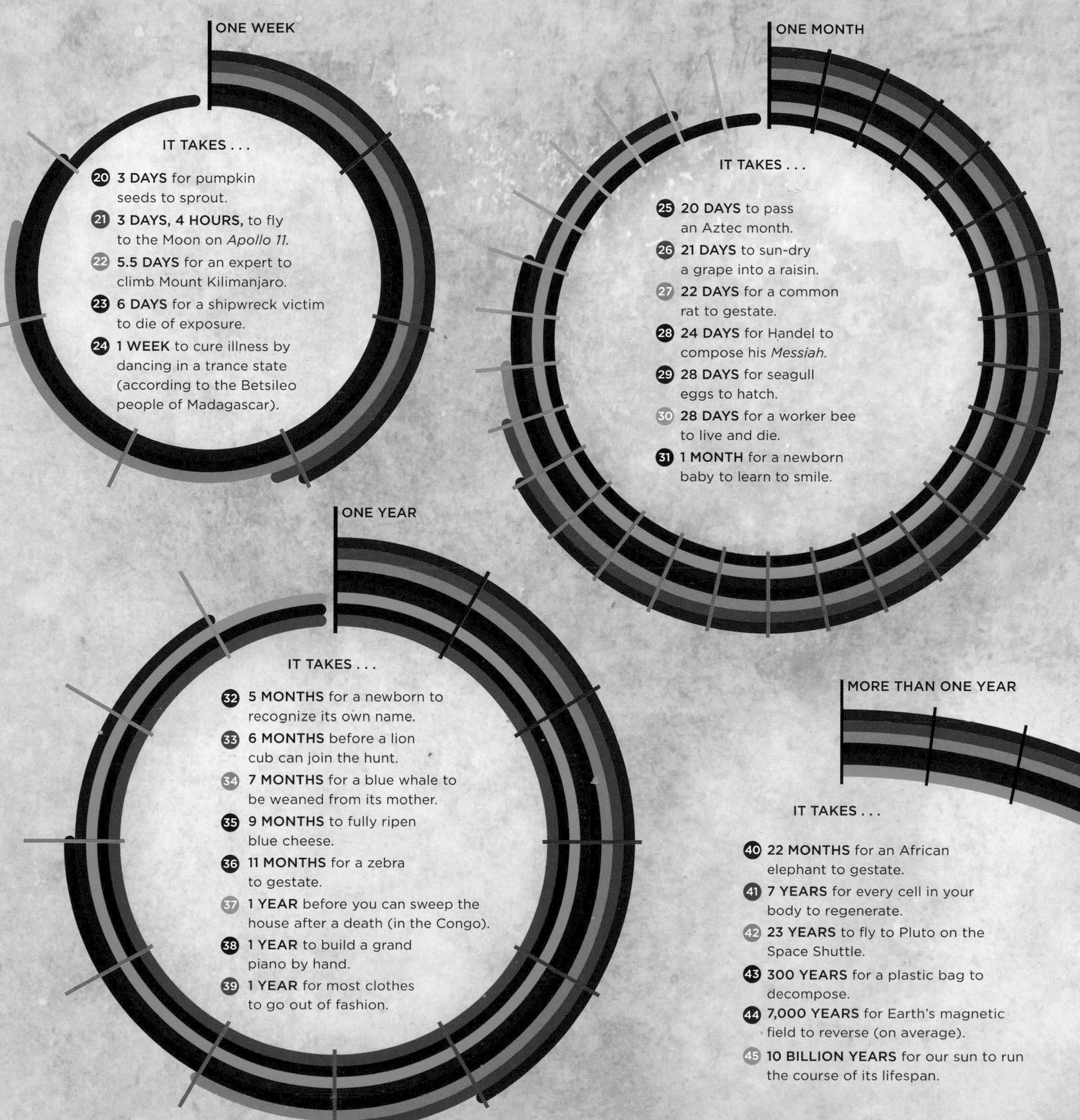
ONE WEEK
IT TAKES . . .
20 **3 DAYS** for pumpkin seeds to sprout.
21 **3 DAYS, 4 HOURS,** to fly to the Moon on *Apollo 11.*
22 **5.5 DAYS** for an expert to climb Mount Kilimanjaro.
23 **6 DAYS** for a shipwreck victim to die of exposure.
24 **1 WEEK** to cure illness by dancing in a trance state (according to the Betsileo people of Madagascar).
ONE MONTH
IT TAKES . . .
25 **20 DAYS** to pass an Aztec month.
26 **21 DAYS** to sun-dry a grape into a raisin.
27 **22 DAYS** for a common rat to gestate.
28 **24 DAYS** for Handel to compose his *Messiah.*
29 **28 DAYS** for seagull eggs to hatch.
30 **28 DAYS** for a worker bee to live and die.
31 **1 MONTH** for a newborn baby to learn to smile.
ONE YEAR
IT TAKES . . .
32 **5 MONTHS** for a newborn to recognize its own name.
33 **6 MONTHS** before a lion cub can join the hunt.
34 **7 MONTHS** for a blue whale to be weaned from its mother.
35 **9 MONTHS** to fully ripen blue cheese.
36 **11 MONTHS** for a zebra to gestate.
37 **1 YEAR** before you can sweep the house after a death (in the Congo).
38 **1 YEAR** to build a grand piano by hand.
39 **1 YEAR** for most clothes to go out of fashion.
MORE THAN ONE YEAR
IT TAKES . . .
40 **22 MONTHS** for an African elephant to gestate.
41 **7 YEARS** for every cell in your body to regenerate.
42 **23 YEARS** to fly to Pluto on the Space Shuttle.
43 **300 YEARS** for a plastic bag to decompose.
44 **7,000 YEARS** for Earth's magnetic field to reverse (on average).
45 **10 BILLION YEARS** for our sun to run the course of its lifespan.

18 REALLY LONG WORDS

NEBEPRISIKIŠKIA-KOPŪSTELIAUDA-VOME

LITHUANIAN
32 LETTERS
"Those that were unable to pick wood sorrels in the past"

Muvaffakiyetsizleştiricileştiriveremeyebileceklerimizdenmişsinizcesine

TURKISH
70 LETTERS
"As though you are from those whom we could not make easily a maker of unsuccessful ones"

Antidisestablishmentarianism

ENGLISH
28 LETTERS
A 19th-century political movement that opposed the disestablishment of the Church of England as the state church

MEGSZENTSÉGTELENÍTHETETLEN

HUNGARIAN
26 LETTERS
Stain-proof

Taumatawhakatangihangakoau-auotamateaturipukakapikimaun gahoronukupokaiwhenuakitana-tahu

MAORI
85 LETTERS
A place name meaning "The summit where Tamatea, the man with the big knees, the climber of mountains, the land-swallower who traveled about, played his nose flute to his loved one"

LLANFAIRPWLLGWYNGYLLGOGERYCHW

WELSH
58 LETTERS
A railway station in Wales that translates to: "St. Mary's church in the hollow of the white hazel near to the rapid whirlpool and the church of St. Tysilio of the red cave"

Hyperneuroakustiskadia fragmakontravibrationer

SWEDISH
45 LETTERS
The technical name for hiccups

SOVRAMAGNIFICENTISSIMAMENTE!

ITALIAN
27 LETTERS
"In a way that is more than magnificent by far"

DZIEWIĘĆSETDZIEWIĘĆDZIESIĘCIODZIEW

Nordöstersjökustartilleriflygspaningssimulatoranläggningsmaterie

KETURIASDEŠIMTAŠTUONIAŠONIUOSE

LITHUANIAN
30 LETTERS
A polygon with 48 sides

Lopadotemachoselachogaleokranioleipsanodrimhy-
potrimmatosilphioparaomelitokatakechymenokich-
lepikossyphophattoperisteralektryonoptekephallio-
kigklopeleiolagoiosiraiobaphetraganopterygon

ANCIENT GREEK
182 LETTERS
A fictional dish composed of all kinds of dainties, fish, flesh, fowl, and sauces that Aristophanes invented for comic effect

DONAUDAMPFSCHIFFFAHRTSELEK-
TRIZITÄTENHAUPTBETRIEBSWERK-
BAUUNTERBEAMTENGESELLSCHAFT

GERMAN
80 LETTERS
An association for subordinate officials of a shipping company operating on the Danube River before World War I

HIPPOPOTO-
MONSTRO-
SESQUIPED-
ALIOPHOBIA

ENGLISH
35 LETTERS
The fear of long words

FLOCCINAUCINIHILIPILIFICATION

ENGLISH
29 LETTERS
The act of estimating something as being worth so little as to be practically valueless

Bestuurdersaansprakelijkheidsverzekering

DUTCH
40 LETTERS
Drivers' liability insurance

RNDROBWLLLLANTYSILIOGOGOGOCH

Chargoggagoggmanchauggagogg-
chaubunagungamaugg

ALGONQUIAN
45 LETTERS
The name of a lake in the US state of Massachusetts meaning "Fishing place at the boundaries, neutral meeting grounds"

ONARODOWOŚCIOWEGO

POLISH
55 LETTERS
"Of 999 nationalities"

erhållsuppföljningssystemdiskussionsinläggsförberedelsearbeten

SWEDISH
130 LETTERS
"Northern Baltic Sea Coast Artillery Reconnaissance Flight Simulator Construction Equipment Maintenance Monitoring Systems Talk Posts Preparation Works"

Kindercarnavalsop-
tochtvoorbereidingswerkzaamheden

DUTCH
49 LETTERS
The preparation activities for a children's carnival procession

CELL PHONE TO LANDLINE RATIOS

THE NUMBER YOU HAVE REACHED

The number of cell phones that exist per landline in countries around the world tells a number of stories, which is why analysts collect the data. A nation with many cell phones and few landlines tends to be a formerly underdeveloped country that's getting tech-savvy quickly. A country where the ratio goes the other way may be geographically unsuited to phone towers, or other cultural factors may be at work.

Country	Ratio
KIRIBATI	0.25
GUINEA-BISSAU	109
ANGOLA	58
CUBA	0.30
LIBERIA	366
GHANA	80
MARSHALL ISLANDS	0.23
DEMOCRATIC REPUBLIC OF CONGO	248
MYANMAR	0.45
TANZANIA	82
RWANDA	79
REPUBLIC OF THE CONGO	81
NIGER	69
KENYA	66
NIUE	0.60

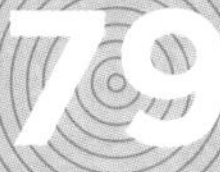

15 FASTEST INTERNET CONNECTIONS AROUND THE WORLD

A NEED FOR SPEED

Internet speed is measured in many ways. Here countries are ranked by the number of megabits that their systems can transfer a second (Mbps) when functioning optimally.

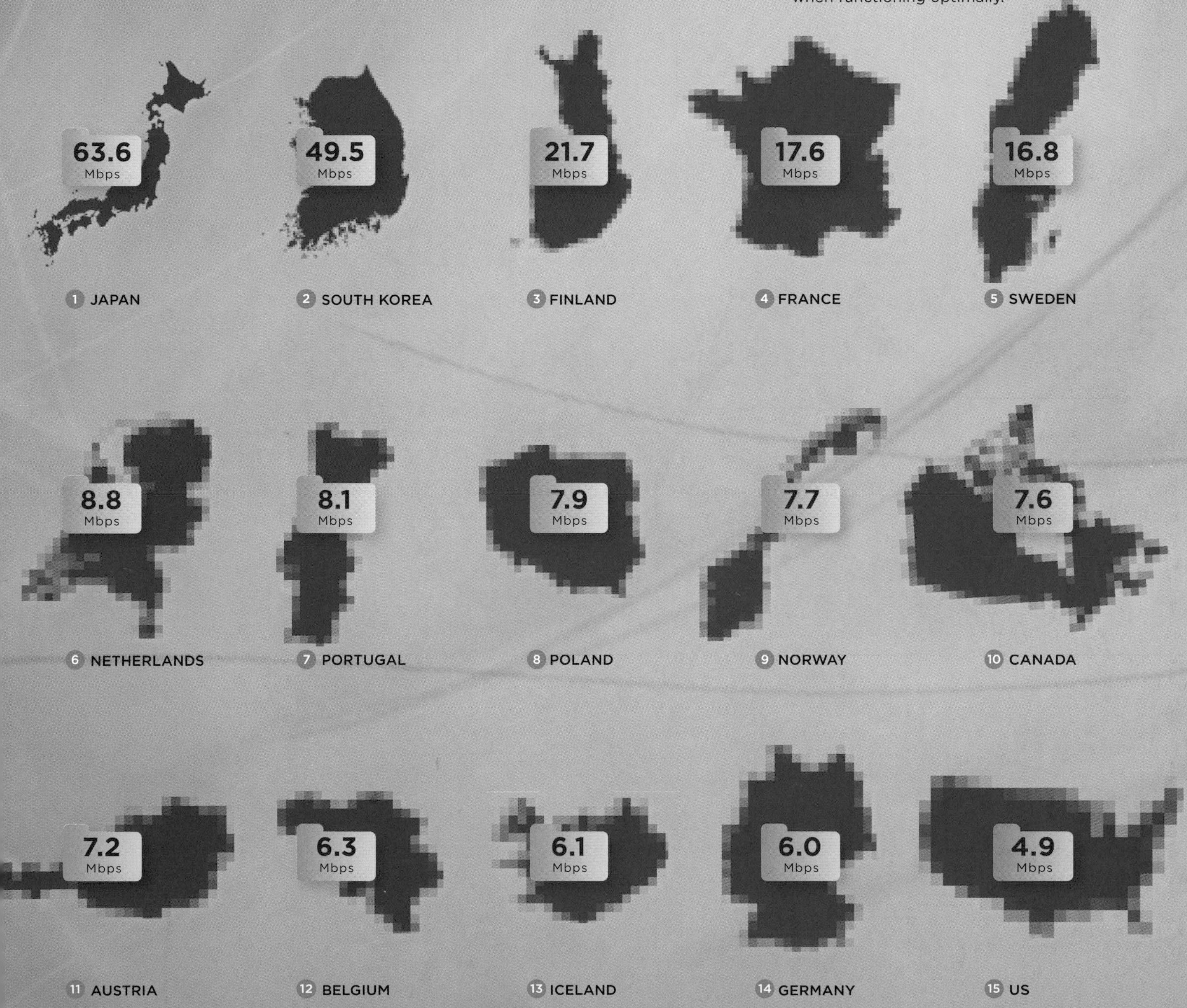

63.6 Mbps
1 JAPAN

49.5 Mbps
2 SOUTH KOREA

21.7 Mbps
3 FINLAND

17.6 Mbps
4 FRANCE

16.8 Mbps
5 SWEDEN

8.8 Mbps
6 NETHERLANDS

8.1 Mbps
7 PORTUGAL

7.9 Mbps
8 POLAND

7.7 Mbps
9 NORWAY

7.6 Mbps
10 CANADA

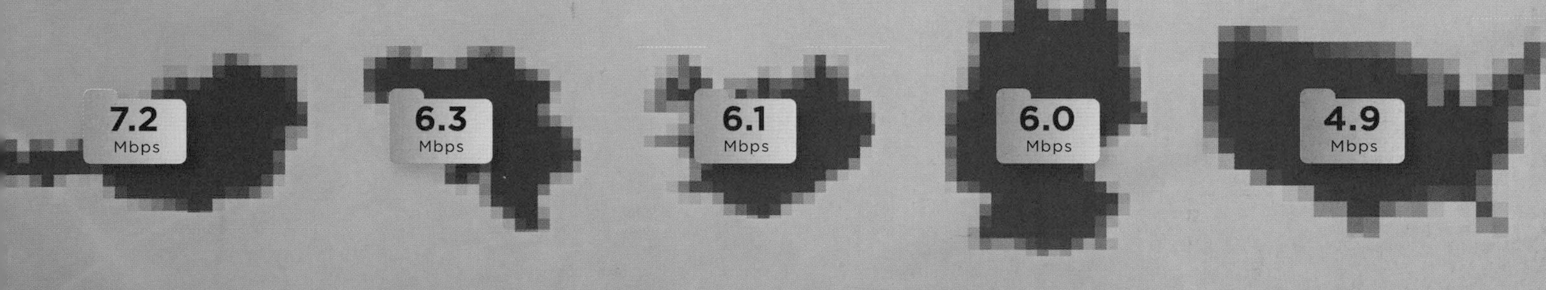

11 AUSTRIA

12 BELGIUM

13 ICELAND

14 GERMANY

15 US

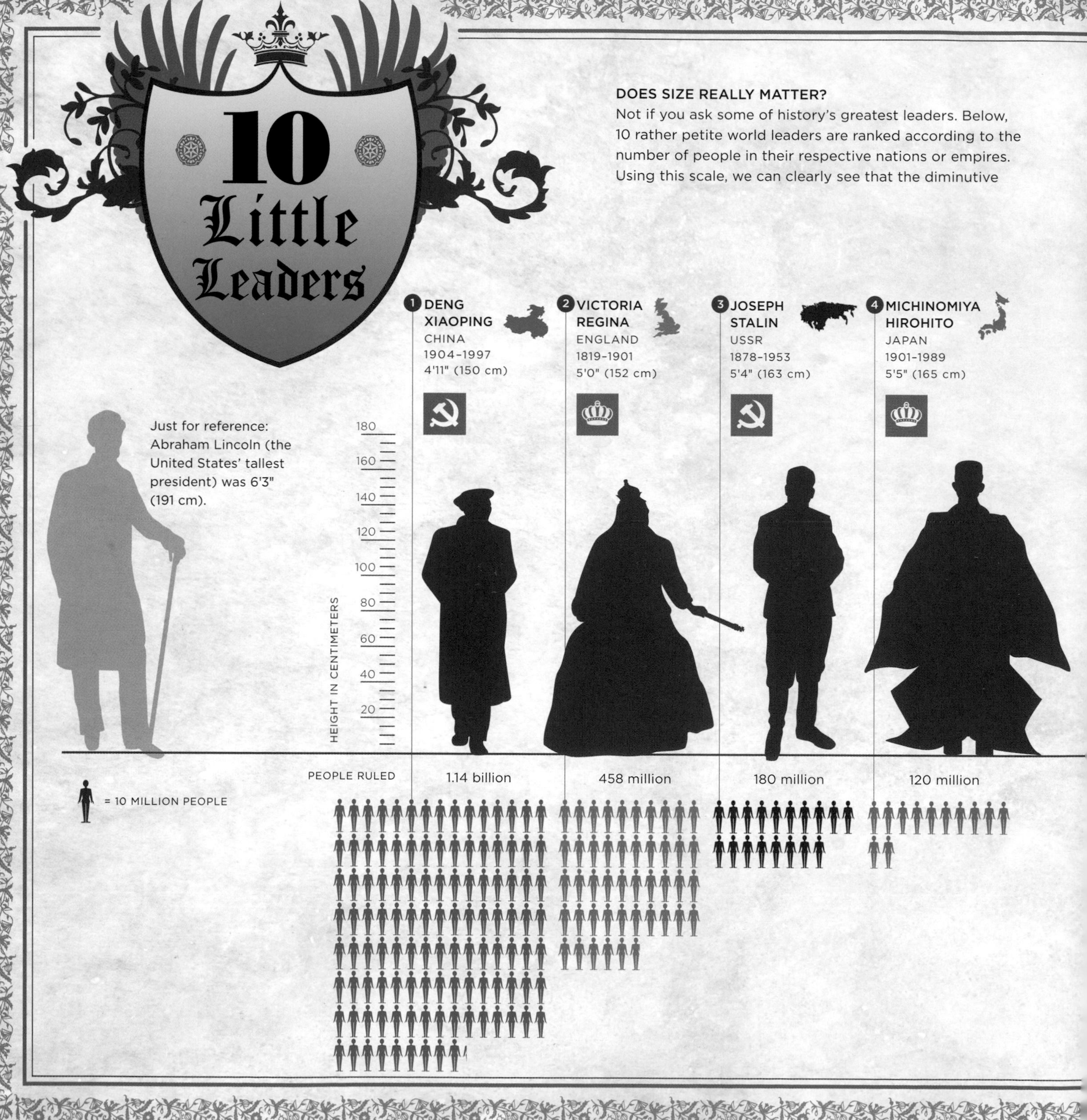
10 Little Leaders
DOES SIZE REALLY MATTER?
Not if you ask some of history's greatest leaders. Below, 10 rather petite world leaders are ranked according to the number of people in their respective nations or empires. Using this scale, we can clearly see that the diminutive
Just for reference: Abraham Lincoln (the United States' tallest president) was 6'3" (191 cm).
1 DENG XIAOPING
CHINA
1904–1997
4'11" (150 cm)
2 VICTORIA REGINA
ENGLAND
1819–1901
5'0" (152 cm)
3 JOSEPH STALIN
USSR
1878–1953
5'4" (163 cm)
4 MICHINOMIYA HIROHITO
JAPAN
1901–1989
5'5" (165 cm)
HEIGHT IN CENTIMETERS
180
160
140
120
100
80
60
40
20
PEOPLE RULED
1.14 billion
458 million
180 million
120 million
= 10 MILLION PEOPLE

Deng Xiaoping leads the field by, well, a head—or several million of them. And what of that famous Napoleon complex? In fact, the emperor was a rather dashing 5'6" (168 cm), a veritable giant in this compact crowd.

5 ADOLF HITLER
GERMANY
1889–1945
5'8" (173 cm)
80 million

6 NICOLAS SARKOZY
FRANCE
1955–PRESENT
5'5" (165 cm)
65 million

7 NAPOLEON BONAPARTE
FRANCE
1769–1821
5'6" (168 cm)
44 million

8 FRANCISCO FRANCO
SPAIN
1892–1975
5'4" (163 cm)
35 million

9 KIM JONG-IL
NORTH KOREA
1941–PRESENT
5'2" (157 cm)
24 million

10 BENITO JUAREZ
MEXICO
1806–1872
4'6" (137 cm)
9 million

HEIGHT IN CENTIMETERS: 20, 40, 60, 80, 100, 120, 140, 160, 180

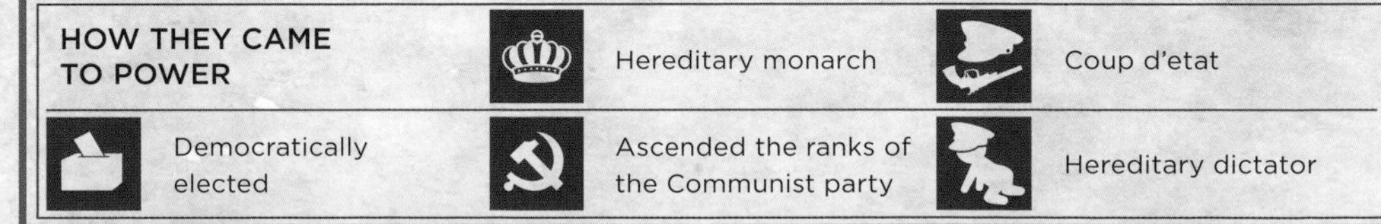

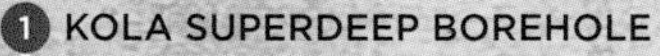

1 KOLA SUPERDEEP BOREHOLE
RUSSIA
7.6 MILES / 12.2 KM
Drilled in 1989 as an experiment as to how deep humans could drill into the Earth's crust, it was made famous by rumors that it was a "well to Hell," and that the voices of the damned could be heard from its depths.

2 ICE CORE DRILLING
ANTARCTICA
2 MILES / 3.2 KM
The European Project for Ice Coring in Antarctica (EPICA) drilled the Dome Concordia hole into the Antarctic ice and got a snapshot of 740,000 years of climate history, geology, and comet strikes.

3 SEAFLOOR DRILLING
NEW ZEALAND
1.25 MILES / 2 KM
The ship called *Joint Oceanographic Institutions for Deep Earth Sampling (JOIDES) Resolution* drilled the deepest hole ever made in the seafloor on a single expedition. The findings chronicle 35 million years of geological history.

4 BINGHAM CANYON MINE
US
0.75 MILES / 1.2 KM
This copper mine is located in the Oquirrh mountains of Utah, right outside Salt Lake City. It is the largest human-made excavation, measuring 0.75 miles (1.2 km) deep and 2.5 miles (4 km) wide.

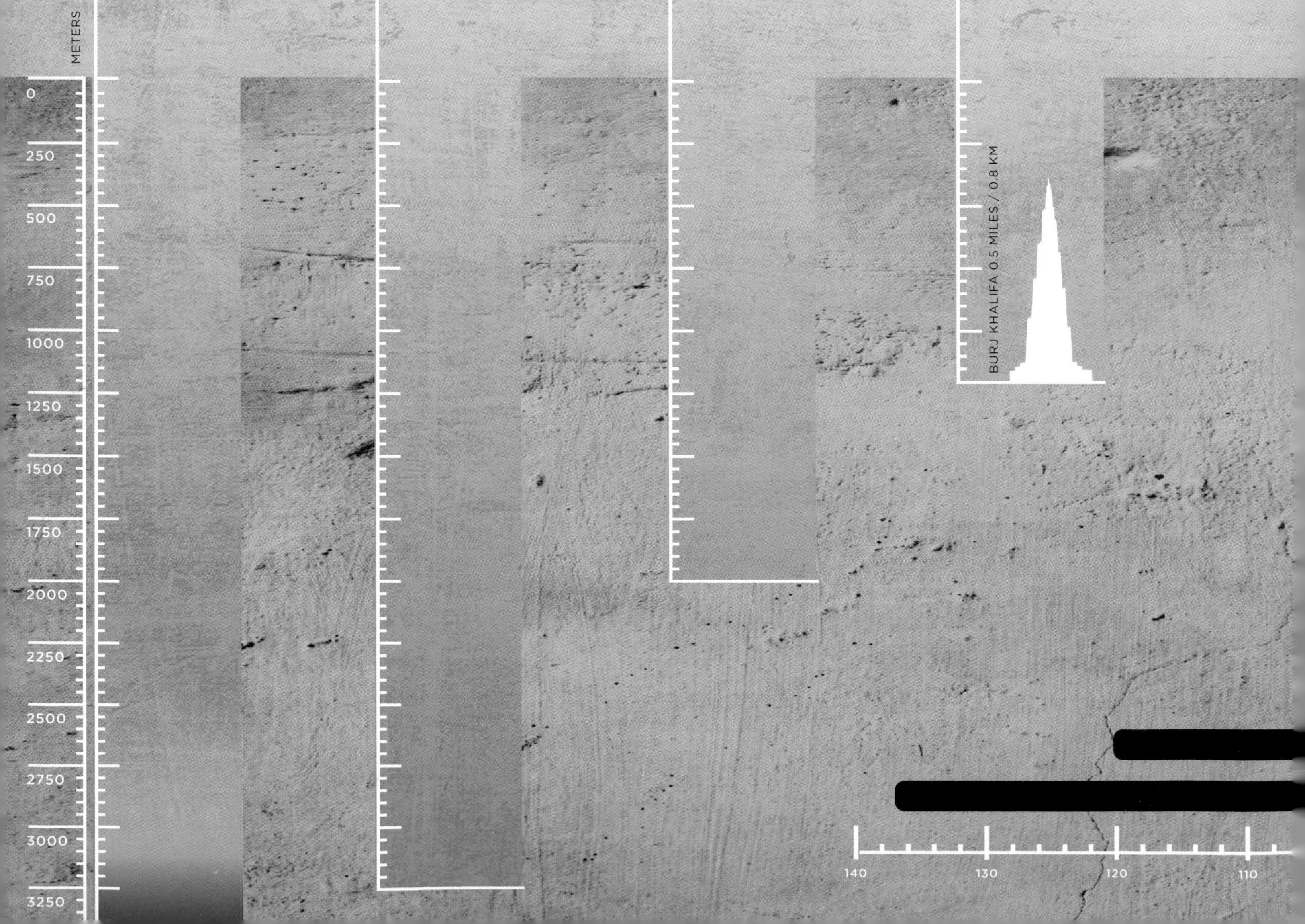

METERS
0
250
500
750
1000
1250
1500
1750
2000
2250
2500
2750
3000
3250

BURJ KHALIFA 0.5 MILES / 0.8 KM

140
130
120
110

5 VRTOGLAVICA CAVE
SLOVENIA
1,978 FEET / 603 M
The deepest vertical shaft in a cave can be found in Slovenia's Monte Kanin. Cavers consider this shaft to be a "vertical pitch," which means that rather than dropping straight down, it descends in long stretches with landings in between.

CN TOWER
1,814 FEET / 553 M

6 MIR DIAMOND MINE
RUSSIA
1,722 FEET / 525 M
The first diamond mine in Russia, this now-abandoned site in Siberia is still the world's second-largest artificial hole. All air traffic above it is prohibited, as the hole's suction has caused many helicopter crashes.

TAIPEI 101
1,670 FEET / 509 M

7 LECHUGUILLA CAVE
US
1,604 FEET / 489 M
The deepest cave in the United States, New Mexico's Lechuguilla Cave is also the fifth-longest cave in the world, stretching 126 miles (203 km) in length. It boasts beautiful and rare stone formations.

SEARS TOWER
1,454 FEET / 443 M

8 EL ZACATÓN CENOTE
MEXICO
1,043 FEET / 318 M
The world's deepest water-filled sinkhole is located in Mexico's Tamaulipas state. One of the first divers to try reaching the bottom died in the attempt; subsequently, NASA sent a robotic vehicle down to measure the hole's extent.

EMPIRE STATE BUILDING
1,250 FEET / 381 M

10 LONGEST TUNNELS

SEOUL SUBWAY LINE 5 / SOUTH KOREA / 29.6 MILES (47.6 KM) / METRO

CHUNNEL / UK AND FRANCE / 31.3 MILES (50.4 KM) / RAILWAY

ŽELIVKA WATER TUNNEL / CZECH REPUBLIC / 31.7 MILES (51 KM) / WATER SUPPLY

SEIKAN TUNNEL / JAPAN / 33.5 MILES (53.9 KM) / RAILWAY

GOTTHARD BASE TUNNEL / SWITZERLAND / 35.5 MILES (57.1 KM) / RAILWAY

BOLMEN WATER TUNNEL / SWEDEN / 51 MILES (82.1 KM) / WATER SUPPLY

ORANGE-FISH RIVER TUNNEL / SOUTH AFRICA / 51.4 MILES (82.7 KM) / WATER SUPPLY

NEW YORK CITY WATER TUNNEL 3 / US / 60 MILES (96.6 KM) / WATER SUPPLY

PÄIJÄNNE WATER TUNNEL / FINLAND / 74.6 MILES (120.1 KM) / WATER SUPPLY

DELAWARE AQUEDUCT / US / 85.1 MILES (137 KM) / WATER SUPPLY

90 80 70 60 50 40 30 20 10
KILOMETERS

DOWRIES AND BRIDE PRICES *from Around the World*

1 MODERN ROMA PEOPLE
Money and a bottle of wine or brandy

8 ANCIENT ROME
Money and an iron ring

2 ANCIENT GERMANY
Trees planted at a girl's birth (for use in building furniture)

9 MEDIEVAL LOWER SAXONY
Land (given to the son-in-law, provided he took the family name)

3 ANCIENT LITHUANIA
Fabric goods, including towels, clothing, and sheets

10 MODERN THAILAND
Gold and money (as much as US $10,000)

4 ANCIENT ATHENS
Money, jewelry, and furniture

11 ANCIENT CHINA
A chamber pot full of fruit and coins, plus other everyday practical items

5 MEDIEVAL EASTERN EUROPE
Furniture (specifically, a bed and a wardrobe)

12 MODERN CHHATTISGARH, INDIA
Nine different species of snake

6 MODERN UGANDA
Chickens, goats, cows, and cash

13 MODERN SEPHARDIC JEWISH PEOPLES
Jewelry (often gold pendants or amulets to ward off evil)

7 ANCIENT EGYPT
Money for furniture and jewelry

14 MODERN POMO TRIBES, NORTH AMERICA
Baskets given to the husband by the bride's mother

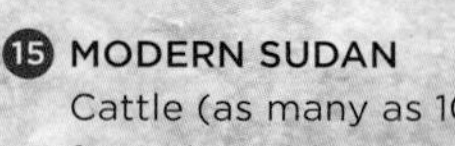

15 MODERN SUDAN
Cattle (as many as 100 for a desirable woman)

MAN'S FAMILY PAYS

WOMAN'S FAMILY PAYS

8 UNUSUAL RANSOMS

1 ASSORTED VALUABLE COMMODITIES
MODERN-DAY ITALY / 408
The Visigoth king Alaric I besieged Rome until the city coughed up 5,000 pounds (2,267 kg) of gold; 30,000 pounds (13,607 kg) of silver; 4,000 silk tunics; 3,000 hides dyed scarlet; and a ton (900 kg) of pepper.

2 FOOD FOR THE HUNGRY
US / 1974
Newspaper heiress Patty Hearst was kidnapped by the Symbionese Liberation Army (which she then joined, in a case of Stockholm syndrome). Her millionaire father, Randolph Hearst, complied with the SLA's demands, donating millions of dollars' worth of food to the poor.

3 THE LARGEST RANSOM ON RECORD
CHINA / 1996
"Big spender" and notorious gangster Cheung Chi Keung kidnapped Victor Li Tzar-kuoi, the son of a Hong Kong business tycoon. Li was released after his father paid a reported astronomical ransom of US $134 million—one of the largest ransoms on record at the time.

4 NAUGHTY CALENDARS
VENEZUELA / 2003
Miss Venezuela 1997, Veruska Ramirez, was car-jacked by a gang of kidnappers. When her assailants noticed a box in her vehicle containing her nude calendars, they simply asked her to autograph the calendars and released her.

5 A PALTRY SUM
US / 2010
Paul Franco changed not only the password on his ex-girlfriend's Facebook account, but also all of her personal information, including her sexual preference and other crucial items. He began spamming friends and family members, and demanded she pay US $390 to release the account.

6 TEA
US / 2010
After killing his estranged wife, Tennessee native and methamphetamine abuser David Cox held his own children hostage for 20 hours. "We got him talking on the phone with the hostage negotiator . . . but he made no sense. He demanded a gallon of tea. He wanted two cups of sugar in the tea," the sheriff on duty recalled.

7 THE COST OF YOUR REPUTATION
THE INTERNET / 2010
The Pirlames Trojan horse scheme entrapped people who downloaded a pornographic game, posting their contact information online and "shaming" victims into paying for the removal of their embarrassing new personal data from the Internet.

8 A CHANGE IN PROGRAMMING
US / 2010
Environmental extremist James Lee took hostages at the headquarters of the Discovery Channel, threatening violence unless the channel changed its programming to combat overpopulation. A sniper shot Lee; no hostages were harmed.

PLACES WE LIVE AND PLACES WE DON'T

From the depths of space to your very own living room, this chapter redefines our ideas about what makes a house a home. (Hint: Pleasingly free of demons is a good start). Zoom in close to see what kind of critter can survive inside a volcano, or take the long view, all the way from the Hubble telescope. Either way, here is a collection of facts about places—ancient, undiscovered, utopian, or otherwise.

TYPES OF HEAVENLY BODIES THAT MIGHT SUPPORT LIFE

IS THERE ANYBODY OUT THERE?

For centuries, the possibility of life on other planets was the realm of science fiction and wild speculation. Recent advances in astronomy have allowed us to discover hundreds of extrasolar planets that might support life, and scientists speculate that there may be a wide range of environments where life could exist. Here are a few planetary environments that we—or other, more mysterious beings—may someday call home.

YELLOW STAR

Every life-supporting planet needs its sun—a source of energy that's relatively stable, lasts long enough for life to evolve (say, at least a few billion years), and provides a habitable zone: an area in which orbiting planets can retain liquid water on their surfaces. Yellow stars do the trick nicely.

1 CRATEROUS WORLD

Planets with harsh surface conditions but plenty of deep craters and caves could provide sanctuary to incipient life-forms.

2 SUPERHOT SCORCHER

A planet located very close to a star might host silica-based life, which could thrive in the extreme heat.

3 VOLCANIC SEA WORLD

Deep-sea thermal vents shoot up substances that can kick-start life, even on inhospitable planets.

4 "GOLDILOCKS" PLANET

A relatively large planet that's "just right." It's fairly close to the star it orbits, and so can both sustain water and gather energy—sound familiar?

5 TIDALLY LOCKED PLANETS
Planets very close to red dwarves might be "tidally locked," with one side in eternal day, the other in eternal night. Only hardy creatures could exist in between the two zones.

RED DWARF
Smaller, cooler, and more stable than yellow stars, red dwarves are the most common stars in our galaxy. Planets would have to orbit them very closely to host life.

6 AMMONIALAND
A planet of liquid ammonia couldn't host carbon-based life, but could host ammonia-based life, which theoretically exists.

7 NEUTRON STAR
Tiny, short-lived nano-beings could flicker into and out of life in this mysterious environment—made entirely of neutrons—that exists after a star dies.

8 GAS GIANT
There's a chance that these huge, yellow star-orbiting gas masses could provide shelter to incredibly light beings in the upper clouds.

9 FROZEN SPHERE
An icy moon could host liquid water under its frozen exterior—and a world of aquatic creatures.

10 VERY SMALL VOLCANIC MOON
Despite its less-than-ideal size, a tiny moon could support microorganisms, if its high volcanic activity pumped life-creating elements into the atmosphere.

12 PLACES YOU MIGHT FIND EXTREMOPHILES

TO BOLDLY GO WHERE NO BUG HAS GONE BEFORE
Most creatures enjoy rather plush lives on planet Earth, but others have adapted to some more grisly habitats, earning themselves the moniker *extremophiles.*

1 2 3 4 5

1 RADIOACTIVE ENVIRONMENTS
Studies of the site of the 1986 Chernobyl nuclear-plant disaster have revealed the unexpected survival of many species, such as the *Anisakis simplex* worm.

2 DROUGHT-RIDDEN ENVIRONMENTS
Arid environments support bacteria and microorganisms, including the "water bear" (*Tardigrades*), which can survive for almost a decade without water.

3 INSIDE ROCKS
As deep as 1.8 miles (3 km) under the Earth's surface live some hardy bacteria and amoebas. They are described as endolithic because they live in rock.

4 HIGH-SALT ENVIRONMENTS
Some salty places are hospitable to bacteria such as *Chromohalobacter beijerinckii*, a type of bacteria that's been found in the Dead Sea and also in salted herring.

5 PITCH-BLACK TERRESTRIAL CAVES
Caves where no light ever penetrates are home to a number of unique millipedes and beetles, including *Neaphaenops tellkampfi tellkampfi* (also known as the cave beetle).

6 VOLCANOES
The Micronesian megapode (*Megapodius laperouse*) is a species of incubator bird that buries its eggs in the hot ash of volcanoes to keep them warm.

7 HYDROTHERMAL VENTS
Undersea vents with temperatures up to 750°F (400°C) are home to bacteria, tube worms, and *Crysomallon squamiferum,* a snail covered in protective iron scales.

8 UNDERSEA CAVES
These lightless, inhospitable areas are called home by fish and crustaceans, including the pale and translucent cave crayfish, *Orconectes australis*.

9 SUBZERO WATER
Some majorly hardy archaea and bacteria, such as *Cytophaga-Flavobacterium-Bacteroides,* can live in salty water as cold as -4°F (-20°C).

10 DEEP BENEATH ICE
The shrimplike species *Lyssianasid amphipods* has been found 600 feet (183 m) under Antarctic ice—a deeper, colder place than had been thought could sustain life.

11 LAVA TUBES
Lava carves channels in volcanoes, and between flows the tubes teem with millipedes and spiders—like the Kauai cave wolf spider, *Adelocosa anops*.

12 OUTER SPACE
OU-20 microbes successfully spent 533 days on the outside of the International Space Station, proving that photosynthesizing bacteria can survive long periods in space.

UTOPIAN EXPERIMENTS

1 BROOK FARM
US / 1841–1847
Brook Farm was partly inspired by the American Transcendentalists, who promoted equality and an appreciation for nature. Noted participants in the community included Nathaniel Hawthorne and Ralph Waldo Emerson.

2 ONEIDA COMMUNITY
US / 1848–1881
This commune was based on the belief that Jesus had already been resurrected and that man could create Heaven on Earth, which for this particular group meant communal living, including group marriage.

3 NEW AUSTRALIA
PARAGUAY / 1893–1894
Australian settlers established this community as a socialist paradise dedicated to communism, racial purity, and temperance. It fell apart quickly, but the basic colony town still remains, with an English-speaking populace.

4 COLONIA FINLANDESA
ARGENTINA / 1906–1940s
Colonia Finlandesa was originally composed of 112 Finnish settlers who arrived in Argentina in 1906. They were fleeing the oppressive Russian regime back home. However, many of them were unused to rural life in the jungle.

5 PENEDO
BRAZIL / 1929–1949
Penedo was established near Rio de Janeiro, Brazil, as a utopian colony by a young Finnish vegetarian group. After the collapse of its utopian ideals, the community began staging "authentic" Finnish traditions for tourists.

6 PADANARAM SETTLEMENT
US / 1966–PRESENT
This fundamentalist Christian community was based around the idea that both sexes have distinct natures and should thus have distinct roles. Man is more wise and woman is more carnal, according to the founder.

7 YAD HASHMONA
ISRAEL / 1971–PRESENT
This spiritual community and "biblical village" was founded by Finnish Christians as a gesture of solidarity with Israel. While the community still exists, its population is now largely native Israeli and Jewish.

8 SVANHOLM
DENMARK / 1978–PRESENT
Located on the island of Zealand, this Danish group was founded on ideals of environmentalism, sustainable living, support for each family by the community, and shared decision-making processes.

Lost Kingdoms

1 ATLANTIS
UNKNOWN
The Greek philosopher Plato is credited with dreaming up the legendary island of Atlantis, although some scholars claim it's an older story. The island is said to have sunk beneath the waves of either the Mediterranean Sea or the Atlantic Ocean.

2 CITY OF THE CAESARS
SOUTH AMERICA
This mythical South American land was known by a number of names, including the Wandering City. It was said to be situated between mountains of gold or diamonds, only sometimes visible, and populated by ghosts.

3 KINGDOM OF SAGUENAY
NORTH AMERICA
According to the Native American Iroquois tribe of the 1500s, there was a northern kingdom of blond men who were rich in gold and furs. It's largely thought to be a myth, but some think it refers to the Vikings' stint in Canada.

4 EL DORADO
SOUTH AMERICA
Sought by the Spanish conquistadores of the 1500s, this land of unthinkable wealth in gold and precious jewels was never found, though it still lives on in lore. Tales placed it on a lagoon, somewhere near present-day Colombia.

5 SEVEN CITIES OF GOLD
NORTH AMERICA
Local tribes told Spanish explorers in the 16th-century American Southwest tales about seven golden cities in the north. The Spanish searched for them and found instead the enchanted land of Nebraska.

6 CANTRE'R GWAELOD
WALES
Said to have perished due to debauchery, Cantre'r Gwaelod is a legendary ancient sunken kingdom, rumored to have existed in what is now Cardigan Bay. Stories say that the kingdom's church bells will ring out in times of danger for the Welsh.

7 THE LOST CONTINENT OF MU
UNKNOWN
An entire continent that sank mysteriously beneath the waves, Mu was also known as Lemuria. Augustus Le Plongeon, a 19th-century writer, popularized the idea that the descendents of Mu generated several civilizations.

8 SHANGRI-LA
ASIA
Shangri-La is a fictional place described in the 1933 novel *Lost Horizon* by British author James Hilton. Since publication, people have theorized that it describes a real, hidden spiritual community somewhere in the Himalayas.

62 ROOMS YOU MIGHT FIND IN A HOUSE
1 ATTIC
2 MUSIC ROOM
3 ALCOVE
4 PLAYROOM
5 NURSERY
6 SOLARIUM
7 FAINTING ROOM
8 CABINET
9 LIBRARY
10 SMOKING ROOM
11 CONSERVATORY
12 COAT CLOSET
13 OFFICE
14 STUDY
15 DEN
16 VESTIBULE
17 HALLWAY
18 SITTING ROOM
19 POWDER ROOM
20 ENTRY ROOM
21 MUDROOM
22 SUN PORCH
23 ANTEROOM
24 PARLOR
25 LIVING ROOM
26 STORM CELLAR
27 ROOT CELLAR
28 UNDERCROFT
29 BASEMENT
30 BOILER ROOM
31 WALK-IN CLOSET
32 LINEN CLOSET
33 CLOTHES CLOSET
34 MASTER BEDROOM
35 BATHROOM
36 BEDROOM
37 GUEST ROOM
38 BILLIARDS ROOM
39 KITCHEN
40 SCULLERY
41 LARDER
42 COLD ROOM
43 HALF BATH
44 WET BAR

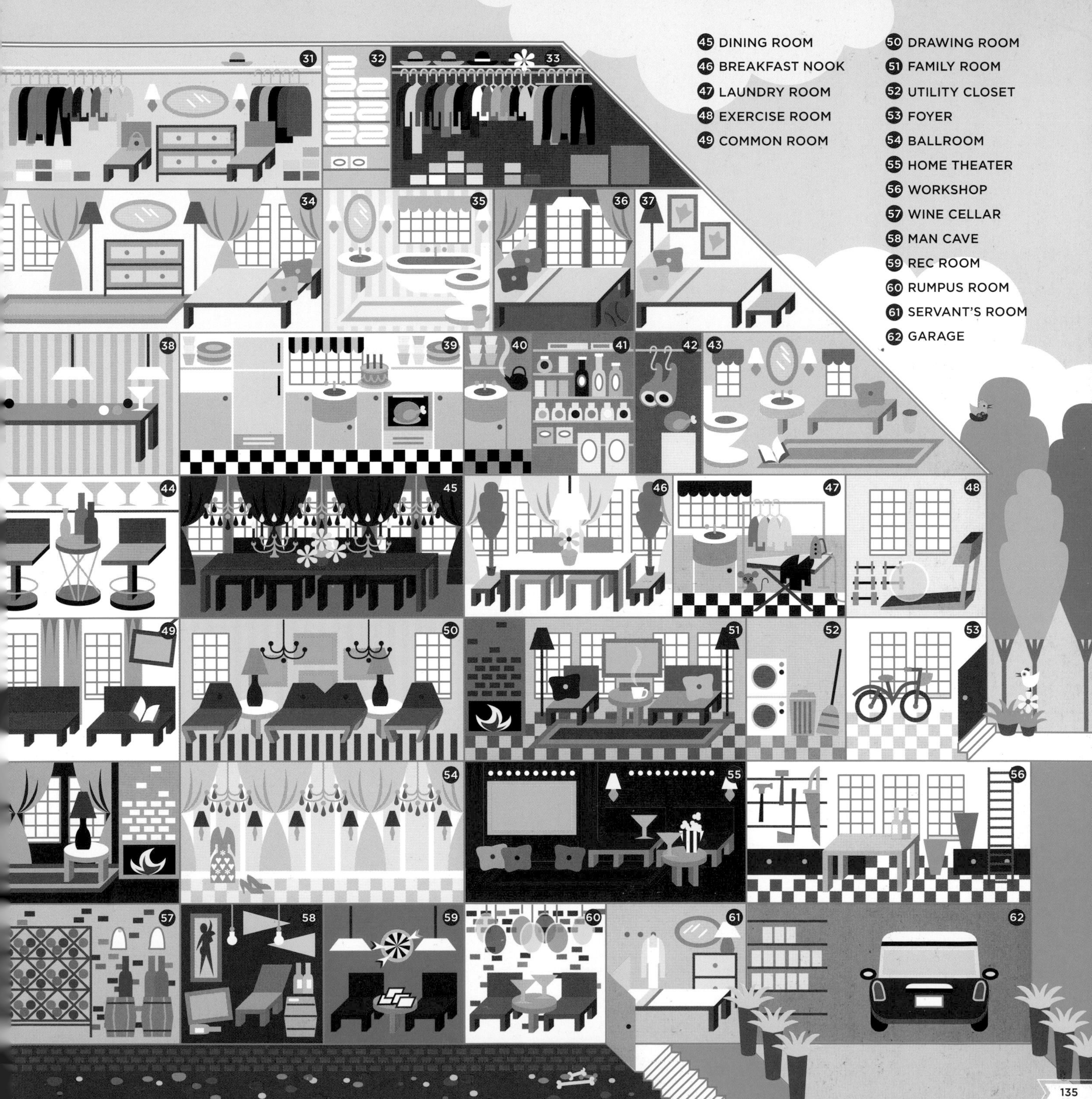

45 DINING ROOM
46 BREAKFAST NOOK
47 LAUNDRY ROOM
48 EXERCISE ROOM
49 COMMON ROOM
50 DRAWING ROOM
51 FAMILY ROOM
52 UTILITY CLOSET
53 FOYER
54 BALLROOM
55 HOME THEATER
56 WORKSHOP
57 WINE CELLAR
58 MAN CAVE
59 REC ROOM
60 RUMPUS ROOM
61 SERVANT'S ROOM
62 GARAGE

21 MICRONATIONS

WHAT IS A MICRONATION, ANYWAY?

It's a tiny, self-defined entity that is unrecognized by mainstream governments. What differentiates it from a secessionist state? Usually its founders have a sense of humor, an unwillingness to use violence, and an eccentric outlook. (Years listed are dates of establishment, and population figures are given where available.)

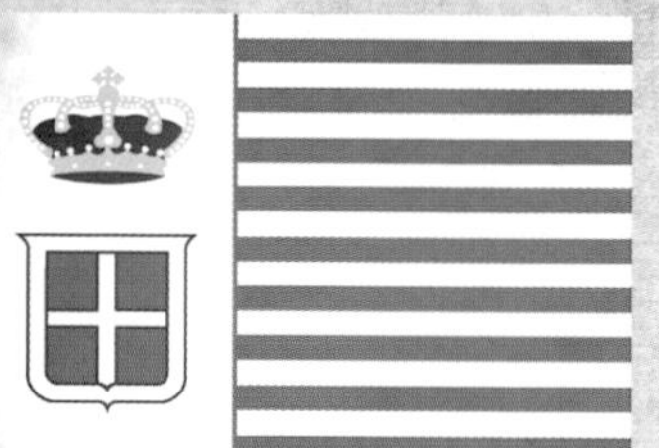

1 PRINCIPALITY OF SEBORGA

ITALY / 954 / POP. 316

This micronation claims independence on the basis of its history as a feudal state.

2 KINGDOM OF REDONDA

THE CARIBBEAN / 1865 / POP. 0

This small uninhabited island was originally claimed by a Victorian-era science fiction writer.

3 AKHZIVLAND

ISRAEL / 1970 / POP. 2

This single-home nation was declared when the government tried to evict an occupant.

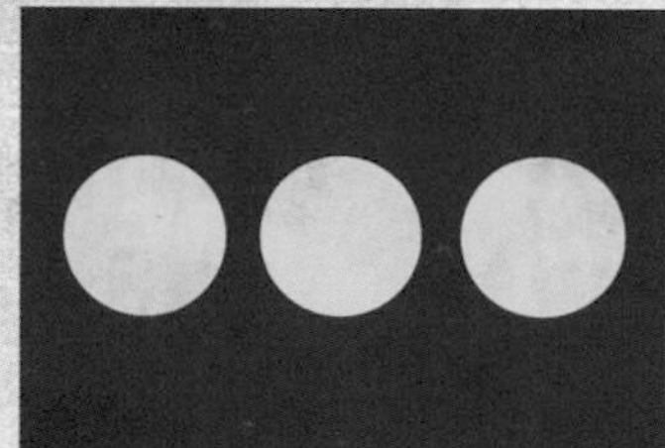

4 FREETOWN CHRISTIANIA

DENMARK / 1971 / POP. 1,000

Hippies established this large commune on a former military base in Copenhagen.

5 SOVEREIGN STATE OF AETERNA LUCINA

AUSTRALIA / 1978

A retiree who claimed he was a baron founded this micronation.

6 KINGDOM OF TALOSSA

US / 1979 / POP. 122

A 14-year-old in Milwaukee established this land and the language to be spoken there.

7 DOMINION OF MELCHIZEDEK

PACIFIC OCEAN / 1986 / POP. 50

Founders were convicted for facilitating large-scale banking fraud in many parts of the world.

8 OTHER WORLD KINGDOM

CZECH REPUBLIC / 1996

This absolute matriarchy and commercial BDSM resort is located in a 16th-century chateau.

9 THE TALLINI FAMILY-KINGDOM OF BUCKSFAN

THE INTERNET / 1998

This country's physical outpost is in Long Island, New York.

10 NOVA ROMA

THE INTERNET / 1998 / POP. 1,200

This Roman revivalist nation celebrates Roman culture, religion, and commerce.

11 BARONY OF CAUX

ENGLAND / 2001 / POP. 102

The rulers of this feudal state claim that it's been in continuous existence since 1069.

12 GAY AND LESBIAN KINGDOM OF THE CORAL SEA ISLANDS

AUSTRALIA / 2004 / POP. 183

Gay-rights activists established it as a symbolic political protest.

13 KINGDOM OF LOVELY

THE INTERNET / 2005 / POP. 60,000

This nation was created in conjunction with the BBC show *How to Start Your Own Country*.

14 CROWN DEPENDENCY OF FORVIK

SCOTLAND / 2008 / POP. 1

The owner of this 2.5-acre (1-hectare) island claims its autonomy.

15 **REPUBLIC OF PERLOJA**
LITHUANIA / 1918
This republic was founded after World War I with its own jail, post office, and army of 300 men.

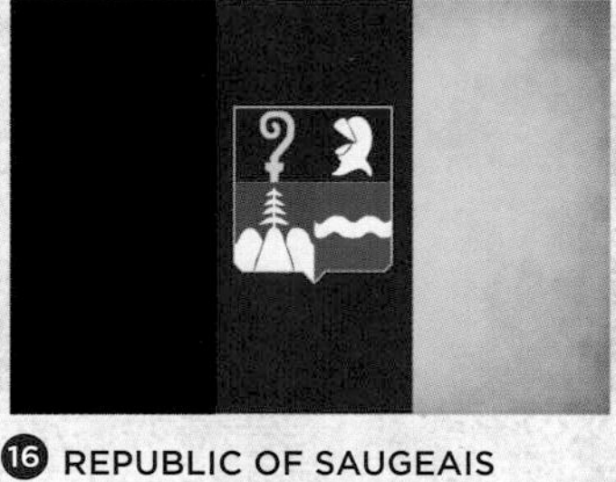

16 **REPUBLIC OF SAUGEAIS**
FRANCE / 1947
This officially sanctioned tongue-in-cheek micronation was invented as a lunchtime joke.

17 **PRINCIPALITY OF SEALAND**
NORTH SEA / 1967 / POP. 5
This country on an offshore oil rig has had a colorful history of conflicts with the British Navy.

18 **PRINCIPALITY OF HUTT RIVER**
AUSTRALIA / 1970 / POP. 30
This country was declared by farmers after a dispute with the government over wheat quotas.

19 **INDEPENDENT STATE OF RAINBOW CREEK**
AUSTRALIA / 1979 / POP. 5
Farmers claimed this land to thwart government appropriation.

20 **GRAND DUCHY OF WESTARCTICA**
ANTARCTICA / 2001 / POP. 0
Settlers claimed land via a loophole in the Antarctic Treaty.

21 **MOST GLORIOUS PEOPLE'S REPUBLIC OF A1**
AUSTRALIA / 2008 / POP. 49
Melbourne students created this country as a classroom project.

12 TYPES OF UNOFFICIAL CITIES

IF YOU BUILD IT, THEY WILL COME
When is a city not quite a city? When it exists for only a week or two, has no official recognition, or is kept secret by its host nation. Below, some types of "cities," with famous examples listed.

1 **RELIGIOUS GATHERING**
HAJJ CITIES / SAUDI ARABIA / POP. 2 MILLION
The Saudi government creates tent cities for pilgrims every year around Mecca.

2 **TEMPORARY SHELTER**
TENT CITY IN TORONTO, CANADA / POP. 300
From 1998 to 2002, hundreds of homeless people lived in this enormous tent city.

3 **TEMPORARY INTENTIONAL COMMUNITY**
BLACK ROCK CITY, US / POP. 50,000
Burning Man has its own temporary infrastructure, laws, and leaders.

4 **FESTIVAL**
GLASTONBURY, ENGLAND / POP. 150,000
Large music festivals often go on for days and have their own infrastructure.

5 **PROTEST CAMP**
FASLANE PEACE CAMP, SCOTLAND / POP. 100
Protesters have created long-standing encampments in a number of locations.

6 **OUTLAW COMMUNITY**
MESA DESERT, US / POP. UNKNOWN
Hippies, bikers, and other "outlaws" create centers where they can make their own rules.

7 **MINE CAMP**
ARGYLE MINE, AUSTRALIA / POP. 300-750
Mine camps far from towns may create their own temporary communities.

8 **GYPSY CAMP**
CAMPS THROUGHOUT EUROPE / POP. UNKNOWN
Due to discrimination against Romani people, their camps are often kept secret.

9 **SECRET RESEARCH FACILITY**
OAK RIDGE, US / POP. 27,000
Part of secret war efforts, this city did not appear on maps and wasn't named for years.

10 **REFUGEE CAMP**
BUDUBURAM, GHANA / POP. 42,000
Camps may exist for decades and become relatively functional cities in their own right.

11 **LEPER COLONY**
SOROK ISLAND, SOUTH KOREA / POP. 646
Sorok Island once had its own special "leper money" and a stand-alone economy.

12 **REBEL SETTLEMENT**
CHIAPAS, MEXICO / POP. UNKNOWN
There are 38 Zapatista Autonomous Municipalities operating outside Mexican law.

11 HOUSEHOLD SPIRITS

1 DOMOVOI
RUSSIA AND POLAND
Traditionally, every house has one domovoi, who won't harass residents unless angered by poor housekeeping, profanity, or neglect. He's a guardian and helps with chores and farmwork. Sometimes neighboring domoviye meet for wild winter parties.

2 ZASHIKI-WARASHI
JAPAN
This childlike, red-faced spirit can be found in well-kept, prosperous homes. They bring the residence good fortune, but if a zashiki-warashi leaves a home, its absence signals the imminent or incipient deterioration of a family's prosperity and fortune.

3 TOMTE
SCANDINAVIA
They take care of farmers' homes and families and protect them from evil, especially at night. When angered (by unnecessary swearing, people peeing in the barn, and the like), they may box your ears or kill your flocks. They also appreciate occasional gifts.

4 CLURICHAUN
IRELAND
Treated well, they will protect a family's wine cellar from thieving servants—among other things. But if they are not treated appropriately, they may do the opposite by souring the wine. Clurichaun are said to be always drunk and sometimes surly.

5 YUNWI DIJUNSTI
NORTH AMERICA
These very mischievous spirits of the Cherokee and Iroquois tribes delight in tripping people and breaking household items. They're invisible to most, but twins can see and speak with them. Conjurers capture them and make them do chores.

6 **HOB**
NORTH ENGLAND AND SCOTLAND
This small creature can be quite helpful—doing work around the house or farm or curing whooping cough, and he's especially fond of children. Take care not to irk him, as he can turn troublesome. To get rid of a hob, simply buy him a new outfit.

7 **BES**
EGYPT
This dwarf god or benevolent demon protects people—especially women and children—from evil. He can kill all manner of beasts with his bare hands and fight off evil spirits in aid of women in labor. He often appears as a lion rearing up on its hind legs.

8 **BOGGART**
SCOTLAND
The boggart may crawl into people's beds at night and put a clammy hand on their faces. He is also implicated in removing bed sheets and in ear pulling. A horseshoe hung on the door of a house will keep a boggart away, but never name one—it'll stay forever.

9 **AITVARAS**
LITHUANIA
The aitvaras appears as a rooster or dragon and steals milk, coins, or grain for its master—acts which might get it in trouble. It may hatch from an egg fertilized by an old rooster, or you can purchase it from the devil for the low, low price of your soul.

10 **KAMUI-FUCHI**
JAPAN
Among the Ainu people, this spirit is a powerful protector of the home and resides in the hearth. To stay in her good graces, families must keep a tidy house and have good familial relationships. They should also never let the hearth fire fully extinguish.

11 **ZAO JUN**
CHINA
An important household god, Zao Jun reports back to heaven once a year on a family's good and bad behavior. He rewards organization around the home and harmony in relationships. Offerings of food and incense are made to him on his birthday.

13 WAYS GLOBAL WARMING COULD AFFECT US

1 KIDNEY STONES MORE LIKELY
As the climate heats up, people will be more prone to dehydration, which often produces kidney stones. The number of cases has been rising since temperatures began to warm noticeably in the late 1970s.

2 WASPS APPEAR IN THE ARCTIC
As the planet warms, wasps will move north into newly hospitable climates. In 2004 a wasp was found inside Canada's Arctic Circle, causing a stir among local Inuits, who had never seen one before.

3 MAPLE SYRUP RUNS OUT
The conditions necessary for sugar maples to produce the sap from which syrup is made are very specific: freezing nights, followed by warm days. Warm nights could spell disaster for pancakes.

4 TURTLES GET LONELY
In most turtles, gender is determined by the temperatures to which eggs are exposed. Warmer weather produces fewer male turtles, which could spell trouble for already devastated turtle populations.

5 MARINE ANIMALS GET CONFUSED
Global warming will increase ocean acidity, causing low-frequency sounds to travel farther. Some marine animals rely on sound to communicate, and they'll be bombarded with more signals from farther away.

6 LONG-DORMANT DISEASES REAPPEAR
Recent discoveries reveal the possibility that dormant diseases like smallpox could reemerge as the ancient dead's corpses thaw along with the tundra and are discovered by modern man.

7 PEOPLE LIVE LONGER
Cold weather seems to be associated with almost every kind of death, from heart attacks to infectious diseases to car accidents. So although it seems counterintuitive, global warming may mean lower, not higher, death rates.

8 RAPID BEE DECLINE
Climate change and air pollution are causing flowers' natural oils to dry faster, resulting in less scent. This means that bees will have a hard time finding nectar and pollinating—and in turn will mean fewer flowers.

9 DRUGS GET STRONGER
Greater concentrations of carbon dioxide may have a drastic effect on the potency of opium poppies. This could create more-potent pharmaceutical painkillers and opiates such as heroin and morphine.

10 BURMESE PYTHONS TAKE OVER
Giant Burmese pythons may migrate north from the Florida Everglades as more of the United States becomes habitable for them. They tend to decimate populations of indigenous animals.

11 VIOLENCE RISES
It is theorized that rising temperatures also increase aggression and aggravation, leading scientists to suspect that as the world gets warmer, it will also make us more prone to murder and assault.

12 TRUFFLE PIGS AND DOGS GET LAID OFF
Truffle farmers are reporting increasingly small harvests each year, and they blame global warming. Trufficulteurs claim that the heat will force them to grow in irrigated plantations, rather than harvesting from the forest.

13 ALIENS ATTACK
UFOlogists warn that aliens may get angry at our poor stewardship of our planet and take matters into their own hands (or tentacles).

COOL THINGS TO VIEW ON GOOGLE EARTH

1 **GIANT HUMAN FINGERPRINT**
UK / 50°50′38.73″N 0°10′19.69″W
A labyrinthine whorl measuring 125 feet (38 m) across

2 **GIANT WHITE LION**
UK / 51°50′43.09″N 0°33′11.03″W
A lion cut into a zoo's lawn

3 **GIANT COCA-COLA LOGO**
CHILE / 18°31′45.21″S 70°15′0.072″W
Etched into a hillside in Chile with 70,000 Coke bottles

4 **VICTORIA FALLS**
ZAMBIA AND ZIMBABWE / 17°55′31.8396″S 25°51′29.6022″E
A giant waterfall

5 **MOUNT EVEREST**
NEPAL AND TIBET / 27°59′9.1176″N 86°55′42.3834″E
Highest mountain above sea level

6 **MILITARY JET IN PARKING LOT**
PARIS / 48°49′30.6588″N 2°11′54.888″E
A large military jet sitting in a school's parking lot

7 **STRANGE MOUNTAINSIDE PATTERNS**
CHINA / 40°27′15.19″N 93°23′33.75″E
A geometric, gridlike pattern carved into a mountain near Tibet

8 **HUGE TRIANGLE**
US / 33°44′17.45″N 112°38′0.17″W
A huge, mysterious equilateral triangle in a hillside

9 **GIZA PYRAMID COMPLEX**
EGYPT / 29°58′35″N 31°7′52″E
The famous pyramids of Egypt

10 **BURJ KHALIFA**
UNITED ARAB EMIRATES / 25°11′49″N 55°16′026.8″E
The tallest building in the world

11 **MYSTERIOUS MODEL**
CHINA / 38°15′56.3472″N 105°57′6.12″E
Believed to be a 1.8-square-mile (4.6-sq-km) scale model of a disputed region on the border of China and India

12 **GIANT PINK BUNNY**
ITALY / 44°14′39.3822″N 7°46′11.0532″E
A rabbit measuring 200 feet (61 m) long that was built by a group of artists

13 **PALM ISLAND**
UNITED ARAB EMIRATES / 25°6′56.1636″N 55°7′56.9418″E
Artificial island in the shape of a palm tree in Dubai

14 **THE BADLANDS GUARDIAN**
CANADA / 50°0′36.2988″N 110°6′46.821″W
A geographical feature resembling a head wearing a full Native American headdress—and earphones

THINGS WE'VE LEARNED ABOUT OUR UNIVERSE FROM THE HUBBLE TELESCOPE

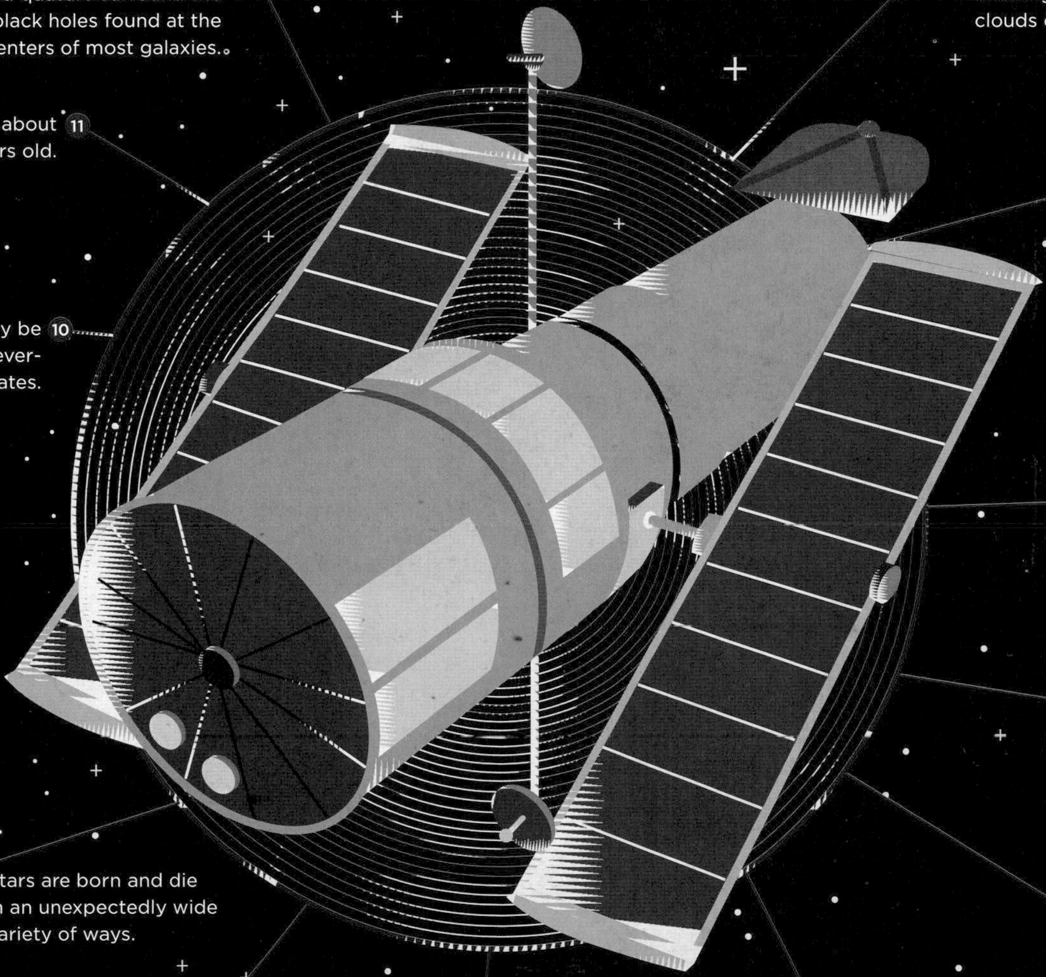

1. Giant galaxies sometimes collide, creating new stars from clouds of gas and dust.
2. Planets are far more common than previously thought.
3. Dust rings around stars most likely transform into planets.
4. Dark matter (matter that doesn't reflect light and is therefore invisible to scientists) really does exist.
5. Black holes probably exist at the center of every galaxy.
6. Jupiter's clouds are made of crystallized ammonia and compounds of carbon, sulfur, and phosphorus.
7. Planets orbiting other stars have organic molecules in their atmospheres.
8. The megastorm that circles Jupiter changes color frequently, partially due to temperature changes.
9. Stars are born and die in an unexpectedly wide variety of ways.
10. The universe may be expanding at ever-accelerating rates.
11. The universe is about 13.7 billion years old.
12. Immensely bright nuclei called quasars surround the black holes found at the centers of most galaxies.

10 Places on Earth THAT ARE STILL UNEXPLORED

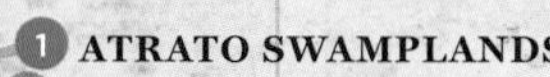

1 ATRATO SWAMPLANDS
BORDER OF COLOMBIA AND PANAMA
This region along South America's Darién Gap is home to swamps that have never been officially explored or charted due to their general impassability as well as a wealth of mosquitoes and alligators.

2 BLACK HOLE OF ANDROS
BAHAMAS
The Black Hole of Andros—which is thought to be some 154 feet (47 m) deep—contains a layer of violet-colored microorganisms that heats the water to 96.8°F (36°C) and makes it pitch black, forming a false bottom. The oxygen-free water below this layer is similar to the water contained in oceans 3.5 million years ago.

3 MERUME MOUNTAINS
GUYANA
While portions of this heavily forested and remote mountain range have been penetrated by humans, the center of the range remains a challenge. The last serious exploration attempt took place in 1992.

4 MAKIRA FORESTS
MADAGASCAR
The forests of Makira, located in the northeast region of Madagascar, adjacent to the Masoala peninsula and its forests, represent one of the largest remaining contiguous areas of tropical rain forest in Madagascar, and are largely unexplored.

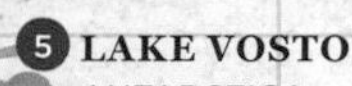

5 LAKE VOSTOK
ANTARCTICA
The sixth-largest lake in the world has never been explored—because it's under a glacier. It covers 5,400 square miles (14,000 sq km) and is up to 3,000 feet (900 m) deep. The lake has been frozen for 25 million years and probably contains diverse and unique forms of microscopic life.

6 DINPERNALASON
TIBET
The mountain of Dinpernalason is just one of a number of Tibet's majestic, challenging, and as-yet-unclimbed peaks. Located in the remote, difficult-to-access Botoi Tsangpo basin, it stands 20,128 feet (6,135 m) high.

7 GANGKHAR PUENSUM
BHUTAN
At 24,836 feet (7,570 m), this is the world's highest unclimbed mountain. It is likely to stay that way for the foreseeable future: The government of Bhutan has outlawed mountaineering entirely on spiritual and ecological grounds since 2003.

8 KIMBERLEY PLATEAU
AUSTRALIA
Access to this area of Australia is difficult due to a lack of roads and a rugged coastline that is battered by strong ocean tides. Islands and coral reefs populate the coastal waters in this area, much of which is as yet unexplored.

9 FOJA MOUNTAINS
PAPUA NEW GUINEA
More than 2 million acres (810,000 hectare) of old-growth tropical forest covers these remote mountains. The heart of the forest has never been charted, and even the outskirts are only now being explored, revealing undiscovered species of plants and animals.

10 CAPE YORK AND THE GULF SAVANNAH
AUSTRALIA
This wild and sparsely populated wilderness area in Queensland was once only accessible during the dry months of April to December. While there are some settlements in the area, harsh conditions have often limited exploration.

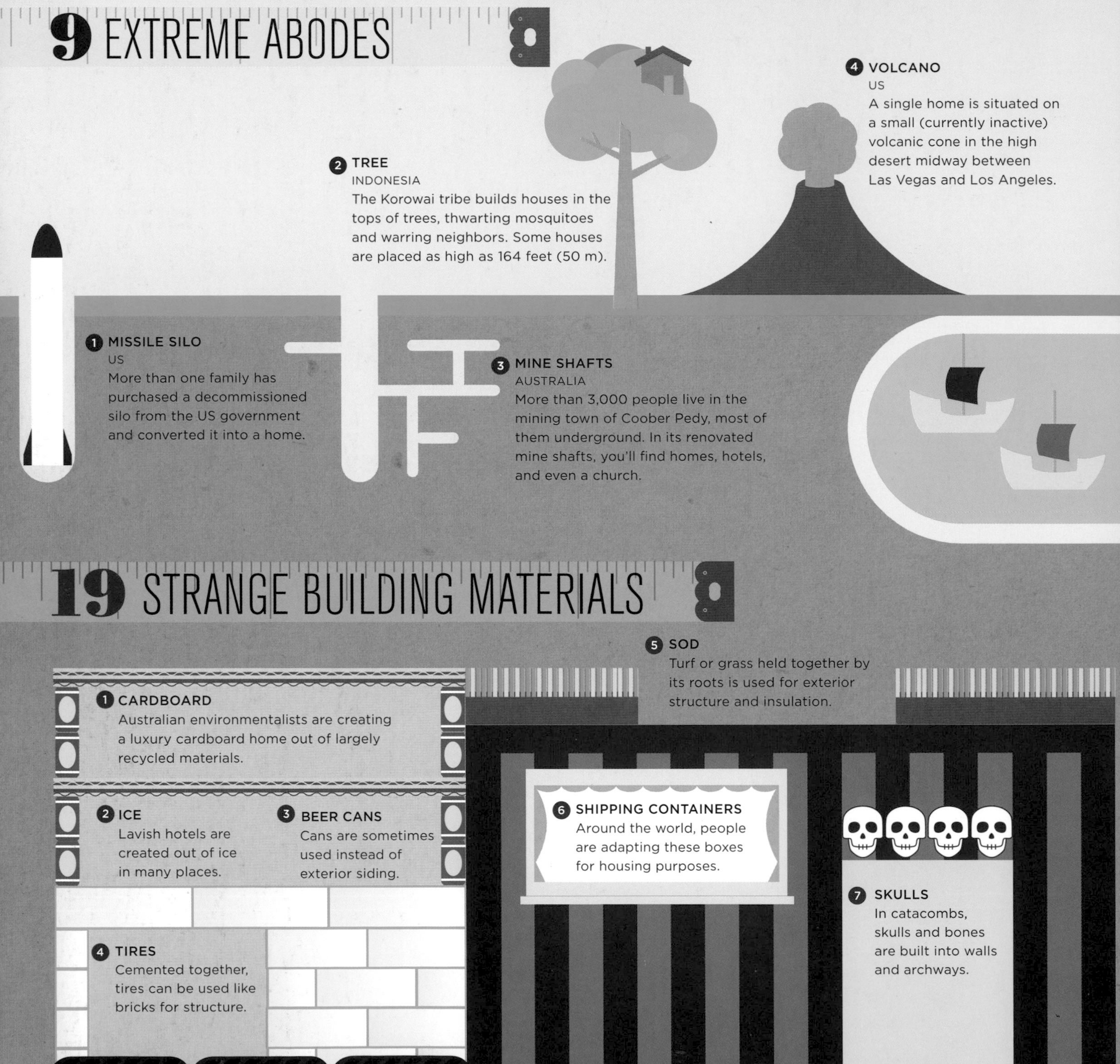

9 EXTREME ABODES
1 MISSILE SILO
US
More than one family has purchased a decommissioned silo from the US government and converted it into a home.
2 TREE
INDONESIA
The Korowai tribe builds houses in the tops of trees, thwarting mosquitoes and warring neighbors. Some houses are placed as high as 164 feet (50 m).
3 MINE SHAFTS
AUSTRALIA
More than 3,000 people live in the mining town of Coober Pedy, most of them underground. In its renovated mine shafts, you'll find homes, hotels, and even a church.
4 VOLCANO
US
A single home is situated on a small (currently inactive) volcanic cone in the high desert midway between Las Vegas and Los Angeles.
19 STRANGE BUILDING MATERIALS
1 CARDBOARD
Australian environmentalists are creating a luxury cardboard home out of largely recycled materials.
2 ICE
Lavish hotels are created out of ice in many places.
3 BEER CANS
Cans are sometimes used instead of exterior siding.
4 TIRES
Cemented together, tires can be used like bricks for structure.
5 SOD
Turf or grass held together by its roots is used for exterior structure and insulation.
6 SHIPPING CONTAINERS
Around the world, people are adapting these boxes for housing purposes.
7 SKULLS
In catacombs, skulls and bones are built into walls and archways.

7 PILLARS
MEDITERRANEAN REGION
In the early years of the Christian era, stylite monks showed their devotion by living atop pillars. The most famous, Simeon Stylites, did not descend for 37 years.

5 AIRPLANE
US
A number of decommissioned commercial aircraft have been transformed into residences.

9 IN A BRIDGE
US
"Homeless" man Richard Dorsay lived in a space he'd created in Chicago's Lake Shore Drive drawbridge for several years until police found and extracted him.

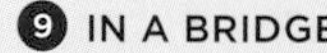

6 FLOATING VILLAGE
CHINA
Aberdeen Harbor in Hong Kong contains hundreds of junks (a type of small boat), which house many local fishing families.

8 TINY ISLAND
CANADA
The Saint Lawrence River is home to thousands of islands. Some are large, and some can only hold a single house—like the famous "Just Room Enough" island.

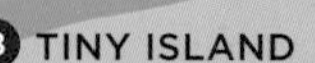

16 MUD AND WEEDS
Soil and weeds are mixed into bricks and stacked to create thick, energy-conserving walls.

8 RECYCLED PLASTIC
Former refuse can be used as insulation and siding.

9 WINE CORK
Corks serve as siding and insulation.

10 TRASH
Added to other materials, trash shores up a home's walls.

15 NEWSPAPERS
Journals are rolled and stacked to create walls, and also used for siding.

17 CLAY
Clay regulates temperatures and can last for hundreds of years. It's often mixed with straw and sand.

18 MANURE
Manure makes an eco-friendly brick used globally in adobe and wattle-and-daub structures. Some tried-and-true suppliers of said manure are horses and cattle.

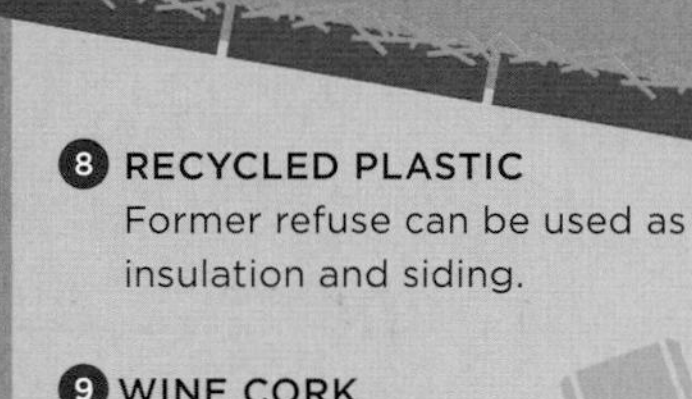

11 BOTTLES
Glass "bottle houses" are made with mortar.

13 STRAW BALES
Hay bales are stacked in a timber frame, then covered with stucco.

19 SEWER PIPE
Concrete drainpipes are reused to create sturdy living spaces.

12 SALT
Mined salt blocks are used as bricks.

14 SEASHELLS
Mixed into mortar, shells are applied to a home's external walls as decoration.

39 PLACE NAMES AND WHAT THEY MEAN

1 COALINGA
CALIFORNIA / ENGLISH
"Coaling Station A"

2 ACCRA
GHANA / AKAN
"Ants"

3 YOGYAKARTA
INDONESIA / SANSKRIT
"Sufficient victorious deed"

4 SUKHOTHAI
THAILAND / THAI
"Dawn of happiness"

5 AMMAN
JORDAN / ARABIC
"Place of tremors"

6 NIN
CROATIA / GERMAN
"Castle of diligence"

7 CARACAS
VENEZUELA / SPANISH
"Snails"

8 TORONTO
CANADA / IROQUOIS
"The place where trees stand in water"

9 MEDITERRANEAN
EUROPE / LATIN
"In the middle of the world"

10 MAHIKENG
SOUTH AFRICA / TSWANA
"Place of stones"

11 TRONDHEIM
NORWAY / NORWEGIAN
"A good place called home"

12 THINGVELLIR
ICELAND / ICELANDIC
"Parliament meadows"

13 DUBLIN
IRELAND / IRISH
"Black pool"

14 ABU DHABI
UNITED ARAB EMIRATES / ARABIC
"Father of gazelle"

15 BUTHA-BUTHE
LESOTHO / SESOTHO
"City of lying down"

16 MANGAUNG
SOUTH AFRICA / SESOTHO
"Place of cheetahs"

17 CHUNGKING
CHINA / CHINESE
"Heavy celebration"

18 ENTEBBE
UGANDA / LUGANDA
"A seat"

19 KHARTOUM
SUDAN / ARABIC
"End of an elephant's trunk"

20 CAIRO
EGYPT / ARABIC
"The victorious"

21 LALĪBELA
ETHIOPIA / AMHARIC
"Person who talks too much"

22 BAGHDAD
IRAQ / ARABIC
"Given by God"

23 SRI JAYEWARDENEPURA KOTTE
SRI LANKA / TAMIL
"Resplendent city of growing victory"

24 HARARE
ZIMBABWE / SHONA
"He does not sleep"

25 AMARAPURA
MYANMAR / PALI
"City of immortality"

26 DOHA
QATAR / ARABIC
"The sticky tree"

12 PLACES THAT YOU MIGHT NOT KNOW WERE NAMED AFTER PEOPLE

1. **CAMBODIA**
   KAMBU SVAYAMBHUVA
   Kambu Svayambhuva was a fourth-century Hindu sage and prince.

2. **CARDIGAN, WALES**
   CEREDIG
   Ceredig was a fifth-century king who ruled the area.

3. **COLOMBIA**
   CHRISTOPHER COLUMBUS
   Named after the man who "discovered" the New World.

4. **EL SALVADOR**
   JESUS CHRIST
   "El Salvador" is Spanish for "The Savior."

5. **ISRAEL**
   JACOB
   Jacob of the Old Testament was renamed Israel after fighting an angel.

6. **KIRIBATI**
   CAPTAIN THOMAS GILBERT
   Kiribati is the native pronunciation of this 18th-century captain's name.

7. **KIRKCUDBRIGHT, UK**
   SAINT CUTHBERT
   The saint's remains were held in a chapel here.

8. **LISBON, PORTUGAL**
   ULYSSES
   Myths say Ulysses founded Lisbon after leaving Troy.

9. **ROME, ITALY**
   ROMULUS
   Romulus was the mythical cofounder of this city, along with brother Remus.

10. **SAUDI ARABIA**
    MUHAMMAD IBN SAUD
    Named for the first head of the ruling House of Saud.

11. **VIRGINIA, US**
    QUEEN ELIZABETH I
    Named in honor of Elizabeth I, the "Virgin Queen."

12. **LORRAINE, FRANCE**
    LOTHAIR
    This Holy Roman Emperor ruled in the first half of the 800s.

27 **ADDIS ABABA**
ETHIOPIA / AMHARIC
"New flower"

28 **KUALA LUMPUR**
MALAYSIA / MALAY
"Muddy confluence"

29 **RIO DE JANEIRO**
BRAZIL / PORTUGUESE
"River of January"

30 **NUKU'ALOFA**
TONGA / TONGAN
"Residence and love"

31 **SINGAPORE**
ASIA / SANSKRIT
"City of lions"

32 **BAMAKO**
MALI / BAMBARA
"Crocodile river"

33 **ISFAHAN**
IRAN / PERSIAN
"Half the world"

34 **ASMARA**
ERITREA / TIGRE
"Live in peace"

35 **THE HAGUE**
NETHERLANDS / DUTCH
"The count's woods"

36 **PODGORICA**
MONTENEGRO / MONTENEGRIN
"Under the small hill"

37 **JAMAICA**
CARIBBEAN / ARAWAK
"Island of water springs"

38 **WOLLONGONG**
AUSTRALIA / ABORIGINAL
"Sound of the sea"

39 **MALDIVES**
ASIA / SANSKRIT
"Thousand islands"

MOST PRO-GAY GOVERNMENTS

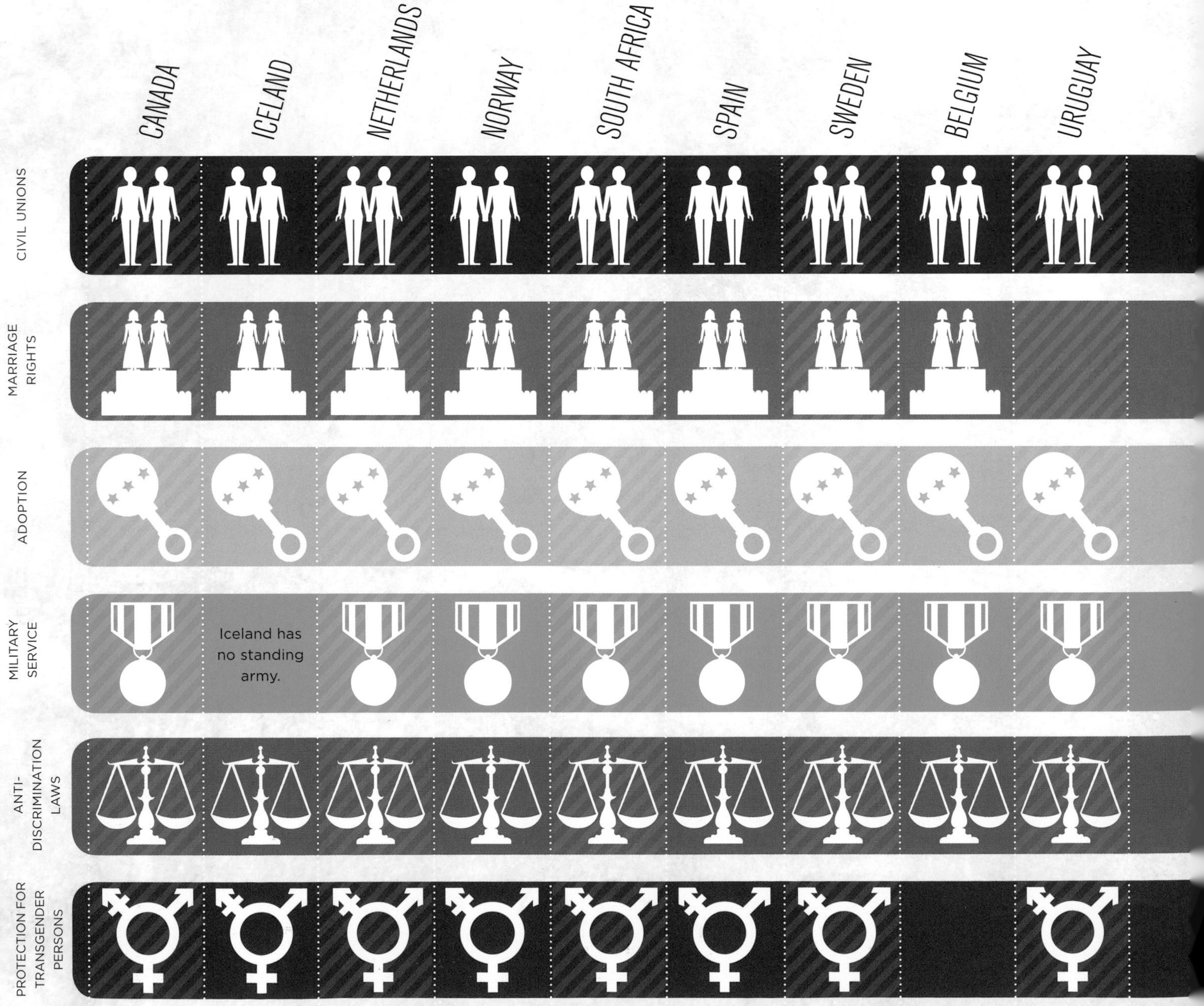

CANADA
ICELAND
NETHERLANDS
NORWAY
SOUTH AFRICA
SPAIN
SWEDEN
BELGIUM
URUGUAY

CIVIL UNIONS

MARRIAGE RIGHTS

ADOPTION

MILITARY SERVICE

Iceland has no standing army.

ANTI-DISCRIMINATION LAWS

PROTECTION FOR TRANSGENDER PERSONS

LIVE AND LET LOVE

It's worth noting that the most gay-friendly *governments* are not necessarily the most gay-friendly *nations.* Some countries have a long-standing history of tolerance, but no official laws to reinforce it. Others have protective policies, but an underlying culture of intolerance. Here's a ranking, from left to right, of nations that have passed the most gay-friendly legislation to date. (Note that the first seven countries indicate a multiway tie for top honors, and that partial credit was awarded to nations where certain rights are protected in only some areas.)

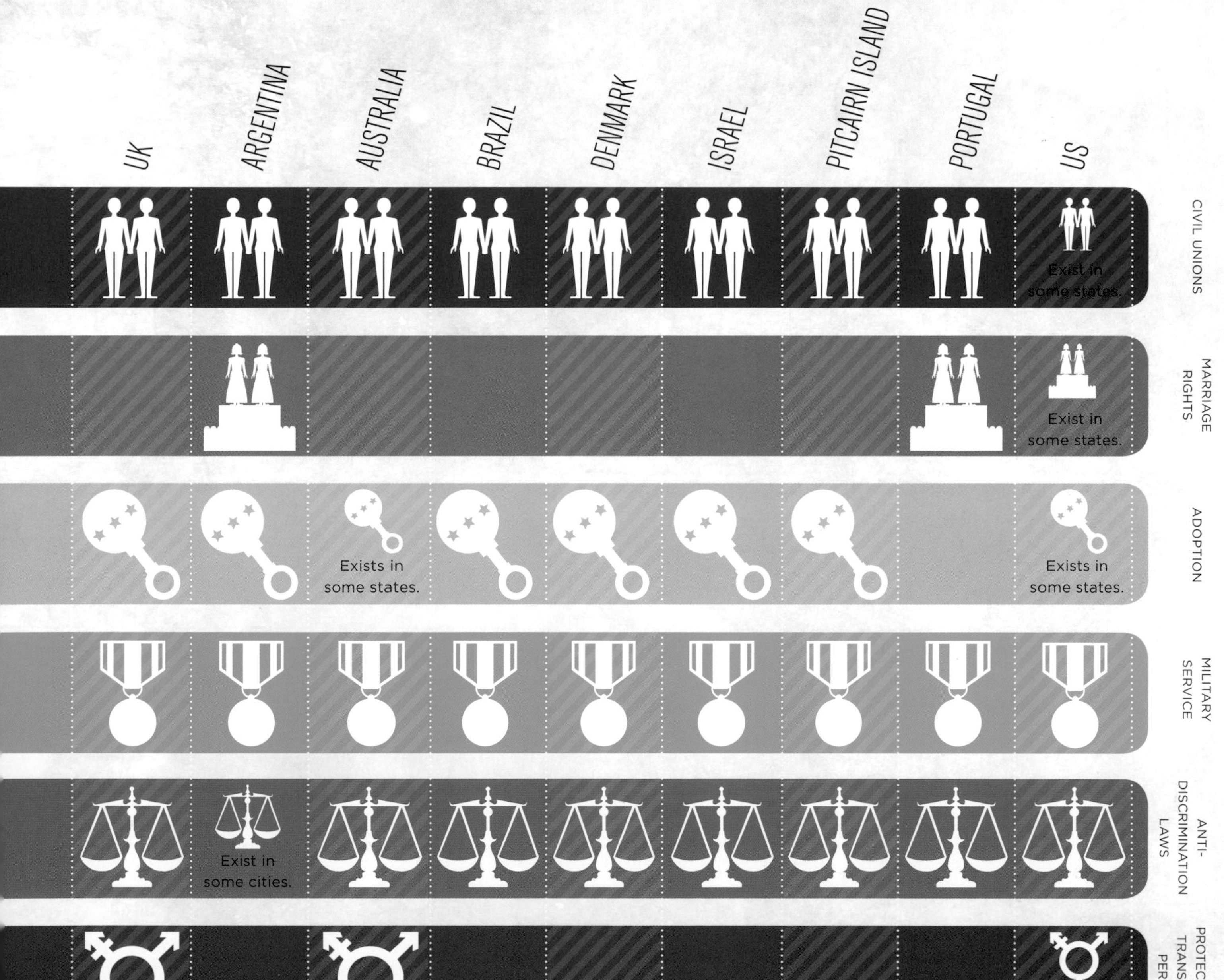

38 ANCIENT CITIES (THAT PEOPLE STILL LIVE IN)

1 **DAMASCUS, SYRIA** 12,000 years old
2 **JERICHO, WEST BANK** 11,000 years old
3 **BYBLOS, LEBANON** 9,000 years old
4 **PLOVDIV, BULGARIA** 8,000 years old
5 **FAYYŪM, EGYPT** 6,000 years old
6 **SIDON, LEBANON** 6,000 years old
7 **SUSA, IRAN** 6,000 years old
8 **GAZIANTEP, TURKEY** 5,700 years old
9 **BEIRUT, LEBANON** 5,000 years old
10 **RAYY, IRAN** 5,000 years old
11 **JERUSALEM, ISRAEL** 4,800 years old
12 **TYRE, LEBANON** 4,800 years old
13 **ARBĪL, IRAQ** 4,300 years old
14 **KIRKŪK, IRAQ** 4,200 years old

Time Line

Present Day
1000 CE
0
1000 BCE
2000 BCE
3000 BCE
4000 BCE
5000 BCE
6000 BCE
7000 BCE
8000 BCE
9000 BCE
10,000 BCE

1 DAMASCUS, SYRIA
ESTABLISHED: 10,000 BCE
POPULATION: 1.7 MILLION

- Damascus was the seat of Islamic power in the seventh century CE; later, the center of the Muslim world moved to Baghdad.
- When Alexander the Great conquered Damascus in the fourth century BCE, he became its first Western ruler.
- The true age of Damascus is lost to history. Archaeological digs show some evidence of settlements in the area as long ago as 10,000 BCE, but it was probably not a full-blown metropolis until 1500 BCE.

4 PLOVDIV, BULGARIA
ESTABLISHED: 6000 BCE
POPULATION: 380,000

- This ancient city was once named Philippopolis, after Philip II of Macedon (father of Alexander the Great).
- Later it went through a phase as a major Roman city before coming under Ottoman rule in the 1400s. Finally, in 1885, the city became part of Bulgaria with the unification of its region and the Principality of Bulgaria.

5 FAYYUM, EGYPT
ESTABLISHED: 4000 BCE
POPULATION: 310,000

- The Greeks founded this city as "Crocodilopolis," so called because the area was the center of the cult of Sobek, the crocodile god.
- Under Roman occupation, the city was known as Arsinoe, and around that time it became famous for producing beautifully painted death masks for mummies.

15 **ALEPPO, SYRIA** 4,000 years old

16 **JAFFA, ISRAEL** 4,000 years old

17 **BALKH, AFGHANISTAN** 3,500 years old

18 **HEBRON, WEST BANK** 3,500 years old

19 **ATHENS, GREECE** 3,400 years old

20 **CHANIA, GREECE** 3,400 years old

21 **LARNACA, CYPRUS** 3,400 years old

22 **THEBES, GREECE** 3,400 years old

23 **LISBON, PORTUGAL** 3,200 years old

24 **CÁDIZ, SPAIN** 3,100 years old

25 **CHIOS, GREECE** 3,100 years old

26 **VARANASI, INDIA** 3,100 years old

27 **XI'AN, CHINA** 3,100 years old

28 **ANURADHAPURA, SRI LANKA** 3,000 years old

29 **GAZA CITY, GAZA STRIP** 3,000 years old

30 **MYTILENE, GREECE** 3,000 years old

31 **CHOLULA, MEXICO** 2,800 years old

32 **HAMADĀN, IRAN** 2,800 years old

33 **NAPLES, ITALY** 2,800 years old

34 **ROME, ITALY** 2,800 years old

35 **YEREVAN, ARMENIA** 2,800 years old

36 **UJJAIN, INDIA** 2,800 years old

37 **CORFU, GREECE** 2,700 years old

38 **SAMARKAND, UZBEKISTAN** 2,700 years old

26 VARANASI, INDIA
ESTABLISHED: 1100 BCE
POPULATION: 1.2 MILLION

- Varanasi, on the banks of the Ganges River, has produced many artists, writers, religious leaders, and philosophers.
- The Buddha gave his first sermon at Sarnath, located near Varanasi.

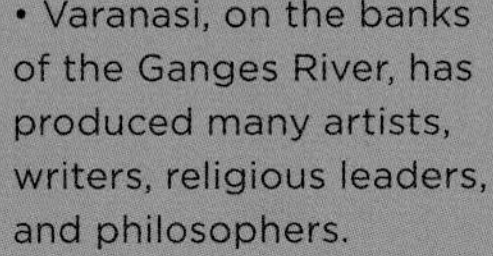

27 XI'AN, CHINA
ESTABLISHED: 1100 BCE
POPULATION: 8.2 MILLION

- The world-famous "Terra-cotta Army" of some 8,000 life-size statues was discovered in Xi'an in 1974.
- The city is famous for its rock music.

31 CHOLULA, MEXICO
ESTABLISHED: 800 BCE
POPULATION: 194,000

- When the Spanish came, Cholula was one of the largest cities in Mexico.
- The city was in part a shrine to the winged serpent god Quetzalcóatl.

*** SYDNEY, AUSTRALIA**
ESTABLISHED: 1788 CE
POPULATION: 4.5 MILLION

* Sydney is the oldest city in Australia, but it's only the 504th oldest city in the world.

- Native people have lived in the area for tens of thousands of years.

PLACES WHERE PEOPLE HAVE LIVED FOR A REALLY, REALLY LONG TIME

The cities noted above represent the oldest continually occupied settlements in each major region. Dates for some of the oldest are approximate.

- Africa
- Asia
- Europe
- The Middle East
- The Americas
- Australia
- Indian Subcontinent

18 WAYS TO BANISH EVIL SPIRITS FROM AROUND THE WORLD

1 **PERFOM A RITUAL DANCE**
In the Kalahari desert, shamans dance to extract spirits, then throw them into a fire.

2 **MAKE FRIENDS**
People in Nigeria call upon a good spirit for protection and offer it food and friendship.

3 **SET OUT STONE LIONS**
Protect your house like a Chinese palace by placing stone lions in front of your door.

4 **GET A SACRED TATTOO**
Have a monk tattoo you with a lucky image, such as a snake, tiger, or Buddhist symbol.

5 **FRIGHTEN WITH GOURD ART**
Do like they do in India: Paint a scary face on an ash gourd and hang it above your door.

6 **TOSS BEANS**
On February 3, the Japanese scatter roasted beans, chanting "Demons out, good luck in!"

7 **GATHER FLOWERS**
Bring Saint-John's-Wort blooms inside on Midsummer's Eve, like they do in England.

8 **DECORATE WITH ANISE**
People in the Mediterranean region put fresh anise leaves around a room.

9 **KEEP THEM AT BAY WITH BAY LEAVES**
Take a cue from Europeans and place a basket of bay leaves at your door.

10 BURN PALO SANTO WOOD
Some people in Peru burn this timber, which has strong purification properties.

11 SWEAT THEM OUT
Spend time in a Navajo sweat lodge, a cedar structure warmed with hot rocks.

12 CONDUCT A CLEANSE
In the United States, some people wash their floors with bitter herbs and lime juice.

13 HOLD A SMUDGING CEREMONY
Burn sage in an abalone shell and wave the smoke with a feather, like Ojibwe tribe members.

14 CALL A PRIEST
In Italy and other parts of the world, priests banish spirits with religious incantations.

15 SAY "BEGONE" WITH A CHARM
Wear the word "abracadabra" on a necklace, as some do in the Mediterranean region.

16 WEAR LAVENDER
In England, people sport a sprig of lavender (or hang a cross of it above their doors).

17 HANG FENNEL
Some people in eastern Europe hang fennel from the rafters and put it in keyholes.

18 FASHION A DILL NECKLACE
Wear charms made of dill leaves around your neck, like they do in northern Europe.

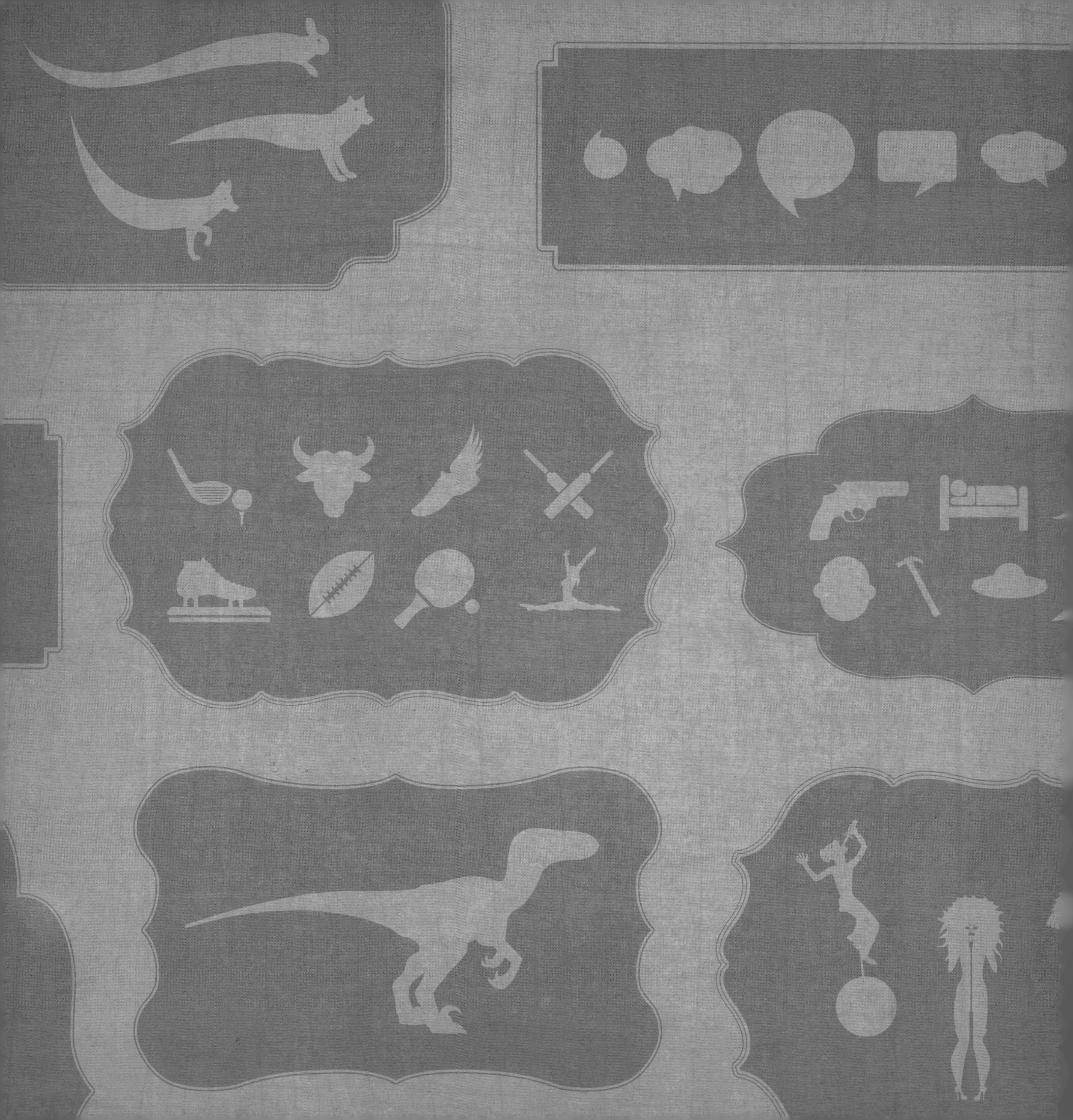

382 GREAT (AND NOT SO GREAT) KINDS OF ENTERTAINMENT

A brush with fame can be enduring (the novel *Fanny Hill* still shocks people after 300 years) or blessedly short (heard the Grover Cleveland gossip? Didn't think so). In this chapter, we present meaningful things people have worn (guess what paisley signifies, besides grooviness), won (from NASCAR races to lawsuits), believed (was Hitler really . . . missing something?), and watched (like tons of robots and cyborgs from the silver screen). Grab some popcorn and dig in.

56 ON-SCREEN ROBOTS AND CYBORGS

- HEROES
- VILLAINS
- SIDEKICKS
- LOVE INTERESTS

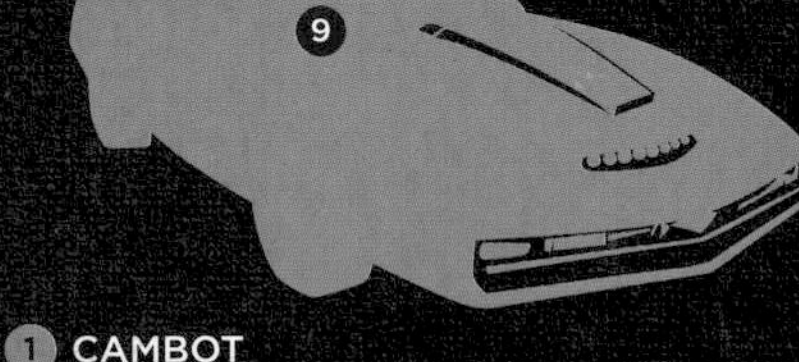

1 **CAMBOT**
MYSTERY SCIENCE THEATER 3000
1988–1999

2 **KARR**
KNIGHT RIDER / 1982–1986

3 **EVE**
WALL•E / 2008

4 **BUBO**
CLASH OF THE TITANS / 1981

5 **DALEK**
DR. WHO AND THE DALEKS / 1965

6 **RACHAEL**
BLADE RUNNER / 1982

7 **GIGOLO JOE**
A.I. / 2001

8 **HUEY, DEWEY, OR LOUIE**
SILENT RUNNING / 1972

9 **KITT**
KNIGHT RIDER / 1982–1986

10 **TWIKI**
BUCK ROGERS IN THE 25TH CENTURY
1979–1981

11 **MECHAGODZILLA**
GODZILLA VS. MECHAGODZILLA
1974

12 **KAY-EM 14**
JASON X / 2002

13 **ROBOCOP**
ROBOCOP / 1987

14 **B9**
LOST IN SPACE / 1965–1968

15 **TIN MAN**
THE WIZARD OF OZ / 1939

16 **MARIA**
METROPOLIS / 1927

17 **MEGATRON**
TRANSFORMERS / 2007

18 **ASTRO BOY**
ASTRO BOY / 2009

19 **V.I.N.CENT**
THE BLACK HOLE / 1979

20 **T-800**
TERMINATOR SERIES / 1984–2009

21 **GORT**
THE DAY THE EARTH STOOD STILL / 1951

22 **OPTIMUS PRIME**
TRANSFORMERS / 2007

23 **BUMBLEBEE**
TRANSFORMERS / 2007

24 **MARVIN**
THE HITCHHIKER'S GUIDE TO THE GALAXY / 1981

25 **GYPSY**
MYSTERY SCIENCE THEATER 3000
1988–1999

26 **ANDREW**
BICENTENNIAL MAN / 1999

27 **BORG QUEEN**
STAR TREK: FIRST CONTACT / 1996

28 **THE FIX-ITS**
BATTERIES NOT INCLUDED / 1987

29 **R2D2**
STAR WARS / 1977–2005

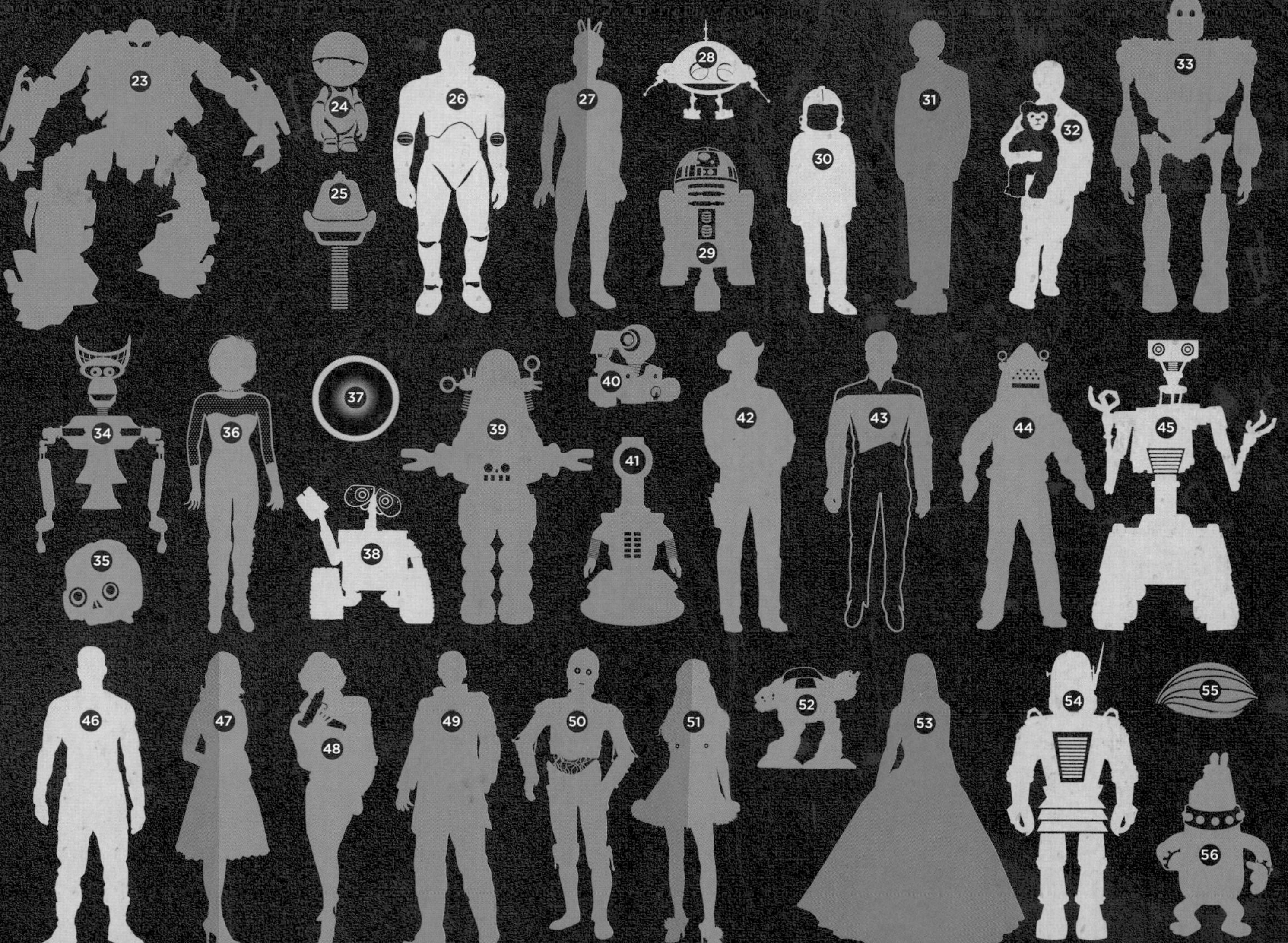

30 DARYL
D.A.R.Y.L. / 1985

31 ULYSSES
MAKING MR. RIGHT / 1987

32 DAVID
A.I. / 2001

33 THE IRON GIANT
THE IRON GIANT / 1999

34 CROW
MYSTERY SCIENCE THEATER 3000
1988–1999

35 M.A.R.K. 13
HARDWARE / 1990

36 PRIS
BLADE RUNNER / 1982

37 HAL9000
2001: A SPACE ODYSSEY / 1968

38 WALL•E
WALL•E / 2008

39 ROBBIE
FORBIDDEN PLANET / 1956

40 ROVER
PLANET 51 / 2009

41 TOM SERVO
MYSTERY SCIENCE THEATER 3000
1988–1999

42 GUNSLINGER
WESTWORLD / 1973

43 DATA
STAR TREK: THE NEXT GENERATION
1966–1968

44 NEPTUNE MEN
INVASION OF THE NEPTUNE MEN / 1961

45 JOHNNY 5
SHORT CIRCUIT / 1986

46 SOLO
SOLO / 1996

47 THE STEPFORD WIVES
THE STEPFORD WIVES / 1975

48 EVE
EVE OF DESTRUCTION / 1991

49 BISHOP
ALIENS / 1986

50 C3PO
STAR WARS / 1977–2005

51 FEMBOTS
AUSTIN POWERS / 1997

52 ED 209
ROBOCOP / 1987

53 LENORE
SERENITY / 2005

54 TOBOR
TOBOR THE GREAT / 1954

55 MAX
FLIGHT OF THE NAVIGATOR / 1986

56 PRESTON
WALLACE & GROMIT IN A CLOSE SHAVE / 1995

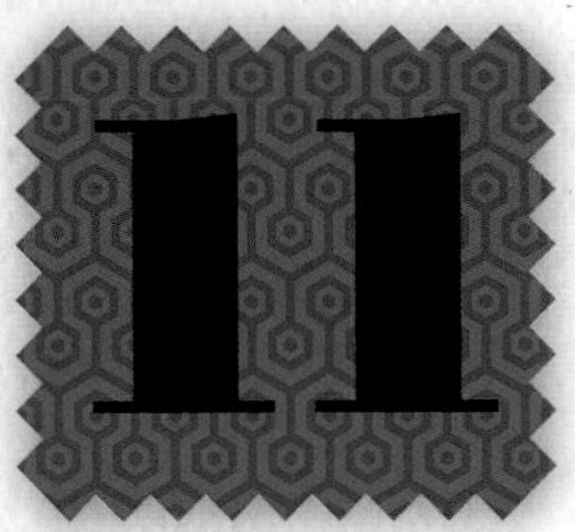

SYMBOLIC FABRICS

1 EYEDAZZLER
NAVAJO

This fabric's pattern is evocative of whirlwinds, desert storms, and the spiritual idea of eternal renewal.

2 PAISLEY
INDIA

This fabric became popular in Europe in the 1500s due to increased trade with the East; it's named for a Scottish town.

3 MUD CLOTH
WEST AFRICA

Mud cloth has many meaningful motifs; this one represents a warrior's belt and tells others that the wearer is brave.

4 TARTAN
SCOTLAND

Tartans come in many patterns; they identify the wearer's region or clan. This is a Royal Stewart, a popular pattern.

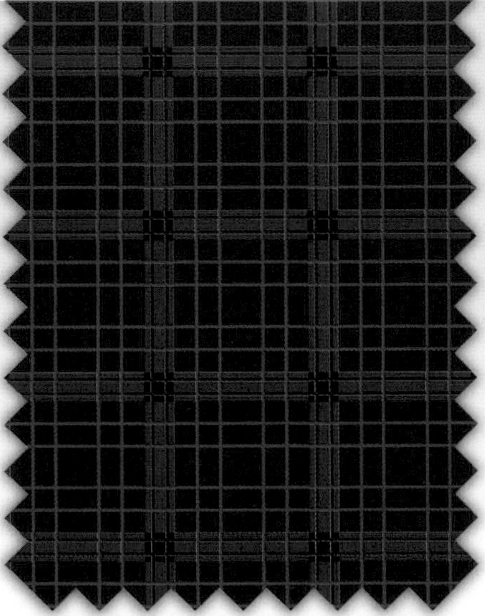

5 KAWUNG
INDONESIA

In the past, this floral pattern was worn to show that one belonged to the royal court of the sultan.

6 **BISKRI**
NORTH AFRICA
Traditional brides wear this pattern. Its symbolic bands are associated with fertility, duty, and domestic harmony.

7 **IKAT CLOTH**
LAOS
Ikat is a dyeing method with many motifs. This particular crab design is meant to invoke a good monsoon season.

8 **SAN ANDRÉS GRAND DESIGN**
MEXICO
This pattern from the Classic Maya Period depicts the sun passing across the sky and re-emerging at dawn.

9 **BINGATA**
JAPAN
In Okinawa's Ryukyu period, royal people wore this painted fabric. Cranes were often seen on wedding attire.

10 **KENTE CLOTH**
IVORY COAST AND GHANA
Kente cloth has many meaningful patterns; this one, the "puff adder," symbolizes exploitation and overwork.

11 **QUESWA**
INCAN PERU
This fabric pattern is used to express the notion of twining together, whether of plants or people.

11 UNUSUAL PERFORMERS

1 LE PÉTOMANE
FRANCE / LATE 1800s–EARLY 1900s
A highly successful "flatulist," Le Pétomane (the stage name means "the farter") entertained posh crowds at Le Moulin Rouge and elsewhere with the amazing sounds created by his gastrointestinal system.

2 CHARLES TRIPP, THE ARMLESS WONDER
CANADA / LATE 1800s–EARLY 1900s
P. T. Barnum hired this Canadian performer after an audition that consisted of Tripp combing his hair. For audiences, he shaved, painted, did wood carving, and wrote in exquisite penmanship using only his feet.

3 OOFTY GOOFTY
US / EARLY 1900s
In this short-lived sideshow, an unknown artist covered himself with tar and horsehair and displayed himself in a cage, where he was fed raw meat. When fed, he would let out a fierce "Oofty goofty!"—hence his name.

4 HADJI ALI, THE GREAT REGURGITATOR
EGYPT / 1920s
This vaudeville sensation was celebrated for his unusual ability to swallow items and regurgitate them on demand—and for his "human flamethrower" routine, in which he spouted burning kerosene.

5 BEN DOVA, THE CONVIVIAL INEBRIATE
FRANCE / 1930s–1970s
Joseph Späh, stage name Ben Dova, performed breathtaking acrobatics either drunk or very convincingly pretending to be so. He was also one of the few passengers to survive the Hindenburg fire in 1937.

6 MARTIN LAURELLO, THE HUMAN OWL
GERMANY AND US / 1920s–1930s
The German-born anatomical wonder was able to turn his head a full 180 degrees, so it faced entirely backward. He toured Europe and the United States with various circuses. He was also a ventriloquist.

7 GALLAGHER

US / 1980s–PRESENT

This comedian's act consists of smashing watermelons and other foodstuffs with a sledgehammer. This popular act has led to more than a dozen TV specials, sold-out arena shows, and other superstar trappings.

8 MARLENE HARING

AUSTRIA / 2005

In her piece "Marlene Hairy or In My Bathtub I Am the Captain," the performance artist donned a suit of long blond hair and had her "audience" follow her home, where she invited them to bathe with her.

9 KEMBRA PFAHLER

US / 1990–PRESENT

This American performance artist and rock musician is the lead singer of The Voluptuous Horror of Karen Black. Pfahler has performed partially naked while cracking paint-filled eggs on her genitals.

10 CHAYNE HULTGREN, THE SPACE COWBOY

AUSTRALIA / 2000s–PRESENT

Famous for swallowing more swords than anyone else, Hultgren has performed other antics, like juggling a sickle, machete, and fire torch while blindfolded on a tall unicycle, and suspending himself from hooks in his flesh.

11 LISA LEVY

US / 2000s–PRESENT

In her stage show "Psychotherapy Live!" Levy invites audience members onstage, has them lie on a couch, and conducts a therapy session. While she's not a real therapist, participants report feeling much better.

14 LIES MOVIES TELL US!!

MORE INSIDE!!

SEX IS PERFECT, WOMEN ARE MODEST

The movies would like us to believe that couples having sex always climax at the same time. And that the woman will always hold a sheet over her breasts when sitting up in bed.

GRAVITY IS THE SAME EVERYWHERE

In sci-fi flicks, humans land on other planets and walk around normally, and their alien costars do the same. Not likely. Consider our own solar system. On Mars, a 180-pound (82-kg) man would weigh just 70 pounds (32 kg). That same guy would weigh 424 pounds (192 kg) on Jupiter. And if he were on the moon? He'd weigh just 30 pounds (14 kg). So, it's wildly improbable that he'd be able to walk the same on different planets, and doubly improbable that all aliens would be as comfortable in our gravitational field as we are—who knows what the gravity on their home planets is like?

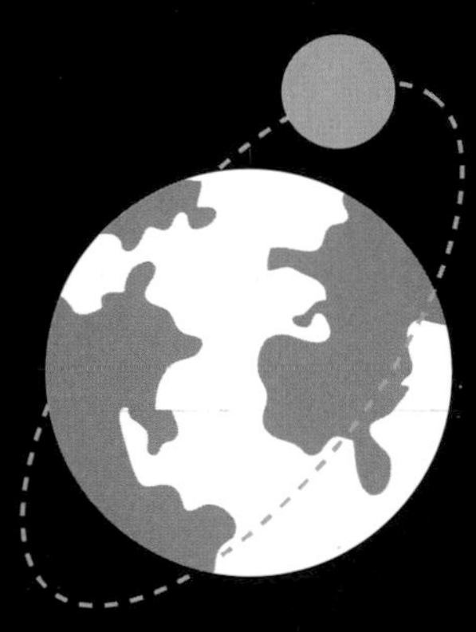

VELOCIRAPTORS ARE HUMAN-SIZE

In reality, these nasty beasts were only 2 to 3 feet (60–90 cm) tall—though still really deadly . . . we think.

COMAS ARE NO BIG DEAL

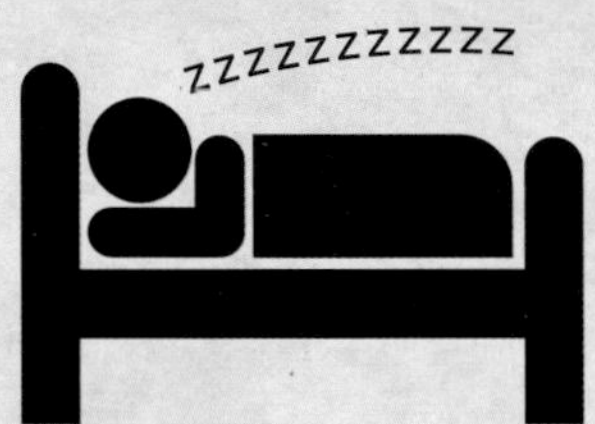

Contrary to movie myth, coma patients don't just wake up after years of deep sleep with no physical or mental problems. Nor do they look gorgeous and fit. Even if someone does come to, he or she will require physical therapy at the very least. And definitely the use of a comb.

ALL TERRORISTS ARE ARAB (OR MAYBE RUSSIAN)

Since the early 2000s, most cinematic terrorists have been from Arab countries. In films from the '70s and '80s, though, they're usually Russian.

ARABS
SEVERE
HIGH
ELEVATED
GUARDED
LOW

HEROES NEVER GET DRUNK

If most people drank the way movie characters do, they'd be unconscious most of the time.

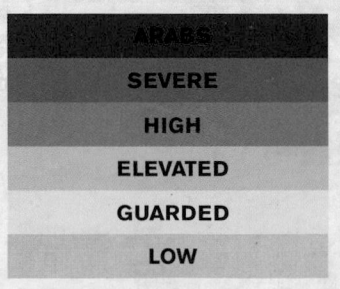

EXCLUSIVE!!! EXCLUSIVE!!! EXCLUSIVE!!!

SHOOT YOUR GUN SIDEWAYS!

IT'S WHAT THE PROS DO

This would be a good tactic if there was no such thing as recoil, which can make for an unpleasant arm injury—hardly "gangsta." Not to mention that shooting sideways makes aiming nearly impossible.

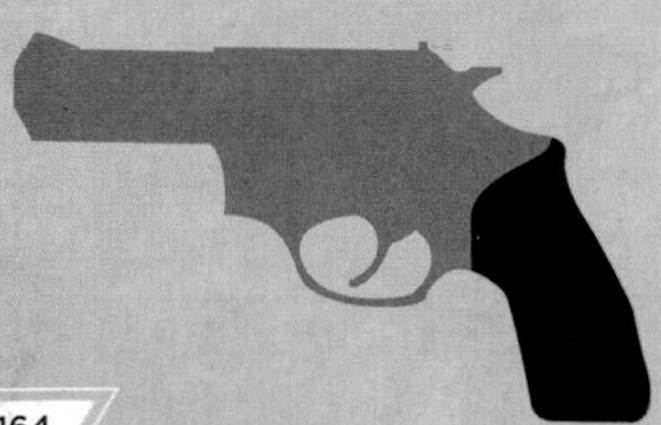

EVERY CAR IS A POTENTIAL BOMB!!

In most movies, cars burst into flame on impact. This is actually pretty rare—in real life, they just get really crumpled. But in other movies, you can jump a car off a bridge, roll it a couple of times, and drive away. In car-crash studies, any pressure of that magnitude on the human body would give you a fifty-fifty chance of surviving, and those who did survive would come away with massive internal trauma.

GRAVITY COMES AND GOES

Film heroes sometimes catch themselves with a rope and a grappling hook while falling, or simply grab onto a spare window ledge. In reality, once any sort of velocity is reached (which happens within a second or two), this sort of abrupt stop would break bones and cause internal injuries.

RUNNING IN HIGH HEELS IS EASY

Sprinting flat out might make some mere mortals breathless. But for women on the silver screen, there's no need to break a sweat or get their hair all messed up. Also, running and performing judo kicks in high heels seem equally effortless for them.

IN SPACE EVERYONE CAN HEAR YOU SCREAM

Actually, space is a vacuum. And without any matter through which to travel, sound waves can't resonate and be "heard." So no one can hear your anguish out there.

HEAD INJURIES ERASE MEMORY

On screen, a conk on the noggin may turn a brutal assassin into an average person and an heiresses into a humble housewife. But profound amnesia (usually caused by neurosurgery, brain infection, or stroke) is quite rare in the general population, and even in those cases, people don't usually lose their identity. Instead, they lose their short-term memory and cognitive ability.

YOU GET ONE PHONE CALL

In the movies, cops must read you your rights when you're arrested in the United States. Also, you get one phone call. Actually, the rights must be read only before someone is interrogated. And while you do have a right to an attorney, you don't technically have a right to a phone call.

PSYCHOPATHS ARE EVIL GENIUSES

Movie psychopaths are intelligent, crafty, calm, calculating, and oh-so-polite. A real-life psychopath is much more likely to be impulsive, disorganized, and short-tempered.

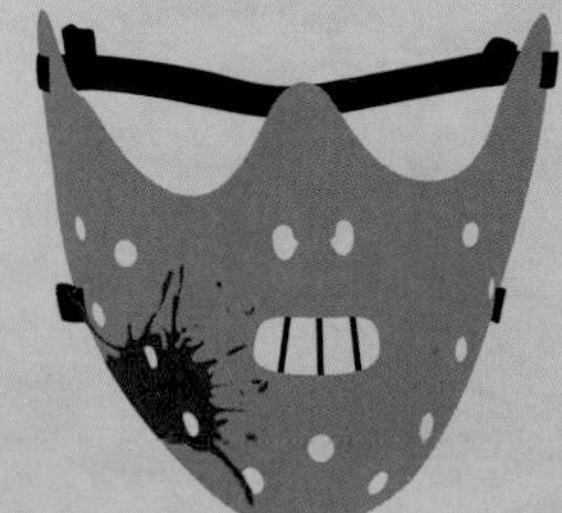

BUNNIES ABOUND

From the bloodthirsty beasts in *Night of the Lepus* to the irrepressible *Harvey,* rabbits are everywhere. Where will they show up next?

1. ***HARVEY***
   1950 / US
2. ***NIGHT OF THE LEPUS***
   1972 / US
3. ***THE TWILIGHT ZONE MOVIE***
   1983 / US
4. ***WHO FRAMED ROGER RABBIT?***
   1988 / US
5. ***AKIRA***
   1988 / JAPAN
6. ***JAN ŠVANKMAJER'S ALICE***
   1988 / CZECHOSLOVAKIA
7. ***BILL & TED'S BOGUS JOURNEY***
   1991 / US
8. ***THE NIGHTMARE BEFORE CHRISTMAS***
   1993 / US
9. ***SEXY BEAST***
   2000 / UK
10. ***AMÉLIE***
    2001 / FRANCE
11. ***DONNIE DARKO***
    2001 / US
12. ***THE SANTA CLAUSE 2***
    2002 / US
13. ***WALLACE & GROMIT IN THE CURSE OF THE WERE-RABBIT***
    2005 / UK
14. ***INLAND EMPIRE***
    2006 / US

8 TRICKSTER ANIMALS

1 CAGN
BUSHMEN, SOUTH AFRICA
Most often appearing as a praying mantis, Cagn is one trickster with major power. In the Bushmen's religion, he is the shape-shifting supreme god and creator of the universe.

2 REYNARD
FRANCE, ENGLAND, AND GERMANY
The trickster of medieval Europe, this crafty fox first cameos in *Ysengrimus,* a mock-epic poem from 1148. In this work, Reynard shows that brains trump brawn by defeating his strong-but-not-so-bright wolf nemesis.

3 BR'ER RABBIT
US
Based on African and Cherokee trickster figures, Br'er Rabbit challenges authority figures and bends social mores in order to slyly thrive in adverse circumstances.

4 *TANUKI*
JAPAN
The *tanuki* (or Japanese raccoon dog) is a jolly shape-shifter, but also gullible and absent-minded. Often depicted with a straw hat, a bottle of sake, an empty purse, and comically large testicles.

5 COYOTE
VARIOUS NATIVE AMERICAN TRIBES, US
Many tribes revere Coyote as an inventive if tricky figure. He's credited with making the universe from mud and stealing fire from the gods for humans. Still, he's not quite trustworthy.

6 SUN WUKONG
CHINA
A monkey who was born from a stone, the superstrong and shape-shifting Sun Wukong wars with heaven until Buddha imprisons him under a mountain. Later Buddha frees him to serve as a guide.

7 RAVEN / YELTH / HOYA
PACIFIC NORTHWEST, US
Credited with pinning the world's first landmass in place with his beak, Raven is seen mostly as a source of good, but his scheming ways can cause trouble for himself and the people around him.

8 ANANSI
ASHANTI PEOPLE, GHANA
Tales of this spider have made it from West Africa to the Caribbean and beyond. According to lore, Anansi mischievously captured many less-clever animals to win all the world's stories from the sky god; hence, the Ashanti refer to most myths as "Anansi stories."

22 BANNED BOOKS

/ RACISM
/ EXTREMISM
/ CRIMINALITY
/ SEXUALITY
/ POLITICS
/ SEXISM
/ RELIGION
/ CULTURAL DIFFERENCES

MADAME BOVARY
FRANCE / 1856–1857
Its depictions of adultery were seen as morally offensive.

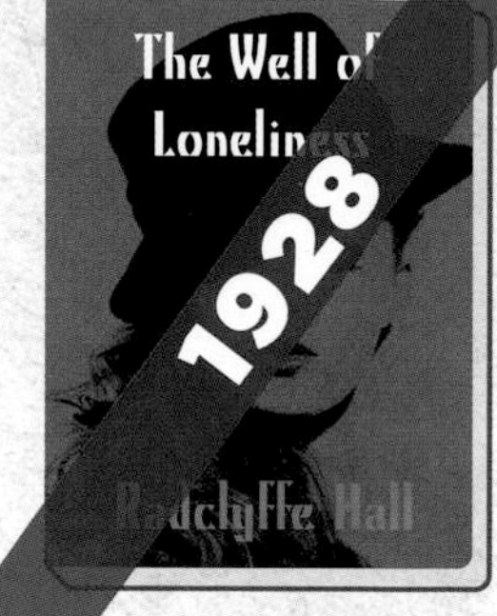

THE WELL OF LONELINESS
ENGLAND / 1928–1949
This novel was banned for its portrayal of lesbian relationships.

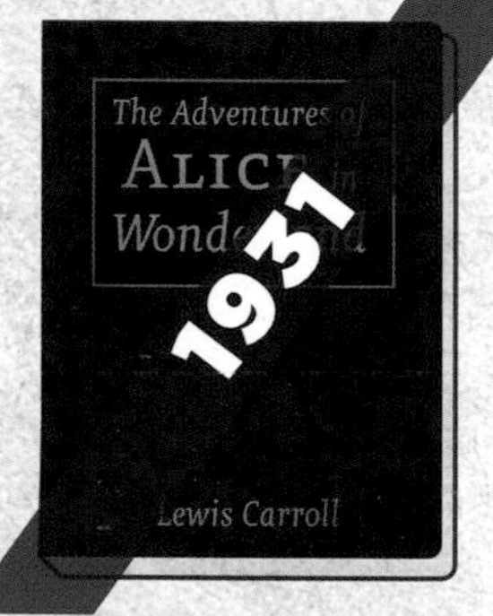

THE ADVENTURES OF ALICE IN WONDERLAND
CHINA / 1931
Anthropomorphic animals were considered inappropriate.

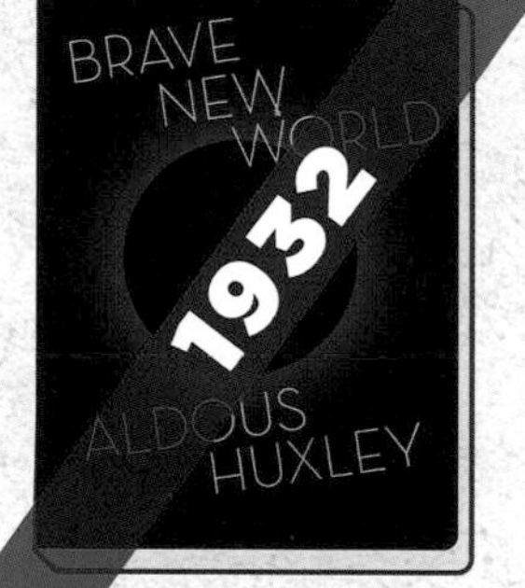

BRAVE NEW WORLD
IRELAND / 1932
The future world's sexual promiscuity was offensive.

TROPIC OF CANCER
US / 1938–1966
The dirty details of the author's expat life shocked Americans.

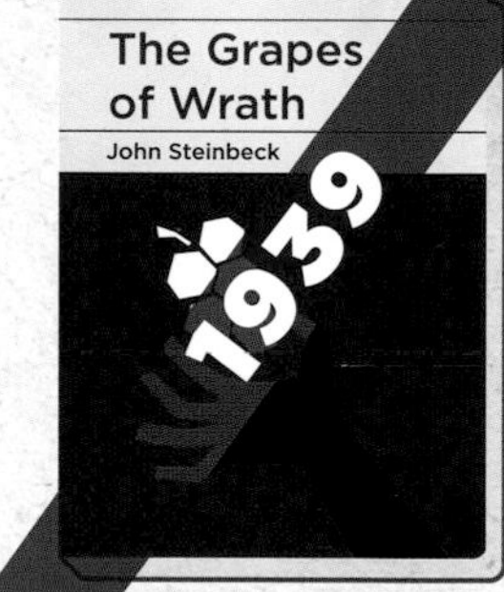

THE GRAPES OF WRATH
CALIFORNIA, US / 1939
Set in California, the book offended the state's leaders.

ANIMAL FARM
USSR / 1945–1990
This novel was viewed, accurately enough, as a critique of communism.

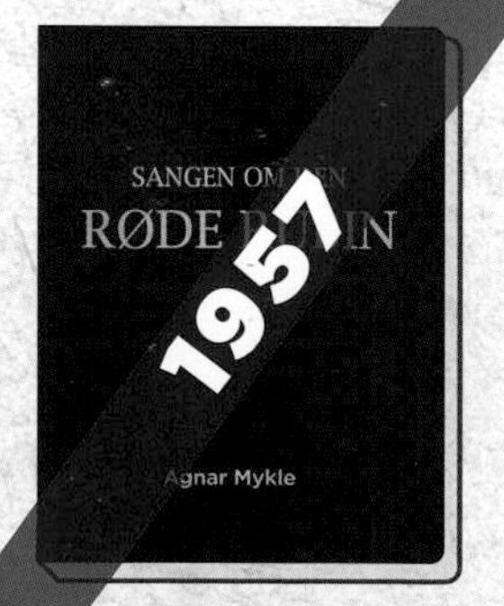

THE SONG OF THE RED RUBY
NORWAY / 1956
This book was briefly banned due to the protagonist's sexual exploits.

NINE HOURS TO RAMA
INDIA / 1962–PRESENT
This title names names in Mohandas Ghandi's assassination.

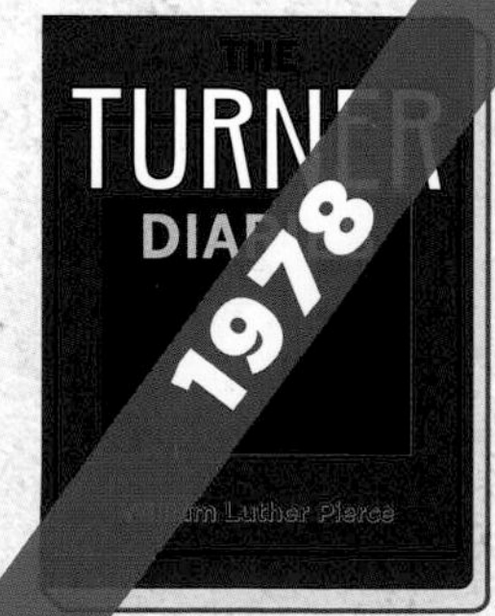

THE TURNER DIARIES
GERMANY / 1978–PRESENT
The author was part of a pro-Nazi political group.

BURGER'S DAUGHTER
SOUTH AFRICA / 1979
This historical novel's treatment of apartheid got it banned for six months.

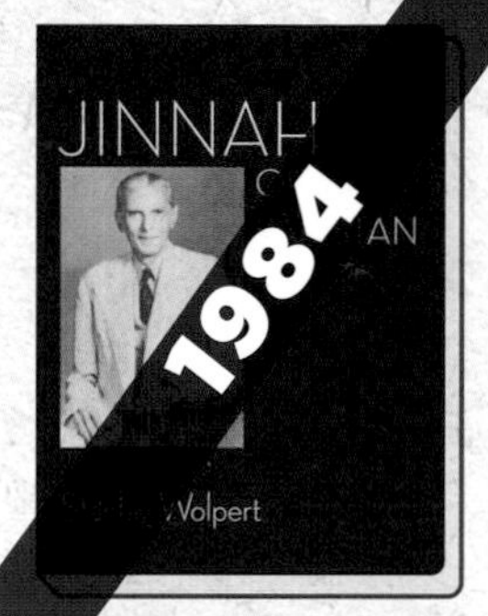

JINNAH OF PAKISTAN
PAKISTAN / 1982–PRESENT
This biography claims Pakistan's founder enjoyed wine and pork.

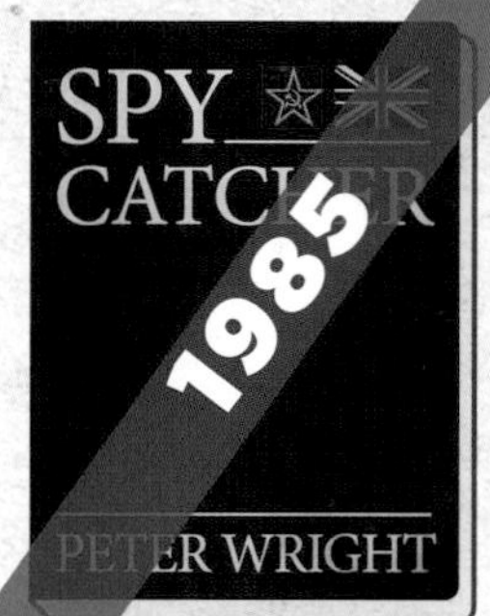

SPYCATCHER
UK / 1985–1988
In this title, a former intelligence officer reveals state secrets.

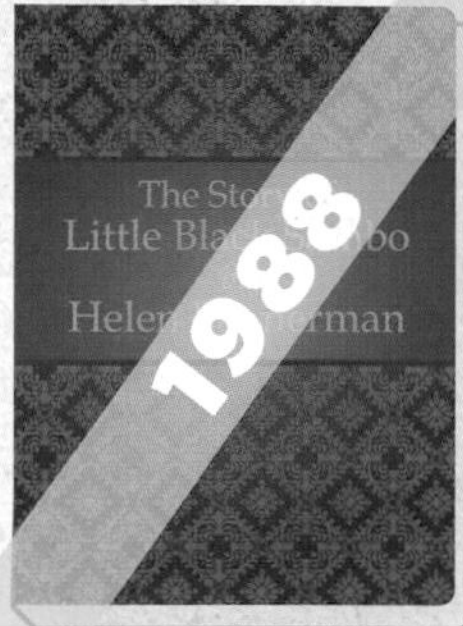

THE STORY OF LITTLE BLACK SAMBO
JAPAN / 1988
This children's book was banned for racist depictions.

THE SATANIC VERSES
THROUGHOUT THE MIDDLE EAST
1989–PRESENT
Rushdie's novel was banned for blasphemy against Islam.

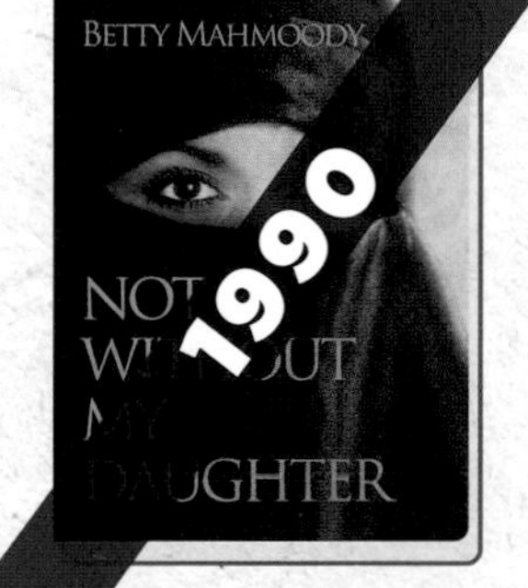

NOT WITHOUT MY DAUGHTER
IRAN / 1990
This memoir is considered critical of Islamic customs.

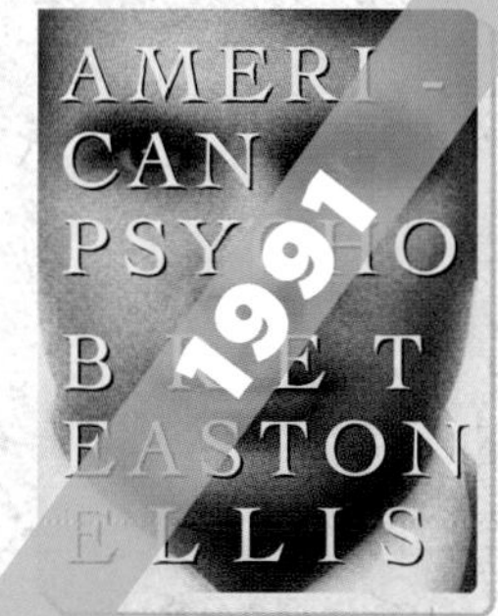

AMERICAN PSYCHO
GERMANY / 1995–2000
The novel was widely criticized for violence and misogyny.

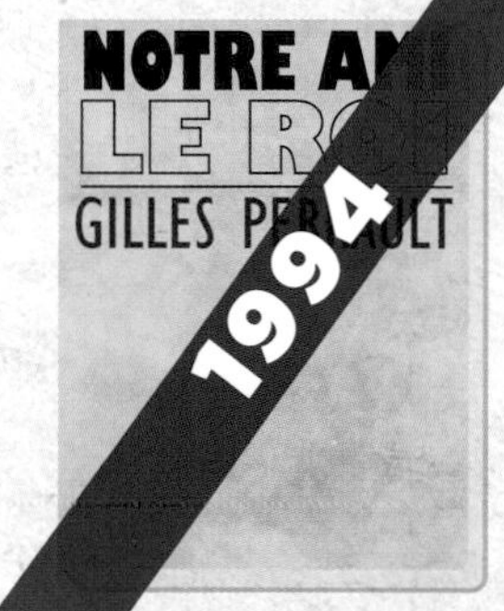

OUR FRIEND THE KING
MOROCCO / 1993–PRESENT
This biography of King Hassan II of Morocco divulged human rights violations.

ZHUAN FALUN
CHINA / 1999–PRESENT
This book details the beliefs of the banned Falun Gong sect.

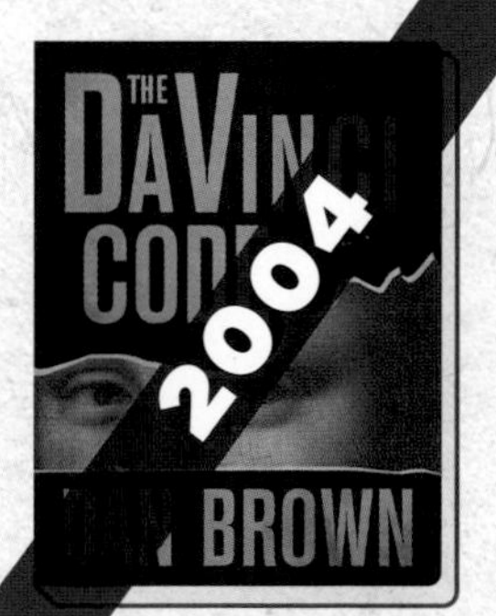

THE DA VINCI CODE
LEBANON / 2004–PRESENT
The Catholic community in Lebanon deemed Brown's novel offensive.

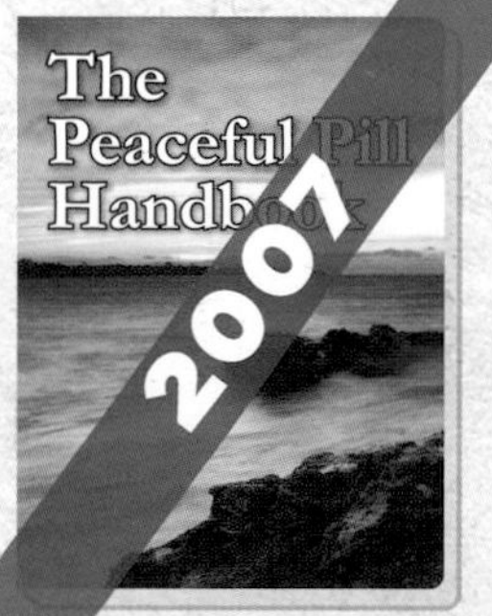

THE PEACEFUL PILL HANDBOOK
AUSTRALIA / 2007–PRESENT
This guide instructs readers how to perform euthanasia.

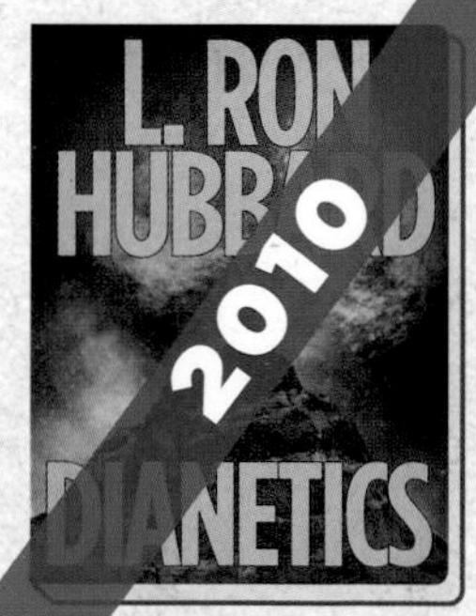

DIANETICS
RUSSIA / 2010–PRESENT
All of Hubbard's books were deemed "extremist material."

11 FAMOUS PEOPLE AND WEIRD RUMORS THEY INSPIRED

1 DIANA SPENCER
PRINCESS / UK / 1990s
Many believe that Princess Di's death in a car accident was actually a stealth assassination ordered by the British royal family. An inquest debunked this rumor in 2008.

2 CLEOPATRA
PHARAOH / EGYPT / FIRST CENTURY BCE
Assumed to be both black and Egyptian, she was actually Greek and Caucasian.

No way!

3 CATHERINE THE GREAT
EMPRESS / RUSSIA / 1700s
Foes spread the rumor that she died in flagrante delicto with one of her horses. In reality, she died of a far-less-titillating stroke.

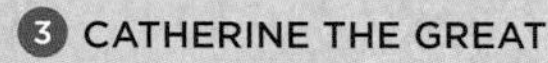

4 BARACK OBAMA
PRESIDENT / US / 2008
Opponents spread the false rumor that he was not actually born in the United States, and so was not eligible to be president.

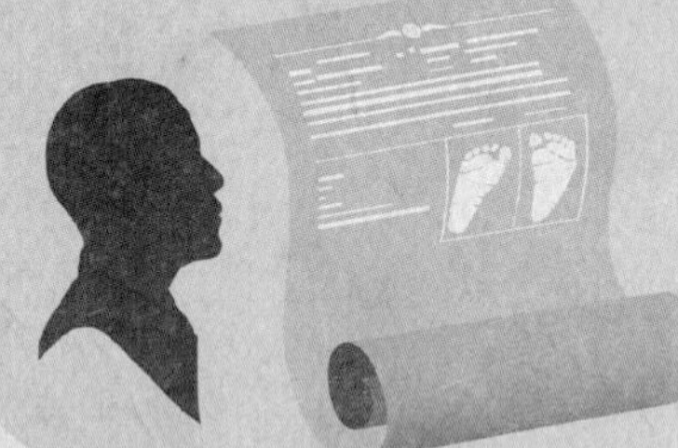

5 ADOLF HITLER
DICTATOR / GERMANY / 1945
Rumors persist that he only had one testicle. Based on a bunk autopsy report, this rumor was disproved by Hitler's lifelong doctors (and an ex-lover or two).

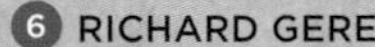

6 RICHARD GERE
ACTOR / US / CURRENT
Rumors persist about his engaging in intimate relations with gerbils, but there are no instances of "gerbilling" in hospital records involving Gere—or anyone else, for that matter.

7 JULIUS CAESAR
DICTATOR / ROME / FIRST CENTURY BCE
Rumor has it that Caesar was born by Cesarean section, but at the time this operation would have killed his mother. She, by all accounts, lived long enough to raise him and six subsequent kids.

8 ELEANOR OF AQUITAINE
QUEEN / FRANCE / 1100s
Scandals state that she rode bare breasted on crusade, slept with her uncle, and murdered her husband's mistress. No actual proof has ever confirmed such bad-girl behavior.

9 WALT DISNEY
ANIMATOR / US / 1960s
It's widely believed that Disney had his head cryogenically frozen so his genius could be revived in the future. Some versions of the myth even say it's stored in Disneyland.

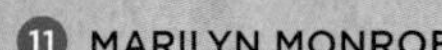

11 MARILYN MONROE
ACTRESS / US / 1960s
There are many conspiracy theories about Marilyn's death, including claims that the family of President Kennedy had her murdered by the Mafia.

10 NERO
EMPEROR / ROME / 64
Contrary to popular belief, Nero didn't fiddle while Rome burned, but organized and personally funded a massive relief effort. Also, fiddles weren't even invented yet.

20 STRANGE ART SUPPLIES

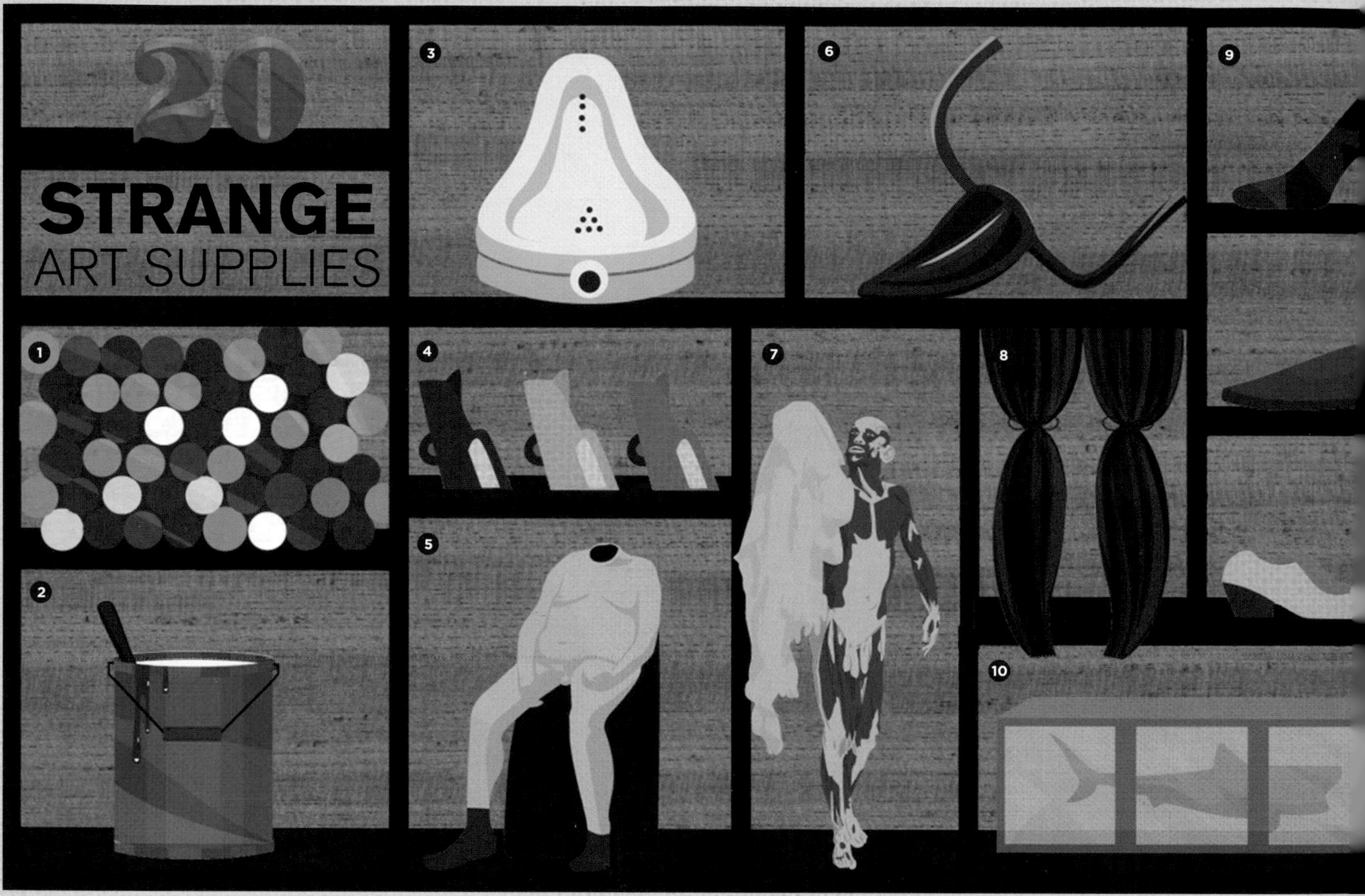

1 OIL BARRELS
CHRISTO / 1962
A blockade of barrels titled *Iron Curtain* caused a large traffic jam in a Parisian street.

2 PAINT AND NAKED WOMEN
YVES KLEIN / 1960s
Nude, paint-covered models imprinted their bodies on canvas to make *Anthropométries.*

3 URINAL
MARCEL DUCHAMP / 1917
Titled *Fountain,* this classic Dadaist piece was just a urinal that Duchamp signed.

4 CADILLACS
ANT FARM GROUP / 1974
Cadillac Ranch is a row of 10 cars painted and buried nose-first in a US desert.

5 DEAD HUMAN BODIES
JOEL-PETER WITKIN / 1960-CURRENT
Witkin poses bodies in a Mexican morgue and photographs them artistically.

6 BICYCLE PARTS
PABLO PICASSO / 1943
Tête de Taureau is a sculptural bull's head made from a bicycle seat and handlebars.

7 MORE DEAD HUMAN BODIES
GUNTHER VON HAGENS / 1995
Body Worlds is an exhibit of "plastinated" preserved and dissected cadavers.

8 HAIR EXTENSIONS
LOREN SCHWERD / 2007-2009
Mourning Portrait uses found hair to depict homes destroyed by Hurricane Katrina.

9 SHOE SHOPS
STANLEY BROUWN / 1960
Brouwn declared that all the shoe shops in Amsterdam were an exhibit of his own art.

10 DEAD SHARK
DAMIEN HIRST / 1991
The Physical Impossibility of Death in the Mind of Someone Living is a shark preserved in a tank of formaldehyde.

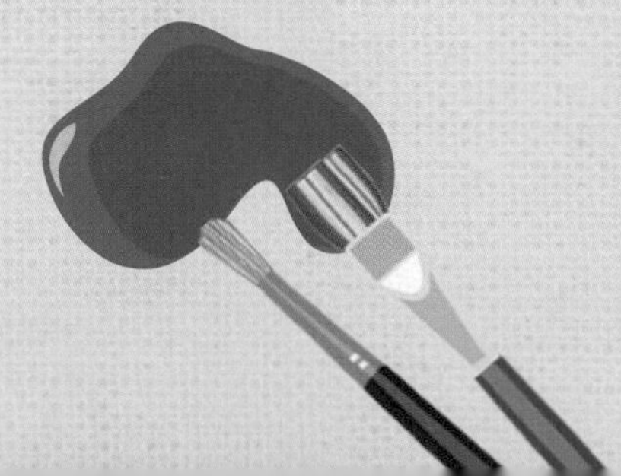

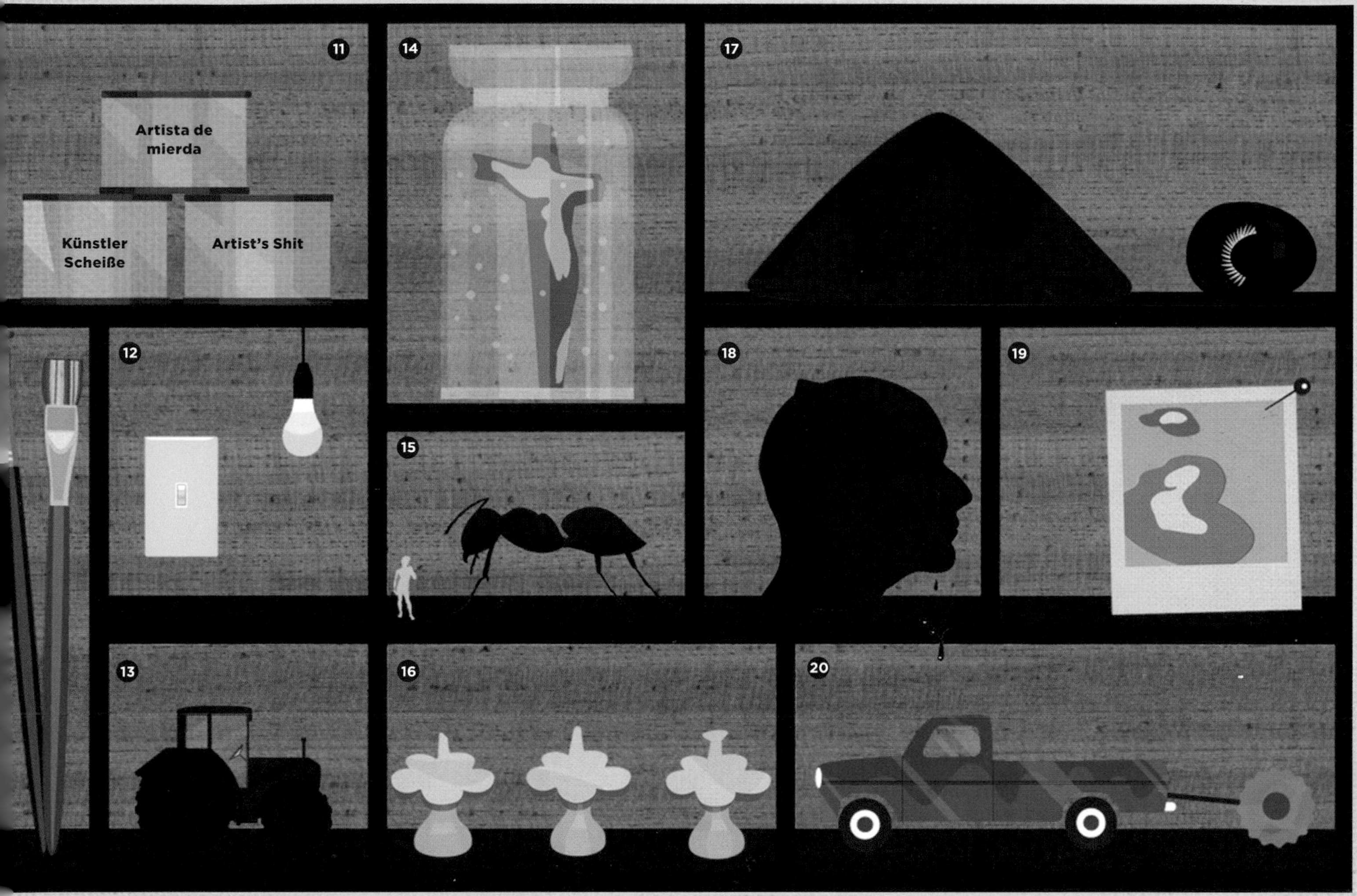

11 CANNED FECAL MATTER
PIERO MANZONI / 1961
The artist's feces are presented in a tin can, in a limited run of 90 tins. Guaranteed fresh.

12 LIGHTS
MARTIN CREED / 2001
The Lights Going On and Off is an empty room in which the lights go on and off.

13 TRACTOR
ANDO / 2001
Ando etched a figure titled *Mundi Man* into the Australian Outback's soil with a tractor.

14 URINE
ANDRES SERRANO / 1987
The infamous *Piss Christ* is a crucifix suspended in a vial of the artist's urine.

15 A SINGLE GRAIN OF SAND
WILLARD WIGAN / 2007
Wigan's sculptures are so tiny that some are no larger than a single human blood cell.

16 URINE AND SNOW
HELEN CHADWICK / 1991–1992
Piss Flowers were cast from cavities made when the artist urinated in the snow.

17 ATOMIZED JET ENGINE
ROGER HIORNS / 2009
This conceptual sculpture is a room full of gray dust that was once an engine.

18 BLOOD
MARC QUINN / 1991
The artist used 9.4 pints (4.5 L) of his blood to make a frozen sculpture of his head.

19 ISLANDS AND PINK FABRIC
CHRISTO / 1983
The artist wrapped 11 Florida islands in vast amounts of pink polypropylene fabric.

20 PICKUP TRUCK AND CHAINS
JIM DENEVAN / 2009
Denevan makes huge "freehand" drawings in the desert by pulling chains over the sand.

46 MOVIES WITH RIDICULOUSLY HIGH BODY COUNTS

836	*THE RETURN OF THE KING** / 2003
610	*KINGDOM OF HEAVEN* / 2005
600	*300* / 2007
572	*TROY* / 2004
558	*THE LAST SAMURAI* / 2003
468	*THE TWO TOWERS** / 2002
310	*GRINDHOUSE* / 2007
307	*HARD BOILED* / 1992
307	*TITANIC* / 1997
305	*WE WERE SOLDIERS* / 2002
256	*STARSHIP TROOPERS* / 1997
255	*SAVING PRIVATE RYAN* / 1998
247	*RAMBO* / 2008
236	*EQUILIBRIUM* / 2002
214	*A BULLET IN THE HEAD* / 1990
199	*A BETTER TOMORROW II* / 1987
187	*BLOOD DIAMOND* / 2006
187	*THE CHRONICLES OF RIDDICK* / 2004
186	*DUNE* / 1984
184	*BRAVEHEART* / 1995
181	*MCBAIN* / 1991
175	*DAWN OF THE DEAD* / 1978
172	*THE LAST OF THE MOHICANS* / 1992
169	*LONE WOLF AND CUB* / 1974
155	*THE MUMMY* / 1999
153	*PEARL HARBOR* / 2001
152	*HERO* / 2002
151	*SHOOT 'EM UP* / 2007
149	*THE KILLER* / 1989
146	*INVASION USA* / 1985
145	*THE WILD BUNCH* / 1969
141	*HOUSE OF THE DEAD* / 2003
140	*BLADE: TRINITY* / 2004
140	*ZULU* / 1964
139	*KELLY'S HEROES* / 1970
131	*DAWN OF THE DEAD* / 2004
127	*RAMBO III* / 1988
127	*VERSUS* / 2000
126	*THE GOOD, THE BAD, AND THE UGLY* / 1966
124	*RESIDENT EVIL: EXTINCTION* / 2007
123	*THE PATRIOT* / 2000
123	*RESIDENT EVIL: APOCALYPSE* / 2004
122	*FROM DUSK TILL DAWN* / 1996
120	*OPERATION DELTA FORCE* / 1997
120	*THE OUTLAW JOSEY WALES* / 1976
119	*AKIRA* / 1988

1 **QUEEN GRIMHILDE**
SNOW WHITE AND THE SEVEN DWARVES / 1937
Known as "the Evil Queen," this onetime fairest of them all set the standard for goth bad girls.

2 **HARRY LIME**
THE THIRD MAN / 1949
A classic noir profiteer and heartbreaker, he has street smarts, charm, and a great hat.

3 **HARRY POWELL**
THE NIGHT OF THE HUNTER / 1955
The con man and murderer woos the ladies with his manliness and sexy Southern drawl.

4 **GENERAL ZOD**
SUPERMAN II / 1980
This Kryptonian criminal is a brilliant natural leader who looks fabulous in a jumpsuit.

5 **JOAN CRAWFORD**
MOMMIE DEAREST / 1981
Arguably the most famous bad mother in film, she's also got drive, power, and style.

6 **KHAN**
STAR TREK II: THE WRATH OF KHAN / 1982
The genetically engineered tyrant is smart, strong, and creative—and his hair is awesome.

7 **JARETH**
LABYRINTH / 1986
The mysterious goblin king has a lot going for him—being played by David Bowie, for one.

8 **STEFF**
PRETTY IN PINK / 1986
He's a mean, upper-crust snob, but he's also popular and hot, and he has a great car.

9 **ALEX FORREST**
FATAL ATTRACTION / 1987
She's blond, professionally successful, and totally dedicated to her man. No matter what.

10 **VALMONT**
DANGEROUS LIAISONS / 1988
Well dressed and smooth, this nobleman is almost always a success with the ladies.

11 **HANS GRUBER**
DIE HARD / 1988
On the downside, he's a terrorist and a thief, but he's also brilliant and has a very sexy accent.

12 **J. D.**
HEATHERS / 1989
This classic high-school bad boy takes it to the next level, what with the murdering and all.

13 **CATWOMAN**
BATMAN RETURNS / 1992
She's a sassy burglar who looks great in leather, only hurts bad people, and is good with animals.

14 **XENIA SERGEYEVNA ONATOPP**
GOLDENEYE / 1995
This classic femme fatale and master assassin has amazing cleavage and killer thighs.

15 **SIL**
SPECIES / 1995
Strong and intelligent, this alien hybrid enjoys getting naked and mating with humans.

16 **SATÁNICO PANDEMÓNIUM**
FROM DUSK TILL DAWN / 1996
On the one hand, she's a deadly vampire. On the other, she's a hot, curvy dancer. It balances out.

17 **COURTNEY SHANE**
JAWBREAKER / 1999
Called "Satan in Heels," this high-school psychopath has a real way with a popsicle.

18 **ASAMI YAMAZAKI**
AUDITION / 1999
This dancer is demurely pretty, shy, and very creative when it comes to dismemberment.

19 **PATRICK BATEMAN**
AMERICAN PSYCHO / 2000
The archetypal yuppie serial killer is rich and powerful, and he looks great in designer suits.

20 **COMMODUS**
GLADIATOR / 2000
A man with serious family connections, he can really rock the leather-skirt-and-sandals look.

21 **MADISON LEE**
CHARLIE'S ANGELS: FULL THROTTLE / 2003
The rogue Angel has looks, skills, a great wardrobe, and a certain cougarish charm.

22 **JADIS**
THE LION, THE WITCH, AND THE WARDROBE / 2005
Coldly beautiful, the White Witch isn't very nice to fauns or lions, but her candy is to die for.

23 **SWEENEY TODD**
SWEENEY TODD / 2007
The Demon Barber is a goth dreamboat with a fabulous cravat and a loyal heart.

 FEMALE CHARACTER

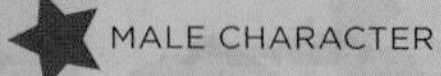 MALE CHARACTER

10 Great Sports Comebacks

1 HENRI COCHET
TENNIS / 1927
French player Cochet was considered seriously overmatched by American Bill Tilden in the Wimbledon semifinal. Tilden, regarded as the world's finest player, quickly took two sets and was winning the third when Cochet rallied and won six games in a row—and, eventually, the title.

2 MANCHESTER UNITED
SOCCER / 1959
In 1958, an airplane carrying the team crashed, killing eight players (including most of its stars), ending the careers of two other players, and putting the manager in a coma. A few months later, Man U was in the Cup Final and, while the team didn't win, it was still an astonishing comeback.

3 NIKI LAUDA
AUTO RACING / 1977
In 1976, after suffering severe burns and inhaling huge amounts of toxic gas after a crash, and later collapsing into a coma, Austrian driver Lauda was back to racing in less than two months. He won the Formula One championship the next year.

4 ERNIE IRVAN
AUTO RACING / 1995
NASCAR driver Irvan was a contender for the Winston Cup in 1994 when a wreck supposedly put him on his deathbed. By 1995 he was back to racing and back to contending for the Cup.

5 DARA TORRES
SWIMMING / 2008
At the age of 41, eight years after her last Olympic games, Torres returned to the pool to compete in the 2008 Summer Games. She won three silver medals, including an individual medal in the 50-meter freestyle.

6 GORAN IVANIŠEVI
TENNIS / 2001
By the 2001 Wimbledon, Ivaniševi was widely thought to be on the verge of retirement and only qualified as a wild card. He went on to win the singles' tournament.

7 MONICA SELES
TENNIS / 1995
Stabbed by a deranged fan of her rival, Steffi Graf, in 1993, Seles did not compete for two years. When she returned, she was back in top form, winning the Australian Open in January 1996.

8 MAGIC JOHNSON
BASKETBALL / 1992
On the eve of the 1991–92 season, Johnson announced he was HIV positive. However, he was selected for the 1992 All Star game and went on to play in the Olympics as part of the gold medal–winning 1992 US "Dream Team."

9 GORDIE HOWE
HOCKEY / 1997
One of Canada's hockey legends began his career in 1946. After retiring several times, he returned for a season at the age of 51, and for one final game at 69.

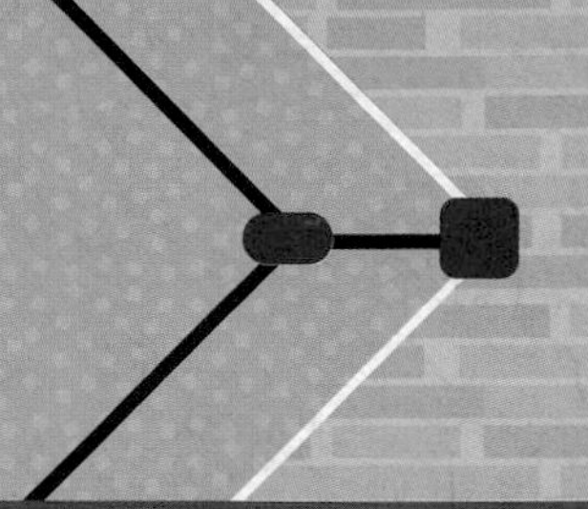

10 **MUHUMMAD ALI**
BOXING / 1974
By the time Ali, the older fighter, was to face George Foreman in the fight known as the "Rumble in the Jungle," he had been beaten by two men whom Foreman had beaten and was considered the underdog. After taking a fairly serious beating, Ali was finally able to knock Foreman out in the eighth round.

11 **LIVERPOOL**
SOCCER / 2005
Heavily outclassed by AC Milan in the Champions League Final, Liverpool trailed 3–0 at the half. The team evened it up, and then won it in an overtime penalty shoot-out, surprising even its fans.

12 **GREG LEMOND**
CYCLING / 1989
On the eve of defending his Tour de France title in 1987, LeMond was severely injured in a shotgun accident. With 37 shotgun pellets in his leg and two near his heart, LeMond took two years off but returned to win the Tour in 1989 and 1990.

13 **LANCE ARMSTRONG**
CYCLING / 1999
Armstrong was an up-and-coming star in 1996 when he was diagnosed with testicular cancer that spread to his brain, lungs, and abdomen. He returned in 1999 to win the first of seven consecutive Tour de France victories.

14 **KELLY HOLMES**
RUNNING / 2004
Suffering from crippling depression, Holmes was unable to take medication. But coming off the worst year in her career, she rallied to win Olympic gold in both the 1,500- and 800-meter races.

15 **LASSE VIRÉN**
RUNNING / 1972
Running the 10,000-meter finals at the 1972 Olympics, Virén tripped and fell on lap 12. This should have eliminated him, but he got up, sped after the pack, and not only caught up but went on to win the gold.

16 **BOSTON RED SOX**
BASEBALL / 2004
The Red Sox were one of the losingest teams in the history of baseball when they met the 26-time champion New York Yankees in a seven-game championship series. The Sox lost the first three games, but won the last four—and the title in the World Series.

17 **EDDIE WAITKUS**
BASEBALL / 1950
Waitkus was shot by a crazed fan during the 1949 season. Still, he returned to finish the 1950 season second in plate appearances and at bats, fifth in hits, sixth in runs scored, and ninth in doubles.

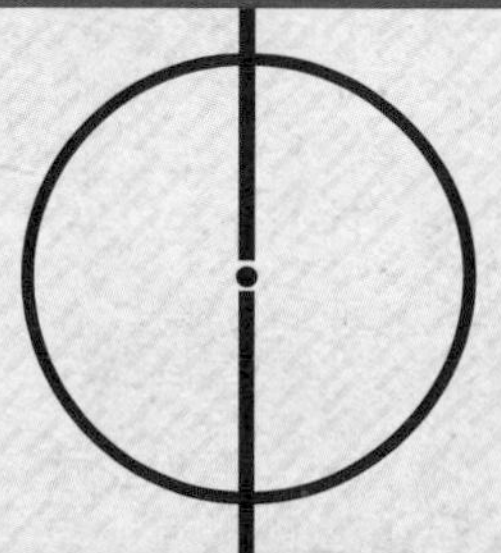

18 **MARIO LEMIEUX**
HOCKEY / 2000
After battling cancer and having several surgeries, the all-star player retired in 1997. He returned in 2000 and led the league in points per game from 2000 until retiring again in 2006.

19 BOOKS with an Animal Protagonist

1. *PUSS IN BOOTS*
   CAT / PUSS / 1697
2. *THE UGLY DUCKLING*
   SWAN / UNNAMED / 1843
3. *THE TALE OF PETER RABBIT*
   RABBIT / PETER / 1902
4. *THE CALL OF THE WILD*
   DOG / BUCK / 1903
5. *THE WIND IN THE WILLOWS*
   MOLE / MOLE / 1908
6. *THE VELVETEEN RABBIT*
   RABBIT / UNNAMED / 1922
7. *WINNIE THE POOH*
   BEAR / WINNIE / 1926
8. *THE STORY OF BABAR*
   ELEPHANT / BABAR / 1931
9. *THE ADVENTURES OF CURIOUS GEORGE*
   MONKEY / GEORGE / 1941
10. *STUART LITTLE*
    MOUSE / STUART / 1945
11. *ANIMAL FARM*
    PIG / NAPOLEON / 1945
12. *CHARLOTTE'S WEB*
    PIG / WILBUR / 1952
13. *MRS. FRISBY AND THE RATS OF NIMH*
    MOUSE / MRS. FRISBY / 1971
14. *WATERSHIP DOWN*
    RABBIT / HAZEL / 1972
15. *THE PLAGUE DOGS*
    DOGS / ROWF AND SNITTER / 1977
16. *BUNNICULA*
    RABBIT / BUNNICULA / 1979
17. *THE SHEEP-PIG*
    PIG / BABE / 1983
18. *TAILCHASER'S SONG*
    CAT / FRITTI TAILCHASER / 1985
19. *THE ROACHES HAVE NO KING*
    COCKROACH / NUMBERS / 1994

16 Books WITH Nameless Protagonists

1. ***FIVE MINUTES***
JOSÉ DE ALENCAR / BRAZIL / 1856
. . . in which the narrator describes his love for a young lady

2. ***A CRYSTAL AGE***
W. H. HUDSON / UK / 1887
. . . in which the narrator is baffled by circumstances

3. ***THE WAR OF THE WORLDS***
H. G. WELLS / UK / 1898
. . . in which the narrator misses his wife and dodges Martians

4. ***ETHAN FROME***
EDITH WHARTON / US / 1911
. . . in which the narrator tells the story of Ethan Frome

5. ***UNDER FIRE: THE STORY OF A SQUAD***
HENRI BARBUSSE / FRANCE / 1916
. . . in which the narrator describes his war experiences

6. ***REBECCA***
DAPHNE DU MAURIER / UK / 1938
. . . in which the narrator dreams she went to Manderley again

7. ***THE SECOND SCROLL***
A. M. KLEIN / CANADA / 1951
. . . in which the narrator searches for his long-lost uncle

8. ***THE UNNAMABLE***
SAMUEL BECKETT / FRANCE / 1953
. . . in which the narrator muses existentially

9. ***MIGUEL STREET***
V. S. NAIPAUL / TRINIDAD / 1959
. . . in which the narrator recounts his childhood

10. ***BEAUTIFUL LOSERS***
LEONARD COHEN / CANADA / 1966
. . . in which the narrator is part of a love triangle

11. ***THE MEMOIRS OF A SURVIVOR***
DORIS LESSING / UK / 1974
. . . in which the narrator learns to traverse space and time

12. ***THE AESTHETICS OF RESISTANCE***
PETER WEISS / GERMANY / 1975
. . . in which the narrator opposes Nazis in 1937 Berlin

13. ***THE LAND OF GREEN PLUMS***
HERTA MÜLLER / GERMANY / 1994
. . . in which the narrator flees a totalitarian government

14. ***CHECKERS***
JOHN MARSDEN / AUSTRALIA / 1996
. . . in which the narrator is a voluntary patient in a psychiatric ward

15. ***FIGHT CLUB***
CHUCK PALAHNIUK / US / 1996
. . . in which the narrator does not talk about Fight Club

16. ***THE CHESS MASTER***
ZHONG ACHENG / CHINA / 2006
. . . in which the narrator observes a chess master's life

36 FAMOUS PEOPLE WHO WERE ADOPTED

FAMILY TIES

Adopted children may be found in a basket by the river, left on a doorstep, rescued from war, or the child of one's new spouse. However parents and children find each other, what they create is a family. Below are some famous adoptees.

- ENTERTAINER
- LITERARY FIGURE
- POLITICAL FIGURE
- RELIGIOUS FIGURE
- ENTREPRENEUR
- ATHLETE
- SCIENTIST
- ARTIST

ARISTOTLE
GREECE

JOHN J. AUDUBON
HAITI / US

JOHANN SEBASTIAN BACH
AUSTRIA

INGRID BERGMAN
SWEDEN

RICHARD BURTON
WALES

GEORGE W. CARVER
US

GARY COLEMAN
US

BO DIDDLEY
US

CARL THEODOR DREYER
DENMARK

JEAN GENET
FRANCE

JOHN HANCOCK
US

DEBBIE HARRY
US

DAMIEN HIRST
ENGLAND

LANGSTON HUGHES
US

MINEKO IWASAKI
JAPAN

JESSE JACKSON
US

JESUS CHRIST
WEST BANK

STEVE JOBS
US

KIRI TE KANAWA
NEW ZEALAND

RUDYARD KIPLING
UK

LORD KRISHNA
INDIA

RAY LIOTTA
US

GORDON LIU
HONG KONG

GREG LOUGANIS
US

NELSON MANDELA
SOUTH AFRICA

JAMES MICHENER
US

MARILYN MONROE
US

MOSES
EGYPT

EDGAR ALLAN POE
US

PRISCILLA PRESLEY
US

NANCY REAGAN
US

JEAN-JACQUES ROUSSEAU
FRANCE

BUFFY SAINTE-MARIE
CANADA

LEO TOLSTOY
RUSSIA

MAURICE UTRILLO
FRANCE

MALCOLM X
US

16 FAMOUS PEOPLE AND THEIR PREFAME JOBS

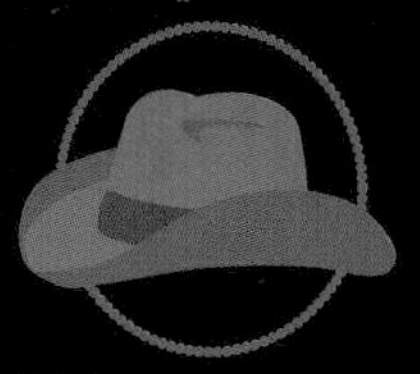

COLIN FARRELL
LINE DANCE INSTRUCTOR

BARACK OBAMA
ICE CREAM SCOOPER

MUGDHA GODSE
PERFUME SELLER

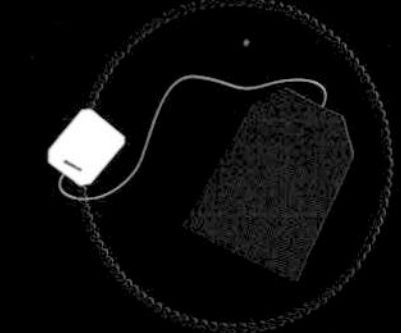

PELÉ
TEA SHOP SERVANT

BJÖRK
WORM EXTRACTOR AT A SEAFOOD PLANT

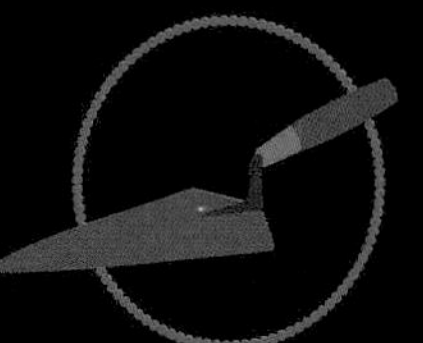

WHOOPI GOLDBERG
BRICKLAYER

POL POT
TEACHER

SEAN CONNERY
COFFIN POLISHER

CHE GUEVARA
MEDICAL STUDENT

SYLVESTER STALLONE
LION CAGE CLEANER

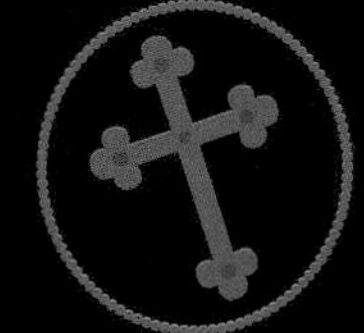

TOM CRUISE
CATHOLIC SEMINARY STUDENT

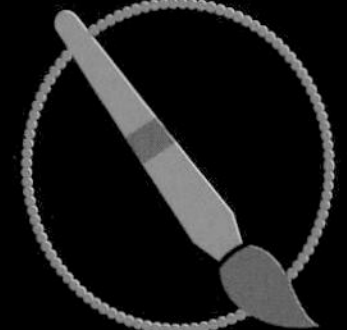

ADOLF HITLER
ART STUDENT

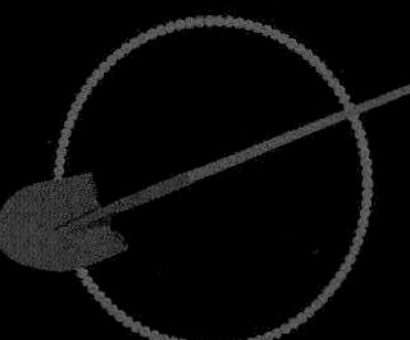

ROD STEWART
GRAVEDIGGER

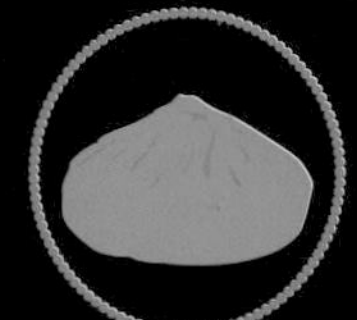

RECEP ERDOGAN
BUN VENDOR

HARUKI MURAKAMI
JAZZ CLUB OWNER

VINCENT VAN GOGH
SOCIAL WORKER

12 STRANGE MUSICAL INSTRUMENTS

1 **AEOLIAN WIND HARP**
Named after Aeolus (the Greek god of wind), this harp is placed so that a breeze strums its strings, which are stretched over a sounding board.

2 **WASHTUB BASS**
This folksy instrument dates from the early 1900s and consists of a string, an overturned metal washtub, and a stick. It's also called a *gutbucket.*

3 **CONTRABASS SERPENT**
Related to the modern tuba but often made of wood, the serpent debuted in the late 1500s. It can be incredibly complex in its twists and turns.

4 **THEREMIN**
Invented in 1928 by Russian professor Léon Thérémin, this electronic instrument is played by waving one's hands through an electrical field.

5 **TSABOUNA**
A sort of bagpipe enjoyed on Greek islands for more than 2,000 years, the tsabouna is made of goatskin and has two pipes that are played together.

6 **HURDY-GURDY**
The hurdy-gurdy is pretty much a fiddle on a wheel, minus the bow. The player coaxes its strings into sound by cranking the rosined wheel by hand.

7 ARMONICA
Glass bowls filled with water are placed in ascending size on a spindle, then agitated to create sound. Benjamin Franklin made a treadle-powered model.

8 JAL TARANG
A traditional Indian musical instrument that is played by striking water-filled porcelain cups with a bamboo stick; varied cup sizes offer different tones.

9 WATERPHONE
Resonant metal rods surround a bowl that's usually filled with water. The waterphonist strikes the rods with mallets to create an ambient sound.

10 KATZENKLAVIER
A "piano" consisting of a line of cats with their tails stretched out underneath a keyboard. Pressing the keys made them squeal.

11 CAJÓN
The first cajónes were simple boxes with a thin frontispiece that players pounded on like a drum. The concept was brought to Peru by slaves from Africa.

12 LASER HARP
This electronic musical instrument simulates a harp, with the performer plucking laser "strings" by blocking them with a hand.

15 SPORTY NATIONS

GO LONG

Some countries dominate a game so brilliantly that it defines their national identity. Other countries contribute a surprising number of valuable players to a sport that's more celebrated in a faraway land. Here are a few examples.

NORWAY / BIATHLON
RUSSIA / CHESS
CHINA / TABLE TENNIS
KENYA / DISTANCE RUNNING
ROMANIA / GYMNASTICS
INDIA / CRICKET
SAMOA / AMERICAN FOOTBALL
NETHERLANDS / SPEED SKATING

14 SCANDALS

THAT JUST SEEM QUAINT TODAY

CROSS-DRESSING PARTY CRASHER

Every year, the Vestal Virgins of Ancient Rome hosted a ladies-only party for the "Good Goddess," Bona Dea. In 62 BCE, politician and known prankster Publius Clodius Pulcher attended in drag to cavort with his girlfriend—who just happened to be Caesar's wife. Pulcher was discovered, scandal erupted, and divorce ensued.

DEPRESSING WEDDING DRESS

Mary Queen of Scots' white wedding dress was considered shocking at the time of her marriage in 1558, as white was the color of mourning.

DIRTY BOOK

John Cleland's 1748 novel *Fanny Hill* is considered the first published pornographic novel. For its time, it was pretty racy, including orgies, sadomasochism, and gay sex. It's one of the most banned books in history.

King of England Gets Divorced

In the 1500s, Henry VIII famously made Protestantism the official religion of England so he could legally get divorced, which had been impossible for him as a Catholic monarch without being excommunicated by the Pope—and risking his mortal soul.

LIFELONG COMPANIONS

The Ladies of Llangollen scandalized Irish high society in 1778 by running away together to avoid being forced into unwanted marriages. They set up housekeeping in Wales, and lived together until death parted them 50 years later.

WITNESS FOR THE DEFENSE

When Lady Mordaunt, the beautiful wife of a British baronet, was involved in a scandalous divorce in 1869, the crown prince (later Edward VII) was accused of being one of her lovers. While he didn't admit guilt, he did testify that he "visited" her while her husband was away.

BIRTH CONTROL

Women's rights crusader Annie Besant was prosecuted in 1877 for publishing a book by birth control campaigner Charles Knowlton.

CHILD OUT OF WEDLOCK

US President Grover Cleveland fathered a child out of wedlock. In his 1884 bid for the presidential office, opponents taunted him with the jingle, "Ma, ma, where's my pa? Gone to the White House, ha ha ha."

Politicians Caught Taking Money from Oilmen

The Teapot Dome Scandal caused outrage in 1922, casting a shadow over President Warren G. Harding's office and going on the books as the first time politicians were influenced by special oil interests.

TEACHING EVOLUTION

John T. Scopes violated a state law that forbade the teaching of evolution in Tennessee public schools. The resulting 1925 "Scopes Monkey Trial" made history.

MARRYING AN AMERICAN

In 1936, Edward VIII of England was forced to abdicate the throne so he could marry Wallis Simpson—a (gasp!) divorcée and (double gasp!) an American.

MARRIED CELEBRITIES BEHAVING BADLY

The tryst between actress Ingrid Bergman and director Roberto Rossellini created such a scandal that Bergman was forced to leave the American movie business for six years.

BLASPHEMOUS ROCK STAR

When John Lennon was quoted in 1966 as saying that the Beatles were "more popular than Jesus," a violent protest broke out in the United States. Records were burned, concerts canceled, and threats made.

Blockbuster Over Budget

The 1979 film *Apocalypse Now* went so far over budget and schedule that director Francis Ford Coppola was forced to borrow nearly US $30 million from the distributor; much derision from the media followed. These days, that's nothing.

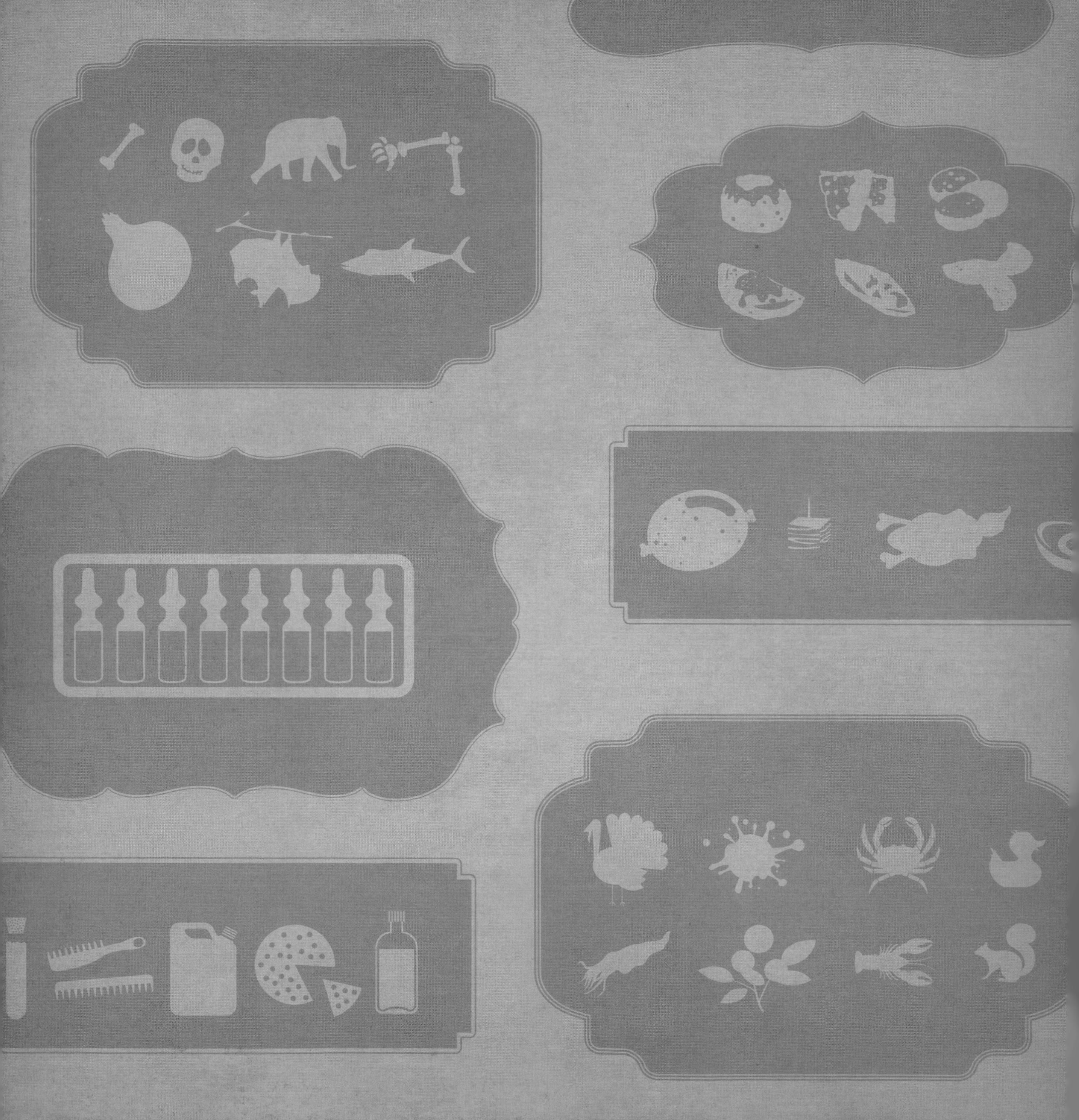

267

THINGS YOU MIGHT **EAT** OR **DRINK** (OR NOT)

Feeling hungry? Perhaps you might enjoy some kangaroo-flavored potato chips, a slice of cow face, or a tasty handful of Soylent Green (good luck with that last one!). If your dinner makes you feel a little ill, this chapter also notes medical treatments of yore, such as cornflakes, ketchup (no, really!), and a nice gin and tonic. And if you overindulge, you can always go on the cigarette diet!

16 MEDICINES WE DEVELOPED A TASTE FOR

1 **HEROIN**
GERMANY / 1898
Ironically, heroin was developed in an attempt to find a less-addictive substitute for morphine.

2 **CORNFLAKES**
US / 1894
A religious group came up with this deliberately bland cereal, which was supposed to lower the sex drive.

3 **KETCHUP "PILLS"**
US / 1937
Dr. Miles Compound Extract of Tomato was ketchup in pill form. It was used to treat a suspiciously wide array of ailments.

4 **GRAHAM CRACKERS**
US / 1829
Graham crackers were invented by American reformers in an effort to reduce carnal desires and curb masturbation.

5 **COCA-COLA**
US / 1886
A pharmacist created this beverage to treat a whole host of conditions, like dyspepsia, headache, and impotence.

6 **COCAINE**
ITALY / 1859
Coca leaves have been used as medicine since prehistory; cocaine was refined as a treatment for drowsiness and flatulence.

7 **ANGOSTURA BITTERS**
VENEZUELA / 1824
Now a cocktail staple, this flavoring first got its start as a digestive tonic, but was also marketed as a cure for scarlet fever.

8 **7-UP**
US / 1929
Originally containing a mood-stabilizing drug, this fizzy soda was marketed as a hangover cure.

9 DR PEPPER
US / 1885
Developed by a pharmacist, Dr Pepper was marketed as a midafternoon pick-me-up—hence the "pep" in its name.

10 BOVRIL
UK / 1871
Bovril was introduced as a "meat drink" to keep soldiers from shivering to death; people today enjoy it as a health tonic.

11 ROOT BEER
US / 1876
This sassafras-based soda was pitched as a "temperance beverage" that purified the blood and gave cheeks a healthy glow.

12 FERNET BRANCA
ITALY / 1845
This digestif is a medley of many different herbs and was believed to cure menstrual discomfort, hangovers, and colic in infants.

13 GIN AND TONIC
UK / 1800s
Quinine (found in tonic water) is a valid malaria preventive; British colonials added gin to make it more palatable.

14 MOXIE SODA
US / 1876
Made with the mythic "moxie" plant, this soda was said to be effective against paralysis, anxiety, and sleeplessness.

15 PEPSI
US / 1898
Pepsi creator Caleb Bradham believed his invention would aid with digestion, as it contained the stomach enzyme pepsin.

16 PEANUT BUTTER
US / 1903
First invented by the Aztecs, this spread was patented in the United States as a way to deliver protein to the toothless.

8 Sacred Foods

1 **COCA LEAVES**
PRE-INCA CULTURE
People of the Andean region chewed coca leaves to achieve some forms of divination. They also offered the leaves to the gods.

2 **COMMUNION WAFER**
CATHOLICISM
In Holy Communion, worshippers eat wafers of unleavened bread that represent the body of Christ.

3 **CHALLAH**
JUDAISM
This braided loaf of bread symbolizes the bread that fell from the heavens and fed the Israelites on their journey from Egypt to the Promised Land.

4 **GHEE**
HINDUISM
According to Hindu belief, Lord Brahma (the god of creation) first made this clarified butter; the Hindus use it in a number of anointment rituals.

TABOO FOODS

1 **ALCOHOL**
RASTAFARIANISM
Many religions prohibit alcohol;

2 **ELEPHANT**
ISLAM
Islam forbids eating animals that have fangs, and tusks count as fangs.

3 **ONION**
HINDUISM
Traditional Hindus consider onions to be impure and so abstain from eating them.

4 **COFFEE OR TEA**
MORMONISM
Prophesy prohibits coffee and tea, but cola drinks are OK.

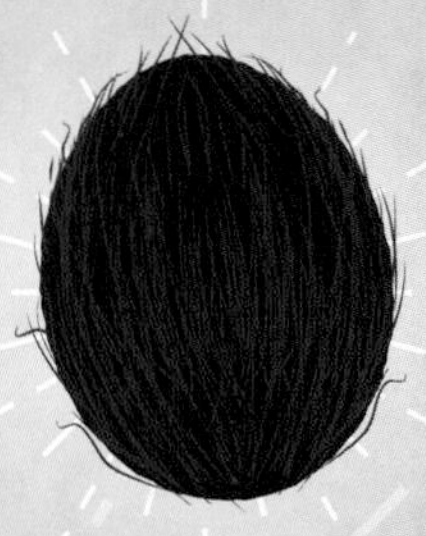

5 **COCONUT**
HINDUISM
Hindus fashion coconuts to look like human heads, crack them open to symbolize breaking the ego, and offer them to Brahma.

6 **CORN**
ZUNI
The Zuni of the southwestern United States revere corn and use it in various spiritual rituals, such as dances and dramatizations.

7 **CACAO**
AZTEC
Aztec nobles consumed cacao as a drink—sometimes mixed with blood. It was also a staple in sacrificial rituals.

8 **HONEY**
ANCIENT EGYPTIAN
Ancient Egyptians offered honey to the fertility god Min. They also used the sweet sticky stuff for embalming.

5 **FUNGI**
HARE KRISHNAS
Mushrooms' status as fungi gets them a no from Hare Krishnas, who won't eat anything grown in dung.

6 **FISH**
SOMALI CLANS
Many Somali clans claim fish are unclean. This belief extends to a refusal to marry into clans who eat fish.

7 **PALM WINE**
YORUBA
After creating people with handicaps and illnesses while drunk on palm wine, the creator god Obàtálá forbade his followers from offering it to him again.

8 **LETTUCE**
YAZIDISM
Members of this Kurdish religion are forbidden to eat lettuce. Legends variously link this prohibition with a martyr who was pelted with lettuce, or with the word for the vegetable itself, which sounds like the name of a sacred group of angels.

10 **GARLIC**
CHINESE BUDDHISM
Chinese Buddhists widely believe that strong-flavored foods inflame the baser emotions.

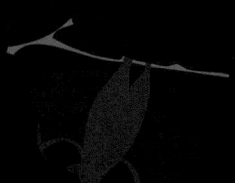

9 **BATS**
JUDAISM
Bats are not kosher, as most Jewish people believe all "flying creeping things" are unclean.

17 Acquired Tastes

1 DURIAN
INDONESIA
This tropical fruit's pungent smell has been likened to the aroma of rotting corpses. Several hotels in Southeast Asia have banned it.

2 KENTUCKY FRIED BUCHES
MEXICO
This delicacy of deep-fried chicken necks and fresh salsa on corn tortillas originated in the restaurant of a Tijuana family.

3 LOCO MOCO
US
This Hawaiian treat consists of rice topped with meat patties (often Spam, everyone's favorite ration), a fried egg, and gravy.

4 POUTINE
CANADA
Quebec's heart attack–inducing signature dish is french fries topped with fresh cheese curds and smothered in gravy.

5 TXIPIRONES EN SU TINTA
SPAIN
For this Basque dish, baby squid are cooked with onions in their own ink, creating a black, murky sauce with a velvety texture.

6 BALUT
THE PHILIPPINES
Enjoyers of *balut* eat a nearly developed chicken or duck embyro that's been boiled and served in the shell.

7 HÁKARL
ICELAND
A basking shark is buried under gravel to ferment, then hung to dry for many months, and then diced and served on toothpicks.

8 HAGGIS
SCOTLAND
A sheep's stomach is steamed and then stuffed with suet, oatmeal, spices, and organs, such as heart and liver.

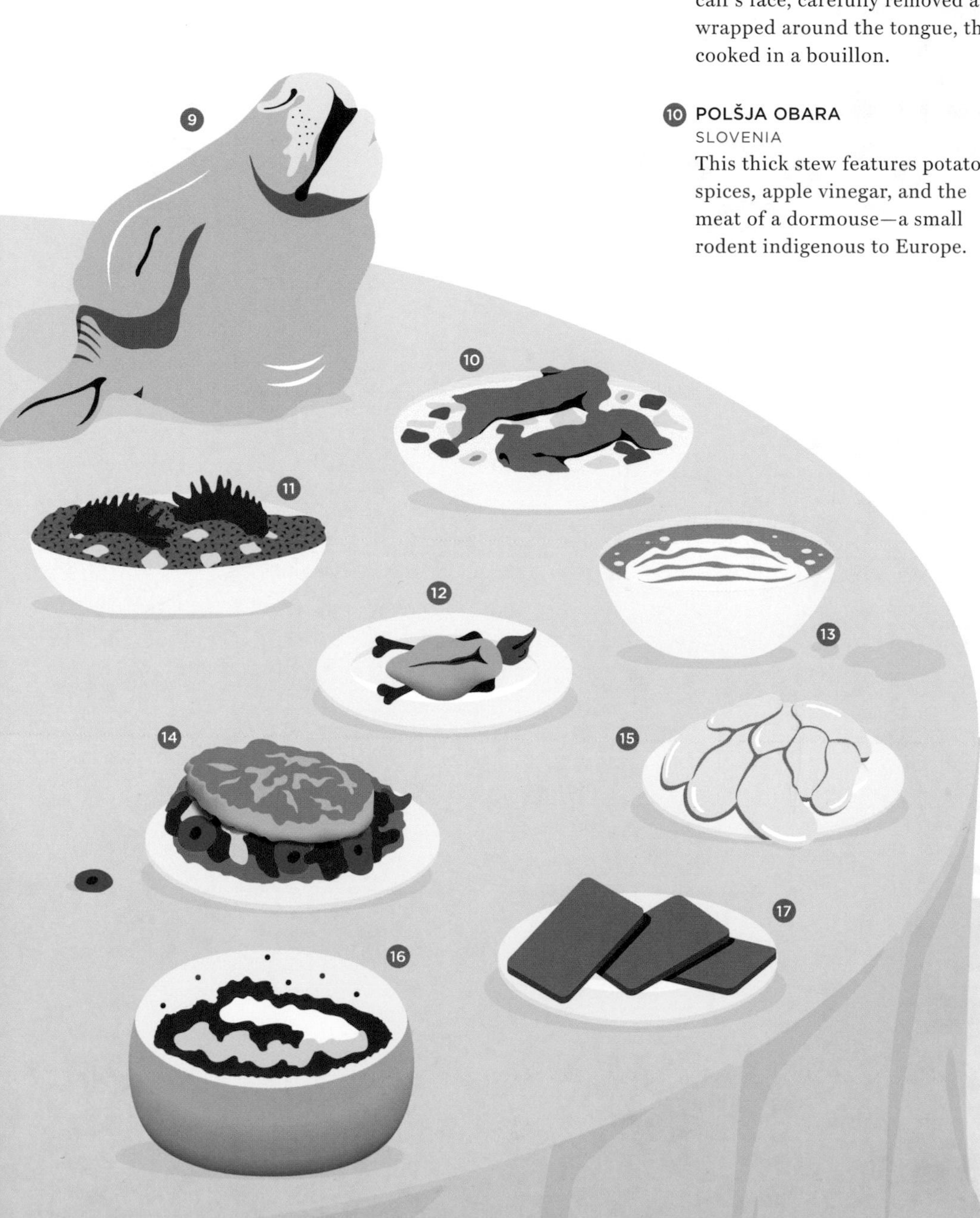

9 TÊTE DE VEAU
FRANCE
A traditional dish, it consists of a calf's face, carefully removed and wrapped around the tongue, then cooked in a bouillon.

10 POLŠJA OBARA
SLOVENIA
This thick stew features potatoes, spices, apple vinegar, and the meat of a dormouse—a small rodent indigenous to Europe.

11 CIBREO
ITALY
Catherine de Medici loved this Tuscan sauce of "extra" chicken parts: the cockscomb, testes, embryonic eggs, and other bits.

12 ORTOLAN
FRANCE
A songbird is drowned in brandy and roasted, then swallowed by a diner wearing a napkin over his head to preserve the "aromas."

13 BIRDS' NEST SOUP
CHINA
This nutritious soup is made from the dissolved nests of the swiftlet, a bird that makes its nest primarily from its own spit.

14 SEAL FLIPPER PIE
CANADA
Newfoundlanders make a traditional meat pie from the flippers of young harp seals hunted each April and May.

15 SHIRAKO
JAPAN
This popular bar food is made of cod milt—also known as "sperm." The semen of anglerfish or puffer fish will also do in a pinch.

16 CASU MARZU
ITALY
The people of Sardinia enjoy this sheep's milk cheese, which is largely rotten and includes live insect larvae for flavor.

17 SCRAPPLE
US
All the parts of a pig not sold or used in other ways are mushed with cornmeal and seasonings to make this semisolid loaf.

15 SUPERFOODS THAT MAY NOT BE SUPER

1 COFFEE

PROS
- Rich in antioxidants
- Reduces risk of Parkinson's disease
- Can improve mental performance

CONS
- Heavy consumption elevates bad cholesterol levels
- May cause difficulty sleeping
- Mild diuretic

2 REFINED SUGAR

PROS
- Better than high-fructose corn syrup
- Can increase energy

CONS
- Refining process adds unhealthy additives
- Habit-forming
- Leading cause of dental deterioration

3 WINE

PROS
- Contains antioxidants

CONS
- Raises blood pressure
- May cause damage to organs

4 SOYBEANS

PROS
- Can lower blood cholesterol
- Good source of protein
- Often high in fiber

CONS
- Difficult to digest
- May affect fertility in men
- Can disrupt thyroid function

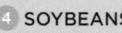

5 CHOCOLATE

PROS
- Rich in antioxidants
- Releases feel-good neurochemicals

CONS
- Packs a lot of calories
- Contains lots of sugar

6 WHEAT

PROS
- High in minerals
- Low in fat
- Good source of fiber

CONS
- Common allergy trigger
- Elevates blood sugar
- Causes celiac disease, which can lead to cancer

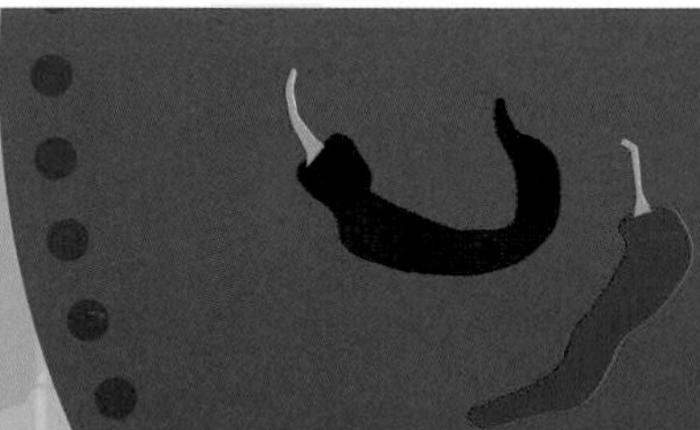

7 SPICY FOODS

PROS
- Can help burn calories
- May aid in reducing cholesterol

CONS
- Too much can cause oral ulcers
- Increased heat in body can cause skin conditions to flare up

8 **OLIVE OIL**
PROS
- Heart-healthy
- Low in cholesterol

CONS
- High in calories
- Not all varieties carry health benefits
- Water used in modern processing may wash away nutrients

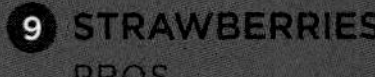

9 **STRAWBERRIES**
PROS
- Low in calories
- High in antioxidants
- Great source of many vitamins and minerals

CONS
- Common vector for deadly *E. coli*
- One of the most allergenic fruits

10 **EGGS**
PROS
- Good source of protein

CONS
- High in cholesterol
- Can carry salmonella

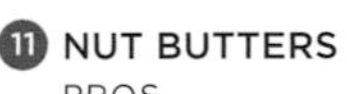

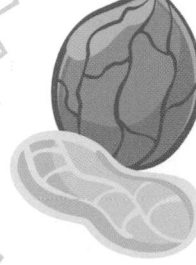

11 **NUT BUTTERS**
PROS
- High in protein
- Low in cholesterol
- Good source of niacin and manganese

CONS
- Very high in calories
- May trigger deadly allergies
- Often high in sodium
- May have added sugars

12 **ENERGY BAR**
PROS
- Packed with protein and fiber
- Easily digested
- Good source of vitamins and minerals

CONS
- Very high in sugar
- High in calories
- Often more protein than the average person needs

13 **FISH**
PROS
- Great source of protein
- Contains essential fatty acids
- Low in fat

CONS
- May be high in mercury
- Possibly tainted by water pollution

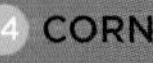

14 **CORN**
PROS
- Good amount of fiber
- High in nutrients

CONS
- Contains loads of starch
- Hard for body to digest

15 **BEEF**
PROS
- A great source of iron
- Full of protein

CONS
- High in fat
- Full of hormones

UNLIKELY INTOXICANTS

1 **URINE**
RUSSIA
To induce visions, Siberian shamans would drink the urine of a person who had eaten fly agaric mushrooms.

2 **PRUNO**
PRISONS WORLDWIDE
Inmates make this alcoholic concoction from ketchup, sugar packets, and fermented fruit, all left to rot in a bag.

3 **TOADS**
WORLDWIDE
Bufotoxin, a compound found in the skins of a number of toad species, can give rise to hallucinations when licked or smoked.

4 **SARPA SALPA**
MEDITERRANEAN
Eating the head of this fish can cause psychotropic effects; one consumer reportedly hallucinated for 36 hours.

5 **COUGH SYRUP**
WORLDWIDE
A number of commonly available cold and cough remedies can produce euphoria when consumed in large quantities.

6 **SALAMANDER BRANDY**
SLOVENIA
This party punch mixes brandy with salamander venom—which also happens to be a hallucinogenic aphrodisiac.

7 **HYGIENE PRODUCTS**
WORLDWIDE
When alcohol is unavailable, some addicts turn to aftershave, perfume, and mouthwash to get their fix.

8 **IODEX SANDWICH**
INDIA
This sandwich made of medicated muscle rub contains morphine and induces a narcotic state. And tastes disgusting.

9 **LIZARD TAILS**
INDIA
Cheap-high seekers capture common lizards, remove their tails, burn them, mix the powder with tobacco, and light up.

10 **STILTON CHEESE**
UK
Participants in a sleep study reported visions after eating 0.7 ounces (20 g) of Stilton.

11 **SNAKE VENOM**
INDIA
Getting bitten on the tongue by certain snakes will induce an epic euphoric experience.

12 **SOUND**
INTERNET
"I-dosing" is a supposed "digital high" obtained by listening to trippy, droning audio tracks.

13 **JENKEM**
ZAMBIA
It's rumored that some street children get high off the fumes of fermented human feces.

14 **NUTMEG**
WORLDWIDE
High doses of this spice produce mild hallucinations for up to several days, plus nausea and rapid heartbeats.

15 **CHANG'AA**
KENYA
This illegal brew of maize and sorghum is often cut with jet fuel to increase its potency. Its name means "kill me quick."

57

INTERESTING POTATO CHIP FLAVORS

LAMB AND MINT
UK

STEAK AND ONION
UK

CHESAPEAKE CRAB
US

TANDOORI CHICKEN
UK

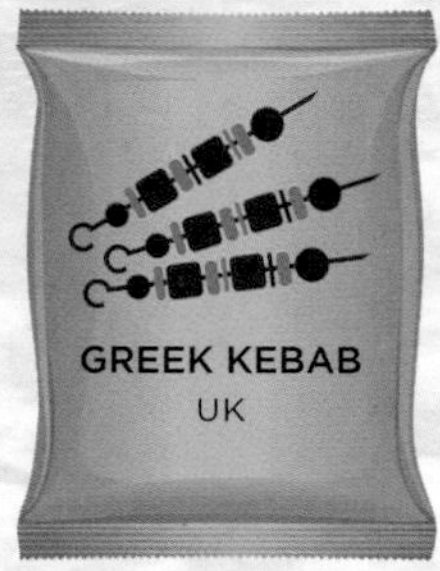
GREEK KEBAB
UK

BBQ KANGAROO
UK

SMOKED SALMON AND CAPERS
NEW ZEALAND

RED CAVIAR
RUSSIA

SPICY CHILI SQUID
THAILAND

SALMON SUSHI
AUSTRALIA

CUTTLEFISH
KOREA

PATAGONIAN LAMB
ARGENTINA

CHEESE CURRY
JAPAN

CREAM CROQUETTE
JAPAN

CHEDDAR BEER
US

KETCHUP
UK

MINT
UK

GARAM MASALA
JAPAN

WORCESTERSHIRE SAUCE
UK

SPICY THAI
AUSTRALIA

BLACK OLIVE AND GARLIC
UK

CILANTRO
AUSTRALIA

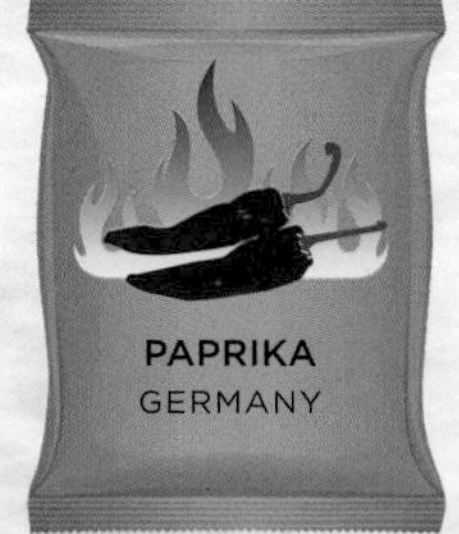
PAPRIKA
GERMANY

KIWI
CHINA

KIMCHI
JAPAN

BLUEBERRY
CHINA

BBQ CORN
JAPAN

PRAWN COCKTAIL
UK

MAYO HAM
IRELAND

CRISPY DUCK AND HOISIN
UK

CAJUN SQUIRREL
UK

TURKEY
USA

CONSOMMÉ
JAPAN

HOT AND SOUR FISH SOUP
CHINA

SAUSAGE AND TOMATO
UK

HAMBURGER
US

GRILLED LOBSTER
THAILAND

TONKATSU (FRIED PORK)
JAPAN

SCOTTISH HAGGIS
UK

PIZZA
JAPAN

POUTINE
CANADA

TZATZIKI
URUGUAY

AMERICAN STYLE CREAM 'N' ONION
PAKISTAN

SEAWEED AND SALT
JAPAN

SWEET CHILE AND RED PEPPER
IRELAND

BLACK PEPPER AND GINGER
UK

MARMITE
UK

MISO
JAPAN

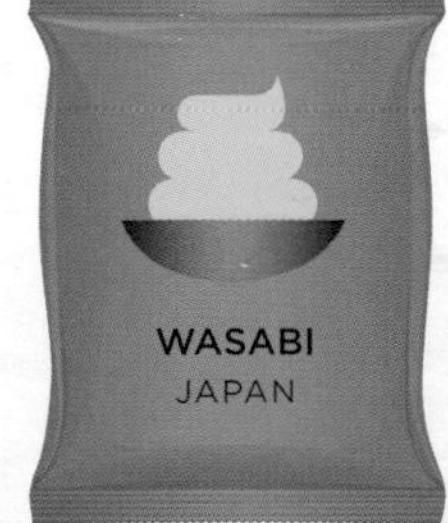
WASABI
JAPAN

CAESAR SALAD
JAPAN

CURRY AND GINGER
JAPAN

DILL PICKLE
US

CHILE AND CHOCOLATE
UK

CUCUMBER
BELGIUM

CHEESECAKE
JAPAN

MARGARITA AND SALT
US

BLOODY MARY
US

13 FAD DIETS

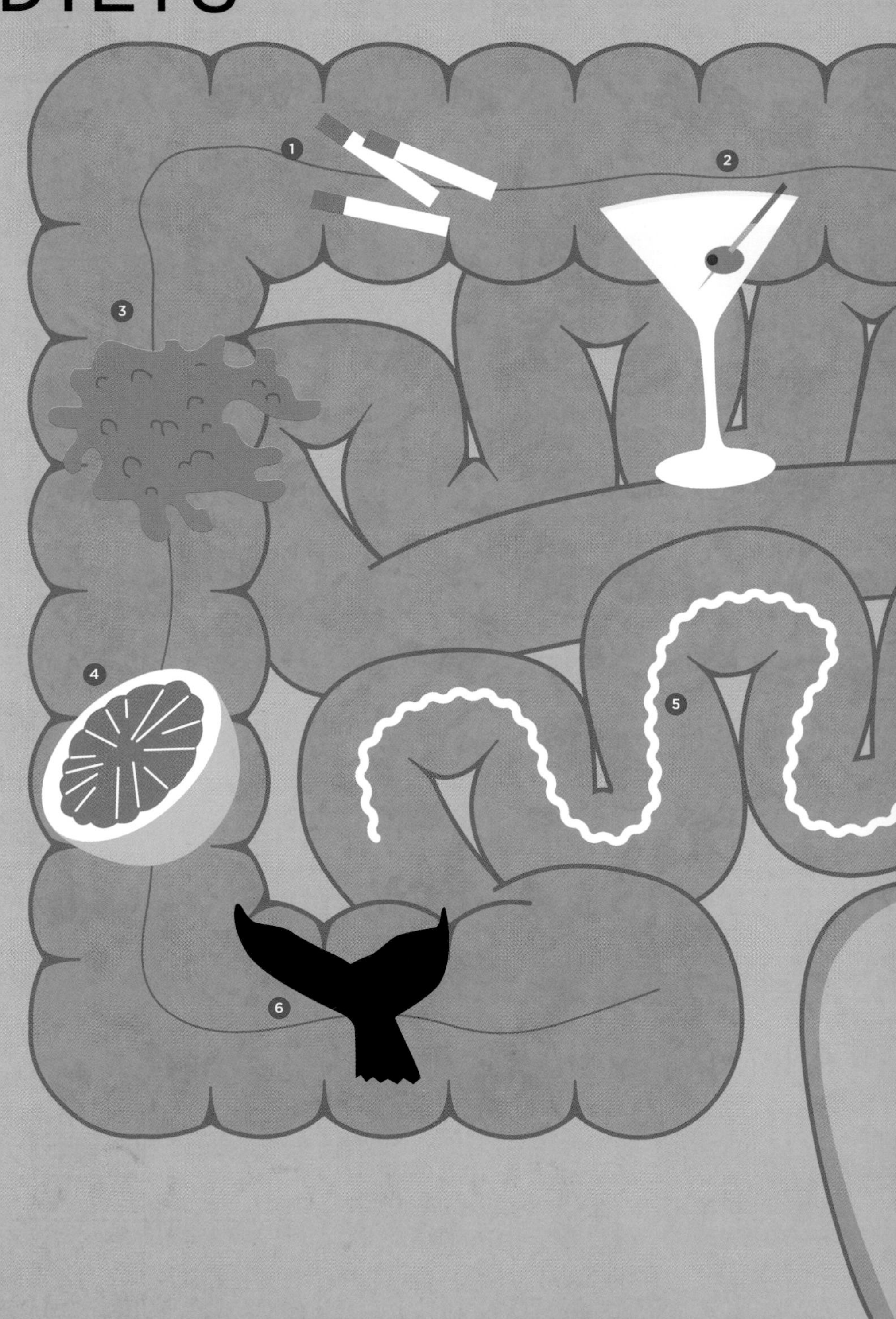

1 **CIGARETTE DIET**
Lucky Strike touted nicotine's appetite-curbing nature with the 1930s slogan "Reach for a Lucky instead of a Sweet," which boosted its sales, annoyed the candy industry, and hooked kids on cigs.

2 **DRINKING MAN'S DIET**
First introduced in 1964, this diet's success hinges on drinking alcohol to quell hunger. It restricts carbohydrates and calls for lots of "manly" protein, but really it's all about the martinis.

3 **FLETCHER DIET**
In 1906, Dr. Horace Fletcher ("The Great Masticator") claimed that chewing all food (even liquids!) 32 times per mouthful aided digestion and led to trimmer waists. The tactic was christened "fletcherizing."

4 **SCARSDALE MEDICAL DIET**
The Scarsdale Medical Diet specifies a strict plan of 850 to 1200 calories per day for about a month. Essential to the diet is a daily breakfast of grapefruit. It went out of vogue in the late 1970s.

5 **SANITIZED TAPEWORM DIET**
It's rumored that in the early 1900s, some figure-mindful women ingested "sanitized tapeworms" to eat up excess calories. The pounds just dropped off while the worm, well, just got bigger.

6 **INUIT DIET**
Native peoples in the Arctic live on a diet of caribou, raw fish, and whale blubber—a protein-rich yet low-cholesterol regimen. The rest of the world was only briefly enamored of this diet in the 1930s.

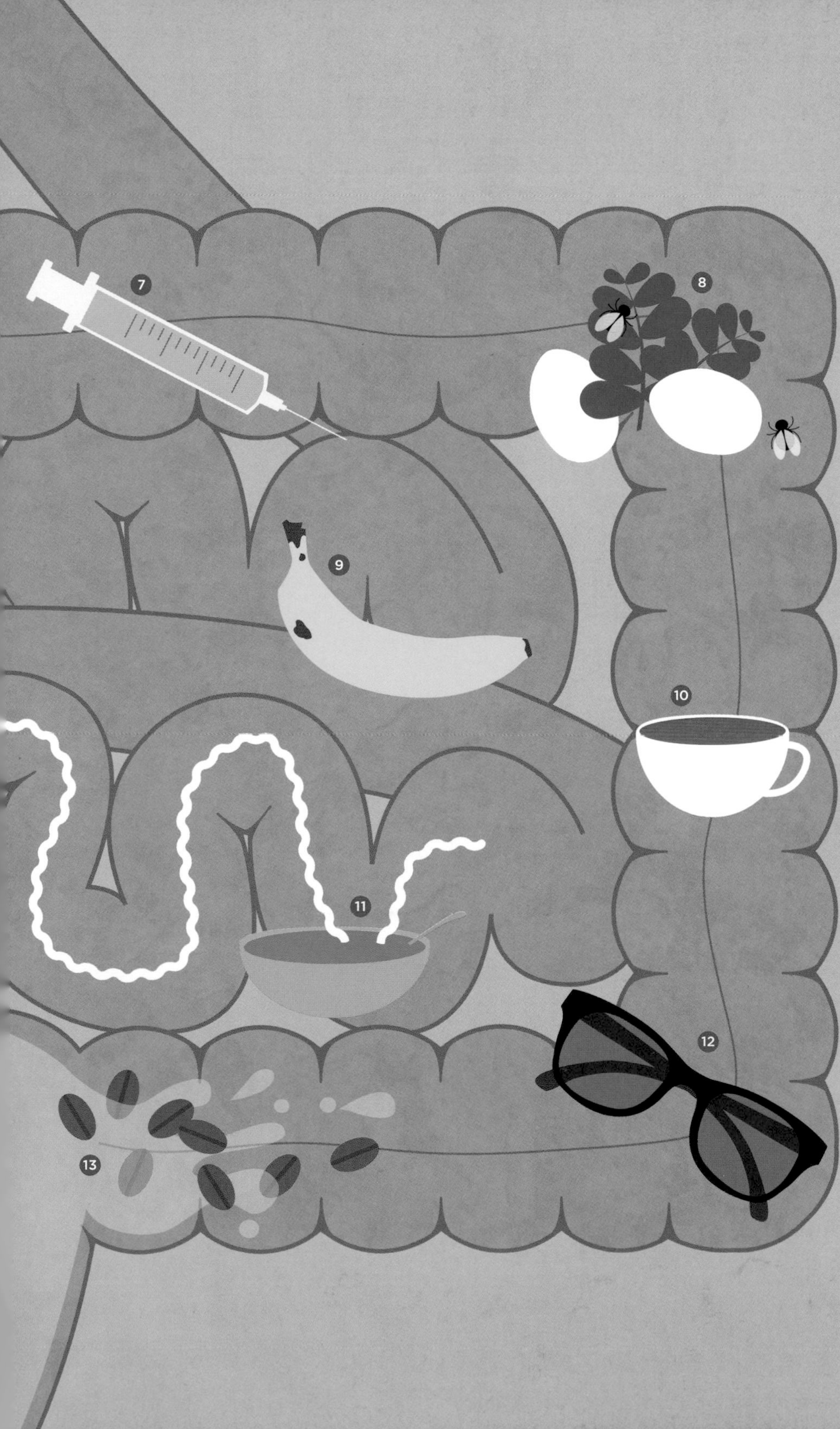

7 HCG DIET
Eat a mere 500 calories a day and undergo injections of the hormone human chorionic gonadotropin (hCG), which is produced by women in early pregnancy. Doctors are still weighing the pros and cons of this recent fad.

8 PALEOLITHIC DIET
"Caveman" dieters eat only foods that can be hunted or gathered, such as meat, seafood, eggs, insects, fruit, nuts, seeds, vegetables, and herbs—no dairy, grains, or processed foods. This diet took off in the 1970s.

9 MORNING BANANA DIET
This diet recently originated in Japan, where it caused a banana shortage. Dieters eat as many bananas as they want for breakfast, and then whatever they like for lunch and dinner—as long as they skip dessert.

10 ISRAELI ARMY DIET
This eight-day regimen was popular in the 1970s and consists of two days eating only apples (plus as much black coffee as desired), then two eating nothing but cheese, two of chicken, and finally two days of salad.

11 CABBAGE SOUP DIET
Basically a modified fast that found followers in the 1980s, the cabbage soup diet is just what it sounds like: Participants eat as many bowls of cabbage soup as they want a day. It causes rapid but unsustainable weight loss.

12 BLUE SUNGLASSES DIET
This diet isn't so bad that you'd actually be advised to ingest eyewear. Since the mid-2000s, some dieters have worn blue-tinted shades, which make food look unappetizing and help people eat less.

13 GERSON THERAPY
This plan was developed in the 1920s as an alternative treatment for cancer patients. Dieters eat raw plant-based meals and organic juices every hour—plus perform enemas with coffee or castor oil.

12 NATIONS' FAVORITE HOT DOG TOPPINGS

1 US
- Mustard
- Ketchup
- Chopped onions
- Relish

2 GUATEMALA
- Various extra meats
- Boiled cabbage
- Guacamole
- Tomato sauce
- Mayonnaise

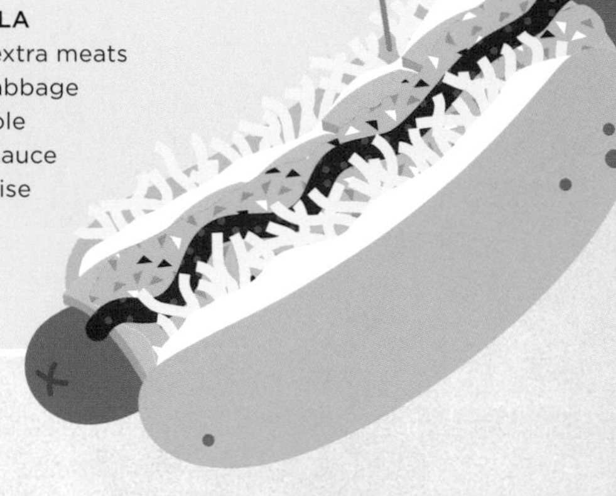

3 CANADA
- Bolognese sauce
- Chopped onions
- Mustard

4 BRAZIL
- Boiled quail eggs
- Corn niblets
- Canned peas
- Mashed potatoes
- French fries

5 CHILE
- Guacamole
- Tomato
- Mayonnaise
- Sauerkraut

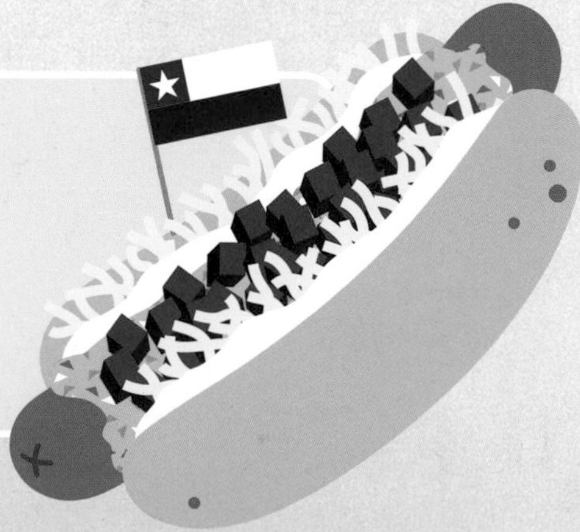

6 MEXICO
- Fried onions
- Bacon
- Chiles
- Beans
- Guacamole
- Cheese
- Salsa

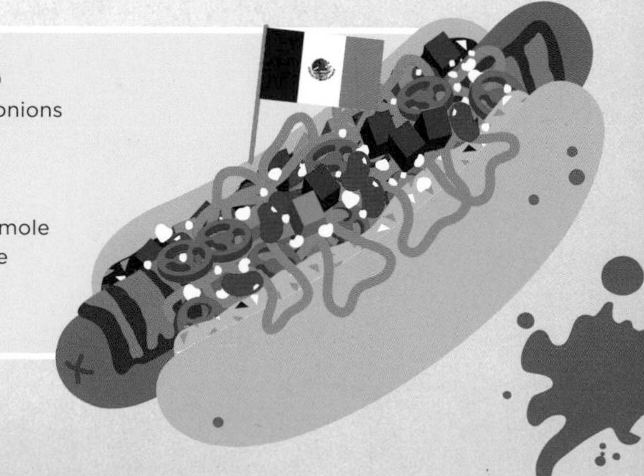

I'LL HAVE THE WORKS, PLEASE

Hot dogs date back to 13th-century Frankfurt, Germany, where the original frank-on-a-bun was served to celebrate coronations. Nowadays, every country has at least one variation on this street-food theme, and, of course, really anything goes.

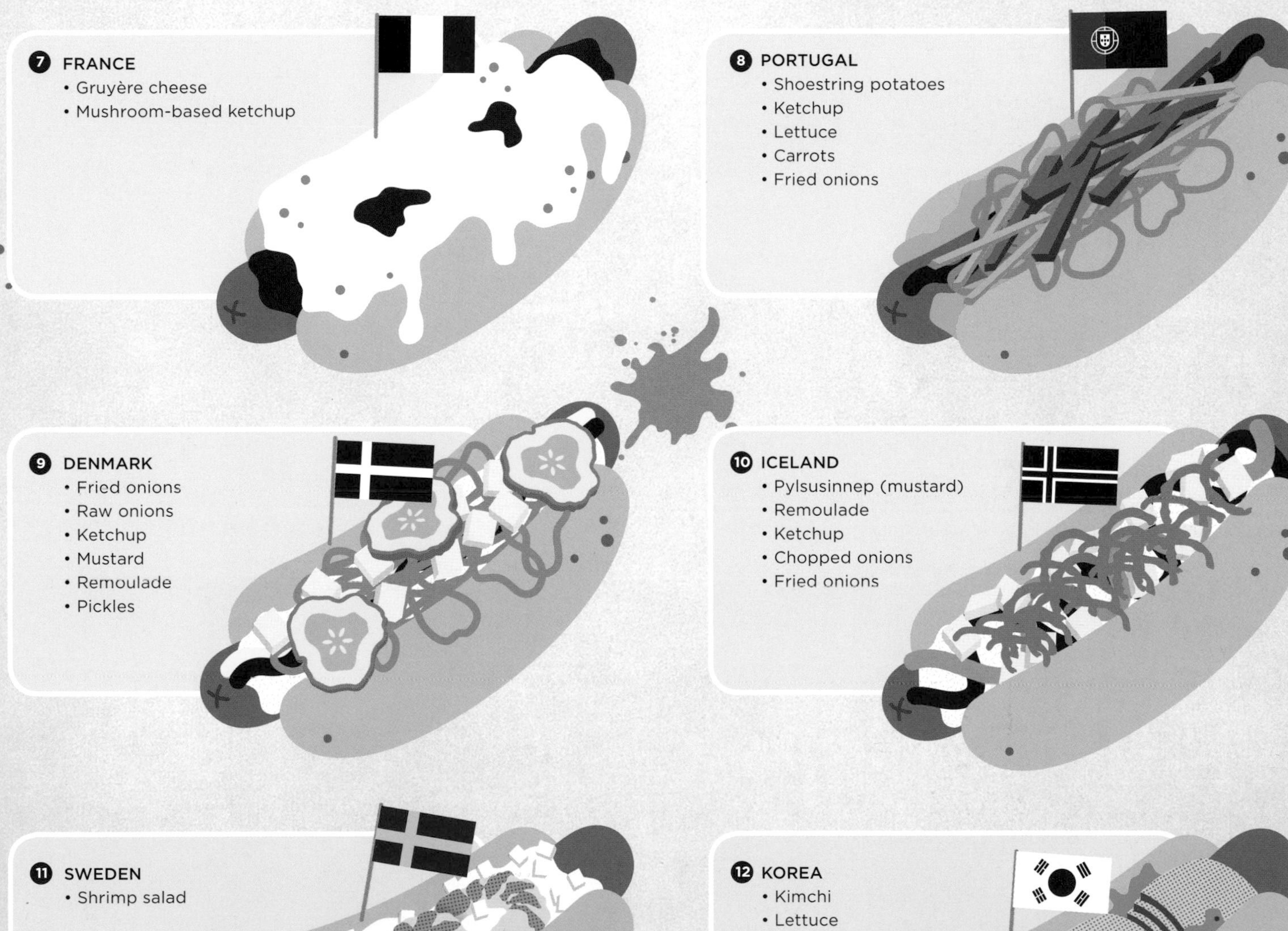

14 AGED FOODS

6 GUNDRUK
NEPAL / 5-7 DAYS
This dish of fermented shredded leafy greens and spices often appears as a side dish and it's a highly popular source of minerals.

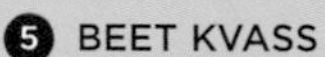

5 BEET KVASS
EASTERN EUROPE / SEVERAL DAYS
Lauded for its nourishing and energizing powers, beet kvass is a drink made of fermented water, beets, salt, and whey.

4 POI
HAWAII AND POLYNESIA / 3 DAYS
A staple in Polynesian diets, poi is a taro tuber that's been mashed to a near liquid state, then mixed with milk and sugar and allowed to ferment.

3 SAUERKRAUT
POLAND AND GERMANY
3 DAYS-SEVERAL MONTHS
This side dish's name means "sour cabbage" in German—it's shredded cabbage and salt left to ferment below 60°F (15°C).

2 KIMCHI
KOREA / 3 DAYS-SEVERAL MONTHS
This dish consists of fermented cabbage and salt, plus any number of spices. Fermentation takes as little as three days, but kimchi was formerly buried underground for months to age it at the right temperature.

1 YOGURT
WORLDWIDE / SEVERAL HOURS
This creamy dairy product is created when milk is heated to about 80°F (27°C), cooled, and then fermented with a bacteria culture.

7 KOMBUCHA

WORLDWIDE / 1–2 WEEKS

A solid chunk of bacteria and yeast—referred to as "the mother"—transforms basic tea into what's considered a highly medicinal drink.

8 PRUNES

WORLDWIDE / 10 DAYS

Dried plums are fermented in a water-and-fruit-juice mixture and used as a condiment (and eaten for constipation relief).

9 PIDAN

CHINA / SEVERAL WEEKS–SEVERAL MONTHS

Duck, chicken, or quail eggs are preserved in a mixture of clay, ash, salt, lime, and rice hulls. This creates an amber-colored, jelly-like white and a dark, creamy yolk.

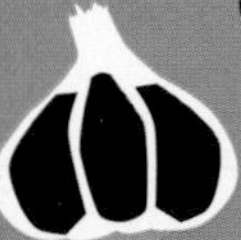

10 BLACK GARLIC

KOREA / 40 DAYS

Whole bulbs of garlic are fermented at a high temperature, blackening the cloves and making them taste sweet and syrupy.

11 MISO

JAPAN / 6 MONTHS–3 YEARS

Rice, barley, and soybeans are aged and fermented, then mixed with fungus. It's used in soups and salad dressings.

12 WINE

WORLDWIDE / 1 YEAR–SEVERAL DECADES

Possibly the most beloved aged food, wine is made of fermented grapes and various strains of yeast, which turn grape sugar into alcohol.

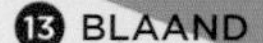

13 BLAAND

SCOTLAND / 1 YEAR

The recipe for this ancient Scottish drink of alcoholic fermented whey varied from family to family. No record of the official process exists; however, a Scottish cheese-maker has developed his own recipe, and it's said to be making a comeback.

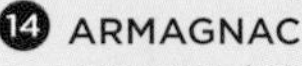

14 ARMAGNAC

FRANCE / 13–15 YEARS

Once consumed for its medicinal benefits, this brandy is distilled from grapes and then allowed to ferment.

10 POISONS WE EAT ANYWAY

1 FUGU
PUFFER FISH / JAPAN
Prepared incorrectly, this fish is deadly. Prepared correctly, its flesh contains just enough of poisonous tetrodotoxin to give diners a bit of a tingle. It is usually served as sashimi, as the toxin is mainly in the organs.

2 CASSAVA
ROOT VEGETABLE / AFRICA AND SOUTH AMERICA
Although cassava is one of the world's main sources of carbohydrates, cyanide compounds in the root make it poisonous. It must undergo a rigorous process to be made safe for eating.

3 TOMATOES
FRUIT / WORLDWIDE
The leaves, stems, and (to a very small degree) unripened flesh of tomatoes contain toxins. In large quantities, these poisons can cause coma or death—but go ahead, put a slice or two on your sandwich.

4 BITTER ALMONDS
SEEDS / WORLDWIDE
Each almond tree yields a few bitter almonds, which are broader and shorter than the sweet almonds that we enjoy. These almonds contain trace amounts of cyanide; they're so deadly that selling them is illegal in some places.

5 NUTMEG
SEEDPOD / WORLDWIDE
The hallucinations caused by eating pure nutmeg just aren't worth it, kids: Large doses of raw nutmeg send your nervous system into overdrive and can cause death.

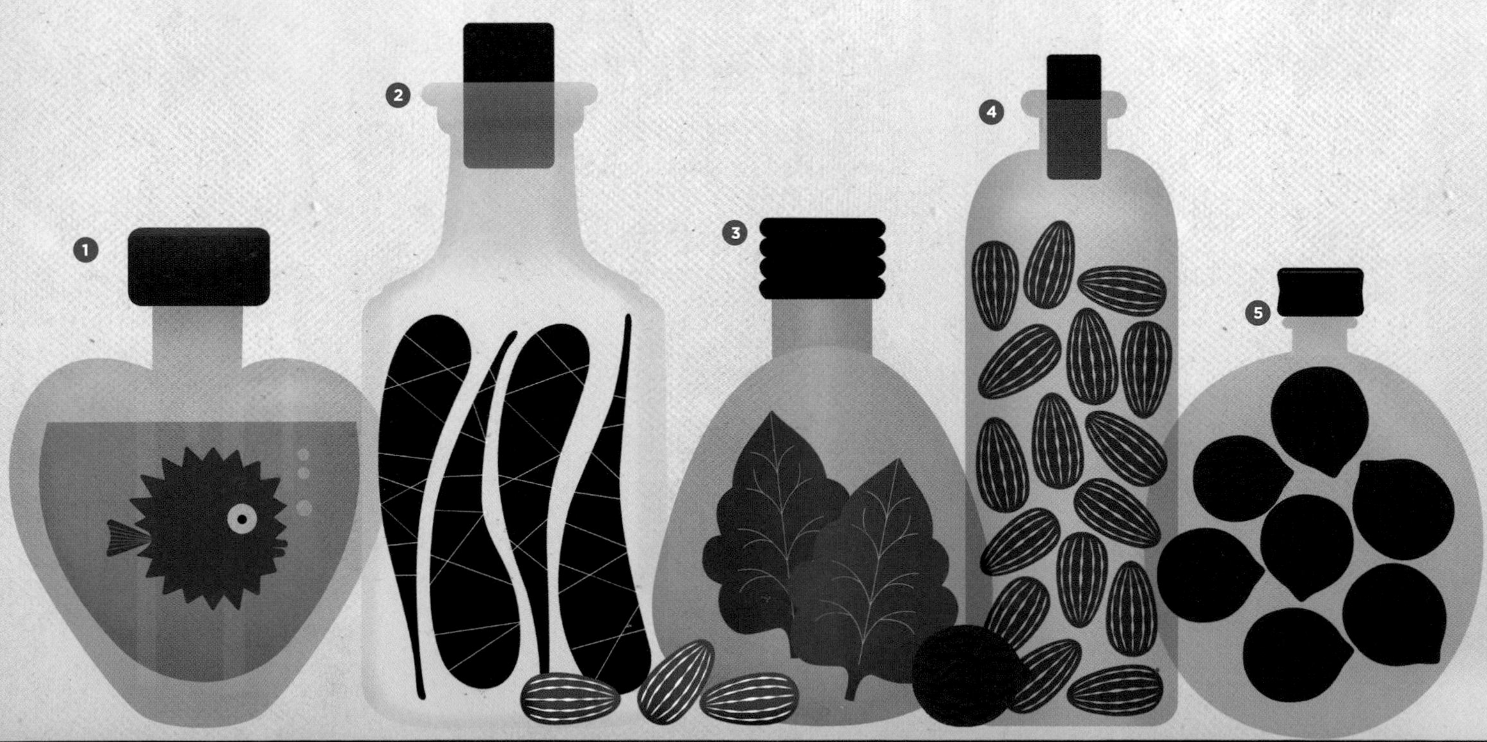

NAME YOUR POISON

It's true: Some of the world's dietary staples are actually toxic in large enough quantities, or when prepared in an unseemly fashion. But rest assured, the commonly consumed foods on this list—like tomatoes and apples—are safe to eat in moderation (which is why we do eat them, and often). The biggest exception is the fugu fish; you're on your own, should you dare try that.

6 SASSAFRAS

BARK / US AND EAST ASIA

This tree bark has been used since antiquity, usually as a painkiller, an insect repellent, or a scent in soaps. It was briefly banned in the United States for containing the carcinogen safrole, but a safe extract is now available.

7 SWISS CHEESE

CHEESE / WORLDWIDE

While this is a rare occurrence, Swiss cheese can be high in histamines (created by pesky bacteria during the cheese-making process), which may lead to rashes and nausea.

8 APPLE SEEDS

FRUIT / WORLDWIDE

Apple pips—that's agriculture speak for "seeds"—contain cyanide, but the amount in a single fruit won't kill a person. Still, don't sit back and pop them like sunflower seeds, as it is possible to ingest a fatal dose.

9 INDIAN PEA

LEGUME / EUROPE, ASIA, AND AFRICA

This pea is easy to grow, making it an attractive food source during a drought. Unfortunately, it contains a nasty neurotoxin, and steady consumption over a long period can result in paralysis and brain damage.

10 CHILES

FRUIT / WORLDWIDE

Some may like it hot, but extremely high, truly over-the-top levels of capsaicin (the stuff that makes chiles fiery to the tongue) can actually cause illness and even death.

15 CURIOUS CANNIBALS

MARCO EVARISTTI 1
CHILE / 2007
In an act of performance art, the artist fed dinner-party guests pasta topped with a meatball made of his own fat (which had been removed via liposuction).

FORE 2
PAPUA NEW GUINEA / 1800s–1950s
The remote Fore people practiced ritual cannibalism as a funeral rite to honor the dead. The tradition was banned in the 1950s, at about the same time a kuru epidemic began to greatly reduce the tribe's numbers. (Kuru is a brain disease spread by eating inflected flesh.)

ARMIN MEIWES 3
GERMANY / 2001
Armin Meiwes posted an ad on the Internet, lookifg for a man willing to participate in a sex game of slaughter and cannibalism. He succeeded in finding his "victim." The details aren't fit for print.

4 **DONNER PARTY**
US / 1846–1847
A group of pioneers set out for California, only to get trapped in the Sierra Nevada mountains during a harsh winter. They ate those in their group who starved, but refrained from eating their own family members.

5 **ISSEI SAGAWA**
FRANCE / 1981
University student Sagawa considered himself weak and ugly, and set out to eat a strong, beautiful woman to gain her qualities. He invited a classmate over, shot her, and ate her flesh.

6 **CAMBODIAN TROOPS**
CAMBODIA / 1960s
There were reports that soldiers in Southeast Asia in the 1960s and 1970s sometimes ate parts of dead enemy soldiers, such as the liver.

7 **URUGUAYAN FLIGHT 571**
CHILE / 1972
A flight carrying 45 passengers crashed in a remote location in the Andes; until they were rescued, survivors resorted to eating the bodies of those who perished.

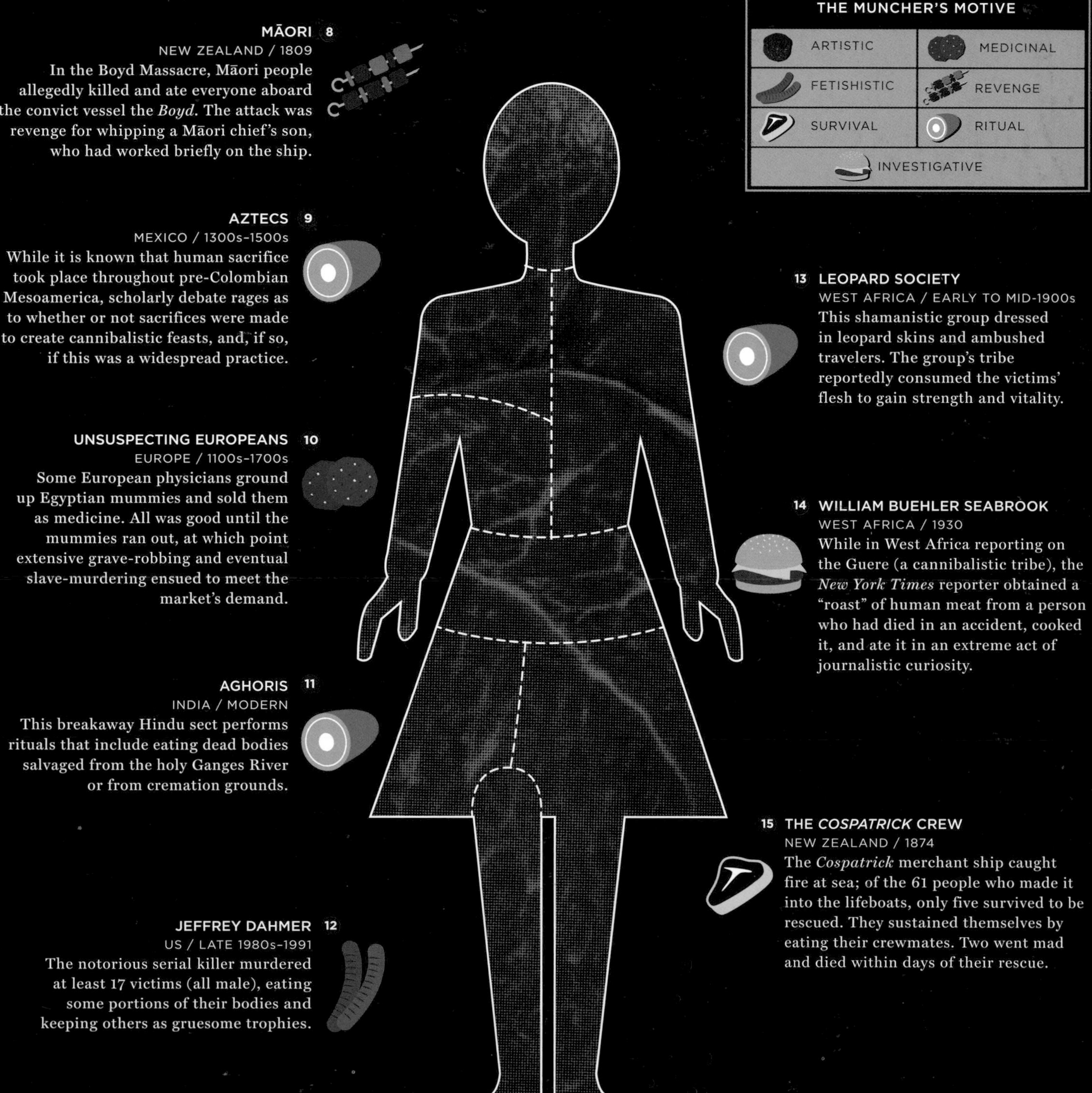
THE MUNCHER'S MOTIVE
ARTISTIC
MEDICINAL
FETISHISTIC
REVENGE
SURVIVAL
RITUAL
INVESTIGATIVE
MĀORI 8
NEW ZEALAND / 1809
In the Boyd Massacre, Māori people allegedly killed and ate everyone aboard the convict vessel the Boyd. The attack was revenge for whipping a Māori chief's son, who had worked briefly on the ship.
AZTECS 9
MEXICO / 1300s-1500s
While it is known that human sacrifice took place throughout pre-Colombian Mesoamerica, scholarly debate rages as to whether or not sacrifices were made to create cannibalistic feasts, and, if so, if this was a widespread practice.
UNSUSPECTING EUROPEANS 10
EUROPE / 1100s-1700s
Some European physicians ground up Egyptian mummies and sold them as medicine. All was good until the mummies ran out, at which point extensive grave-robbing and eventual slave-murdering ensued to meet the market's demand.
AGHORIS 11
INDIA / MODERN
This breakaway Hindu sect performs rituals that include eating dead bodies salvaged from the holy Ganges River or from cremation grounds.
JEFFREY DAHMER 12
US / LATE 1980s-1991
The notorious serial killer murdered at least 17 victims (all male), eating some portions of their bodies and keeping others as gruesome trophies.
13 LEOPARD SOCIETY
WEST AFRICA / EARLY TO MID-1900s
This shamanistic group dressed in leopard skins and ambushed travelers. The group's tribe reportedly consumed the victims' flesh to gain strength and vitality.
14 WILLIAM BUEHLER SEABROOK
WEST AFRICA / 1930
While in West Africa reporting on the Guere (a cannibalistic tribe), the New York Times reporter obtained a "roast" of human meat from a person who had died in an accident, cooked it, and ate it in an extreme act of journalistic curiosity.
15 THE COSPATRICK CREW
NEW ZEALAND / 1874
The Cospatrick merchant ship caught fire at sea; of the 61 people who made it into the lifeboats, only five survived to be rescued. They sustained themselves by eating their crewmates. Two went mad and died within days of their rescue.

21 FICTIONAL FOODS AND BEVERAGES

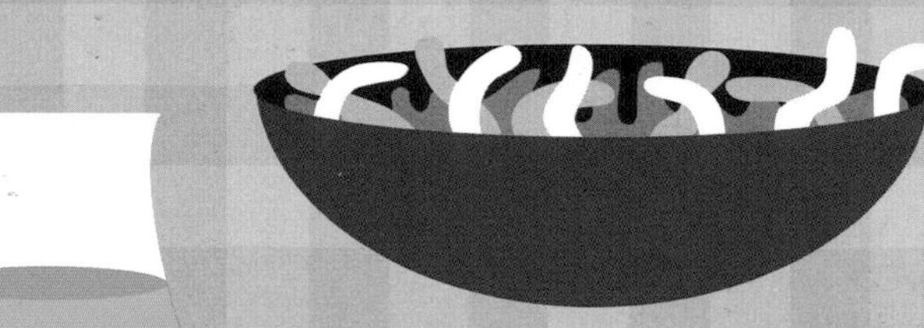

1 SPOO
BABYLON 5
These small, white, pasty, and worm-like creatures were generally regarded as the galaxy's ugliest, but most delicious, animals.

2 SCOOBY SNACKS
SCOOBY DOO
These dog treats are used to incentivize cartoon canine Scooby Doo.

3 BANTHA MILK
STAR WARS
The blue milk from a female bantha, this dairy product is an intergalactic favorite.

4 "DRINK ME" POTION AND "EAT ME" CAKE
ALICE'S ADVENTURES IN WONDERLAND
The drink makes you quite lilliputian, while the cake turns you into a giant.

5 BRAWNDO
IDIOCRACY
This sports drink with a killer marketing campaign "replaces water everywhere."

6 VITAMEATAVEGAMIN
I LOVE LUCY
This tonic was said to contain "vitamins, meat, vegetables, and minerals," but booze is really the secret ingredient.

7 ROMULAN ALE
STAR TREK
The only alcohol that gets Klingons drunk, it's banned under Federation law. Also, it's blue.

8 SLURM
FUTURAMA
This popular, highly addictive soft drink is secreted by a giant worm queen.

9 TOMACCO
THE SIMPSONS
Homer Simpson creates this hybrid between tomatoes and tobacco when he uses plutonium as a fertilizer.

10 EVERLASTING GOBSTOPPERS
CHARLIE AND THE CHOCOLATE FACTORY
Characters with an insatiable sweet tooth were encouraged to "suck on this candy forever," but not to bite it and risk breaking a tooth.

11 LEMBAS
LORD OF THE RINGS
Baked by elves, these thin loaves are wrapped in leaves and carried on long journeys. The elves rarely share a slice—much less the recipe—with non-elves.

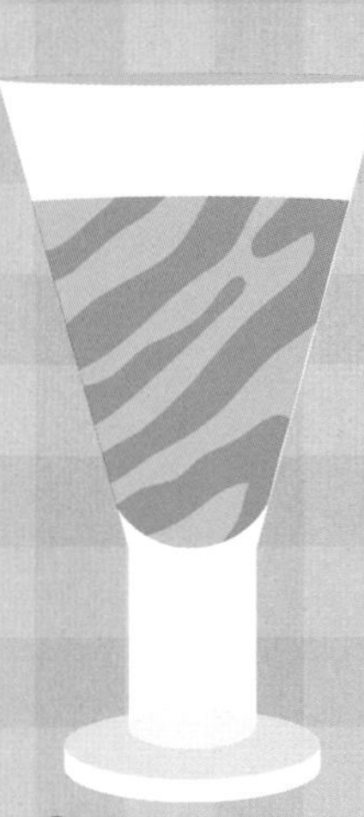

14 ROAST BEAST
THE GRINCH WHO STOLE CHRISTMAS
The mainstay of the cartoon classic's holiday meal is a mysterious though evidently succulent creature.

13 PAN-GALACTIC GARGLE BLASTER
THE HITCHHIKER'S GUIDE TO THE GALAXY
Drinking this highly caustic cocktail "is like having your brain smashed out by a slice of lemon wrapped around a large gold brick."

12 AMBROSIA
GREEK MYTHOLOGY
A thick golden honey, ambrosia imbues the imbiber with ageless immortality.

15 SLIG
DUNE
This genetically engineered cross between a large slug and a pig earns the title of the "sweetest meat this side of heaven."

16 SUBTRACTION STEW
THE PHANTOM TOLLBOOTH
Paradoxically, every bite of this soup makes the diner hungrier and hungrier.

17 MOLOKO PLUS
A CLOCKWORK ORANGE
Drinking this milk cocktail with various added drugs prepares indulgers for "ultraviolence."

18 KRABBY PATTY
SPONGEBOB SQUAREPANTS
The burger-like patty recipe is a closely guarded secret. It is perhaps made of crab.

19 BUTTERBEER
HARRY POTTER
Even young wizards can handle this slightly alcoholic, butterscotch-flavored drink that can be served cold or hot.

20 SCHMOO
LI'L ABNER
This delicious and accommodating beast will happily jump into a frying pan if a human looks hungry.

21 SOYLENT GREEN
SOYLENT GREEN
These green cracker-like wafers are actually made of human flesh.

20 STUFFED DOUGHS

1 PIEROGI
POLAND

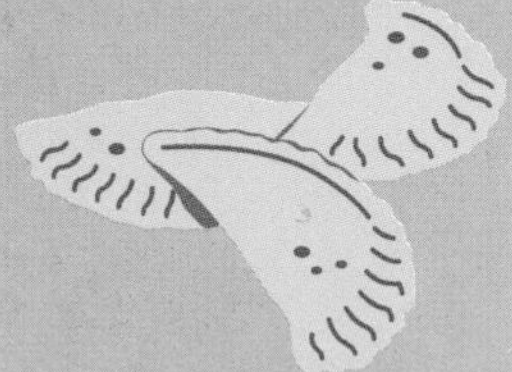

- Mashed potatoes
- Cheese
- Cabbage
- Sauerkraut
- Meat
- Mushrooms
- Spinach or fruit

2 KIBBE
LEBANON

- Minced beef
- Minced lamb

3 CHA SIU BAAU
CHINA

- Pork

4 CALZONE
ITALY

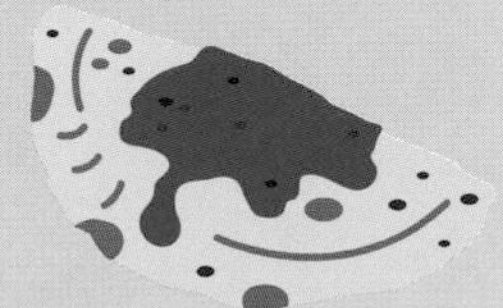

- Tomato sauce
- Mozzarella
- Other traditional pizza toppings

5 PASTY
UK

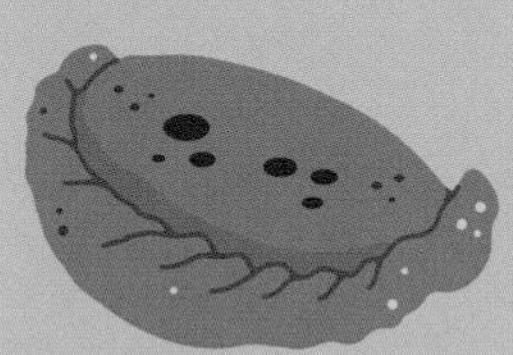

- Beef
- Sliced potato
- Turnip
- Onion
- Other vegetables

6 KARĒ PAN
JAPAN

- Curried meat
- Vegetables

7 ROTI
MALAYSIA

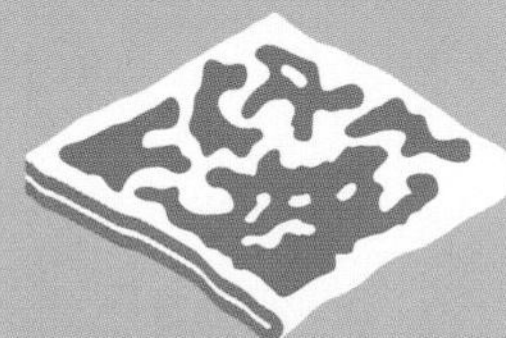

- Pork
- Caramelized onions
- Chinese sausage

8 MASALA KULCHA
INDIA

- Mashed potatoes

9 ALOO PIE
TRINIDAD

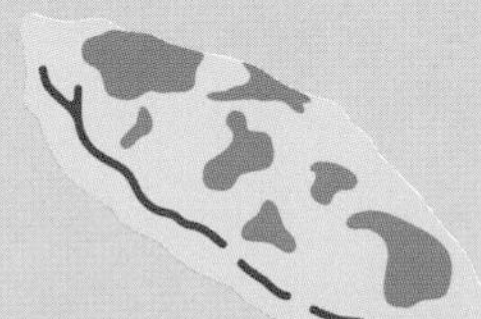

- Mashed potatoes
- Various vegetables, notably peas

10 EMPANADA
SPAIN AND PORTUGAL

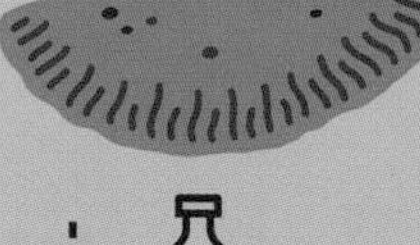

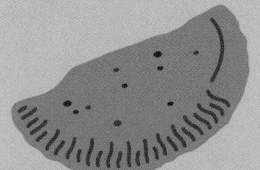

- Wide range of meats
- Vegetables

THE BEST THING SINCE SLICED BREAD

. . . just may be stuffed bread, a dough filled with treats then heated to gooey-on-the-inside perfection. Cultures everywhere enjoy their own versions made with stuffings of their choosing—here are a few examples.

COOKING METHODS

BAKED

STEAMED

BOILED

FRIED

11 BRIDIE
SCOTLAND

- Minced beef
- Onions

12 MOMO
TIBET

- Goat • Buffalo
- Chicken
- Yak meat
- Pork • Onions
- Shallots • Garlic
- Cilantro

13 KNISH
EASTERN EUROPE

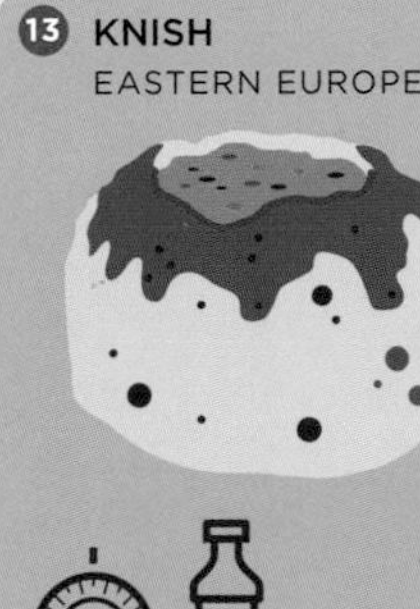

- Mashed potato
- Meat
- Vegetables
- Grains
- Fruits

14 STRUDEL
GERMANY

- Fruit

15 PIROZHKI
RUSSIA

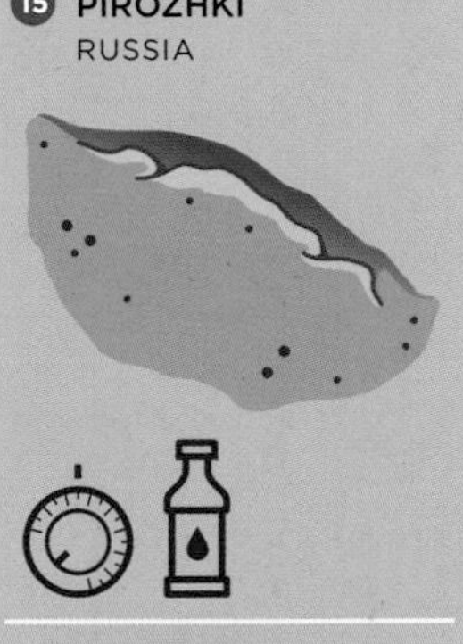

- Mashed potatoes
- Cheese
- Cabbage
- Meat
- Eggs
- Vegetables or fruit

16 BÖREK
TURKEY

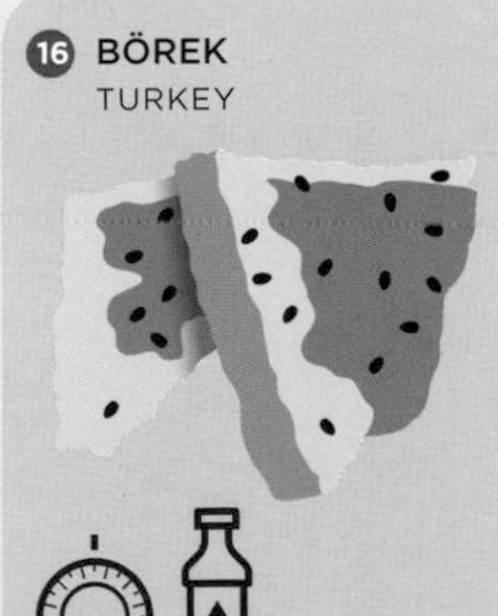

- Cheese
- Minced meat
- Vegetables

17 PAN DE REGLA
PHILIPPINES

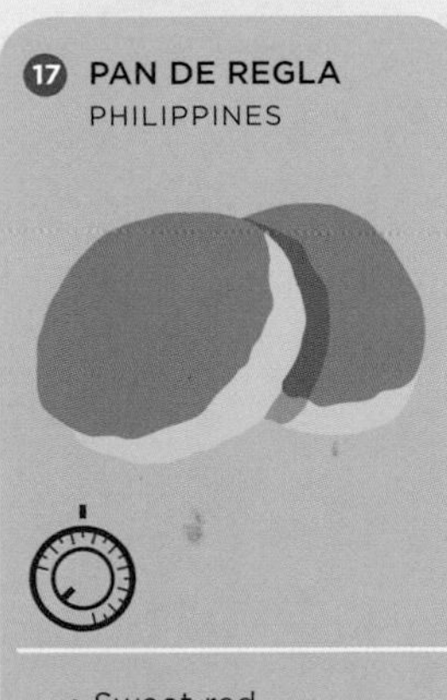

- Sweet red bread pudding

18 GOBHI PARATHA
INDIA

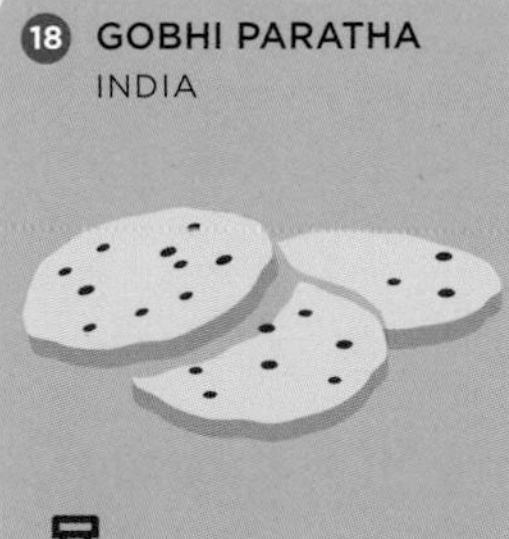

- Cauliflower

19 PUPUSA
EL SALVADOR

- Cheese
- Pork paste
- Squash
- Refried beans

20 BUNNY CHOW
SOUTH AFRICA

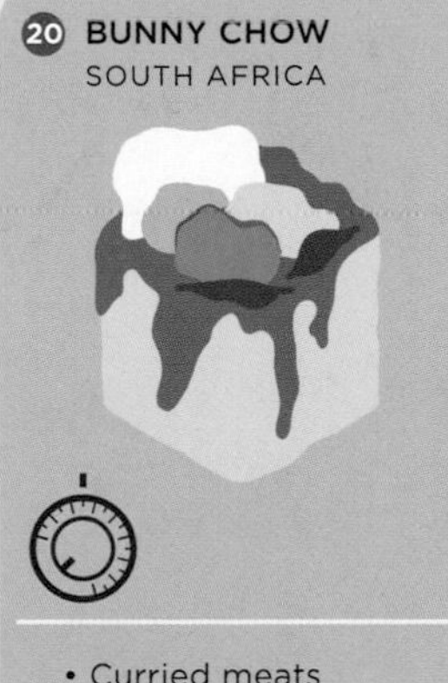

- Curried meats
- Vegetables

6 ANIMALS THAT FETCH US FOOD

1 GOLDEN EAGLES
MONGOLIA
Since the 1400s, the Kazakhs have captured and trained this enormous bird to kill and return with prey, such as foxes and hares. The birds are eventually released back into the wild.

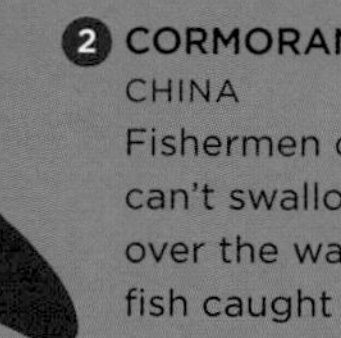

2 CORMORANTS
CHINA
Fishermen collar these birds so that they can't swallow large fish, then send them out over the water. The birds end up with large fish caught in their throats, and the fishermen "help them out"—by snagging their prey.

3 DOGS
EUROPE AND US
Bird dogs scout prey in the sky, then retrieve it after hunters shoot it down.

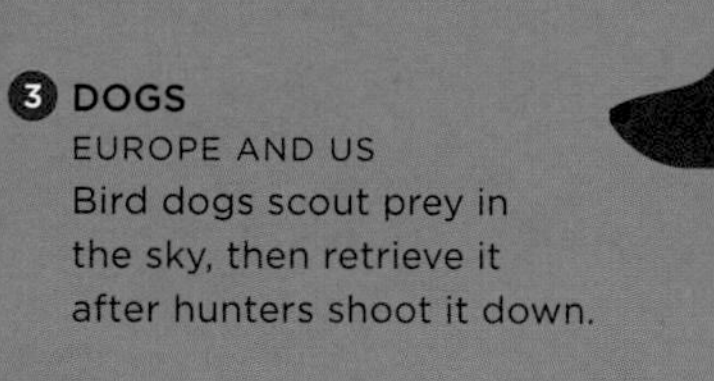

4 MONKEYS
CHINA
Once upon a time, monkeys evidently were kept to pick tea leaves by hand. These days, it seems to be nothing more than a marketing ploy.

5 PIGS
FRANCE
Trained pigs sniff out truffles—tasty, much-desired fungi that are well camouflaged among the roots in which they grow.

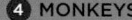

6 CIVET CATS
INDONESIA
This member of the weasel family consumes coffee berries. After the civets have digested and excreted them, the berries are roasted.

8 ARDUOUS EDIBLES

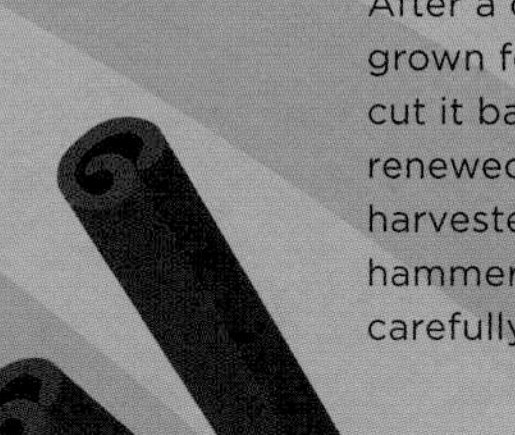

3 CINNAMON

After a cinnamon tree has grown for two years, workers cut it back. The next year, the renewed shoots must be carefully harvested and beaten with a hammer. This way, harvesters can carefully pry out the inner bark.

2 CHOCOLATE

Farmers harvest cacao pods by either knocking them off the tree with a stick or cutting them down with a machete. The pods are then fermented, sun-dried, and processed through an elaborate set of steps.

1 VANILLA

Vanilla is known for being a fussy plant, like most orchids. The plants must grow in precise circumstances to produce seedpods. All commercial vanilla is pollinated by hand.

4 HONEY

Honey must be painstakingly gathered from angry bees who don't really want it taken away. Bees are also quite challenging to nurture and maintain.

5 CHEESE

Many cheeses require a series of steps, any of which can go wrong and ruin the cheese—separating the milk into curds and whey; adding rennet; processing the curds; draining, heating, and aging or ripening, which can last anywhere from a few days to several years.

7 LUTEFISK

Dried white codfish is first soaked for five days in water that must be changed daily. It then must soak in water and lye for another two days, then again in water for another five. The delicate result requires careful cooking to keep it from disintegrating.

6 KOSHER MEAT

Kosher preparation requires ritual slaughter by severing the trachea, esophagus, carotid arteries, and jugular veins using a supersharp blade, and allowing the blood to drain out. If the hindquarters of kosher mammals are to be eaten, they must be stripped of the sciatic nerve, veins, caul fat, suet, and sinews in accordance with a strict procedure.

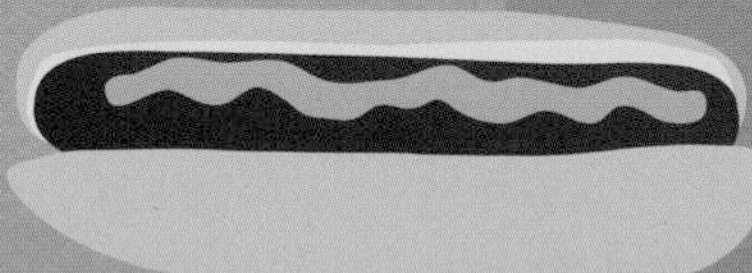

8 SAFFRON

It takes anything from 70,000 to 250,000 flowers of purple saffron crocus to make 2 pounds (1 kg) of saffron. Moreover, the flowers have to be individually handpicked in the autumn when they fully bloom.

10 TOP CHEESE-EATING COUNTRIES

. . . AND THEIR GROSS NATIONAL HAPPINESS

What makes a person—or a nation—happy? The Gross National Happiness project attempts to determine this using complex factors including spiritual values, health, and national wealth. But what about cheese? Does happiness depend on delicious dairy? We think so—sadly, the people of Greece might not agree—but look at Denmark, the happiest, cheesiest nation.

1 DENMARK

57.5 pounds (26 kg) per person per year
Ranked 1st in gross national happiness

POPULAR CHEESES:
DANBO • HAVARTI • MYCELLA

4 FRANCE

53 pounds (24 kg) per person per year
Ranked 62nd in gross national happiness

POPULAR CHEESES:
BRIE • ROQUEFORT • SAINT MARCELLIN

5 ITALY

48.5 pounds (22 kg) per person per year
Ranked 50th in gross national happiness

POPULAR CHEESES:
ASIAGO • GORGONZOLA • RICOTTA

8 GERMANY

44 pounds (20 kg) per person per year
Ranked 30th in gross national happiness

POPULAR CHEESES:
BIERKÄSE • EDELPILZ • QUARK

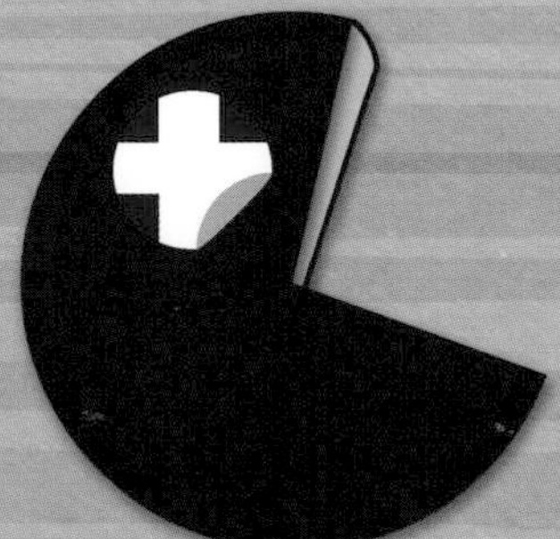

9 SWITZERLAND

42 pounds (19 kg) per person per year
Ranked 2nd in gross national happiness

POPULAR CHEESES:
EMMENTAL • GRUYÈRE • SAANENKAESE

2 GREECE

55 pounds (25 kg) per person per year
Ranked 84th in gross national happiness

POPULAR CHEESES:
FETA • KASERI • XYNOTYRO

3 ICELAND

53 pounds (24 kg) per person per year
Ranked 4th in gross national happiness

POPULAR CHEESES:
AVAXTSKYR • BRAUDOSTUR • RJOMASKYR

6 AUSTRIA

44 pounds (20 kg) per person per year
Ranked 3rd in gross national happiness

POPULAR CHEESES:
KUGELKASE • MONDSEER • SCHLOSS

7 NETHERLANDS

44 pounds (20 kg) per person per year
Ranked 15th in gross national happiness

POPULAR CHEESES:
EDAM • FRIESEKAAS • GOUDA

10 SWEDEN

40 pounds (18 kg) per person per year
Ranked 7th in gross national happiness

POPULAR CHEESES:
GRADDOST • GREVÉ • HUSHÅLLSOST

THE WORLD'S 10 HAPPIEST COUNTRIES

Not every cheese-eating nation is happy, and not every happy place loves dairy. Still, of the top 10 happiest nations, seven eat a lot of cheese (The Bahamas, Bhutan, and Brunei, not so much). Coincidence? We think not.

- Denmark
- Switzerland
- Austria
- Iceland
- The Bahamas
- Finland
- Sweden
- Bhutan
- Brunei
- Canada

218

CREATURES BOTH REAL AND IMAGINARY

From immortal jellyfish to imaginary monsters, this chapter is a veritable menagerie of creatures that lived long ago (hello, rock 'n' roll trilobites), are still living and working today (real-life monkey waiters!), or never actually existed (but should have—like the Honey Island Swamp Monster). Whether you want to snuggle up with a romantic blue crab, unearth signs of alien visits, or know all about ancient shrubberies, read on.

9 MYTHICAL BEASTS

1
2
3
4

❶ ORANG-BATI
INDONESIA
This half-monkey, half-bat creature enjoys flying around its native island of Seram, shrieking and scouring for babies to abduct and eat. It has an apelike head, huge claws on its forearms, and leathery wings that can span up to 10 feet (3 m).

❷ CHERUFE
CHILE
Made of rock and magma, this reptilian beast lives in active volcanoes and causes an eruption or two when peeved. To stave off such fits, locals evidently throw a sacrificial victim into the volcano, and the cherufe often throws the head back out.

❸ HONEY ISLAND SWAMP MONSTER
US
The coastal swamps of the American South are legendarily home to this huge and putrid-smelling "swamp wookie," which may stand 7 feet (2 m) tall and weigh up to 350 pounds (159 kg). It has matted gray hair and oversize amber-colored eyes.

4 YEREN

CHINA

In the mountains of the Hubei Province lives an orangutan-like beast that is covered in red fur (although there have been reports of albino specimens) and walks upright. It is said to have a large belly and emit a terrible odor.

5 AHUIZOTL

CENTRAL AMERICA

According to Aztec legend, the ahuizotl was a slimy, cave-dwelling creature with a dog's head and a handlike appendage on the end of its tail. Sometimes known as the lake guardian, it would cry like a human baby to attract prey.

6 YOWIE

AUSTRALIA

A hominid said to dwell in the Australian wilderness, the Yowie was first spotted by Aboriginal peoples. Early settlers described it as covered in matted hair and standing 5 feet (1.5 m) tall. It's a touch shy and prone to running off when confronted.

7 RUNAN-SHAH

IRAN

This amphibious man-thing makes its watery home in the Caspian Sea; eyewitnesses describe it as sturdily built, with a beak, a protruding gut, webbed hands, gills, and seaweed-colored hair. It converses freely with the fishes of the sea.

8 OWL MAN

UK

Locals of Cornwall, England, occasionally glimpse this massive and mysterious owl beast as it flies through the forest. This winged creature sports a coat of reddish-brown feathers and its eyes glow a bright, sinister red. It enjoys hissing at young girls.

9 FEAR LIATH

SCOTLAND

Since the 1800s, hikers on Ben Macdui Mountain have reported being stalked by a hulking gray humanlike figure that is 10 feet (3 m) tall. The sightings are often accompanied by feelings of paranoia and hearing crunching noises, like footsteps.

28 PREHISTORIC CREATURES NAMED FOR FAMOUS PEOPLE OR COOL THINGS

1 **ATTENBOROSAURUS CONYBEARE**
PLESIOSAUR
Narrator David Attenborough

2 **ANHANGUERA SPIELBERGI**
PTEROSAUR
Jurassic Park filmmaker Steven Spielberg

3 **BAMBIRAPTOR FEINBERGI**
THEROPOD
Disney character Bambi

7 **SERENDIPACERATOPS ARTHURCCLARKEI**
ORNITHISCHIAN
Science-fiction author Arthur C. Clarke

8 **PSEPHOPHORUS TERRYPRATCHETTI**
PREHISTORIC SEA TURTLE
Fantasy writer Terry Pratchett

4 **NORASAPHUS MONROEAE**
TRILOBITE
Cinema and pinup star Marilyn Monroe

5 **GOJIRASAURUS QUAYI**
THEROPOD
Gojira, the Japanese name for Godzilla

6 **DRACOREX HOGWARTSIA**
PACHYCEPHALOSAUR
Hogwarts (the school of wizardry in the Harry Potter series)

9 **ARTHURDACTYLUS CONANDOYLEI**
PTEROSAUR
The Lost World author Arthur Conan Doyle

FILM

11–12 **AVALANCHURUS SIMONI**
A. GARFUNKELI
TRILOBITES
Singing duo Paul Simon and Art Garfunkel

14–18 **ARCTICALYMENE VICIOUSI**
A. ROTTENI / A. JONESI
A. COOKI / A. MATLOCKI
TRILOBITES
Members of the Sex Pistols

10 **AEGROTOCATELLUS JAGGERI**
TRILOBITE
Rolling Stones lead singer Mick Jagger

13 **MASIAKASAURUS KNOPFLERI**
THEROPOD
Dire Straits lead singer Mark Knopfler

19–22 **MACKENZIURUS JOEYI**
M. DEEDEEI / M. JOHNNYI
M. CEEJAYI
TRILOBITES
Members of the Ramones

23–26 **AVALANCHURUS LENNONI**
A. STARRI
STRUSZIA MCCARTNEYI
S. HARRISONI
TRILOBITES
Members of the Beatles

27 **PSEUDOPARAMYS CEZANNEI**
PREHISTORIC RODENT
Post-impressionist painter Paul Cézanne

28 **EFFIGIA OKEEFFEAE**
ARCHOSAUR
Modernist painter Georgia O'Keeffe

14 AMAZING CRITTER COMEBACKS

1 BIG BEND GAMBUSIA
US
3 IN 1957 / 50,000 IN 2004
1,666,567 PERCENT POPULATION INCREASE

2 ASIAN CRESTED IBIS
CHINA
7 IN 1981 / 500 IN 2007
7,043 PERCENT POPULATION INCREASE

3 HAWAIIAN GOOSE
HAWAII
30 IN 1952 / 1,800 IN 2008
5,900 PERCENT POPULATION INCREASE

4 VICUÑA
ANDES MOUNTAINS
6,000 IN 1974 / 350,000 IN 2006
5,733 PERCENT POPULATION INCREASE

5 PRZEWALSKI'S HORSE
CHINA AND MONGOLIA
31 IN 1966 / 1,500 IN 2006
4,739 PERCENT POPULATION INCREASE

6 WHOOPING CRANE
NORTH AMERICA
21 IN 1941 / 513 IN 2006
2,343 PERCENT POPULATION INCREASE

7 BALD EAGLE
CONTIGUOUS US
832 IN 1963 / 20,000 IN 2006
2,304 PERCENT POPULATION INCREASE

8 HUMPBACK WHALE
OCEANS WORLDWIDE
5,000 IN 1966 / 60,000 IN 2006
1,100 PERCENT POPULATION INCREASE

9 SEYCHELLES MAGPIE-ROBIN
SEYCHELLES ISLANDS
16 IN 1970 / 178 IN 2005
1,013 PERCENT POPULATION INCREASE

10 GRAY WHALE
PACIFIC OCEAN
3,095 IN 1968 / 26,635 IN 1998
761 PERCENT POPULATION INCREASE

11 VIRGINIA BIG-EARED BAT
NORTH AMERICA
3,500 IN 1979 / 18,442 IN 2000
427 PERCENT POPULATION INCREASE

12 PEREGRINE FALCON
CONTINENTAL US
648 IN 1975 / 3,400 IN 2000
425 PERCENT POPULATION INCREASE

13 WALIA IBEX
ETHIOPIA
150 IN 1963 / 500 IN 2007
233 PERCENT POPULATION INCREASE

14 GRIZZLY BEAR
CONTIGUOUS US
224 IN 1968 / 500 IN 1998
123 PERCENT POPULATION INCREASE

14 LIVING FOSSILS

ULTIMATE SURVIVORS
A living fossil is an ancient species that still lives in modern times and doesn't look too much different from its first fossil on record. File these critters under the "If it's not broken, why fix it?" school of evolution.

COELACANTH
415 MILLION YEARS OLD

HORSESHOE CRAB
450 MILLION YEARS OLD

COCKROACH
350 MILLION YEARS OLD

VELVET WORM
455 MILLION YEARS OLD

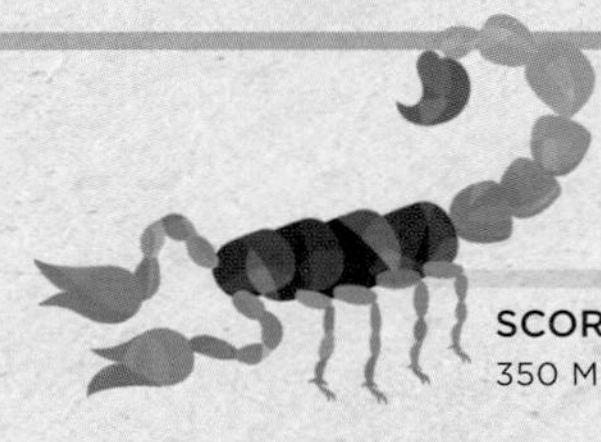

SCORPION
350 MILLION YEARS OLD

MILLION YEARS AGO

500 475 450 425 400 375 350 325 300 275

7 FAST EVOLVERS

1 ADÉLIE PENGUIN
ANTARCTICA
Analysis of penguin DNA—some more than 6,000 years old—reveals that penguins are evolving two to seven times faster than would be expected, perhaps due to climate change.

2 TUATARA
NEW ZEALAND
This creature's DNA has the ability to change very quickly, evidently in response to virtually undetectable variations in its environment. Scientists still do not understand why.

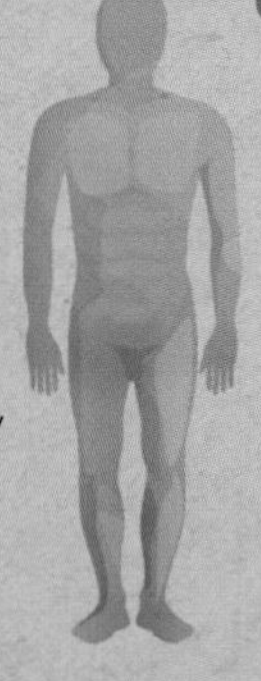

3 HUMAN
WORLDWIDE
Since humans first deviated from chimpanzees around 5 million years ago, we've evolved quickly in response to environmental change. For example, it's thought that humans who migrated to Europe evolved light skin as early as 10,000 years ago, allowing them to absorb more vitamin D during days with less sunlight.

MAGPIE GOOSE
67 MILLION YEARS OLD

FRILLED SHARK
95 MILLION YEARS OLD

RED PANDA
4 MILLION YEARS OLD

QUEENSLAND LUNGFISH
250 MILLION YEARS OLD

IRIOMOTE CAT
2 MILLION YEARS OLD

OPOSSUM
55 MILLION YEARS OLD

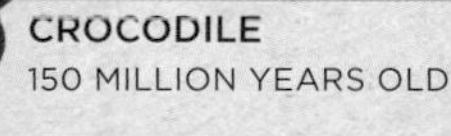

DUCK-BILLED PLATYPUS
110 MILLION YEARS OLD

CROCODILE
150 MILLION YEARS OLD

PURPLE FROG
100 MILLION YEARS OLD

0 225 200 175 150 125 100 75 50 25 PRESENT DAY

4 VANIKORO WHITE-EYE
VANIKORO
White-eyes evolve more quickly than any other bird family. The Solomon Islands boast 13 species of the Vanikoro white-eye, all with various beak lengths and colors on their legs and eyes.

5 DEER MOUSE
NORTH AMERICA
Generally deer mice have dark coats that help them blend into the soil. Mice that migrate to sandier areas, however, turn light faster than might be expected; their DNA evolves very quickly.

6 CICHLID
NICARAGUA
Within 100 years, one species of fish has divided into two: one with thin lips, and another with thick lips, a variation that allows it to feed among sharp, pointed rocks without injury.

7 PEPPERED MOTH
BRITISH ISLES
This moth became darker as pollution increased in its habitat, helping it blend into its dirtier environment. This change happened within the past 200 years.

 SPORTS INVOLVING ANIMALS

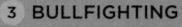

1 **CAMEL RACING**
MIDDLE EAST, INDIA, AND ASIA
This pastime is like horse racing, but with a different speed demon. Spectators bet on camels that run up to 40 miles per hour (64 km/h) and are jockeyed by children.

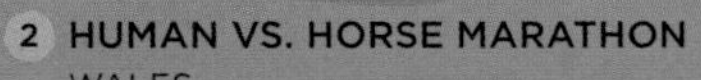

2 **HUMAN VS. HORSE MARATHON**
WALES
Human competitors test their speed and endurance against jockeyed horses, running an obstacle course that's 22 miles (35 km) in length.

3 **BULLFIGHTING**
EUROPE AND LATIN AMERICA
A highly stylized and dangerous battle between man and bull, in which the bull is almost always killed with a single sword thrust.

4 **ELEPHANT POLO**
NEPAL, SRI LANKA, THAILAND, AND INDIA
This variant of the game of polo, which is traditionally played on horseback, unfolds at a much slower speed. Two players ride each elephant: one guiding, the other whacking the ball with the mallet.

5 **IDITAROD**
US
An Alaskan sled race during which mushers (dog-sled drivers) and teams of typically 16 dogs cover 1,161 miles (1,868 km) of icy mountains and tundra in 10 to 17 days.

6 **GREYHOUND RACING**
WORLDWIDE
This betting sport is popular in many places. Dogs chase a lure (usually an artificial rabbit) around a racetrack.

7 **CAMEL WRESTLING**
TURKEY
Specially trained male camels are divided into weight classes and then attempt to make their opponents retreat, scream, or fall. A female in heat is usually called in to inspire rivalry.

8 **COCKFIGHTING**
WORLDWIDE
Roosters are set in a ring to fight, sometimes to the death. The combatants may have razors or other weapons attached to their legs.

9 BEASTLY JOBS

1 **ROASTER**
ENGLAND
In the 1700s, the small turnspit dog was bred to run on a wheel, turning meat to cook it evenly. This terrier-type breed is now extinct.

2 **WARMER**
CHINA
In Imperial China, Pekingese dogs adorned laps and kept royalty warm; some nobles also tucked them inside the sleeves of their silken robes.

3 **MESSENGER**
WORLDWIDE
Due to their ability to home over long distances, pigeons have served as carriers for centuries; 32 won medals for bravery in World War II.

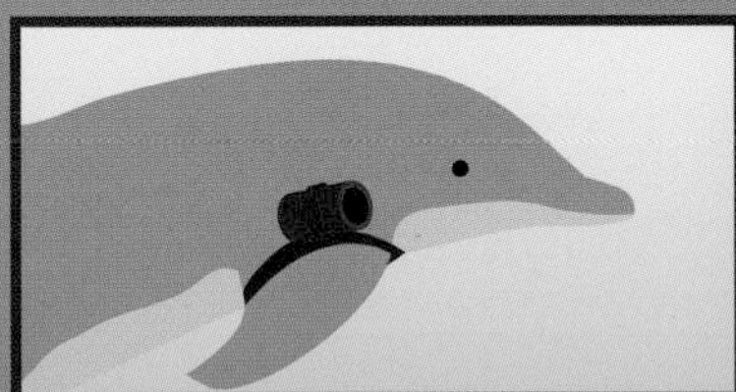

4 **SENTRY**
US
Dolphins use their sonar to detect intruders, report on them, and release an underwater beacon to alert navy security forces.

5 **GUARD**
INDIA
Langur monkeys were employed as guards at the 2010 Commonwealth Games to scare off smaller, much more mischievous monkeys.

6 **HELPER**
US
Capuchin monkeys assist disabled people with everyday tasks, like microwaving food, helping with hygiene, and opening drink bottles.

7 **EXECUTIONER**
INDIA
In ancient times, rulers showed their power over both animal and human by using elephants to brutalize criminals in public executions.

8 **WAITER**
JAPAN
In a bar in Tokyo, a pair of uniformed Japanese macaque monkeys serve drinks to their customers in return for soybeans.

9 **MINE SNIFFER**
MOZAMBIQUE AND TANZANIA
With their amazing sense of smell and high intelligence, rats are used to help sniff out mines—and are light enough that they don't set them off.

11 ANIMALS THAT OUTLIVED EXPECTATIONS

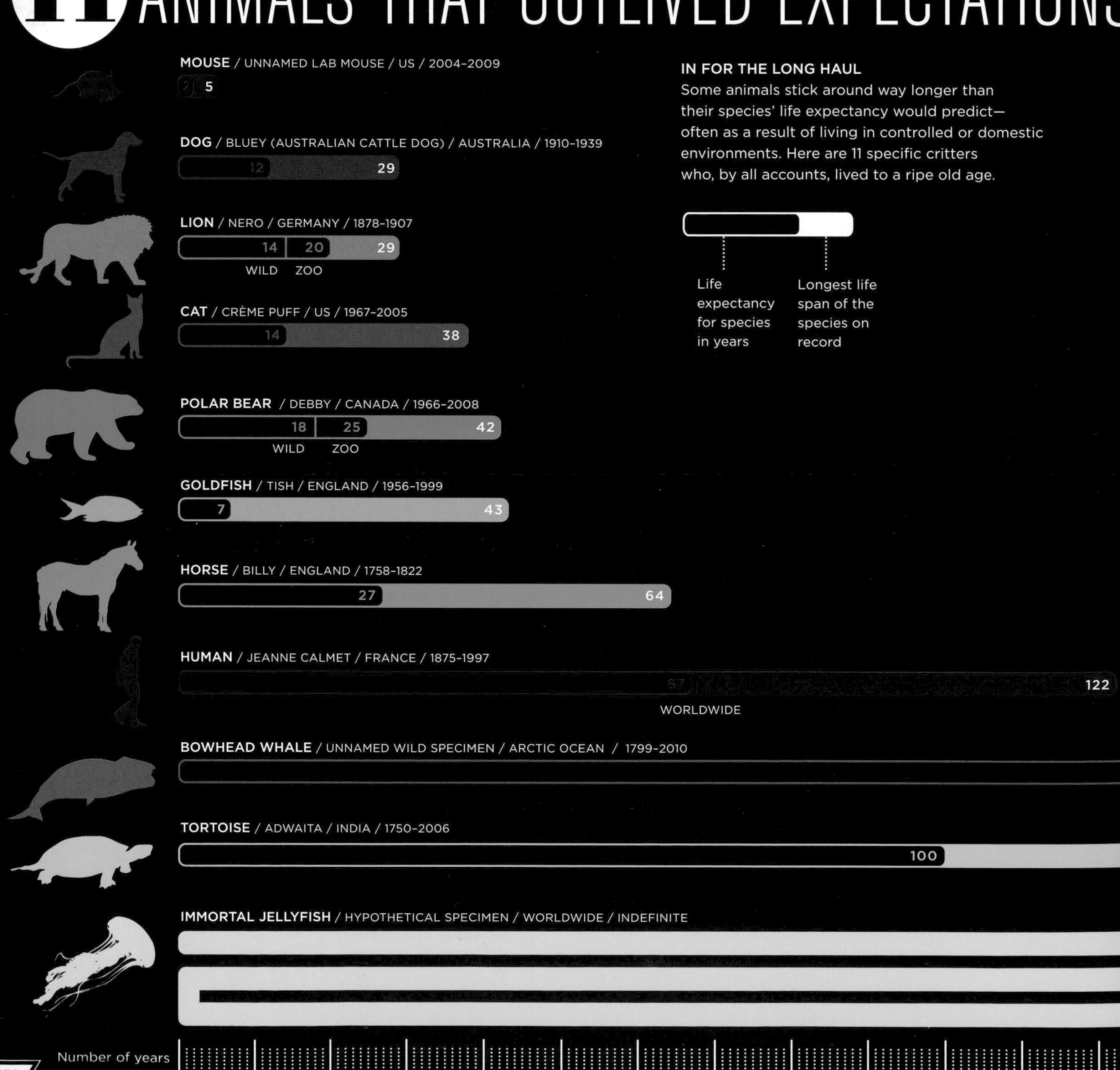
MOUSE / UNNAMED LAB MOUSE / US / 2004–2009
2 5
DOG / BLUEY (AUSTRALIAN CATTLE DOG) / AUSTRALIA / 1910–1939
12 29
LION / NERO / GERMANY / 1878–1907
14 20 29
WILD ZOO
CAT / CRÈME PUFF / US / 1967–2005
14 38
POLAR BEAR / DEBBY / CANADA / 1966–2008
18 25 42
WILD ZOO
GOLDFISH / TISH / ENGLAND / 1956–1999
7 43
HORSE / BILLY / ENGLAND / 1758–1822
27 64
HUMAN / JEANNE CALMET / FRANCE / 1875–1997
67 122
WORLDWIDE
BOWHEAD WHALE / UNNAMED WILD SPECIMEN / ARCTIC OCEAN / 1799–2010
TORTOISE / ADWAITA / INDIA / 1750–2006
100
IMMORTAL JELLYFISH / HYPOTHETICAL SPECIMEN / WORLDWIDE / INDEFINITE
IN FOR THE LONG HAUL
Some animals stick around way longer than their species' life expectancy would predict—often as a result of living in controlled or domestic environments. Here are 11 specific critters who, by all accounts, lived to a ripe old age.
Life expectancy for species in years
Longest life span of the species on record
Number of years
0 10 20 30 40 50 60 70 80 90 100 110 120

6 OLDEST PLANTS

LET IT GROW (AND GROW AND GROW)

Some life-forms can live for thousands of years without attracting too much attention—trees, for example, don't exactly request birthday cake with each passing year. Here are seven organisms (or groups of self-cloning organisms) that have quietly carried on for ages.

1 POSIDONIA OCEANICA

SEA GRASS COLONY / 100,000 YEARS OLD

The Mediterranean Sea hosts a single-organism colony of sea grass that covers 15,000 square miles (38,850 sq km).

2 PANDO

ASPEN GROVE / 80,000 YEARS OLD

This forest of aspen trees in the United States is actually a genetically identical organism with one huge root network.

3 LOMATIA TASMANICA

SHRUB / 43,600 YEARS OLD

Known as "king's holly," this shrub network consists of many 300-year-old plants that have been self-cloning for 43,600 years.

4 QUERCUS PALMERI

OAK BUSH / 13,000 YEARS OLD

This specific shrub—known as the Palmer oak shrub—is 75 feet (23 m) wide. It's been cloning itself since the Ice Age.

5 CREOSOTE BUSH

BUSH / 11,700 YEARS OLD

In the United States's Mojave desert is a ring of extremely old, self-replicating creosote bush; it is known as "king clone."

6 HUON PINE

TREE COLONY / 10,000 YEARS OLD

Huon pines typically live for about 3,000 years; a stand in western Tasmania has lived three times as long.

150 211

255

The *Turritopsis nutricula* is possibly the only creature on Earth that can revert from adulthood to a polyp stage, making it potentially immortal. It's impossible to recognize a jellyfish that's undergone this process, so just take joy in imagining there's one out there.

140 150 160 170 180 190 200 210 220 230 240 250 260 270 280

15 Critters with Strange Mating Rituals

1 **PORCUPINE**
Female porcupines are only in the mood for one day a year. To check if she's interested, a male stands on his hind legs and, from 6 feet (2 m) away, urinates on her. If she's into him, she shows her belly; lovemaking ensues.

2 **SCORPION**
The male and female lock pincers and dance in circles for up to an hour until they come across a perfect spot. The male then lays down a sperm packet and pushes the female over it. She absorbs it, and they go separate ways.

3 **FRIGATE BIRD**
The male can inflate his throat sac into an enormous red balloon that looks a bit like a pompous cravat. He then waggles his head from side to side, shakes his wings, and awaits impressed females.

4 **WHITE-FRONTED PARROTS**
One of the only creatures besides humans to kiss, these birds add their own flourish. After they cuddle, lock beaks, and flick their tongues together, the male vomits on the female to show his commitment.

5 **BOWERBIRD**
The male builds a complex structure called a bower, then decorates it with a variety of gifts: flowers, feathers, stones, and even bits of discarded plastics and glass. Females choose the mates with the best living quarters.

6 **GARTER SNAKE**
A female may be courted by up to 100 males, who form a "mating ball" around her in hopes of getting it on. Only one lucky male gets close enough, but he then has to make a crucial choice: Which of his two penises does he use?

7 **ALLIGATOR**
Alligators announce their interest by bellowing and slapping their heads on the water's surface. Once paired off, the two gators rub snouts together, blow bubbles, and mate. The female then heads to her nest to lay eggs.

8 GALÁPAGOS TORTOISE
In a war to get the girl, males rise up on their legs and stretch their necks to see who has the longest neck. The triumphant turtle then draws the female in with various bellows and aggressive head motions.

9 HEDGEHOG
The male hedgehog's way of attracting a mate involves walking around and around the female hedgehog, sniffling and snorting. This can go on for hours until she decides she is ready to mate; often she just wanders off.

10 ELEPHANT
These massive beasts are actually pretty sweet to each other—nuzzling, twisting their trunks together, and even "french kissing" with their trunks. Oh, he also samples her urine to make sure she's in heat before sealing the deal.

11 AUSTRALIAN REDBACK SPIDER
Females require the males to perform an elaborate dance for more than an hour. During the dance, the male aligns his stomach with her mouthparts. If he stops early, he is eaten; if he finishes in a timely fashion, he is also eaten.

12 BLUE CRAB
Female blue crabs only mate during molting, when their shells are soft. Before and after mating, the male cradles and carries the female to protect her from predators, until her shell hardens and she's safe again.

13 CARDINAL
The male and the female first sing to each other from different perches. The male cardinal then brings the female a seed as a token of his affection. While mating, they sing, repeating each other's phrases and songs.

14 CALIFORNIA LEAF-NOSED BAT
At night, the male sets up a "bachelor pad" in a cave and calls out to potential mates. A female enters and, if she deems him an acceptable suitor, allows the male bat to wrap his wings around her. Then they mate.

15 ANGLERFISH
The male anglerfish attaches himself to a (much larger) female permanently and lives his entire adult life as her sidekick, providing sperm when she requires.

9 THINGS MADE **BY** INSECTS

1 **SILK**
SILKWORMS
In Asia, a 4,700-year-old industry has thrived around the threadlike secretion of silkworm larvae. People incorporate this silk into hypoallergenic sheets, parachutes, and, of course, haute couture.

2 **WEBS**
GOLDEN ORB SPIDERS
The golden orb spider is known for its large, superstrong webs. They're so resilient that fishermen in the South Pacific have been known to incorporate them into their fishing nets and lures.

3 **HONEY**
HONEYBEES
Bees' labor of love is honey. Prior to the global sugar trade and the invention of artificial sweeteners, honey was one of the only natural sources of sweetness around, aside from seasonal fruit.

4 **WAX**
HONEYBEES
Worker bees secrete wax and form it into a comb of hexagonal cells called honeycomb—which makes perfect storage for honey and housing for baby bees. Humans use this wax in a variety of ways: candles, floor finishes, and cheese coatings, to name a few.

5 **SOUNDS**
VARIOUS CRICKETS
Crickets generate a relaxing buzz by rubbing their wings together. Some retail stores play soundtracks of these noises to play up their ecological reputations, and some people play them as sleep aids.

6 **FEVER**
MOSQUITOES
A mosquito carrying malaria is a bad thing—unless you have syphilis. If you do, a doctor may inject you with malaria so the fever it causes can kill the syphilis pathogen. Then quinine will treat your malaria.

7 **ANTIBACTERIAL PROTEINS**
CICADAS
The blood of these insects contains proteins that protect against bacteria. They may someday provide us with protection against germs for which we've developed an antibiotic resistence.

8 **GALLS**
WASPS
Wasps make galls on the surface of oak trees to house their larvae, which secrete chemicals. The galls are harvested and used in astringents, fabric dyes, and a black ink that's been a favorite for centuries.

9 **VENOM**
HONEYBEES
It may sound bizarre, but the venom of honeybees contains strong anti-inflammatory agents. Doctors have harnessed this power to help multiple sclerosis and arthritis patients.

7 THINGS MADE **FROM** INSECTS

1 **RED DYE**
FEMALE COCHINEAL BUGS
Ground-up female cochineal bugs yield a vivid, intense red that's been used in fabrics, cosmetics, and food.

2 **SHELLAC**
FEMALE LAC BUGS
The bodies of female lac bugs and the resin that they secrete are scraped from trees, ground into flakes, and mixed with alcohol to make finishes and glazes.

3 **CANDY**
ANTS
Ants are candied or covered in chocolate and enjoyed throughout South America, though they've spread as novelty treats worldwide.

4 **HERBAL REMEDY**
COCKROACHES
Cockroach brains have antibiotics that kill highly resistant bacteria, including those that lead to severe staph infections.

5 **JEWELRY**
BUTTERFLIES
Jewelers set butterfly or beetle wings in glass and sell them to the masses as pendants, earrings, rings, and cuff links.

6 **APHRODISIAC**
SPANISH FLIES
These beetles (which are called Spanish flies, to the confusion of many) have been ground up and served as an aphrodisiac since Roman times, despite the very real health risks posed by their poisons.

7 **GAG GIFT**
COCKROACHES
Live Madagascar hissing cockroaches are sold as party favors and gag gifts, and sometimes as pets.

1 **ZOMBIE**
HAITI
This reanimated corpse can come into being in a variety of gruesome ways; it can receive the zombie "virus" via a bite or voodoo.

2 **VAMPIRE**
EASTERN EUROPE
The classic "bloodsucker" only comes out at night, stalking his prey and extracting the victim's blood through two fairly sexy fangs.

3 **DRAUGR**
NORWAY, SWEDEN, AND DENMARK
The graves of warriors are each guarded by a Draugr, an undead strongman who keeps robbers and desecrators at bay.

4 **PONTIANAK**
INDONESIA
A woman who dies during childbirth may turn into this spirit, feeding on men and attacking pregnant women out of jealousy.

5 **JIANG SHI**
CHINA
The soul of this undead being is trapped inside its body. At night, it hops after its victims and feeds on their essence.

6 **MYLING**
NORWAY, SWEDEN, AND DENMARK
An unbaptized child's ghost roams Earth, begging for a proper burial and killing those who refuse to comply.

7 **WILA**
POLAND
Women who were mischievous in life float between death and the afterlife, shape-shifting into various beautiful animals.

8 FAMOUS GHOSTS

1. **ANNE BOLEYN**
People have spotted the ghost of this onetime queen of England in a number of locations—most famously the Tower of London, the site of her trial and subsequent beheading.

2. **THE FLYING DUTCHMAN**
The ghost of a legendary Dutch warship that was lost at sea off the coast of South Africa is said to haunt the waves, glowing ominously and trying to send messages to the living.

3. **OKIKU**
The heroine of this traditional Japanese ghost story is a beautiful servant who was pursued by a samurai. She refused his advances, and he threw her down a well.

4. **MARILYN MONROE**
Witnesses claim that visions of Monroe appear in a full-length mirror in her suite at the Roosevelt Hotel in Hollywood. She also apparently makes an appearance in the ballroom.

5. **LA LLORONA**
The Mexican legend of La Llorona tells of a woman who drowned her children in order to follow a lover. Banned from heaven, she now wanders the

6. **FEDERICI**
Opera singer Federici died performing the role of Faust at a Melbourne theater. His appearance during rehearsals for a new show is considered

7. **NYAI RORO KIDUL**
This Indonesian queen jumped from a cliff to her death and turned into a mermaid spirit. Her ghost may imperil swimmers who wear green

8. **JAMES HEPBURN**
The Scottish Fourth Earl of Bothwell was imprisoned in appalling conditions in Denmark's Dragsholm Castle until his death; now his ghost

17 PREHISTORIC GIANTS

LARGER THAN LIFE

Years ago, giants roamed Earth—huge creatures who died out for various reasons. Here are some of the largest of the large, with their modern-day miniatures (plus some everyday objects) shown for scale.

1 GIANT BIRD
23-FOOT (7-M) WINGSPAN
LIVED: 6 MILLION BCE

Argentavis magnificens

Mammuthus sungari

Paraceratherium orgosensis

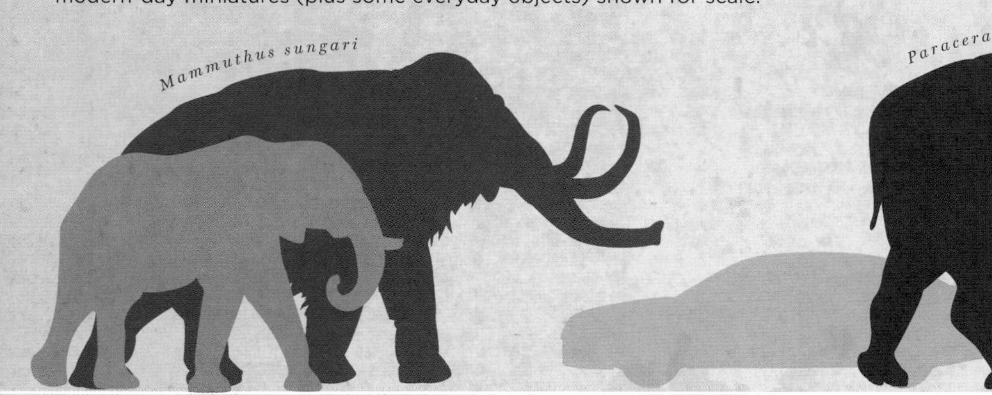

2 SONGHUA RIVER MAMMOTH
17 FEET (5.2 M) TALL
LIVED: 280,000 BCE

3 GIANT RHINOCEROS
18 FEET (5.5 M) TALL
LIVED: 37–23 MILLION BCE

Sarcosuchus imperator

Arctodus simus

4 GIANT CROCODILE
40 FEET (12.2 M) LONG
LIVED: 110 MILLION BCE

5 GIANT BEAR
6 FEET (1.9 M) TALL
LIVED: 800,000–12,500 BCE

Carcharocles megalodon

6 MEGALODON SHARK
52 FEET (16 M) LONG
LIVED: 16–1.5 MILLION BCE

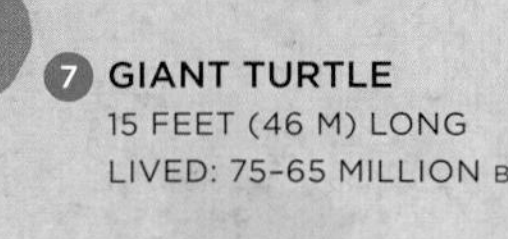

7 GIANT TURTLE
15 FEET (46 M) LONG
LIVED: 75–65 MILLION BCE

Archelon ischyros

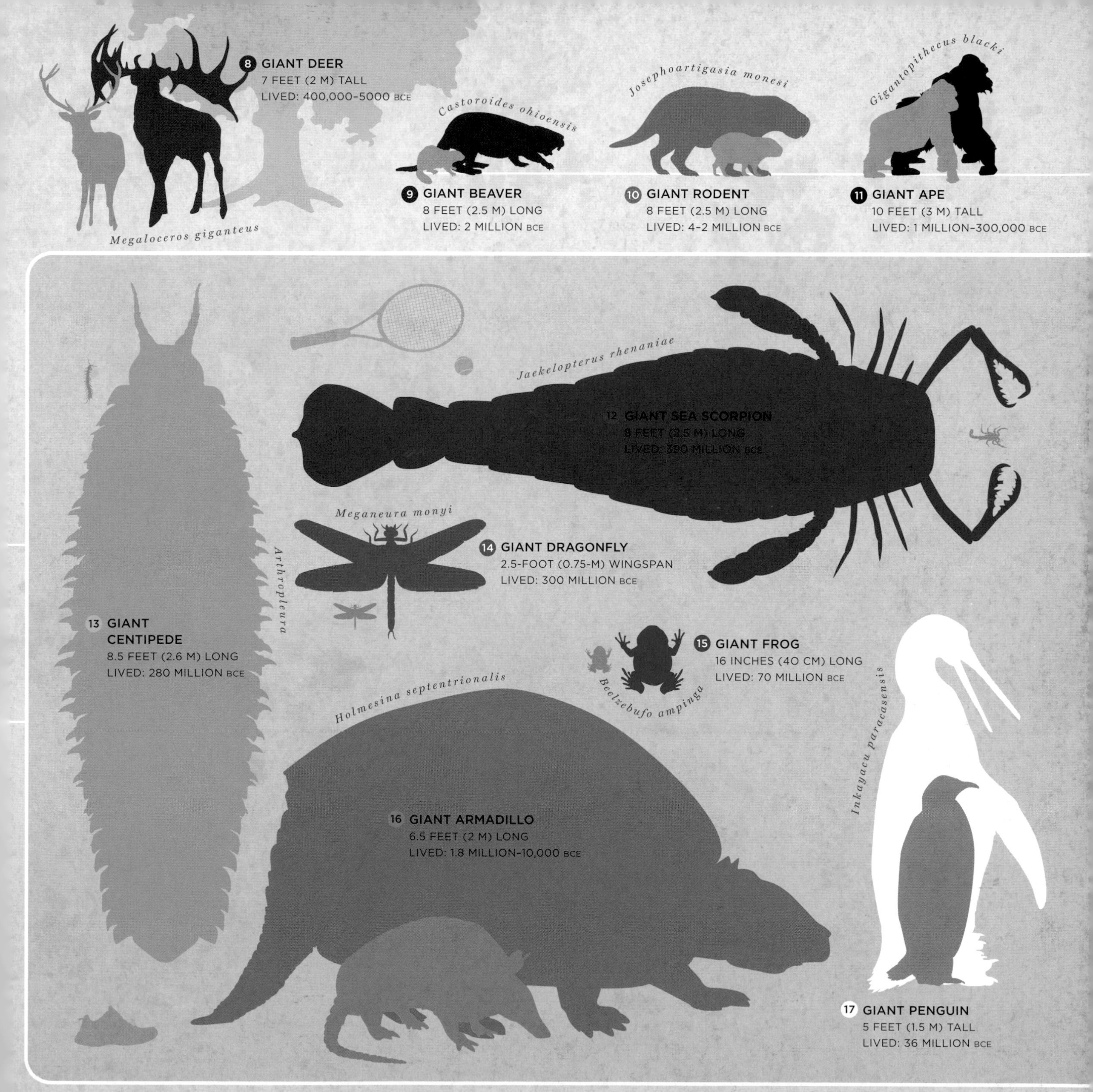

8 GIANT DEER
7 FEET (2 M) TALL
LIVED: 400,000–5000 BCE

9 GIANT BEAVER
8 FEET (2.5 M) LONG
LIVED: 2 MILLION BCE

10 GIANT RODENT
8 FEET (2.5 M) LONG
LIVED: 4–2 MILLION BCE

11 GIANT APE
10 FEET (3 M) TALL
LIVED: 1 MILLION–300,000 BCE

Jaekelopterus rhenaniae

12 GIANT SEA SCORPION
8 FEET (2.5 M) LONG
LIVED: 390 MILLION BCE

Arthropleura

13 GIANT CENTIPEDE
8.5 FEET (2.6 M) LONG
LIVED: 280 MILLION BCE

Meganeura monyi

14 GIANT DRAGONFLY
2.5-FOOT (0.75-M) WINGSPAN
LIVED: 300 MILLION BCE

Beelzebufo ampinga

15 GIANT FROG
16 INCHES (40 CM) LONG
LIVED: 70 MILLION BCE

Holmesina septentrionalis

16 GIANT ARMADILLO
6.5 FEET (2 M) LONG
LIVED: 1.8 MILLION–10,000 BCE

Inkayacu paracasensis

17 GIANT PENGUIN
5 FEET (1.5 M) TALL
LIVED: 36 MILLION BCE

11 THINGS ATTRIBUTED TO ALIENS

1. **CROP CIRCLES**
These detailed, circular patterns cut into wheat- or cornfields started appearing regularly in the United Kingdom in the 1970s, and are believed to be messages from aliens.

2. **COW MUTILATION**
Since the 1960s, US ranchers have occasionally found that their cattle have been assaulted in the night. Sometimes the animals' ears appear to have been cut off with a laser.

3. **NUCLEAR MISSILE FAILURE**
In 1967, a UFO hovered over the Malmstrom Air Force Base in Montana, shutting down all missiles at the site. Allegedly, UFOs have disabled nuclear missile systems on several military bases around the globe.

4. **MACHU PICCHU**
Some believe that aliens must have built Peru's Machu Picchu, as it seems too sophisticated for humans to have created in the 11th century.

5. **EASTER ISLAND HEADS**
Between 1100 and 1680, aliens were apparently stranded on the island and amused themselves by carving these giant statues.

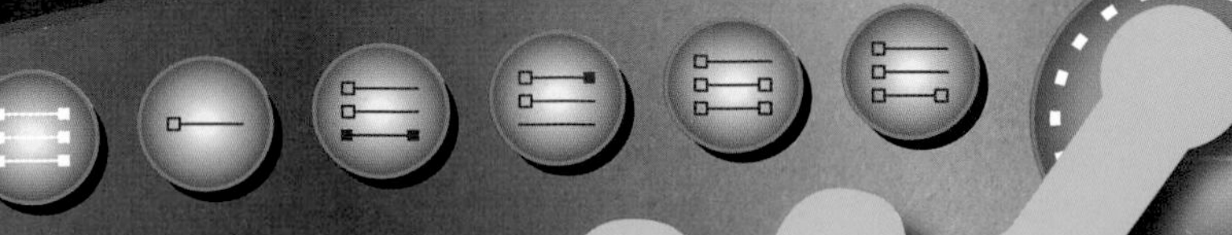

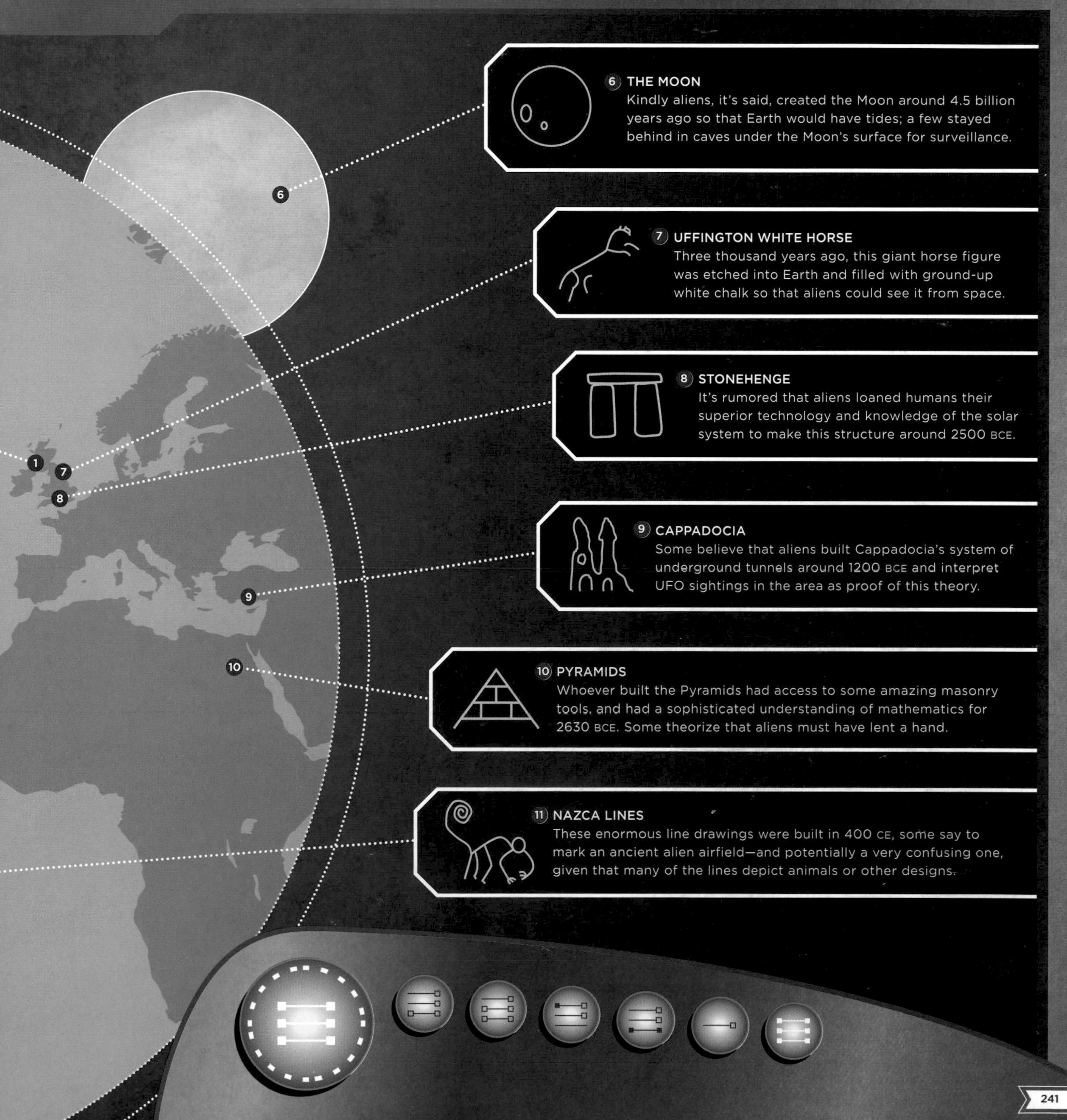
6 THE MOON
Kindly aliens, it's said, created the Moon around 4.5 billion years ago so that Earth would have tides; a few stayed behind in caves under the Moon's surface for surveillance.
7 UFFINGTON WHITE HORSE
Three thousand years ago, this giant horse figure was etched into Earth and filled with ground-up white chalk so that aliens could see it from space.
8 STONEHENGE
It's rumored that aliens loaned humans their superior technology and knowledge of the solar system to make this structure around 2500 BCE.
9 CAPPADOCIA
Some believe that aliens built Cappadocia's system of underground tunnels around 1200 BCE and interpret UFO sightings in the area as proof of this theory.
10 PYRAMIDS
Whoever built the Pyramids had access to some amazing masonry tools, and had a sophisticated understanding of mathematics for 2630 BCE. Some theorize that aliens must have lent a hand.
11 NAZCA LINES
These enormous line drawings were built in 400 CE, some say to mark an ancient alien airfield—and potentially a very confusing one, given that many of the lines depict animals or other designs.
1
7
8
6
9
10

ANIMAL SOUNDS in 8 LANGUAGES

AN OINK BY ANY OTHER NAME

Animals make the same sounds all over the world, but different cultures develop their own fascinating onomatopoeia for each.

MIAO!

KRAW!

BZZZZZ!

	1 COW	2 BEE	3 PIG	4 CAT	5 CHICKEN	6 CROW
AFRIKAANS	MOE-MOE	ZOEM-ZOEM	OINK-OINK	MIAAU	TOK-TOK	KRAW-KRAW
ENGLISH	MOO	BZZZZZ	OINK	MEOW	CLUCK-CLUCK	CAW
FRENCH	MEUH	BZZZ	GROIN-GROIN	MIAOU	COTCOTCODET	CROA-CROA
GERMAN	MMUUH	SUMM-SUMM	GRUNZ	MIAU	TOCK-TOCK	KRÄH-KRÄH
JAPANESE	MAU MAU	BOON-BOON	BUU BUU	NYAN-NYAN	KU-KU-KU-KU	KAR-KAR
RUSSIAN	MU-U-U	ZH-ZH-ZH	HRGU-HRGU	MIYAU	KO-KO-KO	KAR-KAR
SPANISH	MUUU	BZZZ	OINC	MIAO	CACA-RACA	AH-AH
SWEDISH	MU-MU	BUZZ-BUZZ	NÖFF-NÖFF	MJAN MJAN	OCK-OCK	KRA-KRA

TOK!

GRUNZ!

MEUH!

HOU-HOU!

GA-GA!

PIP-PIP!

KERO!

7 DOG	8 DUCK	9 FROG	10 BIRD	11 ROOSTER	12 OWL	13 SHEEP
WOEF	KWAK-KWAK	KWAAK-KWAAK	TJIEP-TJIEP	KOEKELEKOE	HOE-HOE	BÈ-BÈ
ARF-ARF	QUACK-QUACK	RIBBIT	CHIRP	COCK-A-DOODLE-DOO	HOO-HOO	BAA
OUAH-OUAH	COIN-COIN	CROA-CROA	CUI-CUI	COCORICO	HOU-HOU	BÊÊ
WAU-WAU	QUACK-QUACK	QUAAK-QUAAK	TSCHIWITT	KIKERIK	HUUH-HUUH	
WAN-WAN	GA-GA	KERO-KERO	PEE-PEE	KOKEKOKK	HOH-HOH	MEE-MEE
HAV-HAV	KRYA-KRYA	KVA-KVA	FIYT-FIYT	KUKAREK	UH! UH! UH!	BEEE
GUAV	CUA-CUA	CROAC-CROAC	PÍO-PÍO	QUIQUIRIQU	UHH-UHH	BEEE-BEEE
VOV-VOV	KVACK-KVACK	KO-ACK-ACK-ACK	PIP-PIP	KUCKELIK	HO-HO	BÄ-BÄ

ARF!ARF!

MEE-MEE!

11 ANIMAL SENSES

1 **INFRARED SENSORS / SNAKES**
Boas and vipers come equipped with temperature-sensitive organs between their eyes and nostrils, allowing the snakes to sense the body heat of their prey.

2 **ADVANCED TACTILE SENSE / RATS**
Rats have poor vision, but they make up for it with touch. By whisking their hairs across objects they encounter, these rodents form mental pictures of their surroundings.

3 **ELECTRIC FIELD SENSORS / SHARKS**
Sharks have special cells in their brains that are sensitive to the electrical fields other creatures generate. They use this sense to find prey, even when it's camouflaged.

4 **ECHOLOCATION / DOLPHINS**
Dolphins send out high-frequency clicks, which bounce off nearby objects and prey. The sound returns to the dolphins, and they use it to track their next meal.

5 **PHEROMONE DETECTION / MOTHS**
Moths can sniff out chemical love signals, called pheromones, emitted by moths of the opposite sex—sometimes from as far as 7 miles (11 km) away.

6 **ULTRAVIOLET PERCEPTION / DAMSELFISH**
Damselfish can see ultraviolet rays reflected as color, which helps them identify different fish species that would all look the same to the human eye (which can't see UV rays).

7 **SMELL DEFENSE / MINNOWS**
Young minnows learn to associate the smell of ruptured minnow flesh with the sight of pike fish, their most feared natural predators.

8 **NIGHT VISION / CATS**
Cats have special membranes in the backs of their eyes that reflect and increase available light, helping felines see, hunt, and protect themselves in the dark.

9 **SEISMIC SENSORS / TOADS**
Toads have been known to leave a scene before an earthquake hits, only to return a few days later. They may sense changes in the magnetic field or in radon gas levels.

10 **MAGNETIC NAVIGATION / BIRDS**
Many birds, especially those that migrate, have tiny “compass needles” of iron-oxygen in their brains, which they use to stay on course during long flights.

11 **WARNING SYSTEM / ELEPHANTS**
When elephants feel threatened, they stomp their feet, which creates seismic vibrations that travel through the ground and alert other elephants to danger.

14 HUMAN SENSES

1. ESP
2. PAIN
3. SIGHT
4. HEARING
5. SMELL
6. TASTE
7. TOUCH
8. DIRECTION
9. ACCELERATION
10. COLOR
11. LIGHT
12. BALANCE
13. TEMPERATURE
14. KINESTHESIA

193 HEIGHTS AND DEPTHS OF HUMAN BEHAVIOR

When you think of the full realm of human experience, do you ponder whether it's OK for a man to marry a basil plant? Whether Isaac Newton really invented calculus? Or what a good hairdo can do for your soul? Well, maybe you should. From amazing survival stories to magical underwear, this chapter celebrates our proud achievements—plus some not-so-proud and downright bewildering ones.

19 TYPES OF MARRIAGE

1 CICISBEATURA
ITALY / 1700s–1800s
Wealthy women often had an official lover who escorted her to public events and even lived with the pair, all with the husband's consent.

2 COMPLEX MARRIAGE
US / 1848–1881
The 200-person Oneida Community functioned as a group marriage, with older members often initiating younger ones into the joys of sex.

3 SUPERPOLYGAMY
AFRICA / ANTIQUITY–PRESENT
Some African cultures allow wealthy men to take on as many wives as they can support, sometimes siring more than 100 children.

4 ROYAL MARRIAGE
THAILAND / ANTIQUITY–1800s
In days gone by, royalty and the upper classes could have three categories of wife: primary, secondary, and slave.

5 PLURAL MARRIAGE
US / 1830s–1890
Mormon doctrine advised men to take numerous wives. The church banned this practice in 1890, but some still continue the tradition.

6 SORORATE MARRIAGE
INUIT / ANTIQUITY–PRESENT
When a man's wife dies or proves infertile, he may marry her sister in order to have children and maintain the ties formed by the first marriage.

7 PUNALUA
HAWAII, US / ANTIQUITY–1907
In the era before colonization, two or more brothers and their spouses, or two or more sisters and their spouses, could form one marriage.

8 ROYAL INCEST
EGYPT / 332 BCE–395 CE
To preserve the royal bloodline, Egyptian kings often married their sisters—sometimes they would even marry their own daughters.

9 FRATERNAL POLYANDRY
TIBET / ANTIQUITY–700s
In order to keep land and resources within a family, two brothers would often marry the same woman, who was usually in the same class.

10 LEVIRATE MARRIAGE
AFRICA AND ASIA / 4000s BCE–PRESENT
Many ancient codes called for a brother-in-law to marry and provide for his brother's widow; similar rules exist in some modern cultures.

11 HOLY BASIL PLANT MARRIAGE
INDIA / 1100s BCE–PRESENT
According to Hindu lore, the god Vishnu married a pot of holy basil. Hindus start each marriage season with a re-creation of this "marriage."

12 WALKING MARRIAGE
CHINA / ANTIQUITY–PRESENT
In the Mosuo culture, husand and wife lead separate lives; a man visits his wife in the evening and returns to his mother's home in the morning.

13 GHOST MARRIAGE
CHINA / 3000s BCE–PRESENT
When one or both of the betrothed parties die before the wedding, the ceremony may still go on to preserve lineage or wealth.

14 IMPERIAL CONCUBINAGE
CHINA / 1600s–1912
The emperor married a primary wife and then took on several official concubines. In the Qing dynasty, the emperor had 20,000 concubines.

15 SHARIA POLYGAMY
NORTH AFRICA AND THE MIDDLE EAST
800s–PRESENT
A man can have up to four wives, all of whom receive equal support and private living quarters, when possible.

16 FRATERNAL MARRIAGE
TIBET, NEPAL, AND SOUTHERN INDIA
4000 BCE–PRESENT
Two or more brothers may share one or more wives; in some places, sisters may also share husbands.

17 FEMALE HUSBAND MARRIAGE
KENYA / ANTIQUITY–PRESENT
Among the Nandi people, a sonless woman may marry another woman to secure an heir, giving the sonless woman social and economic prestige.

18 LEARNING HUSBAND
BRAZIL / ANTIQUITY–PRESENT
In the Zo'é tribe, a woman has several husbands, including temporary "learning husbands"—young men learning how to be good spouses.

19 HUMAN-ANIMAL MARRIAGE
INDONESIA, INDIA, AND AFRICA
1600s–PRESENT
May be performed as a good-luck ritual or a punishment—in cases of bestiality, the man may be forced to marry the animal and pay a dowry.

12 INFLUENTIAL MISTRESSES *and* CONCUBINES

1 HAGAR
MISTRESS TO ABRAHAM
MIDDLE EAST / 2000 BCE
Hagar was the slave of Sarah, the wife of the Jewish patriarch Abraham. Sarah had difficulty bearing children and arranged for Hagar to sleep with Abraham. This unhappy situation culminated in the exile of Hagar and her son.

2 CLEOPATRA
MISTRESS TO JULIUS CAESAR AND MARK ANTONY
EGYPT / 48–44 BCE AND 41–30 BCE
Powerful in her own right as a Greek ruler of Egypt, Cleopatra was also famous for her amorous and strategic affairs with ancient Rome's leaders. After Caesar's murder, she took up with Mark Antony; they married in 37 BCE.

3 CONSORT YANG YUHAN
CONCUBINE TO EMPEROR XUANZONG
CHINA / MID-700s
Yang Yuhan was first married to the prince, but Emperor Xuanzong arranged for her to become a nun, freeing her up to be his favorite concubine. Sadly, during a military conflict, his troops forced him to kill her as a symbolic act.

4 VANNOZZA DEI CATTANEI
MISTRESS TO RODRIGO BORGIA
ITALY / 1470–1492
This Italian noblewoman was one of the many mistresses of Cardinal—and later Pope—Rodrigo Borgia. Known as his favorite, she bore him four children, whom he acknowledged and lavished with wealth and praise.

5 ELIZABETH "JANE" SHORE
MISTRESS TO KING EDWARD IV
ENGLAND / 1474–1483
King Edward had many mistresses, but Jane Shore was his favorite; indeed, many found her lovely and called her "the Rose of London." After Edward's death, Richard III assumed the throne and publicly ridiculed her for the affair.

6 ANNE BOLEYN
MISTRESS TO HENRY VIII
ENGLAND / 1525–1536
Henry VIII courted Anne for eight years while trying to get his marriage annulled. While it's widely believed they had a chaste relationship in those years, she was pregnant by the time he broke with the Catholic church to marry her.

7 JEANNE ANTOINETTE POISSON
MISTRESS TO LOUIS XV
FRANCE / 1744–1764
A commoner who was well educated in art and conversation, Poisson became the French king's official chief mistress and was dubbed the Marquise de Pompadour. She was quite influential in politics and foreign affairs.

8 LOLA MONTEZ
MISTRESS TO KING LUDWIG I
BAVARIA / 1846–1848
A dancer and actress who dallied in bohemian circles, Montez became Ludwig's mistress and was elevated to Countess of Landsfeld. She was quite the liberal; her political influence over the king made them both unpopular.

9 LILLIE LANGTRY
MISTRESS TO PRINCE ALBERT EDWARD
UK / 1877–1880
The stage actress and noted beauty had affairs with many notable men, but none so exalted as "Bertie," the Prince of Wales and future King Edward VII. He was so taken with her that he introduced her to his mom—Queen Victoria.

10 LUCY PAGE MERCER
MISTRESS TO FRANKLIN DELANO ROOSEVELT
US / 1914–1945
Roosevelt's wife, Eleanor, hired Lucy Page Mercer as a secretary when her husband was a senator. Eleanor discovered the affair in 1918, but Mercer secretly visited Roosevelt at the White House and was with him when he died.

11 VIRGINIA HILL
MISTRESS TO BUGSY SIEGEL
US / 1940s
Hill had lots of mobster boyfriends, but when she met Siegel in Los Angeles, she became his steady gal and partner in crime, couriering cash to Swiss bank accounts. He called her "the Flamingo" on account of her long legs.

12 CAMILLA PARKER BOWLES
MISTRESS TO PRINCE CHARLES
UK / 1970–PRESENT
The long-term affair between Prince Charles and Camilla Parker Bowles began when they met at a polo match. Widely blamed for the breakup of his marriage to Lady Diana, she is now his wife and the Duchess of Cornwall.

9 CASES OF STOLEN GLORY

CREDIT WHERE CREDIT IS DUE

Some of these cases are cut-and-dried, while others are matters of hot debate. Whether a historical figure is a glory hog or a victim of revisionists can be awfully difficult to say for sure. Debate away!

1 THE BIG BANG THEORY

US / 1965

Physicist Robert H. Dicke had a hunch that the universe still contained radiation left over from the Big Bang, which would prove the controversial theory. Before he could measure it, physicists Arno Penzias and Robert Woodrow Wilson accidentally got a reading on it—and with it the 1978 Nobel Prize.

2 DNA

UK / 1953

Rosalind Franklin was the first to discover DNA's double helix structure, for which James Dewey Watson and Francis Crick later won the Nobel Prize in 1962—all thanks to her research. Many feel that they did not properly acknowledge her work; sadly, she later died of cancer caused by radiation from the X-rays that led to DNA's discovery.

3 THE TELESCOPE

THE NETHERLANDS AND ITALY / 1609

Spectacle-maker Hans Lippershey completed the first-ever telescope and attempted to obtain a patent for it in 1608, but was denied. A few countries over, scientist Galileo Galilei heard about Lippershey's work. He went on to built his own telescope, improving on Lippershey's model substantially in 1609.

4 THE TELEPHONE

US / 1876

In 1860, Italian-born Antonio Meucci patented a version of the phone to communicate with his ill wife within their home, but he failed to renew his patent in 1874. Two years later, Alexander Graham Bell registered his own design. Meucci attempted to sue, but his original plans had been lost . . . by Western Union, where Bell had worked at the time.

5 CALCULUS

GERMANY AND ENGLAND / 1675

It is generally accepted today that Gottfried Leibniz and Sir Isaac Newton simultaneously and independently developed calculus. Newton, however, was certain that Leibniz had stolen it from his unpublished works in the early 1670s, and made such a fuss that he became known as its rightful inventor.

6 PENICILLIN

SCOTLAND / 1928

Moldy bread (the original basis for penicillin) has been a folk medicine for infections since at least the Middle Ages. Many scientists also worked with it from the late 1880s on, but only Scottish scientist Sir Alexander Fleming has received credit for its discovery. (However, he did ultimately share the 1945 Nobel Prize with the scientists who developed a version of penicillin that could be used as a medicine.)

7 THE IGUANADON

UK / 1830s

Gideon Mantell uncovered teeth of the then-unknown iguanadon in 1822, but rival Sir Richard Owen stole credit for the discovery and proceeded to ignore his rival's research.

8 RELATIVITY

EUROPE / 1905

The foremost relativity expert in the 19th century, Jules Henri Poincaré was the first to formally present the theory of relativity. Albert Einstein published his findings after Poincaré did—without citing Poincaré's work.

9 ELECTRICITY

US / LATE 1800s

Nikola Tesla was a Serbian engineer who immigrated to the United States and is widely considered to be responsible for radio, microwaves, primitive radar systems, and electricity, for which US inventor and politician Thomas Edison largely gets credit.

11 LIFESAVERS

1 SMALLPOX VACCINATION
ENGLAND / 1796
Although there were treatments for smallpox in ancient India and China, English scientist Edward Jenner introduced the far safer method of vaccination, saving millions of people.

2 BARRY THE SAINT BERNARD
SWITZERLAND / 1800–1814
This Saint Bernard lived at the hospice at Switzerland's Great Saint Bernard Pass—a mountain region that had claimed the lives of many. Barry reportedly rescued at least 40 people from the ice and snow.

3 HANDWASHING IN HOSPITALS
US / 1843

Dr. Oliver Wendell Holmes, Sr., was one of the first to advocate handwashing in hospitals in order to stop physicians from spreading infections. It may seem obvious now, but his idea saved countless lives.

4 DISEASE CONTROL
UK / 1855

When a cholera epidemic broke out in London, John Snow tracked the outbreak's source to a single water pump. He's one of the fathers of epidemiology—the study of disease patterns and control.

5 HOARY TAMARIND TREE
INDIA / 1908

During the devastating floods of 1908 in the Andhra Pradesh state, a tree in the capital city of Hyderabad saved 150 people who quickly climbed it and clung to it for safety as the waters rose.

6 DISEASE-RESISTANT WHEAT
WORLDWIDE / 1944–PRESENT

A Nobel prize-winning humanitarian and agronomist, Norman Borlaug dedicated his life to stopping hunger. The high-yield, disease-resistant wheat he developed has fed millions in developing nations.

7 FAKE SWEDISH PASSPORTS
HUNGARY / 1944

In Budapest, Swedish humanitarian Raoul Wallenberg issued fake Swedish passports and housed Jews in buildings protected by "diplomatic immunity"—which saved an estimated 100,000 people from the Nazis.

8 HELA CELLS
US / 1951

Henrietta Lacks died in 1951, but her cancerous cells have lived on and helped millions. The first such cells that doctors could keep alive and grow, they've aided in research on cancer, AIDS, and more.

9 THE SEATBELT
SWEDEN / 1959

An engineer at Volvo, Nils Bohlin invented the now-standard three-point seatbelt (which crosses the chest and lap, anchoring passengers in their seats). He has saved more than a million lives to date.

10 A "NO" TO NUKES
THE CARIBBEAN / 1962

Soviet naval officer Vasili Arkhipov was serving on a submarine during the Cuban Missile Crisis. The US Navy cornered the ship, but Arkhipov voted against launching a nuclear torpedo—thus saving the world.

11 ONE MAN'S SPECIAL BLOOD
AUSTRALIA / 1953–PRESENT

The world's most generous blood donor, James Harrison has donated 1,000 times since 1953—which is lucky, as his blood contains a rare enzyme that's saved 2 million infants from dying of Rh disease.

17 Holy Hairdos

1 **TONSURE**
ROMAN CATHOLIC MONKS / 700s–PRESENT
Monks shave the tops of their heads, leaving the remaining hair as a "crown."

2 **CHEVE SIMBI**
VOODOO PRACTITIONERS / 1700s–1970
Voodoo leaders wore long braided strands to honor the Simbi Lwa, a Haitian snake spirit.

3 **FEMININE BRAIDS**
ALEUT SHAMANS / ANTIQUITY–PRESENT
Male shamans in these Alaskan tribes adopt a woman's beaded hairdo.

4 **DREADLOCKS**
RASTAFARIANS / 1930s–PRESENT
Long, matted locks of hair represent the wearer's inner spirituality and journey.

5 **"GASH" HAIR STRIP**
CANDOMBLÉ INITIATES / 1500s–PRESENT
Initiates' heads are shaved and cut; later, they grow their hair to mimic this gash.

6 **UNTRIMMED HAIR AND BEARD**
EASTERN ORTHODOX PRIESTS / 300s–PRESENT
After a ritual haircut and shave, a priest never cuts his hair or beard again.

7 **FEMININE HAIR ORNAMENTS**
SIBERIAN CHUKCHI SHAMANS / ANTIQUITY–1400s
Tribal holy men wore feminine hairstyles and clothing, and may have married older men.

8 **MULTIPLE BRAIDS**
RUSSIAN OSTYAK SHAMANS / 1500s
Divided braids symbolized the sale of one shaman's spirit familiar to another shaman.

9 **FLOWING HAIR AND BEARD**
KNIGHTS TEMPLAR / 1119–1312
The knights cultivated long, flowing hair and beards to evoke a Christlike look.

10 **GOAT GALLBLADDER AND BEADS**
NGUNI HEALERS / ANTIQUITY–PRESENT
The initiate healer wears a sacrificed goat's gallbladder in her headdress.

11 **CROPPED HAIR**
ROMAN PRIESTESSES / 600s BCE–300s CE
Vestal virgins had their hair cropped upon their acceptance to the temple.

12 **TOPKNOT**
ORTHODOX HINDUS / 500S–PRESENT
They shave the sides of the head, leaving only the *sikha,* a long lock tied in a knot.

13 **RED AND WHITE RIBBONS**
SHINTO SHRINE MAIDENS / 600s–PRESENT
The Japanese female shaman wears her hair long, tied with red and white ribbons.

14 **PAYOT**
ORTHODOX JEWISH MEN / 4000 BCE–PRESENT
They wear long side curls, as the Bible prohibits cutting the hair's "corners."

15 **SWEETGRASS BRAIDS**
YOUNG CHIPPEWA MEN / ANTIQUITY–PRESENT
Sweetgrass is braided into the hair to banish bad spirits and ill health.

16 **SINGLE LOCK**
BERBER TRIBESMEN / 50 BCE–PRESENT
Tribe members leave one lock of hair long so that angels can pull them up to heaven.

17 **UNGROOMED**
QALANDAR SUFIS / 1100s–PRESENT
These holy men cannot cut or groom their hair for the duration of their lives.

10 UNSOLVED MYSTERIES

1

THE LOST COLONY OF ROANOKE

US / 1587

The first English colony in the New World was established on Roanoke Island off what is now the US state of North Carolina, but disappeared within three years leaving hardly a trace. Some believe the colonists were killed by local Native American tribes or joined them.

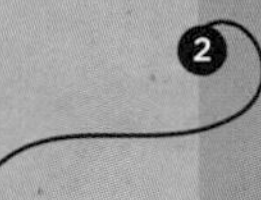

2

THE MAN IN THE IRON MASK

FRANCE / 1669

A masked prisoner held for 34 years until his death, the man in the iron mask was referred to as "Eustache Dauger" (the name of another man doing time elsewhere in France) and was never identified. Some surmise he was an embarrassing relative of royalty.

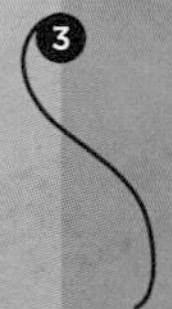

3

OAK ISLAND MONEY PIT

CANADA / 1795

First found in 1795, this sinkhole-like area on an island near Nova Scotia is rumored to contain buried treasure—perhaps even Marie Antoinette's jewels. Explorers unearthed stones with promising inscriptions, but floods and collapses have thwarted excavation.

4

MARY CELESTE

ATLANTIC OCEAN / 1872

This merchant ship was abandoned in the Atlantic Ocean. There had been no storms, the passengers' belongings and cargo were virtually undisturbed, there were plenty of supplies, and there were no signs of violence. The one lifeboat was missing, and was never found.

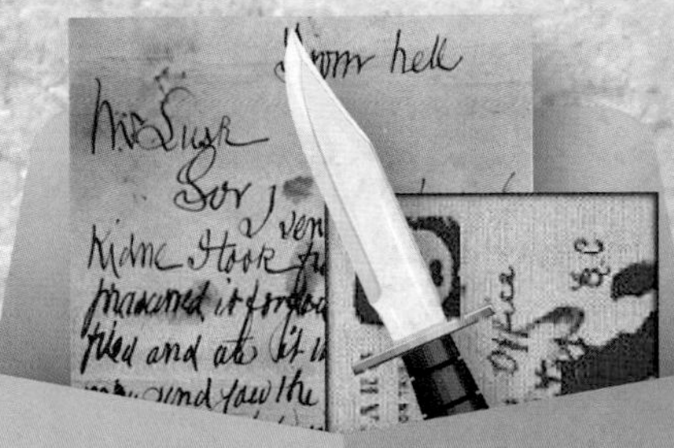

JACK THE RIPPER

UK / 1888–1891

In one of the most famous unsolved mysteries, an unknown man committed a string of gruesome murders and mutilations, all of prostitutes in a poor London district. Letters signed "Jack the Ripper" were sent to the media claiming credit, but the crimes remain unsolved.

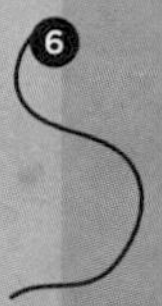

LAS BOLAS

COSTA RICA / 1940

Varying in size from as small as a tennis ball to 8 feet (2.4 m) in diameter and weighing up to 16 tons (14,500 kg), these ancient stone balls are an enigma: No one knows who made them, for what purpose, or how. There are more than 300, and they were discovered in 1940.

SS OURANG MEDAN

INDONESIA / 1948

This Dutch freighter either wrecked mysteriously, or never even existed, depending on whom you believe. Theories about its fate include UFOs (of course) and other less exciting notions, such as an explosion in the cargo hold or carbon monoxide poisoning.

ASSASSINATION OF JFK

US / 1963

While Lee Harvey Oswald is officially believed to be responsible for the assassination of US president John F. Kennedy, theories about who planned and facilitated it—and even who pulled the trigger—have persisted. Many think that the truth has been covered up.

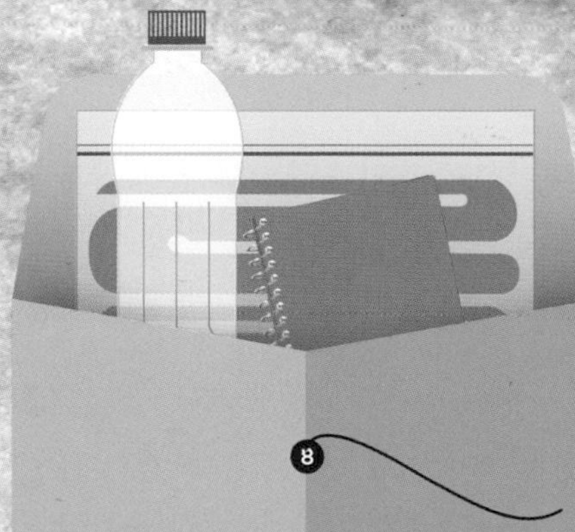

LEAD MASKS CASE

BRAZIL / 1966

Two electronic technicians wearing waterproof coats and lead masks were found dead in a field near an empty bottle and a small notebook that contained weird instructions regarding orange capsules and "awaiting a sign." Autopsy results were inconclusive.

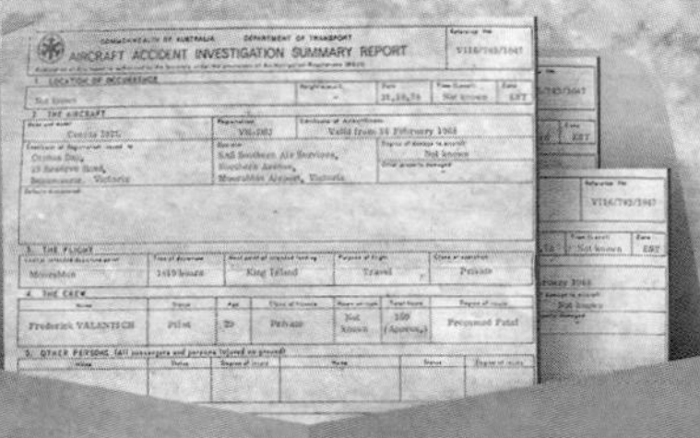

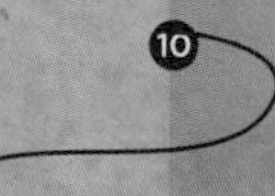

FREDERICK VALENTICH

AUSTRALIA / 1978

While flying in optimal conditions, Valentich disappeared without a trace after radioing in that he'd seen mysterious lights in the sky and that an aircraft was hovering above him. This case is much beloved by UFOlogists.

14 FAMOUS BODY PARTS

2 SAINT BONAVENTURE'S ARM
ITALY / 1274
This saint believed that all ideas flowed from God; thus, his writing arm was the vehicle through which he made God's ideas manifest. After his death, this arm was placed in a silver arm-shaped reliquary.

1 LAZZARO SPALLANZANI'S BLADDER
ITALY / 1799
After this priest and biologist died of bladder cancer, physicians removed the cancerous organ for medical study. It's on display in a museum in Pavia.

14 JESUS'S FORESKIN
ISRAEL / 1
The holy prepuce—aka, holy foreskin—is one of several relics attributed to Jesus, which many European churches have claimed to possess throughout history.

13 JOSÉ RIZAL'S VERTEBRA
THE PHILIPPINES / 1913
During the transport of the Philippine revolutionary hero's body 17 years after his death, a single vertebra was enclosed in a glass reliquary for display—the single bullet that killed him struck it.

12 CHE GUEVARA'S HANDS
UNKNOWN / 1967
When this Argentine Marxist revolutionary was executed in Bolivia, his hands were severed for identification purposes. His body and hands went missing for nearly 30 years; the corpse was found, but the hands were not buried with it.

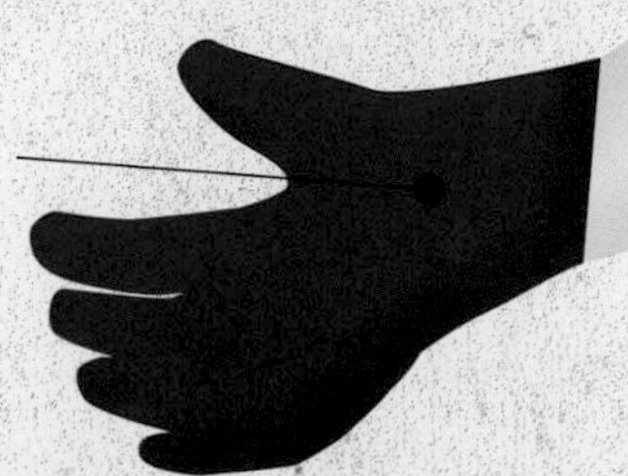

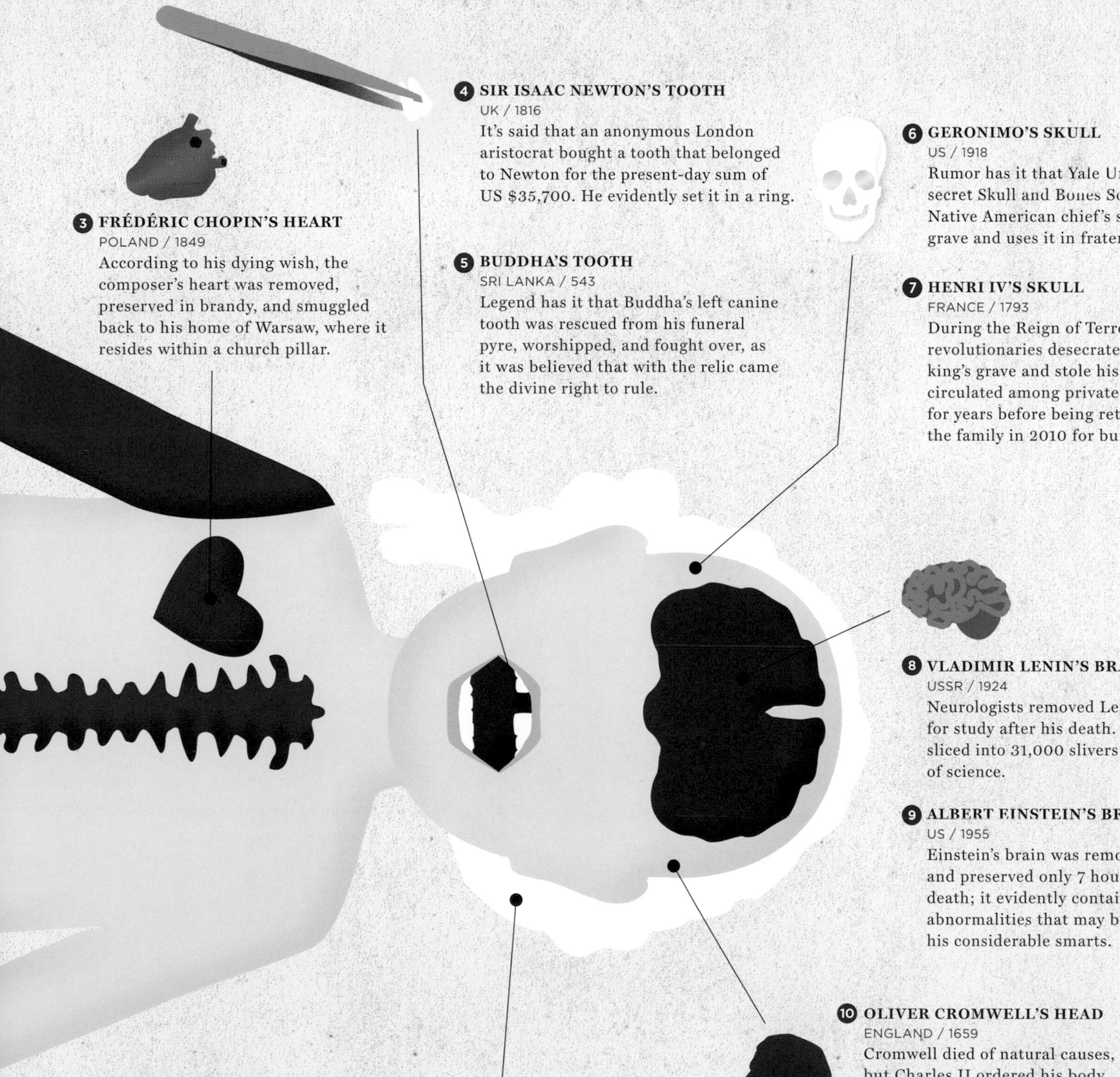

3 **FRÉDÉRIC CHOPIN'S HEART**
POLAND / 1849
According to his dying wish, the composer's heart was removed, preserved in brandy, and smuggled back to his home of Warsaw, where it resides within a church pillar.

4 **SIR ISAAC NEWTON'S TOOTH**
UK / 1816
It's said that an anonymous London aristocrat bought a tooth that belonged to Newton for the present-day sum of US $35,700. He evidently set it in a ring.

5 **BUDDHA'S TOOTH**
SRI LANKA / 543
Legend has it that Buddha's left canine tooth was rescued from his funeral pyre, worshipped, and fought over, as it was believed that with the relic came the divine right to rule.

6 **GERONIMO'S SKULL**
US / 1918
Rumor has it that Yale University's secret Skull and Bones Society stole the Native American chief's skull from his grave and uses it in fraternity rituals.

7 **HENRI IV'S SKULL**
FRANCE / 1793
During the Reign of Terror, French revolutionaries desecrated the king's grave and stole his head. It circulated among private collectors for years before being returned to the family in 2010 for burial.

8 **VLADIMIR LENIN'S BRAIN**
USSR / 1924
Neurologists removed Lenin's brain for study after his death. It's been sliced into 31,000 slivers in the name of science.

9 **ALBERT EINSTEIN'S BRAIN**
US / 1955
Einstein's brain was removed and preserved only 7 hours after his death; it evidently contains several abnormalities that may be linked to his considerable smarts.

10 **OLIVER CROMWELL'S HEAD**
ENGLAND / 1659
Cromwell died of natural causes, but Charles II ordered his body exhumed and publicly hung for a day, after which his head was placed on a spike to eerily reside over Westminster Hall for decades.

11 **GEORGE WASHINGTON'S HAIR**
US / 1800
Martha Washington gifted a lock of the deceased president's hair to the young Eliza Wadsworth (later aunt of Henry Wadsworth Longfellow). It now resides in a gold locket in the Maine Historical Society.

5 GAME-CHANGING EQUATIONS

❶ **PYTHAGOREAN THEOREM**

PYTHAGORAS / GREECE / 500s

This theorem states that for any right triangle, the square of the hypotenuse—the side opposite the right angle—is equal to the sum of the squares of the other two sides. It proved the existence of irrational numbers, advancing ancient mathematics.

❷ **NEWTON'S LAW OF UNIVERSAL GRAVITATION**

ISAAC NEWTON / ENGLAND / 1687

Newton found that the gravitational force exerted by two objects is directly proportional to those objects' masses and inversely related to the distance between them. It explains the movements of the planets, but probably wasn't inspired by an apple dropping on Newton's head.

$$P_1 + \tfrac{1}{2}pv_1^{\,2} + pgh$$

3 SPECIAL RELATIVITY

ALBERT EINSTEIN / GERMANY / 1905

Given that both the speed of light and the laws of physics are constants, Einstein set out to explain why various bodies seem to move at different speeds to people in different frames of reference. From this theory, Einstein proved that energy equals mass multiplied by the square of the speed of light—thus, energy and mass are interchangeable. His ideas have affected everything from nuclear fission to radiocarbon dating.

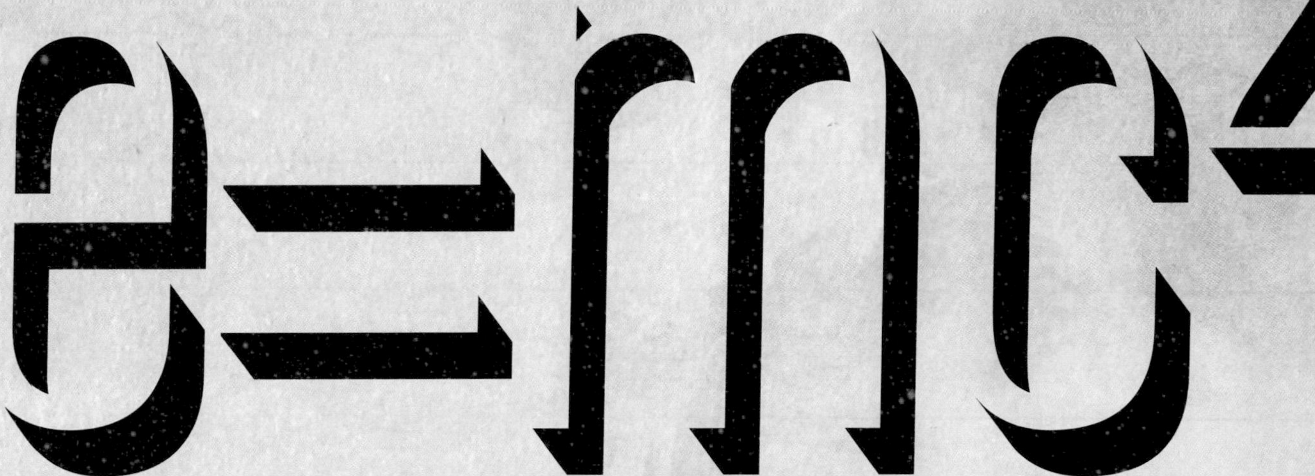

4 HEISENBERG'S UNCERTAINTY PRINCIPLE

WERNER HEISENBERG / GERMANY / 1927

This cornerstone of quantum physics states that at the quantum level, it is impossible to observe a phenomenon without affecting it: The more an observer measures a particle's present state, the less the observer knows about where it's going.

$$\Delta x \Delta \rho \geq \frac{\hbar}{2}$$

5 BERNOULLI'S PRINCIPLE

DANIEL BERNOULLI / SWITZERLAND / 1700s

Bernoulli's principle shows the inverse relationship between fluid velocity (whether of a liquid or a gas) and pressure. His ideas proved important for many applications of fluid motion, including airplane wing design.

$$= P_2 + \tfrac{1}{2} p v_2^{\,2} + p g h_2$$

1 **HEADLESS ANIMALS HEALED**
EGYPT / 2500 BCE
According to lore, the conjurer Dedi entertained King Khufu by seemingly cutting off and then restoring the heads of a goose, a pelican, and an ox. (He refused to demonstrate this skill on a human.)

2 **AN EARLY SHELL GAME**
GREECE / 200 BCE
The philosopher Alciphron told of a street magician who placed three small cups on a table, then made pebbles appear under each cup, then in his mouth, and then in the ears and noses of amazed bystanders.

3 **TINY WONDERS**
ENGLAND / LATE 1700s
An impressive showman, the Prussian Gustavus Katterfelto used microscopes to reveal tiny microbes in water to a riveted audience. He claimed that they were responsible for the flu epidemic of 1782.

4 **THE HOLLOW-LEG GAMBIT**
HOLLAND / 1793
After his leg was amputated due to a wartime injury, Eliaser Bamberg began using his hollow wooden prosthetic to make objects disappear. He was dubbed *Le Diable Boiteux* ("the lame devil") as a result.

5 **MAGIC MAGNETS**
FRANCE / 1840s–1850s
For his act, Jean-Eugène Robert-Houdin invited spectators to lift a lightweight box. Secretly, he then activated a magnet under the stage, which attracted metal hidden inside the box, making the box "immovable."

6 **WHERE'D THE KID COME FROM?**
US / 1898
Ching Ling Foo breathed smoke and fire and produced ribbons from his mouth, but his grand finale was making a huge bowl of water appear out of nowhere, and then pulling a small child out of it.

7 BURIED ALIVE
US / EARLY 1900s

African-American magician Benjamin Rucker (who went by Black Herman) faked his own death, allowing showgoers to touch his "corpse" and watch his coffin be buried. Days later, he would rise from the grave.

8 CUTTING A LADY IN HALF
UK / 1921–1938

P. T. Selbit invented the now-classic "cutting a woman in half" trick. He made his version especially dramatic by having the box that held her bound in ropes to prevent his "victim" from escaping.

9 THE FLOATING LIGHTBULB
US / 1930s

The most famous trick of magician Harry Blackstone, Sr., involved removing a light-bulb from a lamp and making it "float" through a small hoop—without losing its glow. It would then float over the audience.

10 MYSTERIOUS ROPES AND CARPETS
INDIA / 1933–1971

Bengali magician and scholar of magic Pratul Chandra Sorcar popularized or invented many now-classic magic acts, including a number of rope tricks and a flying carpet illusion.

11 Technologies Based on Nature

1 EIFFEL TOWER
BASED ON THE HUMAN FEMUR
The round head of the human thigh bone isn't solid bone—it's a lattice of tiny criss-crossing struts that support the natural curve of the femur. Engineer Gustave Eiffel studied skeletons and applied the lessons to Paris's Eiffel Tower, which was finished in 1889.

2 SUSPENSION BRIDGE CABLES
BASED ON TENDONS
Tendons are made up of multiple muscle fibers twisted together to provide both strength and flexibility. Bridge makers have copied this natural phenomenon, crafting load-bearing cables composed of smaller cables that allow suspension bridges to span greater distances.

3 BATTLE ARMOR
BASED ON SPIDER SILK
Spider silk is amazingly light, strong, and easy to work with. Scientists are trying to replicate it in the lab so they can build body armor that's tougher than steel and much more flexible.

4 UNDERWATER EXPLORATION ROBOT
BASED ON CRABS
A prototype robot that functions underwater and on land was modeled on crabs. Its eight legs easily scurry over rocks and change direction—perfect for deep-sea exploration.

5 VELCRO
BASED ON THE BURR OF THE BURDOCK PLANT
In the 1940s, Swiss engineer George de Mestral returned from a hike covered in burdock burrs, fascinated with how they attached to his clothes and dog. The thistle's tiny, hook-tipped burrs inspired his invention of Velcro.

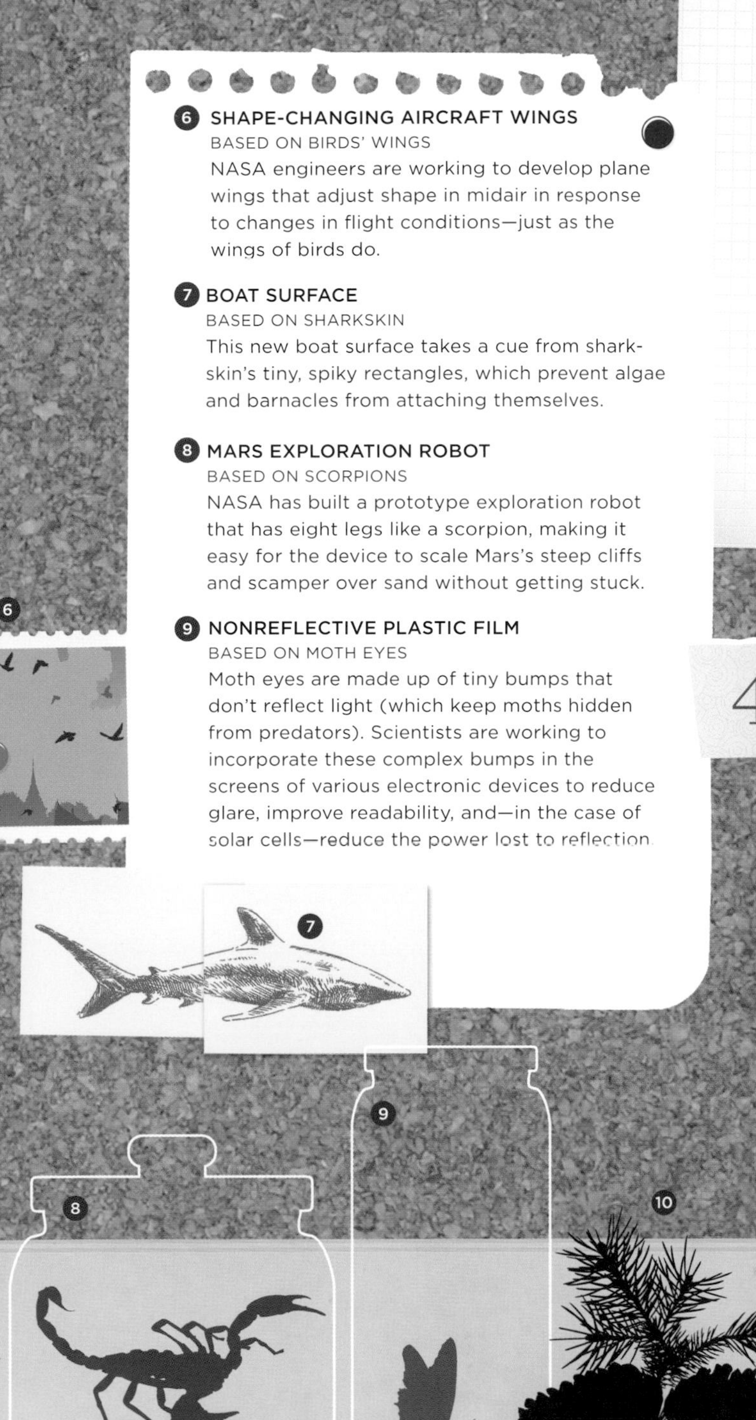

6 SHAPE-CHANGING AIRCRAFT WINGS
BASED ON BIRDS' WINGS
NASA engineers are working to develop plane wings that adjust shape in midair in response to changes in flight conditions—just as the wings of birds do.

7 BOAT SURFACE
BASED ON SHARKSKIN
This new boat surface takes a cue from sharkskin's tiny, spiky rectangles, which prevent algae and barnacles from attaching themselves.

8 MARS EXPLORATION ROBOT
BASED ON SCORPIONS
NASA has built a prototype exploration robot that has eight legs like a scorpion, making it easy for the device to scale Mars's steep cliffs and scamper over sand without getting stuck.

9 NONREFLECTIVE PLASTIC FILM
BASED ON MOTH EYES
Moth eyes are made up of tiny bumps that don't reflect light (which keep moths hidden from predators). Scientists are working to incorporate these complex bumps in the screens of various electronic devices to reduce glare, improve readability, and—in the case of solar cells—reduce the power lost to reflection.

10 SMART FABRIC
BASED ON PINECONES
Inspired by pinecone scales' ability to open when it's warm and close when it's cool, designers have invented a fabric with a layer of tiny wool spikes that similarly open and shut, adjusting to fluctuations in body temperatures and keeping the wearer comfortable.

11 ANTONI GAUDÍ'S BASÍLICA I TEMPLE EXPIATORI DE LA SAGRADA FAMÍLIA
BASED ON PLANT STRUCTURES
Architect Gaudí began work on this "forest of stone" in 1884, inspired by nature's geometric forms. In particular, he based the basilica's trunklike columns on the oleander plant's stems, and covered the ceiling in stone "leaves."

4 DEVICES INSPIRED BY ORIGAMI

1 SATELLITE SOLAR PANELS
In 1995, a massive solar sail was folded into a compact shape, packed on the Japanese *Space Flight Unit,* and launched into space, where it was unfolded with one elegant tug—all thanks to the Miura-ori origami technique.

2 HEART STENT
Scientists in the United Kingdom created a heart stent that increases in diameter by more than six times when unfolded inside the artery.

3 TELESCOPE
In 2002, Dr. Robert J. Lang used origami to make a telescope that fit inside a rocket and expanded to the width of a soccer field once in space.

4 AIR BAG SIMULATION
Dr. Lang was at it again, developing a computer algorithm based on origami that was then used in the simulation of air bag folding and dispersal.

28 Sacred Outfits

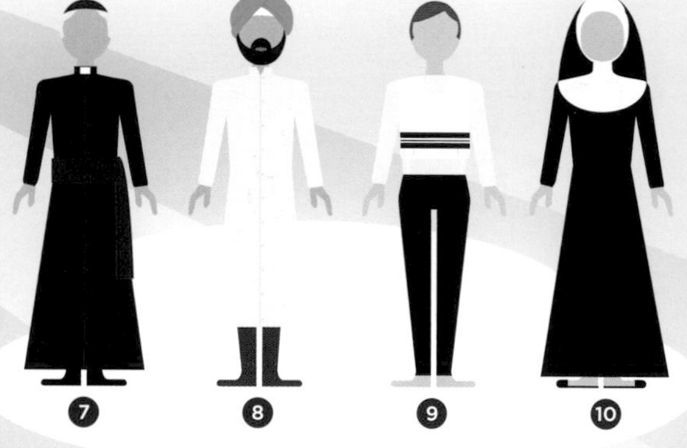

1 HIJAB
ISLAM
Islam prescribes modest dress for both men and women. This code of dress, called the hijab, is also used to refer to the headscarf worn by moderate Muslim women.

2 KASA
JAPANESE BUDDHISM
A traditional hat worn by Buddhist monks, it is large and rounded, covering most of the wearer's face. This provides anonymity and guards against distraction.

3 MITRE
CHRISTIANITY
A mitre, a term derived from the Greek word for "headband" or "turban," is a headdress worn by bishops in Catholic and other Orthodox dioceses during high ceremonies.

4 TSONGKHAPA HAT
TIBETAN GELUG BUDDHISM
Named for the monk who founded the school, this hat is decorated with fringe that resembles a horse's mane; monks of three denominations wear it.

5 EPHOD
JUDAISM
Worn by high priests, this vestment is similar to an open-sided tunic. It's constructed of fine linen and dyed thread, with shoulder straps and a sash belt.

6 BURKA
ISLAM
The most extreme example in Islamic female dress, the burka is a head-to-toe garment that hides all of a woman's body and face except for her eyes.

7 ZUCCHETTO
CATHOLICISM
A small skullcap similar in appearance to a Jewish kippah, the zucchetto is color-coded liturgical headgear for the pope, cardinals, bishops, and sometimes priests.

8 TURBAN
SIKHISM AND ISLAM
Adult Sikh males are required to wear a turban, called a dastar. Muslim males may wear turbans, but it is typically not required, save on pilgrimages to Mecca.

9 TALLIT KATAN
ORTHODOX JUDAISM
Jewish men can wear the tallit katan, which looks somewhat like a poncho, over or under other garments. The knotted fringes on the corners are called tzitzit.

10 NUNS' HABIT
CATHOLICISM
The nuns' habit makes them recognizable to the world, but its elements can vary. Most distinctively, it includes a full-length dress and a square, white, starched coif covering the hair.

11 CASSOCK
CHRISTIANITY
The traditional liturgical garment of Catholic, Orthodox, and Reformed churches, the cassock is generally a simple ankle-length robe. It can be close- or loose-fitting.

12 DHOTI
BUDDHISM, HINDUISM, AND JAINISM
Many males wear this unstitched cloth wrapped around both legs and waist. Jainism especially requires followers to avoid stitched clothing in the name of ahimsa (nonharming).

13 AMISH CLOTHING
AMISH
The Amish show their commitment to their faith with simple, unadorned garments, without belts or zippers. This attire also attests to their nonconformance to outside fashions.

14 KASAYA
INDIAN AND ASIAN BUDDHISM
Originally made from discarded fabric and named for the reddish-brown dye used to color them, these robes consist of three rectangular cloths. Various Buddhist monks wear them.

15 CULT GARMENTS
HEAVEN'S GATE CULT
For their mass suicide, each cult member wore a blue shirt, sweat pants, athletic shoes, and armband patches, and covered himself or herself with a purple square cloth.

16 TALLIT
JUDAISM
Worshippers wear this square prayer shawl over their clothes during their morning prayers and on the Shabbat. It features similar fringes and knots to the tallit katan.

17 SARI
BUDDHISM, HINDUISM, AND JAINISM
This rectangular piece of cloth is anywhere from 13 to 29 feet (4–9 m) long. Women wear it in all sorts of artful folds, such as wrapped around the legs and draped over the shoulder.

18 MONKS' HABIT
CATHOLICISM AND ANGLICANISM
Monks' habits vary by religious order and sect. Typically, though, a monk's robes tend toward drab colors—brown, black, gray—and unadorned simplicity.

19 TEMPLE GARMENT
MORMONISM
Adults must wear special underwear to enter a temple. Most Mormons wear it daily as a personal symbol of their faith. (It's referred to by outsiders as "Mormon underwear.")

20 SHEITEL
HASIDIC JUDAISM
A sheitel is the Yiddish term for a wig or half-wig worn by married Orthodox Jewish women. Jewish law requires that they cover their hair, but it doesn't say with what.

21 TEMPLE ROBES
MORMONISM
Mormons wear these robes, modeled on those worn by Hebrew priests in Exodus, during their ceremonial rites of passage. Each element is white, except for the green apron.

22 TAQIYAH
ISLAM
Many Muslims today wear this short, round hat—which is a similar cap to the one the Prophet wore—in order to be closer to holiness. It's often worn under a turban.

23 MANTILLA
CATHOLICISM
Some Spanish Catholic women wear this scarf, particularly in church, where women are required to cover their heads. They also typically wear it when seeing the Pope.

24 SHTREIMEL
HASIDIC JUDAISM
A fur hat, similar to the hats worn by Tatars, it's worn mostly by married Hasidic men. Wearing a shtreimel is considered a sign of orthodoxy and honor.

25 PAPAL TIARA
CATHOLICISM
This ornate three-tiered crown is covered in jewels and coats of arms, and is a distinctive symbol of the papacy. The Pope usually wears it only for high ceremonies.

26 GIRDLE (CINCTURE)
CHRISTIANITY AND JUDAISM
This knotted belt secures the robe of clergy members, and it serves as a symbol of chastity, purity, and authority. It's often made of simple rope, and is most often white.

27 ROBE
WICCA
White is the most common shade, but these robes come in all colors. They serve mostly as a cue to observers that a magical ritual is about to take place.

28 CANTERBURY CAP
ANGLICANISM
A square cloth hat with four sharp corners, the Canterbury cap is soft and foldable, and all members of the Anglican clergy wear them.

9 AMAZING TALES OF SURVIVAL!

1 STRANDED ON A DESERTED ISLAND

JUAN FERNÁNDEZ ARCHIPELAGO / 1704–1709

Sailor Alexander Selkirk elected to stay behind on a deserted island with only a musket, gunpowder, a few carpenter's tools, a knife, a Bible, some clothing, and rope. He was rescued by a British privateer; his story probably inspired Daniel Defoe's *Robinson Crusoe*.

2 ADRIFT IN A HURRICANE

SOUTH PACIFIC / 1983

A boat carrying Tami Oldham Ashcroft and her boyfriend was hit by a category 4 hurricane. He was lost at sea; she was knocked unconscious. She woke to a broken mainmast, a dead motor, and no radio. With a makeshift sail and few supplies, she headed to Hawaii, 1,500 miles (2,415 km) away, and arrived 41 days later.

3 ESCAPING THE NAZIS

GERMANY / 1943

A Norwegian commando in World War II, Jan Baalsrud was on a mission when Nazis discovered and sunk his boat. He swam ashore, shot a Gestapo officer, cut off nine of his own toes to avoid gangrene, and traveled two months in the snow to neutral Sweden.

4 ATTACKED BY A BEAR AND LEFT FOR DEAD

US / 1823

After a female grizzly mauled fur trapper Hugh Glass, his companions left him for dead, taking his knife and gun. He awoke unable to walk due to a broken leg and suffering from serious wounds, 200 miles (320 km) from safety. He set his leg, cleaned his wounds, and six months later crawled into the nearest settlement.

5 STRANDED IN ANTARCTICA
ANTARCTICA / 1912–1913
When half their dog team (and all their food) fell into a crevasse, explorer Douglas Mawson and another surviving team member headed for base, eating their dogs to survive. Poisoned by dog liver, his friend died, but Mawson made it—but had to wait a year for a rescue boat.

6 DROPPED OFF A MOUNTAIN
PERU / 1985
During a never-before-achieved ascent, British mountaineer Joe Simpson broke his leg; his partner tried to lower him by ropes, but accidentally dropped him and assumed that he was dead. Days later, Simpson crawled into base camp as his partner prepared to leave.

7 SHOT NINE TIMES
MEXICO / 1915
A soldier in the Mexican Revolution, Wenseslao Moguel was captured and set before a firing squad. He was shot nine times—including a coup de grâce to the head from the officer in charge. He survived, escaped after they left him to die, and lived for decades afterward.

8 CRASHED IN THE JUNGLE
PERU / 1971
The only survivor of a plane crash, 17-year-old German Juliane Köpcke was on the way to visit her father, a zoologist. She remembered his survival tips and—despite suffering from a broken collarbone and having no shoes—followed a stream for 10 days until she found a hunter's hut.

9 LOST IN THE DESERT
MOROCCO / 1994
During a 145-mile (233-km) race in the Sahara, Italian runner Mauro Prosperi got lost in a sandstorm. After days without water, he caught bats and drank their blood. Suicidal, he tried to slit his wrist but was so dehydrated that his blood didn't flow. He was rescued five days later.

20 Ignoble Deaths

1 Legend has it that the Greek philosopher secretly jumped into a volcano, hoping to make it look as if he had "vanished" and was therefore divine.

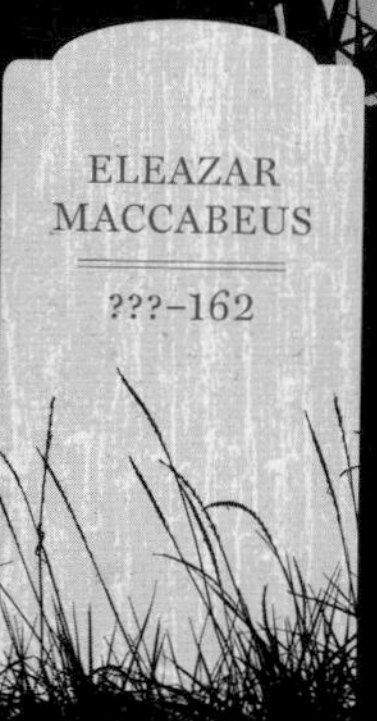

2 This Hebrew soldier was crushed by an elephant immediately after he killed it during battle.

3 According to legend, the Chinese poet drowned after falling from his boat while trying to embrace the moon's reflection in the Yangtze River.

4 This king of Hungary died when his throne's canopy collapsed. Rumors persist that it was not an accident.

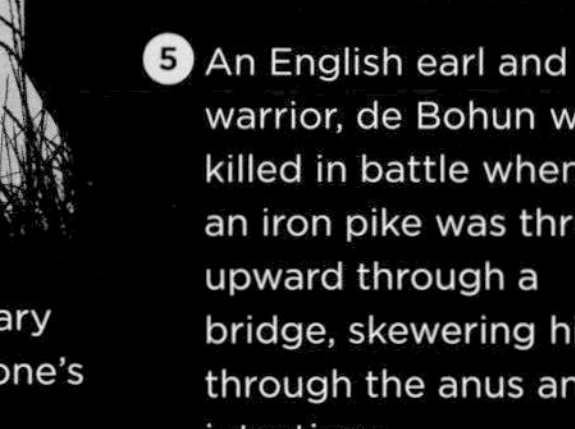

5 An English earl and warrior, de Bohun was killed in battle when an iron pike was thrust upward through a bridge, skewering him through the anus and intestines.

HUMAYUN
1508–1556

6 The emperor of India died when his foot got caught in the folds of his long robes, causing him to tumble down the stairs and fatally hit his temple on a rock.

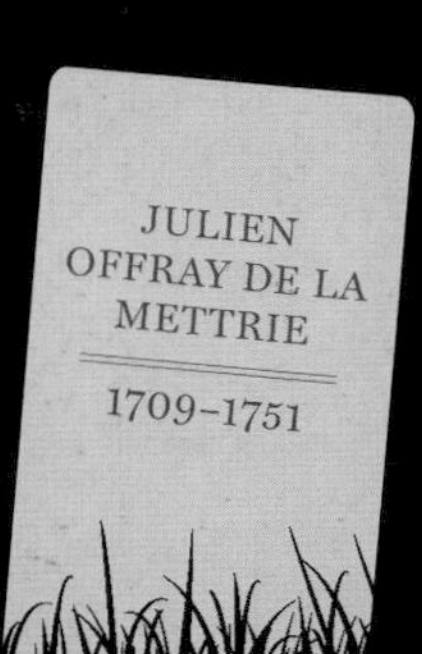

7 The French philosopher and physician died from eating too much truffle pâté at a feast held in his honor by a man he had cured of an illness.

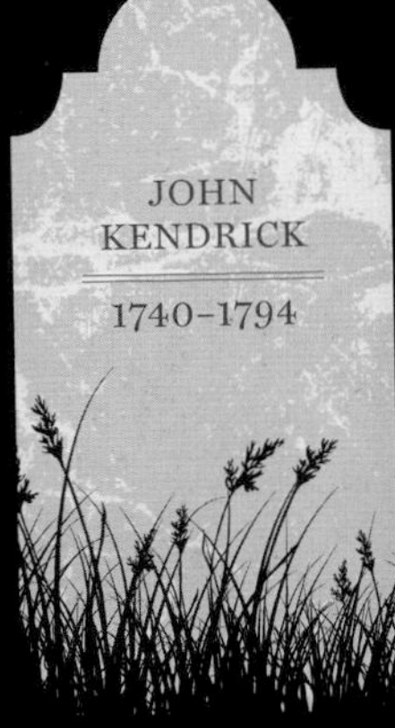

8 This American sea captain was killed when a British ship mistakenly fired live ammunition while saluting Kendrick's vessel.

9 While prepping to defend a murder, the American lawyer accidentally shot himself as he demonstrated how one could accidentally shoot oneself. He died of his wounds, and the defendant was acquitted.

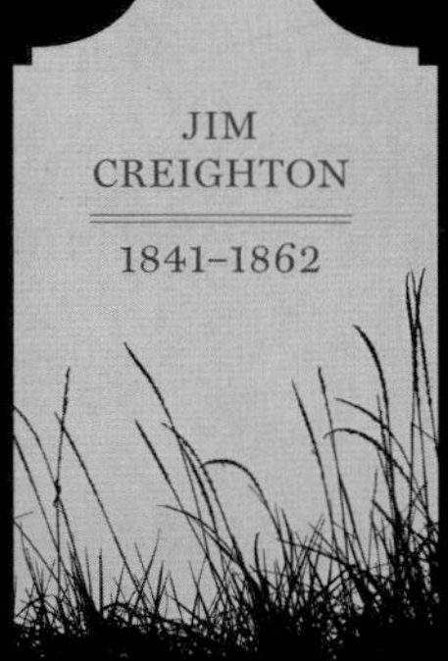

10 Creighton was an early baseball star who died days after he swung a bat too hard, causing internal injuries.

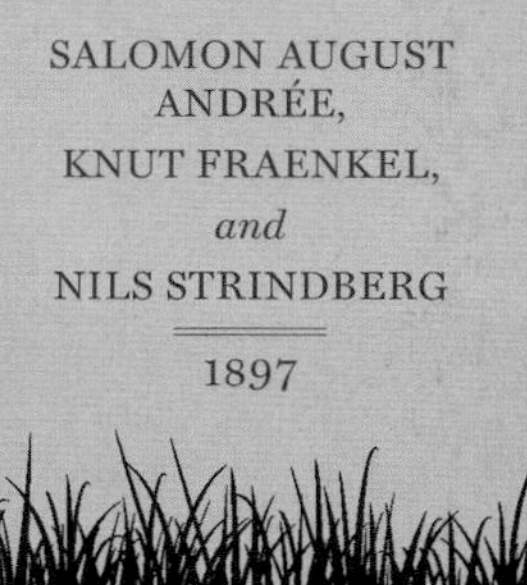

SALOMON AUGUST ANDRÉE,
KNUT FRAENKEL,
and
NILS STRINDBERG
1897

11 These Swedish explorers set out for the North Pole in a hot-air balloon, which crashed on the ice during a storm. Their bodies were recovered in 1930; it's believed that they died from eating undercooked polar bear meat—some of which was still at the site where their bodies were found.

LADY RANDOLPH CHURCHILL

1854–1921

12 Jeanette Jerome (Winston Churchill's mother) broke her ankle descending a staircase while wearing high heels. Gangrene set in, and her left leg was amputated. She died anyway.

13 This Russian physicist died after performing a blood transfusion on himself . . . using blood infected with malaria and tuberculosis.

ISADORA DUNCAN

1877–1927

14 The modern dance icon died when one of her signature long silk scarves caught on the wheel of a car in which she was a passenger, breaking her neck.

15 This Austrian-born tailor fell to his death from the Eiffel Tower's first deck. He was testing his invention, the coat parachute.

16 The New York City recluse died when he set off his own booby trap and was crushed by an avalanche of books, newspapers, and other objects.

17 A circus strongman and Jewish folklore hero, Breitbart died after a performance in which he accidentally pierced his knee with a rusted spike—which led to blood poisoning, the amputation of both legs, and his death.

18 The lead singer and harmonica player for '60s band the Yardbirds got electrocuted because his amplifier was not properly grounded.

19 The South Korean gaming enthusiast died of cardiac arrest after playing the video game StarCraft for almost 50 straight hours in an Internet café.

SERGEY TUGANOV

1981–2009

20 The Russian man bet two women US $4,300 that he could have nonstop sex with them for 12 hours. He won, but promptly died of a heart attack—probably because he'd taken an entire bottle of Viagra.

14 NOTED ENDINGS

A MASSIVE METEOR IMPACT *WAS THE END OF*

THE FORCED ABDICATION OF ROMULUS AUGUSTUS *WAS THE END OF*

"THENCE WE CAME FORTH TO REBEHOLD THE STARS" *WAS THE END OF*

THE EXECUTION OF KING ATAHUALPA *WAS THE END OF*

A FINAL DODO BIRD'S DEATH *WAS THE END OF*

THE DEATH OF ANTONIO STRADIVARI *WAS THE END OF*

VICTORY IN THE PACIFIC *WAS THE END OF*

THE RELEASE OF *THE JAZZ SINGER* *WAS THE END OF*

"AFTER ALL, TOMORROW IS ANOTHER DAY" *WAS THE END OF*

"DON'T LET IT END LIKE THIS. TELL THEM I SAID SOMETHING." *WAS THE END OF*

THE RECORDING OF "I ME MINE" *WAS THE END OF*

THE DEATH OF JANET PARKER *WAS THE END OF*

THE FALL OF THE BERLIN WALL *WAS THE END OF*

PAGE 288 *IS THE END OF*

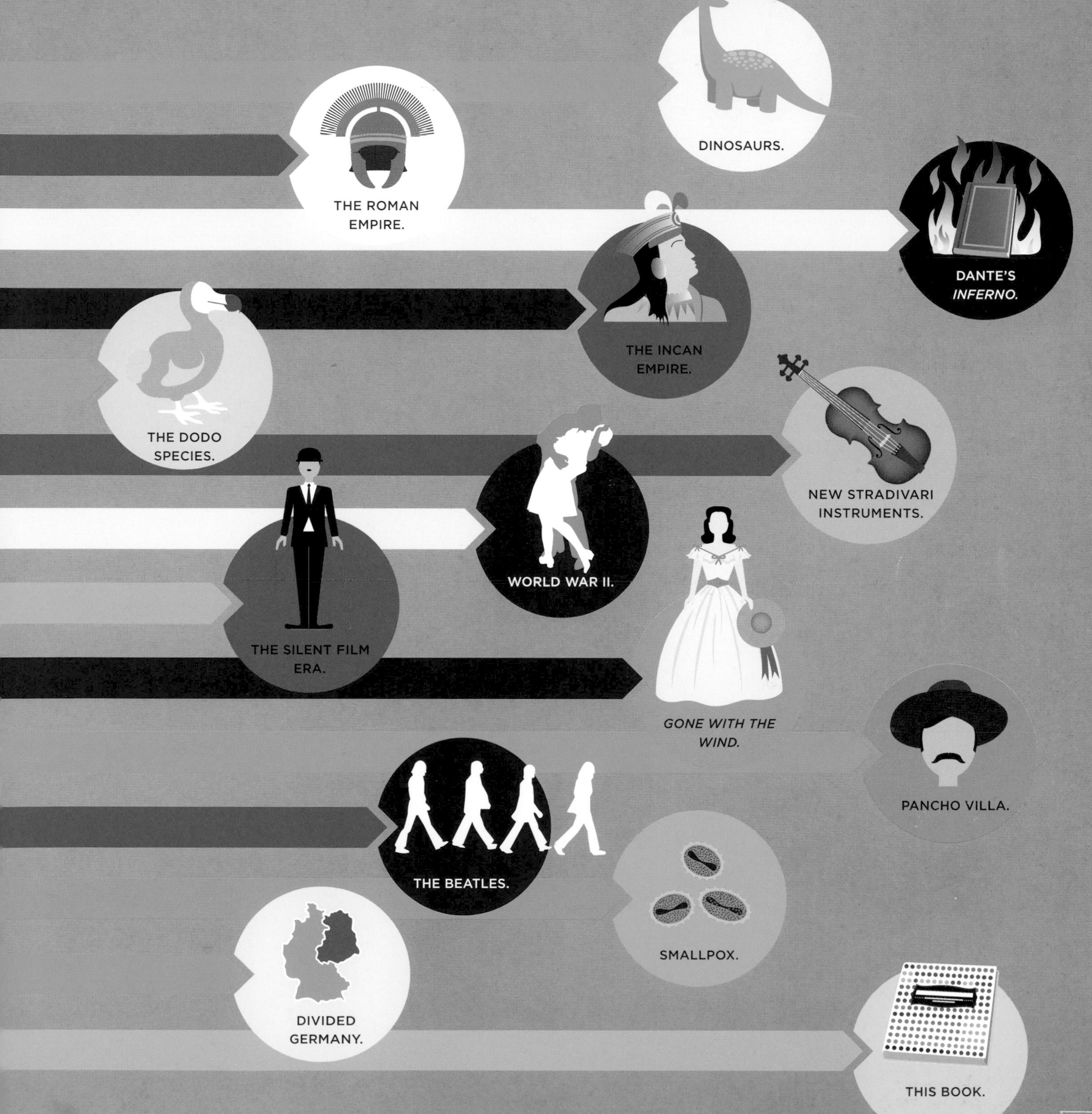
DINOSAURS.
THE ROMAN EMPIRE.
DANTE'S *INFERNO.*
THE INCAN EMPIRE.
THE DODO SPECIES.
NEW STRADIVARI INSTRUMENTS.
WORLD WAR II.
THE SILENT FILM ERA.
GONE WITH THE WIND.
PANCHO VILLA.
THE BEATLES.
SMALLPOX.
DIVIDED GERMANY.
THIS BOOK.

1,333 AMAZING THINGS ABOUT THIS BOOK

Congratulations—you are now quite erudite! But let's face it: It's been a whirlwind of information, and you will want to—at a moment's notice—be able to locate certain facts and share them with others . . . whether near and dear loved ones or know-it-all business associates, bored strangers in waiting rooms or alluring ones at cocktail parties. We've recapped it all for you in the next few pages.

70 RECURRING THEMES IN THIS BOOK

PLACES
RELIGIONS
ANIMALS
CONSUMABLES
INDIVIDUALS
GROUPS
MODERN TECHNOLOGY
CULTURAL ARTIFACTS
THE SUPERNATURAL
BAD SCENES
GROSS THINGS

US
138 OCCURRENCES

JUDAISM
13 OCCURENCES

THE INTERNET
7 OCCURRENCES

THE FLU
2 OCCURRENCES

CANADA
15 OCCURRENCES

BLOOD
2 OCCURRENCES

GUNS
5 OCCURRENCES

DUNE
2 OCCURRENCES

VACCINATIONS
3 OCCURRENCES

SPIDERS
6 OCCURRENCES

LSD
4 OCCURRENCES

GEORGE ORWELL
3 OCCURRENCES

ANTARCTICA
5 OCCURRENCES

INDIA
32 OCCURRENCES

THE BEATLES
4 OCCURRENCES

JESUS CHRIST
7 OCCURRENCES

FUTURAMA
2 OCCURRENCES

HENRIETTA LACKS
2 OCCURRENCES

ESP
2 OCCURRENCES

TELESCOPES
3 OCCURRENCES

ANCIENT EGYPT
13 OCCURRENCES

SNAIL SLIME
3 OCCURRENCES

CHEESE
12 OCCURRENCES

THE CIA
3 OCCURRENCES

BUDDHISM
7 OCCURRENCES

JELLYFISH
2 OCCURRENCES

MUMMIES
5 OCCURRENCES

JAPAN
36 OCCURRENCES

CORPSES
22 OCCURRENCES

ELEPHANTS
9 OCCURRENCES

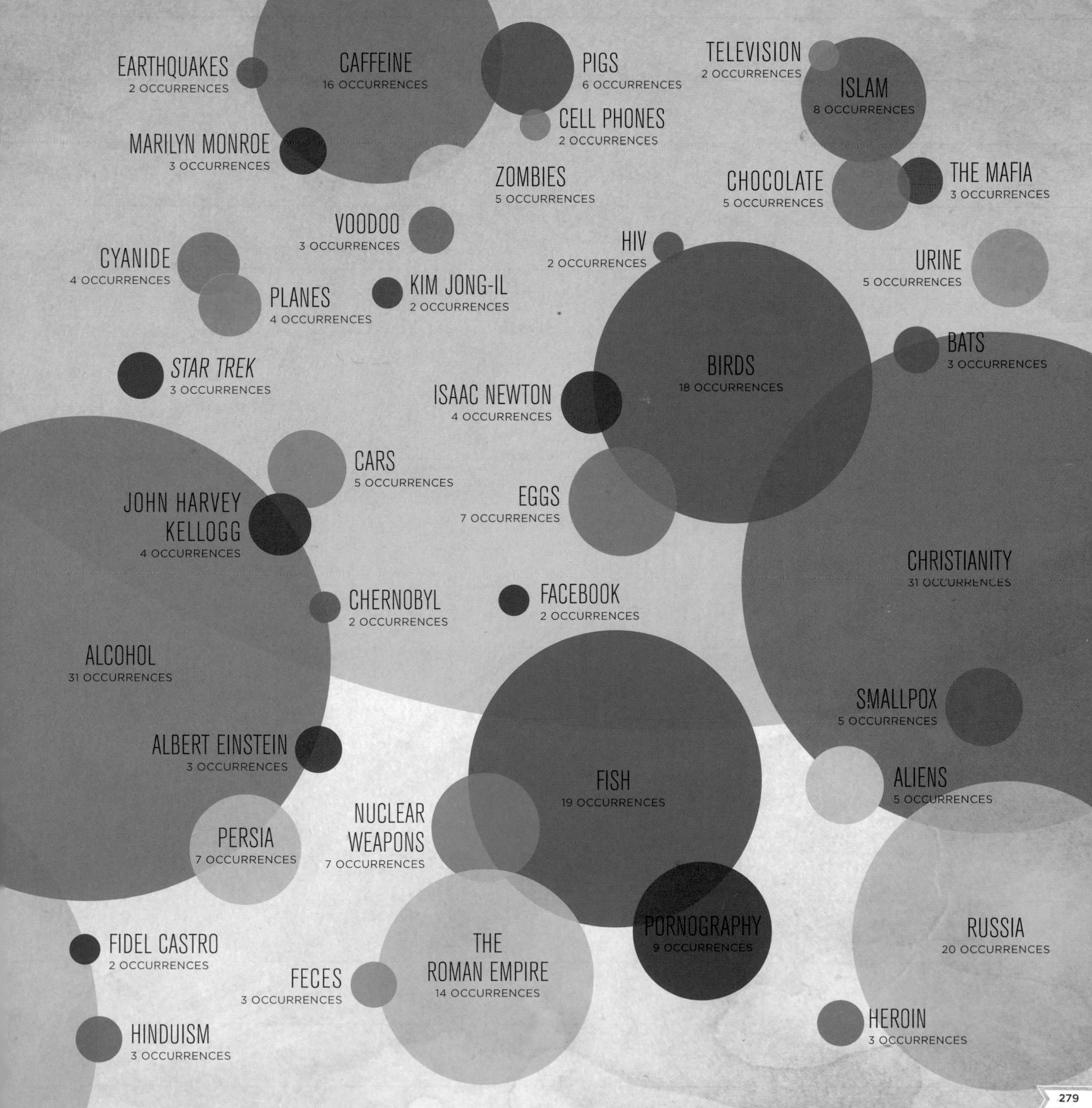

CAFFEINE
16 OCCURRENCES
EARTHQUAKES
2 OCCURRENCES
PIGS
6 OCCURRENCES
TELEVISION
2 OCCURRENCES
ISLAM
8 OCCURRENCES
CELL PHONES
2 OCCURRENCES
MARILYN MONROE
3 OCCURRENCES
ZOMBIES
5 OCCURRENCES
CHOCOLATE
5 OCCURRENCES
THE MAFIA
3 OCCURRENCES
VOODOO
3 OCCURRENCES
HIV
2 OCCURRENCES
CYANIDE
4 OCCURRENCES
URINE
5 OCCURRENCES
PLANES
4 OCCURRENCES
KIM JONG-IL
2 OCCURRENCES
BATS
3 OCCURRENCES
STAR TREK
3 OCCURRENCES
BIRDS
18 OCCURRENCES
ISAAC NEWTON
4 OCCURRENCES
CARS
5 OCCURRENCES
JOHN HARVEY
KELLOGG
4 OCCURRENCES
EGGS
7 OCCURRENCES
CHRISTIANITY
31 OCCURRENCES
CHERNOBYL
2 OCCURRENCES
FACEBOOK
2 OCCURRENCES
ALCOHOL
31 OCCURRENCES
SMALLPOX
5 OCCURRENCES
ALBERT EINSTEIN
3 OCCURRENCES
FISH
19 OCCURRENCES
ALIENS
5 OCCURRENCES
NUCLEAR
WEAPONS
7 OCCURRENCES
PERSIA
7 OCCURRENCES
PORNOGRAPHY
9 OCCURRENCES
RUSSIA
20 OCCURRENCES
FIDEL CASTRO
2 OCCURRENCES
THE
ROMAN EMPIRE
14 OCCURRENCES
FECES
3 OCCURRENCES
HEROIN
3 OCCURRENCES
HINDUISM
3 OCCURRENCES

1,214 INDEXED ITEMS

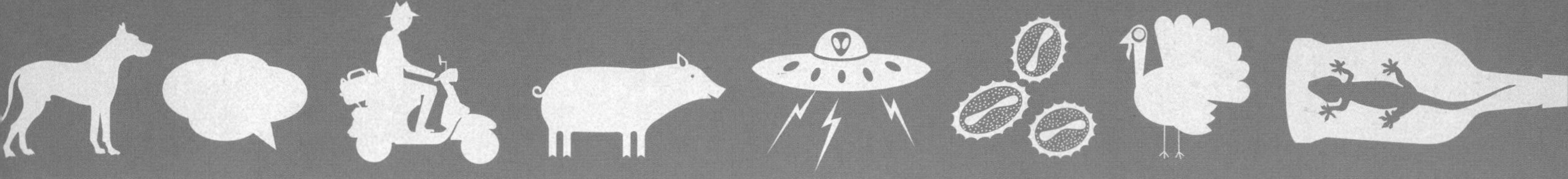

C

D

E

F

G

S

T

U

V

W

Z

22 AWESOME ILLUSTRATORS AND DESIGNERS

1 **JON ADAMS**
PAGES 42-43, 60-61, 138-139, 164-165, 202-203, 240-241, 254-255, 270-271, 274-275

2 **BOOKISH DESIGN**
PAGES 236-237, 264-265

3 **CONOR BUCKLEY**
PAGES 158-159, 181, 182-183, 238-239, 256-257, 268-269

4 **WILFRED CASTILLO**
PAGES 48-49

5 **COLUMN FIVE MEDIA**
PAGES 66-67

6 **ROBERT DI IESO**
PAGES 184-185, 194-195, 204-205, 214-215

7 **ELSORA**
PAGES 154-155

8 **ERNA GYLFADOTTIR**
PAGES 162-163, 172-173, 190-191, 208-209, 222-223, 226-227, 234-235

9 **HUM CREATIVE**
PAGES 206-207, 242-243, 260-261

10 **TRACY SUNRISE JOHNSON**
PAGES 14-15, 76-77, 144-145, 174-175, 178-179, 186-187, 196-197, 250-251, 266-267, 272-273

11 **SUPRIYA KALIDAS**
COVER, PAGES 16-17, 18-19, 32-33, 46-47, 52-53, 62-63, 70-71, 82-83, 84-85, 92-93, 98-99, 100-101, 104-105, 112-113, 120-121, 122-123, 124-125, 128-129, 140-141, 142-143, 158-159, 166, 180, 182-183, 198-199, 200-201, 226-227, 230-231, 245, 258-259, 268-269, 274-275, 278-279

12 **DAVID MACK**
PAGES 18-19, 88-89, 136-137

13 **WILLIAM MACK**
PAGES 10-11, 20-21, 24-25, 28-29, 30-31, 36-37, 38-39, 56-57, 72-73, 74-75, 78-79, 86-87, 88-89, 90-91, 96-97, 106-107, 108-109, 110-111, 114-115, 116-117, 118-119, 132-133, 136-137, 148-149, 150-151, 152-153, 167, 168-169, 176-177, 181, 184-185, 194-195, 197, 210-211, 218-219, 224-225, 238-239, 242-243, 262-263

14 **ALYSSA NASSNER**
PAGES 50-51, 54-55, 64-65, 74-75, 130-131, 160-161, 167, 192-193, 212-213, 216-217, 228-229, 232-233

15 **OMNIVORE MEDIA**
PAGES 22-23, 26-27, 134-135, 248-249

16 **MATT OWENS**
PAGES 58-59, 86-87

17 **JESSICA TAICH**
PAGES 170-171, 252-253

18 **STEPHANIE TANG**
PAGES 12-13, 40-41, 68-69, 94-95, 126-127, 156-157, 188-189, 220-221, 246-247, 276-277

19 **TRACY WHITE TAYLOR**
PAGES 34-35, 78-79, 102-103

20 **TY DESIGN**
PAGES 244-245

21 **TALIN WADSWORTH**
PAGES 10-11, 80-81, 164-165

22 **ALLISON WEINER**
PAGES 44-45, 146-147

All photographs courtesy of Shutterstock Images—with the following exceptions, which are courtesy of WikiCommons: pages 28-29 (all), page 56 (Hotel de Bilderberg), pages 180-181 (all), pages 250-251 (all).

27 PEOPLE WHO MADE THIS BOOK POSSIBLE

WELDON OWEN INC.
CEO, President Terry Newell
VP, Sales Amy Kaneko
VP, Publisher Roger Shaw
Creative Director Kelly Booth
Executive Editor Mariah Bear
Editor Lucie Parker
Editorial Assistant Emelie Griffin
Senior Designer William Mack
Designer Supriya Kalidas
Production Director Chris Hemesath
Production Manager Michelle Duggan
Color Manager Teri Bell

SPECIAL THANKS
Illustration and Design Support: Conor Buckley, Michel Gadwa **Editorial and Research Support:** Sarah Lynn Duncan, Alex Eros, Jann Jones, Marianna Monaco, Katharine Moore, Gail Nelson-Bonebrake, Frances Reade, Michael D. Shannon, Marisa Solís, Brandi Valenza, Astrea White, Charlie Wormhoudt, and Mary Zhang.

weldon**owen**
415 Jackson Street, Suite 200
San Francisco, CA 94111
Telephone: (415) 291-0100
Fax: (415) 291-8841
www.wopublishing.com
A division of

BONNIER

HarperCollins books may be purchased for educational, business, or sales promotional use. For information, please write: Special Markets Department, HarperCollins*Publishers*, 10 East 53rd Street, New York, NY 10022.

First published in 2011 by:
Harper Design,
An Imprint of HarperCollins*Publishers*
10 East 53rd Street
New York, NY 10022
Tel: (212) 207-7000
Fax: (212) 207-7654
harperdesign@harpercollins.com
www.harpercollins.com

This edition distributed throughout the world by:
HarperCollins*Publishers*
10 East 53rd Street
New York, NY 10022
Fax: (212) 207-7654

Library of Congress Control Number: 2011925881
ISBN: 978-0-06-208283-1
Printed in Singapore by Tien Wah Press
10 9 8 7 6 5 4 3 2 1